FRANCES
HODGSON
BURNETT

FRANCES
HODGSON
BURNETT

Gretchen Gerzina

Chatto & Windus
LONDON

Published by Chatto & Windus 2004

First published in the United States of America by Rutgers University Press 2004

2 4 6 8 10 9 7 5 3 1

First published in Great Britain in 2004 by
Chatto & Windus
Random House, 20 Vauxhall Bridge Road,
London SW1V 2SA

Random House Australia (Pty) Limited
20 Alfred Street, Milsons Point, Sydney,
New South Wales 2061, Australia

Random House New Zealand Limited
18 Poland Road, Glenfield,
Auckland 10, New Zealand

Random House (Pty) Limited
Endulini, 5A Jubilee Road, Parktown 2193, South Africa

The Random House Group Limited Reg. No. 954009
www.randomhouse.co.uk

A CIP catalogue record for this book
is available from the British Library

ISBN 0 7011 6892 7

Papers used by Random House are natural, recyclable products made from wood
grown in sustainable forests; the manufacturing processes conform to the environmen-
tal regulations of the country of origin

Printed and bound in Great Britain by
Biddles Ltd, Kings Lynn

For Penny Deupree

CONTENTS

Prologue   ix

PART ONE: *The Coming Woman*

1   The New World, 1865   3

2   A Manchester Childhood, 1849–1865   12

3   A Shabby Genteel Story, 1866–1868   25

4   Vagabondia, 1869–1872   36

5   The Reluctant Bride Abroad, 1872–1876   48

6   Piracy and a Play, 1876–1878   62

7   A City of Groves and Bowers, 1877–1880   77

8   In the Company of Women, 1880–1884   87

9   Fauntleroy, 1884–1887   103

10   Return to Europe, 1887–1888   114

11   Lionel, 1889–1890   127

PART TWO: *A Lady of Quality*

12   Drury Lane, 1891–1892   145

13   "Great London Roars Below," 1892–1894   157

14 The New Woman, 1894–1896   171

15 Ladies of Quality, 1896–1897   189

16 Maytham Hall, 1897–1900   202

17 Stephen, 1900–1902   215

18 Recovery and New Thoughts, 1902–1906   231

19 The End of an Era, 1907–1911   251

20 At Home and Abroad, 1911–1918   267

21 Elizabeth, 1919–1924   290

    Epilogue   304

    Notes   309

    Acknowledgments   341

    General Index   343

    Index of Works   355

PROLOGUE

I N APRIL 1925, six months after the death of Frances Hodgson Burnett, several of her friends met in the Manhattan apartment of the writer and magazine editor Elizabeth Garver Jordan to plan a memorial to their late friend. Those who formed the memorial committee were united in their wish to honour the extraordinary woman they loved. Little else bound them, and it was inevitable that they would fall out over design, fundraising, publicity—in short, over who got to control the public representations of Frances's life and work.

Just about the only things they did agree on may surprise modern readers: that the memorial would depict the best known of her child characters at that time, Cedric of *Little Lord Fauntleroy*, Sara Crewe of *A Little Princess*, and Glad of *The Dawn of a To-morrow*, and that it would be in New York's Central Park. With surprising foresight, Jordan instead commissioned a fountain featuring Mary Lennox and Dickon Sowerby from *The Secret Garden*, which was far less well known at that time but whose characters, like that book's English setting, have kept Frances Hodgson Burnett's name alive today.

Old memories die hard, however, and the legend that held Frances responsible for the "untold pain and sorrow" that *Little Lord Fauntleroy* had inflicted on "thousands of little boys" nearly prevented the tribute. The park commissioner himself had to come to her defence, declaring that the book "is a beautiful, wholesome piece of fiction, and if hysterical parents chose to inflict upon their children the fictional costume of Fauntleroy I think the blame should be placed on them and not on Mrs. Burnett. I know my mother also read the book and she did not insist or even conceive of having me wear long curls or a velvet suit."[1]

It was not until April 1937, twelve years after Frances's death, that the elfin reclining figure of Dickon, flute in hand, and a graceful and nubile Mary, the uplifted bowl in her hand serving as a birdbath, was finally installed. It is an oddity and an irony that a park in New York is the location of a tribute to a woman whom British readers consider one of their own, who was Manchester born and partly bred, who was passionate about English gardens, who grew into southern American womanhood, and who went nowhere near India or "the colonies" in her life. One can walk through— and indeed get married in—the gardens she so carefully nurtured at her house in Kent, see the blue plaque on her London house in Portland Place, and watch her work transformed into West End musical theatre.

She spent her life as neither British nor American but revelled in straddling both countries' opportunities and attitudes. The characters in her books and plays delighted in breaking down class and continental divisions, bringing American independence of thought and speech into the English drawing room, or Yorkshire dialect into the books read by American southerners. Even her name differed on each side of the Atlantic. American friends knew her as Mrs. Burnett, with the emphasis on the second syllable; the English at the time called her Mrs. Hodgson Burnett, a dual surname with the emphasis on the first syllable of "Burnett." (The former pronunciation is correct, because it is the pronunciation of her husband's American family.)

Like the rival claims that Britain and America have on her, the discrepancies between her private friendships and public reputations plagued Frances, and continued past the grave. How would she wish to be remembered? Did friends and acquaintances from one part of her life carry more weight than those from another? Who would control for posterity the public depiction of her life and work? These are, of course, questions that face a biographer no less than those preparing a different kind of memorial, and they are no less important when the biographer is a relative. Immediately after her death, her son Vivian rushed to complete the first biography of his mother, hoping to circumvent the gossipmongers who would otherwise leap to publish a racier version of the way the author of *Little Lord Fauntleroy* spent her life. His wife, Constance Buel Burnett, wrote an even more romanticized version for young adults. Even so their children, Frances's beloved granddaughters, grew up to be women who never spoke of "that woman," even though their financial security resulted from her hard work and her literary and dramatic successes.

Frances lived an enormously varied and unexpected life, from her childhood in Manchester to adulthood in America, where she arrived in 1865 when she was just fifteen, and up to her death at seventy-four. Between those years she published fifty-two books and wrote and produced thirteen plays, married and divorced an American doctor, then married and separated from an English doctor. She was wildly successful in both America and Britain. That success began when she was just eighteen, and in the fifty-six years of her professional writing life, no publisher in either America or Britain ever turned down her work. She came to believe, as did many who knew her, that her stories simply materialized from some unnamed and powerful force. She rarely revised, and stories and novels were sent off to the publishers virtually as they emerged from her pen. She crossed the Atlantic no fewer than thirty-three times, and when the ships on which she travelled docked in the New York or Boston harbour, she was invariably met by crowds of newspaper and magazine reporters who asked about her latest play or novel, her marriages and separations, her relationship with her children, and her often fragile health.

Publicly conventional, Frances led an unconventional life. She married twice and probably had unrecorded lovers. She saw herself as a transatlantic person, someone who longed for one place whenever she was in the other. She viewed America as a place of vigour and ingenuity, England as a place of cultural accomplishment and erudition, and rest. One was inherently entrepreneurial, the other bound by traditions in need of shaking up, but also worthy of respect—particularly important because, as a Victorian woman living for years apart from her husband in entire independence, her public persona dictated her ability not only to make a living but to remain a publicly "respectable" woman. At a time when so many moneyed people shuttled back and forth across the ocean, and transatlantic cables wove the countries together in an unprecedented way, her dual lives were seen as somewhat exotic, and certainly admirable. She professed to crave solitude and a retired life but lived in a social vortex often of her own making. In a class-bound society she counted nobility and newsboys, aristocrats and actors, publishers and poor relations among her private circle. She was as likely to spend a day with a local gardener as an evening with a lord. It was no accident that nearly all of her stories and books would have to do with reversals of fortune and shifts in class status.

The deepest gulf has to do with her modern reputation. She would be astounded to learn that today she is considered almost entirely a writer of children's books. Many of her novels dealt with adult subjects: unhappy marriages and marital infidelity, illegitimate births, spousal abuse, women who refused to be limited by societal dictates, crossings of class lines. *Little Lord Fauntleroy*, in 1886, was her eighteenth published book and the first she ever wrote that involved or appealed to young people. Like *The Adventures of Huckleberry Finn* or *Robinson Crusoe*, it was intended for a wide audience at a time when there was less demarcation between books for children and adults than there is today. Indeed, by far the greatest number of readers for *Fauntleroy* was adult, most notoriously mothers who tried to foist its fashions upon their resisting sons. *The Secret Garden*, which regularly tops lists of most influential books, passed nearly unnoticed by critics and readers when it appeared in 1911, and during its composition she does not discuss it in any of her letters as she did her other works. Elizabeth Jordan's shifting of the memorial's focus to Dickon and Mary was, therefore, eerily prescient. Few visitors to the bronze figures in Central Park can know that when first cast, it would have been far less recognizable to those who saw it than the figures of Fauntleroy, Sara, and Glad would have been.

Even when adjusting for the difficulties of a failed marriage unsuccessfully kept secret from her family and from the press, the modern reader finds it hard to understand the ironic rift between her reputation as the writer of some of the best literature ever written about childhood and the undeniable fact of her being a largely absent if adoring mother who was stricken with guilt only after terrible tragedy struck. Jordan, probably her closest friend in the last years of her life, recalled that "as soon as her success made it possible she transformed her life into a sort of fairy-tale, deliberately shutting out the sordid, the sad, and the unlovely. Nevertheless, when life called on her to face tragic realities she always did it with high courage."[2]

Throughout her life, Frances was known for five things: her unrelenting literary production, which often drove her to illness; her love of beautiful clothes and domestic surroundings; her inability to remain settled in any one place, or even in one country; her wonderful gardens; and in the second half of her life, compassion and enormous generosity to friends and strangers alike. To these traits a modern biographer would add several others: border crossings of all kinds, and transformations through self-determination and nature; a fierce independence, coupled with a sometimes disastrous sympathy for others; a tendency to romanticize herself and her life, equally matched by her warmth and compassion for others; a refusal to read newspapers, but a temper that rose up against wrongdoers and led her to conduct battles in public; an often debilitating need to work in order not only to support herself but to help support a host of family members, including her children, her sisters and their families, her brothers and their families, and at least one of her husbands. She was a passionate and loving person who inspired the devotion of nearly all who knew her. Many who met her thought she lived a fairy tale existence, but shortly after her death her son said that "one of the most surprising things" that people would learn about his mother was "the fact that her life was not a happy one." He told an audience in Knoxville that "Frances Hodgson Burnett had a great deal of physical and mental suffering, and many sorrows that the world did not know about." In her final hours she told him "that she had never wanted to add more sorrow to the load that people carried. She wanted to bring real joy into the lives of other people. She was a real romanticist."[3] Indeed, most of her many books "had been written under great physical difficulties."[4]

In 1927, the same year that Vivian Burnett published the biography of his mother, Virginia Woolf wrote that "there are some stories which have to be retold by each generation."[5] At the end of Frances's life, modernism was supplanting her kind of fiction, for, as Kitty Hall Brownell put it, "fashions change, fashions in writing like other fashions. Form forged with labor and pain in a hard material has, we are told, the better chance of survival. Literary immortality is short at its longest."[6] The books she wrote were often formed from the labour and pain of her own life. Understanding Frances requires us to look at her life and work through different eyes, to see a woman who worked within and against the restrictions of Victorian life to develop her own code of spiritual and moral behaviour; who wrote love stories but ardently believed in a woman's right to independence; and who became one of the wealthiest woman writers of her time on either side of the Atlantic. She may be memorialized as the author of *The Secret Garden*, but neither her life nor her works were only for children.

Frances Hodgson Burnett's life, like that of her literary Manchester predecessor Mrs. Gaskell, reminds us that before our time there were women struggling to combine work and family, and that just as it does today, enormous and public success often carries with it a private price. In her final book, *In the Garden*, she declared that "I love it all. I love to dig. I love to kneel down in the grass at the edge of a flowerbed and pull out the weeds fiercely and throw them into a heap by my side. I love to fight with those who can spring up again almost in a night and taunt me. I tear them up by the roots again and again, and when at last after many days, perhaps, it seems as if I had beaten them for a time at least, I go away feeling like an army with banners."[7]

The image of the triumphant gardener wrestling with life itself and emerging victorious has inspired legions of girls on both sides of the Atlantic to believe that they could discover secret gardens and bring order to the chaos of adolescence. As she wrote hopefully from her deathbed in October 1924, one month away from her seventy-fifth birthday, "As long as one has a garden, one has a future; and as long as one has a future one is alive."[8] It is fitting that a memorial exists in one of the best-known gardens in the world, and that it represents in its design another whose name has become a universal phrase for the unseen and the redemptive.

Throughout her life, Frances Hodgson Burnett was known by many names to many people. Those close to her, her adult family and friends, always called her Fluffy. Her sons called her Mammy or Dearest. In America she was known formally and professionally as Mrs. Burnett, in England as Mrs. Hodgson Burnett. I have chosen to call her Frances.

PART ONE

~

The Coming Woman

I conclude that no biography is ever definitive, because that is not the nature of such journeys, nor of the human heart which is their territory. Sometimes all one achieves is another point of departure.

—RICHARD HOLMES,
Sidetracks: Explorations of a Romantic Biographer

Perhaps it is rather to my advantage that I never had any 'dear old days'.

—FRANCES HODGSON BURNETT
to her son Vivian, 14 November 1906

It began with a description of a garden in May—a garden so full of wonders of color and form and fragrance, of wings and glitter, shadows and shine, music of birds and insects, that the impression was of something so precious as to seem outside of our workaday world, to suggest some elaborate and superlative garden of exclusive royalty. . . . And then . . . the story was to lead one very gradually to understand that such a place was accessible to us, she had herself found it—amazingly!— in the plot of this very Park named the Ramble. There it stood . . . but the secret of seeing it lay with the eyes that looked.

—KITTY HALL BROWNELL,
speaking at the dedication of the Central Park memorial to Frances Hodgson Burnett, of a story that Burnett narrated but never wrote.

~

CHAPTER I

THE NEW WORLD

1865

I

T MIGHT SEEM THAT ONLY the most desperate and naïve of English widows could have believed it was a good idea to take her five children from economically depressed Manchester to war-ravaged Tennessee in the spring of 1865—but then where could an impoverished widow take her family? East Tennessee was perhaps as good a place as any. Frances recalled Manchester as a place where "all the human framework of the great dirty city was built about the cotton trade. All the working classes depended upon it for bread, all the middle classes for employment, all the rich for luxury."[1] In cutting off the supply of cotton to Manchester's textile industry, the American Civil War had caused the local English economy to falter. Wearied from trying to keep her late husband's business afloat, depressed by repeated moves, each a bit further down the economic scale into what the characters in her famous daughter's early potboiler stories would bitterly term "shabby genteel" life, Eliza Boond Hodgson chose to believe the boasts of wealth and ease that her brother William Boond sent from his new home in the American South.

The excitement of Eliza's two cocky teenaged sons and her three diminutive adolescent daughters ran high. They approached the move with a "delicious sense of adventure and wild, young, good spirits and fun."[2] They were not, however, oblivious to or necessarily even neutral about the war that had devastated Manchester's economy: Herbert, at eighteen the oldest child, went ahead of the others. His British passport, issued by Viscount Amberley on 5 October 1864, was "good for the voyage to New York, or any port not under blockade." When he arrived in Knoxville he apparently acted, for a time, as a Confederate spy. He got a job with a local jeweller, Joseph Wood, another English transplant who had arrived in Knoxville in 1860 after a stay and a marriage in New York. Wood was a secessionist later described as someone who had chosen the wrong side in the war, and his sympathies may have influenced Herbert, who like his brother John became a lifelong southerner, although there is no record that Herbert's political leanings remained with the Confederacy.[3]

Back in Manchester, the rest of the Hodgsons stayed with a cousin's family while their house and most of its contents were disposed of, finding that "two families in one house filled it to overflowing and produced the most hilarious results. There was laughing nearly all night, and darting in and out on errands and visits all day, there was a buying of things and disposing of things, the seeing friends, the bidding good-bye."[4] Fifteen-year-old Frances had to leave behind some of her most precious possessions: a long story, "the pride of her heart," called "Céleste, or Fortune's Wheel," was consigned to the fire along with most of her other unfinished stories. To the older male friend of a cousin she bestowed her beloved little Italian greyhound named Florence, not knowing she could have taken the dog with her; her mother had given her the greyhound when Fanny seemed unable to get over the disappearance of her Newfoundland puppy, Rollo.[5]

On a Thursday morning, after a long and largely sleepless night spent with the relatives who had filled two railroad carriages in order to travel with them to Liverpool to see them off, Eliza and the other four of her children boarded the SS *Moravian*, taking little more with them than their carefully tailored clothing and their middle-class manners. The date 11 May was not particularly auspicious; the day they sailed away, most of them never to return, the Liverpool newspaper reported Abraham Lincoln's April assassination. None of this fazed the Hodgsons, and even on board ship Frances made friends who talked to her about books. A teacher bound for Montreal lent her all the books he had with him, including a volume of Carlyle's essays, and tutored her in English literature, to the amusement of her siblings.

Abandoning her country and extended family was an act of faith and courage for a gentle and tired woman who had become increasingly beaten down by the difficulties of raising her brood on a constantly diminishing income. Within five years she would be buried in a Knoxville cemetery, the ancestor of generations of Americans, literally worn out by the years of effort and deprivation. For Frances, too, this departure marked a permanent change, for it brought to an end the only period in her life when she was financially supported by others rather than working tirelessly to support not only herself but a host of family members.

The three-week crossing from Liverpool to Quebec was cheaper than a direct crossing to the United States. Throughout the voyage, Frances was alert and animated with what her sister Edith called "a unique way of noticing things." Normally she talked non-stop, but the two-week train journey that took them from Canada to Knoxville rendered her nearly speechless. Gifted with the ability to create riveting serial stories for her sisters and young friends, nothing she read or narrated as a child prepared her for the vast lakes and forests of Canada and America, nor for the village of New Market, Tennessee. For it was in New Market that Eliza's brother William, pleading the vagaries of his Knoxville dry goods business, housed them in a log house not much bigger than a cabin, twenty-five miles from the city. There, with quiet and proud British reticence, they nearly starved.

East Tennessee was one of the hardest hit regions of the country during the war. Geographically located in the South that had voted to secede from the nation, most of its inhabitants allied themselves politically with the Union rather than with the Confederacy. They sent their crops and their livestock to the northern army, but when the Confederate army encamped on their doorstep and took what little food and supplies were left, the citizens were left destitute. Knoxville, whose ordinary citizens and newspaper sided with the North while many of its leading residents sympathized with the South, seesawed between northern and southern occupations, with some of the war's fiercest battles fought on its soil. In 1864 the desperate citizens directly petitioned Congress and Lincoln for relief, citing a heartrending list of miseries endured by their young men, who "have been butchered, others shot down in their own homes or yards—in the highroad, or the fields, or in the forests; others still have been hung up by the neck to limbs of trees, without judge or jury—there is no single neighborhood within the bounds of East Tennessee, whose green sod has not drunk the blood of citizens murdered."[6]

With a population of around twenty thousand white people and more than two thousand black people, Knox County fought hard to maintain its Union and antislavery loyalties even while cut off from supplies. African Americans, who had been freed in 1863 by Lincoln's Emancipation Proclamation, worked alongside other East Tennessee Union sympathizers to repair the earthworks that protected Knoxville. The white women, older men, and boys who remained at home struggled to keep their farms and businesses going, while the *Knoxville Whig* complained of a steady stream of up to twenty thousand English and Irish emigrants conscripted throughout the South into the rebel army, a fate that might well have befallen Frances's brother John had he not arrived in the final moments of the war. Shortly after the Hodgsons arrived, haggard white soldiers moved out by train, calling to Frances and her sisters from the windows, jokingly offering them locks of hair from their shorn and bandaged heads.

"A gambler in business adventures," Eliza's brother William Boond made and lost several small fortunes in America. In June 1865, when his sister and her family arrived, he was advertising himself in the *Knoxville Whig* as "William Boond, Grocer, Provision Dealer and Commission Merchant," with a store on the corner of Gay and Union Streets in Knoxville.[7] During the years of the war, he had made a great profit by providing provisions for the armies and supplying the ceaseless stream of Union and Confederate soldiers who poured through Knoxville. With the end of the war his lucrative business slowed considerably, and the best he could do for them when they arrived was to arrange for them to live in the little New Market cabin, and to find employment for Herbert in his grocery and for John George at his gristmill in nearby Dandridge. Towards the end of her life, Frances spoke of her Uncle William with "amusement at the conservatively shocked awe with which her family then regarded him," seeing him as being "on the order of a business gambler" whose fortunes rose and sank with the times.[8]

This was New Market shortly after the Hodgson family arrived: a single unpaved street of wooden houses, white or log, surrounded by forest and hills. It had an attorney, several general stores and blacksmiths, three shoemakers, three churches, one carpenter and one brickmason, one saddler, and a postmaster. The residents were cash poor but friendly and welcoming, surviving through small businesses in which many of the goods and services were bartered, and a bit of farming. Eliza and her children found a rural economy, a strange diet, a language that was English but unfamiliar. The villagers were naturally curious about the new family, and particularly about their speech, their clothing, and linen and tableware, which seemed to indicate an apparent urban material comfort oddly out of step with their untried hardscrabble life in a rustic cabin.

Like most bookish English children, Frances had received most of her ideas about America and Americans from fiction. From James Fenimore Cooper she learned of Native American people, and expected to find Indians, particularly those of a heroic and elegant style, living nearby; she was disappointed to learn that those few she might encounter were likely to be poor and hungry, begging for work or food at local back doors. From Harriet Beecher Stowe she learned of American slavery. *Uncle Tom's Cabin*, which sold over a million and a half copies in Britain and appeared in hundreds of theatrical versions all over Britain, was published in 1852 when Frances was three. Stowe's book made such an impression on Victorian England that nurseries were decorated with Uncle Tom wallpaper and countless girls owned Topsy dolls. Eliza was stunned to come upon her daughter one day "apparently furious with insensate rage, muttering to herself as she brutally lashed with one of her brother's whips, a cheerfully hideous black gutta-percha doll who was tied to the candelabra stand and appeared to be enjoy-ing the situation." She was "talking to herself like a little fury"; she had been reading *Uncle Tom's Cabin* and was pretending that the doll, which she nor-mally referred to as Topsy, was now "poor Uncle Tom, and that the little fury with the flying hair was the wicked Legree" who had treated Tom so cruelly in the novel. When the decision was made to go to Tennessee, she was thrilled to go to "the land of Uncle Tom's Cabin! Perhaps to see planta-tions and magnolias! To be attended by Aunt Chloes and Topsys!"[9] Despite some surprises and disappointments, her impressions of America's people and landscapes remained in her earliest years there as fully romanticized as her previous notions had been.

East Tennessee was profoundly lush and beautiful in its mountains and vegetation. The child from a manufacturing city whose coal fire smoke continually rained down smuts and ashes from a sunless sky found herself able to wander at will through acres of green, to lie on her back and watch the clouds for hours at a time. It was a far cry from the Manchester that Elizabeth Gaskell had described in her 1848 novel, *Mary Barton,* as a city where "there are no flowers, the rain had only a disheartening and gloomy effect; the streets were wet and dirty, and the people were wet and dirty. Indeed, most kept within doors; and there was an unusual silence of foot-steps in the little paved courts."[10] It was as though Frances had been living in a bad dream of exile and now, at last, found herself at home. "Strange as it may seem," she later wrote about her new Tennessee life, "to do, to feel, to see and hear all this was somehow not new to her. She was not a stranger here—she felt she had been a stranger in the Square in Manchester when she had lifted her face to the low-hanging, smoky clouds, talking to them, im-ploring them when they would make no response. Without knowing why—because she was too young to comprehend—she felt that she had begun to be alive, and that before, somehow, she had not been exactly living."[11]

All of this seems to indicate an adolescent who viewed her neighbours and surroundings romantically and remotely, but in fact Frances and her siblings tumbled easily into local life. She found the countryside overwhelmingly lovely and the people delightfully "primitive." Thirty years earlier Frances Trollope wrote of her experiences as an English mother travelling America with her children and her discomfort with the American expansiveness of manner, rusticity of speech, and informality, all of which she found crude and uncouth. She described a neighbour "whose appearance more resembled

a Covent Garden market-woman than any thing else I can remember. . . .
Her look, her voice, her manner, were so exceedingly coarse and vehement,
that she almost frightened me."[12] Trollope and her children found such
encounters with overly friendly country folk amusing, and Frances too saw
them as literary fodder. "I studied them because it was my natural bent to
delight in human beings, and study them without being aware that I was
doing so," she later wrote. "Not until after I was twenty did I find out that
during those years spent among the woods and mountains of East Tennessee
I had been accumulating material out of which I could build and from
which I should draw as long as I lived."[13] So at home did she feel there that
she "delighted in conversation with the natives—the real native, who had
a wonderful dialect. As she had learned to speak Lancashire she learned to
speak East Tennessean and North Carolinian and the negro [sic] dialect.
Finding that her English accent was considered queer, she endeavoured to
correct it and to speak American. She found American interesting, and
rather liked it."[14] What would her English relatives and friends say, she
wondered, if they could hear her using phrases like "I guess" and "I reckon"?
The varieties of American speech intrigued her as much as the varieties of
English speech had in Manchester, and she practised writing out scraps
of stories and Bible passages in a variety of dialects in what remained of
her mother's ledger books. When she began her publishing career only three
years later, she was so adept at transplanting southern people and situations
into Lancashire settings and dialect that her first editor wondered whether
she was English or American.

During the year that the Hodgsons remained in New Market, the gentle
and reserved Eliza tried to re-create in their cabin the life of a respectable
Victorian family for whom appearances counted as much as truth. The five
red-haired children—the teasing but responsible nineteen-year-old Herbert,
the frustrating and doomed eighteen-year-old John, the gifted fifteen-year-
old Frances, gentle and fiercely loyal thirteen-year-old Edith, and the resourceful eleven-year-old Edwina, called Teddy by her older siblings—were
properly dressed in shoes and stockings and good linen, and ate with silver
and pristine napkins, even though they lived in the poorest house in a village whose children sometimes had no footwear at all. They became a house
of women during the week, with Herbert working in Knoxville and John at
the gristmill, and were a complete family only at weekends, when the brothers brought home their own food supplies of cornmeal, bacon, and molasses.

It quickly became clear to the neighbours that the Hodgsons, for all their
fine accoutrements, needed feeding. The Jenkins and Peters families took to
stopping by to visit and leaving behind a bit of pork or baked goods, as

though by afterthought, to save the women from embarrassment. Frances later called "graduating angels" those who dropped by with gifts of food, keeping them one step away from debilitating hunger. These hungry days made a lasting impression on her attitude towards money, even in the future when it flowed like water from her purse. "When I have bills to pay & no more money than will pay them I pay them & *go without* the things I want," she scolded her son when he was in college. "It is in the feminine part of our family at least, to do this & I do not think the men make debts to any extent. Do you know that in those awful starving days in New Market we never owed anyone a farthing."[15]

When the cold weather set in, it became clear that more must be done, and Frances, as the oldest child remaining at home, decided to set up a small school, a Select Seminary for Young People. She was practically a child herself, not only in years but in appearance. Always short, with auburn curls that frequently defied control, she was lively and imaginative and active— just the sort of teacher that her much younger pupils enjoyed for their lessons in music and basic instruction. Kind and hardworking as the villagers were, however, few of them could pay cash for lessons, yet the eggs, butter, and meat that the handful of students used in its stead helped get the family through the winter.

A picture emerges of Frances in these first American years as a playful young woman who was resourceful, popular, and versatile, attractive in a spirited and original way, and willing to shoulder the domestic burden in order to increase their general welfare. With a mother who seems to have faded into the background after the great effort of arranging the emigration, two brothers whose work kept them away from home for most of the week, and two younger, less resourceful sisters, it fell upon Frances to find ways to help make ends meet. These circumstances combined in that first New Market year, partly out of necessity and partly out of chance, into the things that would define the rest of her life: a love of nature, a willingness—indeed, a compulsion—to work hard to support others as well as herself, and an equally strong compulsion to write.

A generation later, a newspaper reported on her forty-second birthday that "[t]he spirit of the grand mountain scenery and the subtle influence of the romantic and historic environment, working upon a temperament naturally ardent and imaginative led the girl of sixteen to essay imaginative writing."[16] In one sense they were wrong. The scenery and the environment undoubtedly moved her, but the craving to put stories down on paper had begun back in Manchester when she first learned her letters. What was different about her new life in East Tennessee was a sort of physical opening up that nature, in combination with a loosening of social rules, allowed. Language and words and writing were already deeply formed in her, and nearly everyone who knew her since her earliest childhood until old age believed that she had a gift. Stories and conversation flowed unchecked from her, and even she could not explain their source. Her education at a small school run by three sisters in Manchester had ended shortly before she left for America; she was a voracious reader but not a particularly discriminating one. Neither of her parents was especially literary, although her late father had written verse on occasion and sent infrequent letters to the editors of newspapers, but none of her brothers or sisters felt any notable urge to write or otherwise invent or imagine. Even when Frances was a child, however, they all believed that her scribblings and storytelling sprang from some mysterious and endless source.

The *Boston Traveller* of 11 July 1889 puzzled over this evident lack of instructed ability.

> Mrs. Burnett's literary achievements are in the line of the wonderful, not because they are so intrinsically great, but because her work is produced from no apparently adequate power; that is to say, here is a woman without education in any trained sense, without the culture of thought that is achieved by severe study; with only a limited acquaintance with literature and the great productions of art, and who has no marked intellectual ability; there are none of the positive and logical mental causes for mental production, yet the quality of the production far exceeds, in flexibility, vividness, and spontaneity, that of any other American woman writer of fiction. The solution of this problem is in her possessing, in an amazing degree, the impressionable temperament. Her mind takes an impression as a mirror does the reflection of an object before it, and she has the alchemy of genius to transmute it into artistic form. . . . Altogether, her literary personality is a rather curious study in human nature.

Her real apprenticeship was coming up, but in a sense the year she spent in New Market, rejoicing in the hand that fate dealt her, was the bridge between her old life and a new one. It saw her uniting her two lives, becoming both English and American, and this was reflected in her writing.

Both countries now claim Frances as their own, and even she never satisfactorily answered the question of whether she was English or American. During her adult life she had houses in Washington and London, on Long Island, in rural Kent, and in Bermuda. She married an American doctor in Tennessee, and two years after their divorce she married an English doctor in Genoa and lived with him in England. Referring "to a general indefiniteness as to whether I am an Englishwoman or an American, I can only say that I do not wonder that such doubts exist," she told an audience at London's Vagabonds Club in 1895.[17] She believed that the move changed the whole colour of her life and could perhaps give no better answer, yet anyone who wrote about her tried to resolve the conundrum. *Harper's Bazar* described her in 1900 as

> below the average height, rather too much flesh for her small frame, her face blessed with an English woman's complexion, an American woman's animation, and framed in an aureole of auburn hair, its chief interest a pair of eyes that are blue changing to a very deep violet with the play of her emotions. She speaks after the manner of an English woman and talks like an American. Her voice is much better than ours; her views are broader in their nature than are theirs—more quickly taken and adhered to with an independence of spirit eminently American.[18]

Many writers leave behind some scrap, some indication of childhood talent, or some early literary attempt. If we're lucky enough to find these bits, they may also provide a glimpse into the life that gave rise to the talent, a thumbnail history. In Frances's case she left behind an extraordinary artefact, a memento that hints at the extensive and breathless stream of language that seems always to have flowed from her, and one that in later life even she forgot existed. Among the few personal items that made the voyage across the Atlantic with the Hodgson family was a ledger book with the accounts of the family business sadly revealed in its columns. As the business folded, the book was handed to Frances. In it, in pencil and blotchy ink, she dashed off some of her first stories, many of them the earliest drafts of her novels. There, in her doodles and distractions, she hinted at her dreams, worries, desires, and even at her later marriage to Swan Burnett, whose family lived across the road from them in New Market.

At the end of the year in which they "lived in the village long enough to gain a great deal of atmosphere . . . she went with the family to another place."[19] They took with them their clothes and tableware, a clearer sense of belonging, and the book into which she scribbled traces of her past, present, and future. The question is how these abilities—a gift of the gab and observation, determination and drive—combined with what she called the "Force" that controlled the universe and channelled stories through her pen, and with geography, to make her one of the most admired and prolific writers of her time and one of the most influential of our own.

CHAPTER 2

⌇

A MANCHESTER
CHILDHOOD

1849–1865

"I ALWAYS KNEW THAT MY SISTER Frances was different, even
when we were children, though, of course, at the time I could not
have told you why," said her sister Edith. "There was something
about her thatset her apart from other people."[1] From the beginning Frances
was a passionately imaginative child, at times rather fierce, with a bit of a
temper that flared when she was teased or mocked, but generally affectionate with a desire to please and a fear of doing wrong. She seemed to be one
of those talented changelings, "a distinct little individual," dropped into
middle-class, mid-Victorian families to the surprise of their kind but rather
unremarkable parents.[2]

Her parents, Eliza Boond and Edwin Hodgson, both came from solid local
Lancashire families. The Boonds in particular had a long lineage and some
prominence in Manchester society. The name is not a particularly common
one, and for hundreds of years the Boonds clustered around Manchester
and Salford; in Frances's time it meant she was surrounded by an extended
family and a loving household. Edwin's only surviving letter, written to his
new in-laws from the honeymoon at York on 28 November 1844, reassures
Hanna and William Boond that "Eliza is very well & happy & sends her
dear dear love to you—father" and offers them "the best of wishes from my
dear wife for your health & happiness." He signs it "yours very aff[ection-
ate]ly." There was no reason to expect that he wouldn't be a good provider,
and with the seemingly unlimited supply of cotton and coal to fuel local
fortunes, the couple prospered. The booming textile and mining industries
surrounding Manchester produced a thriving middle and upper middle class
that built and furnished new homes. Edwin's self-owned firm on King Street

in Deansgate supplied the brasses, chandeliers, door handles, and decorative ironworks that adorned the houses of the up-and-coming and of "the rich men in Manchester who were known everywhere as Cotton Lords."[3] The Hodgsons lived comfortably, employing twenty-eight-year-old Ellen Parry as a house servant and nineteen-year-old Elizabeth Mottram as a nurse. They also kept a stylish carriage and a "fine" pair of horses.

Edwin and Eliza's first two children were sons—Herbert, who was born at their first home at 30 Moreton Street on 20 February 1846, and John George, born only eighteen months later at what is now 358 Cheetham Hill Road. Frances Eliza, the third child and first daughter, was born there too, on 24 November 1849. A few months before Edith, the next child, was born in 1852, the family moved a bit further along Cheetham Hill Road to St. Luke's Terrace, which was backed by fields owned by the earl of Derby, leading Frances to think of it as being in the "back garden of Eden." It seemed a place of gardens and perpetual summer, where she could lie beneath trees, ignoring the industrial city that surrounded this suburb of light and air. It was here that her devotion to gardens began and her discomfort with the rush and dirt of cities. There were farms and country cottages close by, and she became friendly with the Rimmers, market gardeners who kept pigs. They had a small daughter, Emma, with whom Frances was allowed to be friends, despite the girl's humble circumstances and pronounced Lancashire accent.

Like most mid-Victorian children, Frances spent most of her time in the nursery, where her father was only a visitor, albeit a playful and welcome one. She remembered little of him, but in many ways she resembled him. Like her, he had curling hair and was quick to laugh; he was good-humoured and affectionate. Like her too he held himself erect with a posture that seemed to give him greater height than he possessed. His portrait shows a pleasant round face that his children inherited, but they were disrespectful enough to use the dark picture as a target for their indoor games He was a "bookish" man and kept a library of sorts in the house. He sang well and played the piano. Eliza was less clever but equally affectionate, not quite a "charming but helpless ornament to society" but certainly a woman who had been educated for marriage and motherhood rather than self-sufficiency.

Frances's first memory was of February 1852 and the infant Edith, who was being tended by a nurse near the fire in a comfortable bedroom, where Eliza Hodgson was resting in her carved four-poster bed with red draperies. A visiting neighbour sat in a chair near her, and the talk between the two women was of their new babies. As they spoke, two-year-old Frances marched over to the nurse and demanded to hold the baby on her knee. The result was a compromise: the nurse knelt on the floor, placing the baby on the toddler's little lap, but continued to support the tiny body instead of allowing Frances to take the whole weight. She knew she'd been duped, as children often were by adults, and in recollection saw this as "an infant indication of a nature which developed later as one of its chief characteristics, a habit of adjusting itself silently to the inevitable."[4] This served as an occasion for self-reflection, for it suggests that even as a small child she wanted to carry the weight and independence of holding others. Edith, who became her mainstay through-out their adult life, benefited from and adored her for this.

Many of her other early memories have a similar cast: the differences between wanting to have her way and, simultaneously, to do the correct thing, without causing offence, for "her inward desire was to be a good child. . . . She did not want to be 'naughty,' she did not want to be scolded, she was peace-loving and pleasure-loving, two things not compatible with insubordination. When she was 'naughty,' it was because what seemed to her injustice and outrage roused her to fury. She had occasional furies, but went no further."[5] The visiting woman said her baby's name was Eleanor; wasn't that a nice name? Frances did not think so but knew it was wrong to contradict adults. Finally she blurted out that it wasn't as pretty a name as Edith, which pleased everyone. Her memoir of her childhood is a litany of such small recollections of her mind's awakening at a time "when the child mind was a region unexplored and the child brain regarded as a semi-inert mass to be awakened to activity only by the passage of a decade or more."[6]

The family apparently sat for no photographs, and because she could not recall studying her face in the mirror, her recollections of her young self were vividly internal and experiential rather than visual. As a toddler she stood by the table with John or Herbert and learned to read capital letters pointed out in the newspaper advertisements. At three she stood at her grandmother's knee in the nursery and slowly sounded out her first sentence in a large-print Bible. Her grandmother Boond also helped her learn to read from an alpha-bet flower book, a gift she desired more than any toy. Her grandmother, who was "stately but benevolent" with "silver-white hair [and] a cap with a full white net border [and] carried in her pocket an antique silver snuff-box, not used as a snuff-box, but as a receptacle for . . . 'sweeties,'" did not quite understand the preference for a book over a doll but was won over, and Frances got her first book from "a tiny shop on a sort of country road."[7]

When Frances was not quite four years old, the comfortable and secure life came to an end. Edwin, only thirty-eight, suffered a stroke and, after lin-gering for some months, died on 1 September 1853. The children were kept ignorant of the severity of his illness, instead being sent to stay in a country house open to the public in a nearby estate, where she experienced her first recorded sense of terror when she realized that the policemen who strolled through the park and chatted up her nurse could also put her in prison should she mistakenly tread upon or fall onto the grass—something the policeman solemnly assured her could occur. She felt a similar fear a year or so later when she and her friend Emma Rimmer encountered a table of cakes and sweets on offer for a halfpenny. No one was watching the table, and Emma convinced the hungry Frances to take a parkin "on trust." Unable to pay back the halfpenny, and knowing that her mother, a lady, would never approve, Frances suffered agonies before confessing to Herbert, a "combative little fellow with curly hair," who marched himself to the Rimmers and paid for the borrowed feast.

Barely had she recovered from her fear of the police when the Hodgson children were returned home. There they saw their father's corpse lying in the bed with the crimson curtains, looking as though he had fallen asleep. When someone explained to her that he had "gone to Heaven," she felt no fear or sorrow but "looked down with quiet interest and respect."[8] The youngest child, Edwina, was born posthumously and named after a father she never saw, a man whom Frances recalled only as being jocular in the way that adults are to children, with brown curls and a pleasant laugh.

The formerly dependent Eliza, "Mamma," made the brave decision to take over the running of his business. She sent out light blue flyers announcing herself as "Eliza Hodgson (widow of the late Edwin Hodgson)," and her profession as "general furnishing ironmonger, lamp and chandelier manufacturer, electro-plate and fancy warehouse." Her business, with its large showroom, sold and even often made an impressive array of household fittings that must have required a substantial workforce to produce them. They were authorized gas fitters and offered everything from lighting fixtures, silver tea sets, and papier-mâché dressing cases to fenders and fire irons.

With five children and no husband, she needed the income, but she was an unlikely person to succeed in the demanding business world. Described by Frances as resembling Amelia Sedley, the pretty but helpless young widow in William Makepeace Thackeray's novel *Vanity Fair*, Mamma was a gentle, angelic soul whose mind remained until her death "like that of an innocent, serious, young girl—with a sort of maidenly matronliness."[9] She was neither talkative nor clever, and could be vague and unworldly. The children adored her ability to soothe and calm them in their nursery life, an ability less useful in the larger world of commerce. Within months it became clear that they could not continue to live as they had, so dismissing some of the servants, Eliza made the first of several downward moves into a house in Seedley Grove, Tanner's Lane, Pendleton, where Frances attended the Hague sisters' school. A year later they moved again, to the decidedly less genteel neighbourhood of Islington Square, Salford, which backed onto the rougher neighbourhood of miners' families. Eliza preferred that they literally turn their backs on the less reputable and more dangerous occupants behind them, attend school, and accompany her on visits to the nearby art gallery at Peel Park. The children were fascinated by the people with their strong Lancashire accent and dialect, "the men and women who worked at their looms, the swarms of smoke-begrimed children who played everywhere [and] began to work in the factories as early as the law allowed."[10]

Like all studies of persons who go on to be writers, Frances's childhood autobiography describes the important stepping-stones taken towards her literary awakening: the first alphabet book of flowers given to her by a grandmother who came to stay with them; the first book of stories, lost and rediscovered in adulthood; the first original poem, read to an adoring and astonished mother; the search for books containing the short lines that indicated dialogue and therefore fiction; the repeated requests to her friends and relatives for things to read; the visits to houses, where she would read their books rather than play with the other children. Late in life she recalled "wandering about the house on long, rainy days, like a little ghost sighing desolately under my breath 'if I just had something to read'; and the word 'just' was a sort of a small wail which nobody really heard."[11] Nevertheless, she was "from her very infancy making everything into a story, reading voraciously from less than five years of age, absorbing the symbol, adopting the method, becoming expert at the trick, and steadily educating herself to set forth her own ideas—or imitate others' ideas—in romance form."[12] By today's standards, Frances's was a minimal education, one that did little to prepare her for a literary career. The Seedley Grove school for small children, which she first attended, was run by two sisters named Mary and Alice Hague. She loved to read, and their reward to her for her good behaviour was a copy of a storybook, a prize they intended to replace later on with something less frivolous. Frances threw what was possibly her first temper tantrum and burst into tears, begging to keep the book. She memorized the stories in it, and by seven she was writing her own, which adults admired as being "remarkably clever for a child."[13] In retrospect she thought little of her stories' quality, even though she knew, early on, that she had an ease of expression that grew out of her reading, her imagination, and her innate comfort with ideas.

Her reading, like her education, was as slapdash as it was fervent, and this was to colour her literary output for years into her writing career until she gained sufficient discrimination and guidance to produce more informed and sophisticated work. "I wonder how many—or how few—of those who have written books the world knows well, were educated for literature?" she later remarked. "I was not. I lived among the educated, but not among literary, people until I was taken to America."[14] She was as likely—and indeed, happier—to read the romantic potboilers in the *Ladies' Halfpenny Journal* in England and *Godey's Lady's Book* in America than to struggle with more formidable and complicated books, and to imitate them on slates or scraps of paper left over from the cook's kitchen accounts. She read popular favourites Sir Walter Scott, Captain Mayne Reid, and Harrison Ainsworth, and her sense of drama led her to use her dolls in the most melodramatic ways: they were beheaded, buried, revived, beaten, and adored in scenes out of all these stories, and in ways that concerned her mother and amused her brothers (once they found that, inspired by a pamphlet on Aztecs she had found in her late father's desk, she used the underneath of a draped table to enact human sacrifices with her dolls), but it was done with such good humour on her part that it never indicated anything more than a lively mind.[15]

Even from the earliest age, Frances committed to paper her imaginings, scraps of poems, and stories. She and her sisters were given free rein to draw and scribble in old ledger books, cooks' accounts, and random scraps of paper. Frances loved clothes—two of the most detailed memories in the autobiography of her childhood concern dresses she either owned or wished to—and one sketch on an early page of the surviving ledger book shows "Frances as she appears in her new dress and Hat." The early drawing is alongside the name "Colonel Scarborough," who became a character in a story she wrote in the book at a later time, probably after her move to America, "How Donna Scarborough Married for Money," about a jaded young woman who rejects true love with a poorer man for an empty life with someone who can maintain her fashionably in her accustomed comfort.

After the move to Islington Square in 1855, Frances, along with her siblings, spent her days until she was thirteen or so at the primly named Select Seminary for Young Ladies and Gentlemen run by Henry Hadfield's nineteen-year-old daughter Sarah and her sisters Jane and Alice, where the emphasis was on learning by rote. Their younger sister Annie became Frances's closer friend, and through them she was exposed to a finer and more cultured life than she had known. There were only six children at the school in addition to the Hodgsons. Henry Hadfield, a drawing and painting master, had anticipated a brighter future through an expected inheritance but instead spent fifty years teaching at the Mechanics' Institute. The Hadfields remembered Frances as "an exceedingly precocious . . . and very romantic" child who was "full of animal spirits" and very popular with the other children at the school, for whom she made up stories, keeping them spellbound.

> She could read very well, and knew the multiplication table off, when I first taught her; but was never cleaver [sic] at Arithmetic; and, when learning history, could never remember dates, and such things as County towns, rivers, and lakes &c—though any historical event, or incident, which occurred anywhere, she could remember clearly enough—in fact, whatever was connected with literature she was passionately fond of—Grammar, Analysis, &c were no trouble to her, though she never struck me at the time as being a very deep thinker; but naturally quick of comprehension—seeming to understand a subject at once. She was a great reader when even a very little girl; but not at all particular as to the subjects she read. If it were a book she would wade through it. She wrote one or two little stories when at school, so did several of the other girls; which they used to bring to me to be read before the pupils—her productions, however, were the most romantic and sensational; containing, as they did, such glowing discriptions [sic] of beautiful girls, with heavenly blue eyes &c—and one particular I remember—she had always a strong character and a weak one.[16]

Frances knew from her haphazard reading that characters had to be minutely described, with a checklist of physical attributes such as "a straight, delicate nose, large pellucid violet eyes, slender arched eyebrow, lashes which swept her softly-rounded, rose-tinted cheek, a mouth like Cupid's bow, a brow of ivory on which azure veins meandered, pink ears like ocean shells, a throat like alabaster, shoulders like marble, a waist which one might span."[17] None of this described Frances herself in the least. She was small and plump, with rather unruly curling reddish hair. She was so active and bouncing that her brothers likened her to India rubber. A Manchester boy recalled her as "a little lady dressed in short muslin frock and velvet tippet, whose face was attractive and interesting always . . . with a red-lipped, sensitive mouth, pretty inquisitive eyes, and head crowned with an abundance of rich auburn hair, worn in long, thick curls." She drew admirers from both the boys and the girls at the school, including a boy whose unlikely name of Marmaduke Mudieman seems uncannily like those she gave to her stories' characters.[18] In addition to the serial stories, she wrote numbers of poems, mostly for occasions, and always to amuse. When she was twelve she wrote a poem about Bacchus:

King Jove had given a dinner,
To his courtiers handsome and bold,
And as his friend, Bacchus, had sat by his side,
He took too much wine, I am told.

For such a sweet Goddess attended him,
So brightly bewitching and clever,
A sort of compound of Venus,
Aurora, Clyte, and Minerva.

And Bacchus had musically observed,
Tho' at first he professed to be shy,
That Jove was a jolly, good fellow,
Which nobody could deny.

It went on for many verses, concentrating on several issues that would become themes throughout her own life—marital discord and fashion. She signed this with the name under which all her earliest stories would be published, Fannie E. Hodgson.[19]

Despite all the anecdotes about her penchant for reading and inventing, it is also true that she lived an active social life and was in that respect certainly similar to many young girls whose talents do not interfere with their relationships. The only surviving letter of her youth is one written on 4 June 1862, when she was twelve, begging her mother to let her go on various visits with friends or to a lonely cousin:

My Dear Mother:
I hope you will let me go to Rhyl with Miss Emma on Whit Wednesday. If I may not go there, let me go to Blackpool with Lizzie Farrar and Ada Renshaw.
We break up next Friday and are going to have five weeks' holiday.
I hope it will be fine during Whit week so that you can take us to Miss Watson's to see the scholars walk.
I am going to write to cousin Lillie to-day. I am sorry you do not wish us to visit her this month. I am sure she will feel very lonely, as she does not know any one there.
I am glad to inform you that we are going to say no more lessons until after the holiday.
With kind love, I remain, my dear Mamma,
Your loving daughter,
Frances[20]

She was frequently out and about with friends and family members, and returned home to write about her excursions. After attending the festivities occasioned by the marriage of Prince Edward and Princess Alexandra on 10 March 1863, she wrote a poem for her cousin Emily White about the fine time she'd had with another cousin, Emily Boond, when they went to see the illuminations, or fireworks. It included a literary promise:

> Some very fine day I will step up your way,
> At least, if to it you agree.
> With two tales I've been writing, full of murders and fighting—
> So I hope you'll be glad to see me.[21]

She kept all her young friends amused by making up episodic stories such as "Millicent's Romance" and the deeply missed "Celeste, or Fortune's Wheel." The longest running of her serial stories, narrated to her classmates over their stitching or on the way home from school, was "Edith Somerville." Like the others, this was a typically adolescent romance, and the children, amazed at her ability to conjure up tales and episodic adventures, were enthralled. Her teachers, like her fellow students, recognized "her extraordinary powers as an Improvisatrice; she being able to commence, and spin out, a yarn at a moment's notice—and it was an interesting sight to see, when she was so engaged, the children sit or stand around her, spellbound, like the listeners to the tale of the 'Ancient Mariner,' as she proceeded to work out one of her, to them, exciting and wonderful tales."[22] Frances, as she spun out these stories, felt a sense of exhilaration at the stories themselves but also at the response. She loved an audience, and one of her greatest evening pleasures in adulthood was to sit in the living room, chain-smoking and reading her day's work to Edith or her house guests. As a girl she shared a fantasy life with the boys and girls at the academy and with her cousins, even keeping a copy of Lemprière's *Classical Dictionary* on her desk, "so that I could dip into it and snatch a legend while I was looking for pencils or geographies."[23]

Because Eliza reacted with a sort of stunned awe to her daughter's first poetic effort, Frances was never shy about continuing or sharing her work, except with her teasing older brothers. The real problem, one that persisted until her first publishing successes, was how to write them down. Never a compact writer, she always found that her imagination outpaced her materials. Slates simply did not provide enough space to complete a story; the cook's old butcher's books were greasy, and most of the pages were used up so that the heart-wrenching lines spoken between lovers were always interrupted by grocers' accounts. It makes sense, then, that she developed a quick and verbal way of telling stories, one "not limited by a slate-frame" but with "the stimulus of an enraptured audience. She told 'Edith Somerville' all the afternoon, and when she left the school-room her friend Kate followed her while she related it on the way home, and even stood and told some more at the front gate. It was not finished when they parted. It was not a story to be finished in an afternoon."[24] The story ran on for weeks, with a devoted circle of listeners who secretly brought an odd assortment of refreshments— green apples, jugs of water, and even raw turnips—in "a sort of Bacchana-lian orgie [which] added to the adventures of Edith Somerville just the touch of license needed. The Small Person's enjoyment was a luxurious thing."[25]

Frances was clearly a gifted, lively, and voluble child, so admired by her sis-ters and friends that she was in danger of never moving beyond her natural gift for exuberant storytelling into any further critical thinking. Her hunger for reading and mental expansion went undernourished at a time when the "child who was found furtively and pathetically—for there was pathos in it—reading volumes intended for the perusal of its elders, was regarded as an abnormality and a persistent display of interest in such literature aroused doubts of health and safety."[26] With no one seeing a need to do more than indulge her passion for words and books, one of the best things that could happen to her was to have someone of taste call her up short and force her to examine her judgment.

When Frances was nine, a friend rushed to her with the news that a wonderful family, consisting of a woman and her adult daughter and three "grown-up" sons, was living nearby, that they had in fact been there for a year without anyone in the neighbourhood making friends with them, and that they seemed to like children. The girls made a point of bumping into them and, over time, were each more or less adopted by a son as his special small friend. At first Frances belonged to the musical son who played piano, but as her literary aspirations became known, she drifted closer to the laughing one in his twenties who cared for books. It was at a time when there was tacit acknowledgment of the distance between adults and children, a time during which it "would be impossible for a child brought up in the freedom of an American nursery" to understand "the respect for ripe years which dominated ours."[27] Each girl became the devoted and reverent "pet" of one of the brothers, ready to engage in whatever conversation and atten-tion the young man was willing to spare when they encountered him in the square.

Frances's young man was in his late twenties and had no intention of being either a mentor or an instructor to her. The small chatterbox who accosted him in the square, breathlessly recounting the latest story she had read, amused him. When he had time, he would lean against the railings, adjust his monocle, and watch her, smiling, while he stroked his moustache. He knew she was very fond of him; "he could not have helped knowing, but that I regarded him with adoration as the most brilliantly accomplished, the most dazzlingly witty and undoubtedly profound of his sex, would have filled him—if he had for a moment realized it—with an intensity of amusement which he could not possibly have concealed, and a knowledge of which would have crushed me to the earth with indignant humiliation when it had revealed itself to me."

As much as she worshipped him, she also over the five or six years of their friendship thought of him as her adversary. Unlike her young friends who were dazzled by her bottomless well of tales, her adult friend took a much more critical view of her reading habits, often gently chastising for what he recognized as her weak points: a "voracious appetite for books of all sorts, without the least tendency toward discrimination; that there were jocular legends about what I read and vague rumors that I very furtively tried to scribble myself; that I was wildly romantic in secret and that I had a fiery and most rebellious little spirit, which revealed itself at once when I was twitted about these hidden weaknesses." Frances was accustomed to the mockery of her brothers, who tormented her about her ceaseless writing and were "immensely exhilarated by the idea, and indulged in the most brilliant witticisms at her expense," pretending to quote the most purple of passages from her overblown manuscripts when others were around to hear.[28] Even though the boys meant no harm, her new friend's amusement prompted in her a similar reaction. Often, to his enjoyment, she turned red in the face, spat out her anger, and ran off, only later to become humiliated when she recognized the justice of his criticism. One day, excited by a story of an orange-seller surrounded by marquises who wanted to marry her but whom she was rejecting in favour of a duke, she accosted her friend in Islington Square. A housemaid had shown her the story in a penny weekly paper, and Frances was so desperate to know the end that she revealed to him her plan of saving her pennies to subscribe to the paper. He stared for a moment, then broke into a series of short disbelieving laughs that infuriated her. Becoming serious, he advised her to "throw it in the kitchen fire, and I will get you something worth reading."

Even though he delighted in watching her explosions, theirs was also a friendlier relationship between two readers. Meeting Frances in the square as he returned home in the evenings, he often asked casually whether she had read a particular book or story, or mentioned that "There is a story in

'Cornhill' this month you ought to read," or "Come to the house and I will read you some verses you will like in the last number of 'Once a Week.'" After she'd read them, they discussed them, and slowly she gained insight into what made good writing good. He "cleverly parodied sentimental things I might have leaned toward . . . jeeringly made light of lurid romances. . . . [His] ironical view of certain things made me burn with uncomfortable blushes when I realized that I had regarded with secret respect sentiments and situations which could be so brilliantly derided. There was a great deal of derision in it all, but as it was really clever derision[;] it certainly developed my sense of humor." At no point did he either act like a schoolmaster or treat her like "a fool," even when making fun of her youthful penchant for lurid romances.

It was an education that no one else around her could offer. The Hadfield sisters' school taught the basics, as well as dancing, sewing, and comportment. Although certain subjects were taught separately, the boys received no more in the way of what one might term a "cultural" education than did the girls. Often the lives of literary men begin with their formal training with a tutor, at a grammar school, and perhaps later a university; with the classic books and classical languages under their belts, they make their first youthful forays into poetry. Even many of the women writers from whom formal education was withheld grew up in households with libraries they could raid, with educated fathers who were clergymen or scholars. Frances, a nice mid-Victorian girl in a middle-class family, had a gift but no literary advantages or direction. Her "bookish" father was in trade and died when she was barely out of her infancy. Her mother's efforts were desperately concentrated on clutching at whatever financial security she could, and although she was a loving parent, she was also a distracted one whose clever daughter's imaginative antics puzzled and even worried her. Frances's two older brothers were uninterested in the life of the mind, and their teasing meant that "she should take precautions about secreting [her attempts at writing] safely" out of their sight.[29] Her two adoring but even younger sisters admired her gift and encouraged the "Edith Somerville" types of creation, breathlessly calling her, as did the other girls in their school, "an auth'ress" and a regular "Charles Dickens," but were unable to help her grow in her craft. Her schoolyard successes led her to believe that her untrained talent was sufficient in itself, yet she continued to hone it in private, without guidance. There simply was no one to direct and mould her inquisitive young female mind. Girls were brought up to be good wives; to offer more was not only simply beyond the financial means of Eliza Hodgson but also beyond her immediate understanding.

Brave as she was in taking over Edwin's business, Eliza was no match for the combination of hard work and general economic downturn of the early 1860s. The American Civil War had begun to affect Manchester in ways that its recent and growing prosperity made seem impossible. In 1863, when Frances was in her early teens, Eliza finally sold the business to the firm of Penman and Butt and out of necessity took an even smaller house on Gore Street. In that same year the Hadfields moved to Strawberry Hill, closing the school, and Frances's formal education came to an end.

Even after the sale of the firm, it was clear that Eliza still could not make ends meet. At about this time she received a letter from her brother William, boasting of his latest American successes. Why, he asked her, did she not give up on England and join him in Tennessee? The income from his Knoxville grocery and provisions business was strong and growing, and he could use one of her sons as an assistant. The gristmill just outside the city prospered enough to offer work to her other son. They should all join forces so that she would no longer have to face her difficulties alone. Even though she had no other ideas on how she could continue to provide for her family, she did not decide immediately. Family and friends surrounded her in Manchester, and in those days a move to America seemed a permanent move. "When we went out to Tennessee," Frances recalled in middle age, "every one said good-bye to me as if for life, as if taking leave of us forever, convinced that they would never see us again. And it looked just as serious to us as it did to them."[30] To her and her brothers and sisters, the move to America was an adventure.

For several months Eliza conferred with her relatives and at last, in early 1865, decided to sell their furniture and emigrate. Fifteen-year-old Frances broke the news to her "enemy" at his mother's house. He expressed no emotion, but after a pause exclaimed, "'Oh, I say!' he added, with the half-chafing lightness to which I was quite inured. 'Confound America, you know, in fact, hang America!' And he laughed the short laugh again, and I—sitting upon the hearth-rug—responded by a sad little grin." Shortly before they left England, his sister invited Frances to spend the night with the family, so that their good-byes could be made at leisure. The next morning he walked her back to the Grove Street house. Pausing under the church clock in the square, they shook hands and he repeated "Good-by, and—confound America, you know!" They never met again, even though she was to return to Manchester several times, each time with a greater and wider literary reputation. He would be shocked to learn, she said, that he was the person who most influenced her in the world, although he must certainly have discovered how famous she became.

CHAPTER 3

A SHABBY
GENTEEL STORY

1866–1868

T HE HODGSONS REMAINED in New Market for only a year and
a half before moving closer to Knoxville to an area called Clinton
Pike in 1866, where they would remain until moving into Knoxville
proper in 1869. They may have been closer to the city in Clinton Pike, but
in many ways they now lived a more rustic life. Whereas New Market was
a village with next-door neighbours and a small station running trains in
and out of Knoxville several times a day, Clinton Pike seemed to back right
up to mountains. The new house was a small "planked up arrangement with
crude windows and doorways that were practically covered with morning-
glory vines . . . it was neat and home-like, and nestled among the pines that
stretched their gnarled arms in a most friendly manner toward the little
primitive home."[1] Frances lost no time in christening it "Noah's Ark" and
the hill behind it "Ararat," and was enthralled with its seemingly untouched
primeval beauty. Even so, it was only a half hour's walk into Knoxville, and
the site, only a few years later, of Knoxville College, one of the South's
oldest historically black colleges. In Frances's time it combined the best of
tumble-down rural life with easy—and free—access to town.

The Hodgson boys and girls found that animals as well as people attached
themselves to them, and they had what Frances referred to as "colonies of
dogs." An irascible one they called Pepper followed one of the Hodgson boys
home and spent a year or two seesawing between their family and another
one, whenever he felt offended. Edith enticed a large yellow one, Mr. K, to
follow her home. He was perfect in every way except for a tendency to fight
with other dogs, particularly Tige, owned by a nearby black family. "The
children could not decide whether or not it was a matter of race prejudice,"

but the two dogs feuded constantly, ending when Tige's canine friends attacked Mr. K, leaving him nearly dead but reformed.[2] The Hodgsons found themselves fully immersed in country life, in a place where the vegetation grew so fast that the war's battle scars were all but obliterated from the land.

Their view was of the Smoky Mountains, hills covered in spring and summer with wildflowers, and old oak trees. Times remained extraordinarily difficult financially, but somehow Frances remained optimistic and confident. Unlike Britain, America seemed to her a place of opportunity, and she eventually used the family's slow descent into poverty in the fiction she would create as she matured. She did not yet narrate out of her own experience, and at sixteen she found it as easy to imagine the Indians who had lived there before as it had been to write unfinished stories about Londoners marrying dukes. In good weather she dragged Edith and Edwina, and later her new friend Ada Campbell, as well as local children, on long walks by the Tennessee River, throwing herself down on the rocks to tell them stories.

In fact, the native people of the region had a horrifying history. A New Market neighbour's uncle, on his eightieth birthday in 1890, confessed to his family his shame at having been forced to take part in the 1838 slaughter and removal of the Cherokee from their lifelong homes. Asked to join the mission because of his ability to speak their language fluently, he "witnessed the execution of the most brutal order in the History of American Warfare. I saw the helpless Cherokees arrested, dragged from their homes, and driven at bayonet point into the stockades, and in the chill of a drizzling rain on an October morning I saw them loaded like cattle or sheep into six hundred and forty five wagons and started toward the West."[3] Calling it "the blackest chapter on the pages of American History," he declared that watching a brutal driver use his whip on an old and nearly blind Indian caused him to strike the teamster unconscious with a hatchet he kept in his belt.

Frances, having missed the war, plantation slavery, and the forced relocation of Indians, was sheltered from the appalling history and circumstances of many of the places around her. For all her reading she was young and had lived a rather sheltered life. Despite its grinding poverty, life in New Market and Clinton Pike seemed an adventure, and she charmed her young sisters and friends with the stories she invented as they lay on their backs after their hikes, modelling the American stories on those she'd made up in England about lost loves and romance. One, about a Cherokee brave whose tribe was camped outside Knoxville and who thought he'd lost his beloved to a white man who had rescued her from a white settlers' attack, brought tears to the eyes of the girls who accompanied her.[4]

The Hodgson girls never lacked companions. In New Market, Mary Johnson, whose mother befriended the family, became friendly with Fannie, as the Americans all called Frances. Their nearest neighbours, the Burnetts, were quite well off compared to the Hodgsons, but in fact they were the poor relations of a well-regarded family of long American lineage. The Burnett family was descended from Huguenots who had escaped religious persecution by emmigrating to Charleston, South Carolina, and their Bible entries recorded births and deaths back to the seventeenth century. It was a proud and successful family line with whom the New Market branch remained connected by the repeated use of recognized Burnett first names. Between 1844 and 1858, Dr. John M. Burnett and his wife, Lydia Ann Peck Burnett, had seven children, three of them dying young. Their son Swan, whom Frances would eventually marry, was their third child, born on 16 March 1847, less than two years before Frances. The Hodgsons lived in a comfortable but unimposing wooden frame house across a clearing from the Burnett cabin. As a local physician, Dr. Burnett would often be gone for days at a time because he visited on horseback, with his supplies in saddlebags, his patients in the surrounding hills. With poverty so pervasive in those years, the doctor was little better off than his new neighbours and, like Frances running her short-lived seminary, was often paid in goods such as bacon, grits, and feed for the mules Jenny and June, rather than cash.

Swan Burnett was a quiet young man whose adolescence had been spent in the deprivations of a war economy. What had been a thriving small town became during that time an extremely poor backwater that, except for its daily trains to and from Knoxville, felt cut off from the wider world. He was, as Edith said, both "studious and ambitious" and expected to have a successful medical career. Into this mundane life dropped a family from England, with a daughter who amused everyone with her chattiness and her storytelling, and most of all her laughter—she told people that her "first glimpse of Swan was watching him from a window on the turnpike outside, contending with a refractory mule."[5] A little afraid of her, and never really relaxing in her presence, he nevertheless fell for her immediately.[6]

It is much less easy to see what attraction he held for her. Swan perhaps had the better formal education, but Frances introduced him to the books of all her favourite novelists. Charles Dickens, Sir Walter Scott, and William Makepeace Thackeray were all new to him, but to her they, along with the less reputable writers of stories in ladies' magazines, were her lifeblood. She undoubtedly told him about her early investigation, in Manchester, of her parents' mahogany bookcase, containing "rows of volumes called 'The Encyclopaedia,' rows of stout volumes of *Blackwood's Magazine*, a row of poets, a row of miscellaneous things with unprepossessing bindings, and two rows of exceedingly ugly brown books." It wasn't until a dull, rainy day when she was seven or eight that she climbed the unpromising piece of furniture in search of something to read and discovered that *Blackwood's* contained not dry arithmetic but stories, and that "the secrétaire" was full of treasures in the form of Scott's novels, the poetry of Keats and Coleridge, and Shakespeare's plays. I "was perched in Paradise," she recalled. "No one could fall from a Secrétaire filled with books, which might all of them contain Stories!"[7]

She delighted in long walks in the hills, while Swan, less physically sturdy, found enjoyment in his studies and in reading the books she recommended to him. He walked with a pronounced limp, the result of a childhood injury: some said that he was walking through a cornfield and swinging a large knife at the stalks when the knife glanced off into his leg, others that he was playing "mumble the peg" when the knife fell into his knee, causing infection and permanent damage that left him unable to participate in outdoor activities. Always sympathetic to those with physical handicaps, she enjoyed his attentions but wavered in her commitment to him, feeling nowhere near to promising her future to anyone. She repeatedly confessed in later life that she never wanted to marry anyone—marriage was too confining, especially for a woman as independent as she.

This craving for domestic autonomy was incompatible with a soft heart, though. "Fannie, with her tenderness for any sort of disability or disadvantage," wrote Edith, "well, knowing Fannie, can't you see how inevitably it came about?"[8] Frances herself confirmed this to a friend some years after the marriage formally ended, even though at that point she rarely discussed Swan. "He was lame," she said. "That was enough for me."[9] For the time being, however, there was no need for either of them to make a commitment to the other because Swan had just completed his studies at New Market Academy and was about to follow in his father's medical footsteps. Shortly after the Hodgsons' move to Clinton Pike, Swan left for Cincinnati, Ohio, to begin his medical studies.

Everyone's recollections of Frances in these years come through the filter of her later successes. In their later years, friends from her time at New Market, Clinton Pike, and Knoxville filled local newspaper columns with their memories of a young woman who "possessed a lovable nature, [was] romantic, full of sunshine, optimistic and saw the funny side of everything."[10] The stories of this time became apocryphal, and in their repetitions over the course of more than 130 years became so filled with error and idealism that it is difficult to extract the determined young woman from the portrait of the happy-go-lucky adolescent who inspired her friends to practise their own writing on their reminiscences of her youth. Some of this occurred because of the times: a young woman who landed in their yards like an exotic breeze at the end of the worst slaughter America had yet known, who became extraordinarily famous for her writings, lent memory an idealistic glow. Mistakes have a way of perpetuating themselves. Several articles claimed that she met Swan when she went to his house to sell berries in order to buy paper and pencils; that he was already a doctor; that he became instantly infatuated with her and financed her education. That he was still a local student only slightly older than she and that her education had already ended before they met became lost in this fairytale version of their meeting.[11]

There is no doubt of her originality and playfulness, and in later years she may have encouraged this naïve depiction of her early life. She selected Reginald Birch, another transplant from England to America, to illustrate the autobiography of her youth, *The One I Knew the Best of All*, in 1893 when she was forty-three. She enthusiastically approved of his drawings, which depicted what she called "the Small Person" in a state of perpetual childhood, even in those pictures representing her at nearly twenty, because she wanted the book as a whole to represent the years when she "went through all those queer little mental processes."[12] The book was to take her from infancy to adulthood, through the lens of a developing psyche. The new interest in psychology meant that she and her readers concentrated on her earliest years, and that remained its draw when the book was reissued more than twenty years later. The circumstances of her life had changed in adulthood, she wrote in the foreword to the new edition, but her essential character had not:

> What I myself find suggestive & recognize every day of my life is the characteristics of the Small Person—her emotions, her faults, her strengths, her raptures, her dislikes have accompanied through a lifetime the individual she was—in the "Back Garden of Eden"—preparing to become. I see very little change in her. She has accumulated more facts & knows more of the relative sizes of things but she does today exactly the *kind* of thing she would have done in nursery days if life could then have called her up to confront the conditions it now presents. I could not say that I consider her much wiser.
>
> And there is a degree of illumination in a fact like that after all—to the unbiassed & searching mind.[13]

The interior view of those years—the revelling in the countryside, the desire to please and entertain, the certitude of better times to come—is borne out in the views of her friends. She referred to these times as her dryad days, a term she repeated in her stories with southern settings.[14]

What is missing in their accounts is her silent vow to succeed in escaping the dreariness of a poverty that had loomed ever nearer since her father's death, privation that, although kept hidden from the children in their younger years, was now staring them in the face. Missing too are her sporadic but lifelong battles with depression, usually triggered when she was overworked and exhausted, or struggling with family or financial difficulties. She made this clear to Swan, whom she had now rechristened by the more masculine name Jerome, shortly after the Hodgsons moved from Clinton Pike into Knoxville proper:

> There is a very strong feeling deep in my heart, telling me that something must be done to raise us all a little from the dust, and the very strength of that feeling lies in the fact that I am *sure, sure* I must do it. You have no need to smile. Nobody else will do it, because nobody else cares a cent whether we drag through our wretched lives as shabby, genteel beggars, or not. We are not shabby, genteel beggars, says Bert, when I fire up a little—but we *are* shabby, genteel beggars, I say. We are not respectable people in our own eyes, whatever we may be in any one elses. I would as soon be a thief as feel like one, and I do feel like one. . . .
>
> Respectability doesn't only mean food and a house—it means pretty, graceful things; a front street *not* close to the gas works; an occasional new book to provide against mental starvation; a chance to see the world; a piano and fifteen cents spending money (not to be squandered recklessly of course). "Man cannot live by bread alone," said the minister to his drunken old parishioner. "No," said the apt non-convert, "He mun hae' a few wedgetables," which is my opinion. What I want is a "few wedgetables."
>
> What is there to feed my poor, little, busy brain in this useless, weary, threadbare life? I can't eat my own heart forever. I can't write things that are worth reading if I never see things which are worth seeing, or speak to people who are worth hearing. I cannot weave silk if I see nothing but calico—calico—calico. It is all calico, it seems to me. Ah, me! Ah, me! see what a tangled skein of thread for one poor little woman to unwind.[15]

The theme of shabby gentility, probably taken directly from Thackeray's novella *A Shabby Genteel Story* set in a boarding house whose owners have higher aspirations, appears over and over in her ledger book stories, and the desire to escape it drives many of her early characters. A desire to marry money motivates Lisabel Cray, who cannot forget "the shabby genteel little personage who [studied] at the third rate French boarding school . . . . It makes me shudder to think of it." Theo is the "daughter of a shabby genteel English solicitor" and "cut bread & butter in the shabby genteel house on the shabby genteel street until the outer world had been only a dream land to her."[16] Frances began to view the storytelling, formerly her party piece, as a way to stave off destitution and rise in the world. Once she learned that she could make money by her pen, the aim for the next decade was to keep the wolf from the door, sometimes turning a deliberately blind eye to quality in an effort to churn out quantity. Within five years she would became what she bitterly called a "pen driving machine" whose health was permanently affected by the unrelenting hard work.[17]

Frances regularly spent part of her days at the Clinton Pike house sequestered in the attic, writing. "I cannot remember a time when I did not write," she told a reporter,

> and I have a distinct recollection of employing my time while the rest of the family were at church in writing down some verses. I must then have been seven years old. When I was about fifteen I accompanied my mother to America, and you can easily imagine the effect that such a change of scene produced on a sensitive girl. We settled in one of the wildest and most beautiful districts of Tennessee. But this utter change only seemed to stimulate my ardour for literary work, and I went on writing steadily, though still without any thought of publishing, till it became necessary for me to be able to earn some money.[18]

Edith confirmed that "it was here that she began to write. To write for publication I mean."[19]

As in England, the Hodgson girls read the monthly magazines whenever they could get hold of them. The American market supported a number of magazines for women, most of them a combination of sewing patterns, short stories, poems, and household hints. Each had a staff of regular editors and contributors, but they also published pieces by outsiders. As the girls pored over magazines such as *Frank Leslie's Illustrated Newspaper*, *Peterson's Monthly Magazine*, and *Godey's Lady's Book and Magazine*, Frances, Edith, and Edwina noticed at the back messages from the editors directed towards readers who had submitted their work for publication. "Elaine the Fair.— Your story has merit, but is not quite suited to our columns. *Never* write on both sides of your paper." "Christabel.—We do not return rejected manuscripts unless stamps are enclosed for postage." None of the family had ever imagined the possibility of Frances's stories being worth money, but as they grew poorer, Edith and Edwina encouraged her to submit her work to the magazines.[20] At this stage in her life her brother Herbert was still tormenting her, "asking her how she was getting on with her tale of 'The Gory Milkman and the Blood-Stained Pump.'"[21] She was willing to face rejection if there were a chance she could be paid, but she was shy about her work and loath to face the taunts of Bert and John, who "ridiculed my literary productions, and on many occasions, to tease me, would pretend to have found my manuscripts, and would quote most ridiculous things which they said were extracts from a new book about to be published by Francis [*sic*] Hodgson." Moreover, it was clear from the columns that she needed good paper and postage, two things fairly hard to come by in their cash-strapped household. They could have found a way to pay for the stamps, but not without letting Herbert and John, who brought home the only hard cash, into the plan. "They were poor, but they weren't that poor," Frances's nephew Bert later confirmed. "She didn't want anyone to know she had sent the story off; was afraid she'd be teased."[22]

One of the regular visitors to the Clinton Pike frame house was a middle-aged man, "Mr. S—, a charming man, who used to ride out frequently to the Noah's Ark, just to talk with her. She could hold her own with anybody."[23] They talked philosophy and history, and her envious sisters huddled at the top of the winding staircase, eavesdropping. One evening Edith was straining forward to listen and lost her balance, sliding partway down the stairs as Edwina tried to pull her back, to Frances's utter embarrassment. As in Manchester, Frances found herself taken up by an adult man who enjoyed her company and challenged her in conversation; unlike the youthful Swan, he was not only too old for her but "far too comfortably placed to arouse her protecting tenderness, so there was no love affair on her part."[24] It is likely that "Mr. S—" was the same unnamed schoolteacher who assisted her in sending her first stories off to a magazine by offering to take them to the post office and to let her use his address. The postage problem itself was solved by a black family who lived nearby. "Aunt" Cynthy—African American women, including mulattoes like Cynthy, were never at that time in the South allowed the title of Mrs. but were commonly referred to as Aunt by southern whites— had two daughters who sometimes made money by picking wild grapes and selling them in the Knoxville market. Hearing of this, Frances and Edith consulted the girls, then went out themselves to pick grapes and arranged for Cynthy's daughters to sell the fruit for them. They made enough to buy the needed paper and the stamps required to cover the return postage.

Despite her later assertions, not all of her writing was consigned to the fire before leaving Manchester, and Frances chose as her first submission a story called "Miss Carruthers' Engagement," which she had written there. She copied it out in the chilly attic room at the Clinton Pike house where she regularly retired, a cat on her lap, to write in the afternoons and evenings. True to her youthful style, she included in the story's first paragraph the laundry list of physical characteristics of her heroine Georgie, "who, playing the part of heroine, of course needed particular description." She endowed her with "large, heavily-fringed brown eyes, and a crown of amber hair, [she was] a girl with a little haughty curve on her velvet mouth, and a slightly *superbe* manner of holding her white neck."[25] The tone quickly changes in the first paragraph to something surprisingly accomplished and astute for a fifteen-year-old, even though she revised it at eighteen. Georgie Carruthers was

> in disposition, warm-hearted and affectionate. A great favorite with her own sex, though not a "sweet young lady" in the common acceptance of the term. By this I mean, one of the sweet young ladies of the present day, who, so wisely averse to wasting their saccharine properties on the desert air, dispose of them to so much advantage, lending them out at interest, as it were, cooing and lavishing endearments on each other, in public, in a manner which, to persons of Mephistophilean temperament, might appear to insinuate an excess of amiability. Certainly not of this class my brown-eyed heroine.[26]

In fact, were it not for the evidence of Frances's pencil-scrawled stories from this time, one would suspect that a more worldly and experienced mind was at work. Georgie Carruthers has many of the traits that Burnett called upon for her growing stable of heroines: too proud, seemingly rather cool and controlled in the social world, but warm and even inwardly tortured. She had broken an engagement to the man she loved after receiving letters that had been mistakenly switched in their envelopes. Because all these early stories rely on a happy ending and the overcoming of obstacles to love, Georgie inadvertently learns her mistake and the couple tearfully resume their engagement.

The men in these stories come from a similar stable of characters. Not quite comfortable in the noble realm, Frances frequently drew on military officers as having the rank and panache to handle the accomplished women who challenged them. Georgie's betrothed is Captain Standish, a military title she had tried out in the pages of the ledger book. There too are Captains Vesey, Chesebro, and, in her pencilled story "Little Polly Landsell" (published in 1872 as "Little Polly Lambert"), a Captain Fergus. A Captain Beswicke appears in "Aunt Portia's Diamond." She fluctuates between Colonel and Major Carmichael in "Lisabel Cray's Punishment," with the title of Major ultimately winning out. In "How Denis Scarbrough Married for Money," Denis is a colonel. Miles Cardovan is "the son of an Irish colonel & a gentleman at leisure" in the same story. As she practised her stories or wrote out later drafts for publication, she sprinkled them with occasional lords and ladies, but relied on titles that could occur on either side of the Atlantic and were accessible to those, like her, who could not aspire to the noble classes but who might find a well-born young officer within matrimonial reach. And even though "Miss Carruthers' Engagement" takes places at a country house presumably in England, Georgie is English and her hostess and friend, Mrs. Baynton, is American, an early example of her nudging the continents closer together as she would do so often in her novels.

Frances only sent the story out in an effort to generate income, as she made clear in her cover letter to *Ballou's Magazine*, chosen because the lesser quality of the stories offered more chance of hers being accepted. *Godey's Lady's Magazine* intimidated her too much. "I enclose stamps for the return of the accompanying MS, 'Miss Carruthers' Engagement,' if you do not find it suitable for publication in your magazine," she wrote to *Ballou's*. In case this was not direct enough she added, "my object is remuneration." She signed ambiguously as "F. Hodgson."

What exactly happened next is unclear. When the anxiously awaited response arrived via the schoolteacher, Frances tore open the envelope in the presence of her sisters and mother, none of whom could quite understand the message; the letter praised the story and made editorial suggestions but made no mention of payment. In 1887 she recalled a somewhat different scenario: that the editor of *Ballou's* "wrote me a most flattering note, offering to publish, but saying that he thought it hardly good enough to pay for; but I thought differently and asked for the return of my story."[27] Either way she requested the story's return and sent it off to the more prestigious *Godey's Lady's Magazine*. The editor liked the story but could not make the English subject matter jibe with the East Tennessee address of the androgynous "F. Hodgson." Was the author English or American, female or male? "Sir, Your story, 'Miss Carruthers' Engagement,' is so distinctly English that our reader is not sure of its having been written by an American. We see that the name given us for the address is not that of the writer. Will you kindly inform us if the story is original?" Frances replied by the next post that "The story is original. I am English myself, and have been only a short time in America." The editor, worried about the story's provenance but inclined to publish, responded, "Before we decide will you send us another story?"

Frances retired to her attic room and wrote a second piece, "Hearts and Diamonds," a story with an American theme dealing with issues of class. "Aristocracy was a curious hereditary failing" of the heroine Valerie, who early on in the story is admonished for her class snobbery by her friend Jettie. "'That sort of people!' she exclaimed. 'Are you an American, my dear, or the descendant of a three-tailed bashaw, or is it possible you are only a very charming little goose? I had the temerity to imagine myself living in a republican age, but, as I find I am mistaken, I am happy to say I am not ashamed of my forefathers. I believe one of my grandmothers was washerwoman to a nobleman's wife; in my opinion an infinitely more exciting position than that held by the lady herself. Imagine the fun on scrubbing days!'"[28] Like "Miss Carruthers' Engagement," it was a romantic melodrama that depended on misunderstandings, authorial asides to the reader, and, despite its American setting, toyed with Dickensian names such as Mr. Flutterby, Miss Waterfall, Mrs. Shoddy, and Mademoiselle Chignon. In both stories, she showed her trademark ease with dialogue. The editor's response to this second story was unequivocal. A cheque arrived for thirty-five dollars—fifteen dollars for "Hearts and Diamonds," published the following June 1868, and twenty dollars for "Miss Carruthers," which appeared in October 1868. "That first check of Fannie's!" exclaimed Edith. "Never did one for twice as many thousand dollars, such as she was by way of receiving in afterlife, seem so enormous a sum, produce so great a thrill, as did that first cheque of Fannie's! Above all, it meant that she was accepted as a writer, and women weren't writing then as they are today!"[29]

The rejoicing in the household was universal, with her brothers as delighted as Eliza and the girls at her success. She did not yet take public credit for her work, publishing her first three *Godey's* stories under the pseudonym "The Second." A second cheque for forty dollars for her next stories turned the family's fortunes, and even later in life she remained amazed at her early naïveté and success. "I was a baby!" she exclaimed. "I had been brought up in an English nursery. Do you know what that means? It means that in all my life I had talked with hardly one person except my family and my schoolmates. I knew nothing about life."[30]

With Frances now making more money than her brothers—her daughter-in-law later claimed that her output averaged six stories a month in the ladies' magazines—in 1869 the family moved to Knoxville, into a house in which her natural gregariousness and popularity found an outlet, and at only eighteen years old "she had crossed the delicate, impalpable dividing line."[31] Her life as a working writer began, and from that time on no publisher ever rejected her work.

CHAPTER 4

~

VAGABONDIA

1869–1872

I N WHAT WOULD PROVE TO BE her last year of life, Eliza was delighted with the way things were looking up for Frances although worried about her children's futures. The young Hodgsons were very popular, and with more space in the Knoxville house than they had had at Clinton Pike, and a bit more money, they were able to entertain. Eliza helped them to bake cakes and, because the older girls had nothing suitable to wear, Frances bought a length of silky alpaca "from that timely check," which "Mama, who was a wonderful needlewoman, helped us to make [into] frocks. Fannie's was straw-color with blue scallops, and [Edith's] was blue with straw-color scallops."[1]

Welcome as Frances's cheques were, the boys, now young men, still needed to work. Herbert was respectably employed by Joseph Wood, the jeweller and watchmaker on Marby and Crozier Streets, and eventually he built a profession out of what he learned there. John, however, shocked his mother in 1869 by going to work as a bartender at the Lamar House, a bustling social centre that advertised it kept "constantly on hand a large assortment of the choicest of Foreign and Domestic Brandies and Whiskies," as well as the "choicest brands of Domestic and Rhine Wines."[2] Although Lamar House itself was frequented by all levels of Knoxville society (Frances herself attended a number of parties there), it was quite a different matter to have a son tending bar. Eliza was mortified, and perhaps with good reason; John, the only one of her children to remain in Knoxville, descended later in life into alcoholism and destitution, which she fortunately did not live to see. It was Herbert, though, who was the more social brother, in demand at parties and dances, to which Frances often accompanied him.

Like her, he was "a jovial spirit among the young folk" and found himself surrounded by a cheerful group of friends.³ He was a friendly, responsible, and multi-talented young man, as good a musician as he was a jeweller.

Although the Knoxville house was a brick structure in a state of disrepair, there was plenty of space, they were in town, and there was a back garden running down to the banks of the Tennessee River, or the Houlston, as it was then known. Herbert and John bought a boat and held water parties in the moonlight. They christened the house Vagabondia Castle, and in some ways it served as a model for the rest of Frances's homes throughout her life. As time went on and her finances improved, her homes became increasingly elegant, but they never lost this familiar aura of happy social gatherings of artistic friends and family. It was an unconventional household from the outset, one that Frances portrayed as a bohemian paradise in her first novel-length work, a serial story called "Dolores," published in January 1873 in *Peterson's*, and in another iteration in *Lippincott's Monthly Magazine* as "Dorothea," and later reprinted as the novels *Vagabondia* and *Dolly*.⁴ *Dolly* described the place cheerfully as "queer and nondescript" and in a state of artistically tattered disarray, "as inviting as [it was] disreputable in appearance; there was manuscript music among the general litter, a guitar hung from the wall by a piano, and yet, notwithstanding the air of free and easy disorder, one could hardly help recognizing a sort of vagabond comfort and luxury in the Bohemian surroundings. It was so very evident that the owners must enjoy life in an easy, light hearted, though, perhaps, light headed fashion; and it was also very evident that their light hearts and light heads rose above their knowledge of their light purses."⁵

In her ledger book, in which she still drafted stories or experimented with dialogue, Frances tried out an earlier version of this opening in a fragment she called "Bohemia."

A poor little square parlor with a queer . . . look about it, a threadbare & jaded but once rich carpet on the floor its large medallions oddly out of place taken into consideration with the size of the room, numberless pictures hanging on the walls, numberless books & papers scattered upon tables & chairs, numberless sheets of music manuscript & otherwise lying here & there near various musical instruments all this mixture of shabbiness, untidiness incongruity . . . first presents itself. Not a very promising one truly but withal a scene not wholly without its redeeming points. Shabbiness as a rule is depressing. A shabby room is as apt to give one a vague sense of secret melancholy, as a shabby person & yet here was a room truly making no pretensions on earth to anything but shabbiness,

overpowering & irredeemable & still at the same time impressing the
beholder in defiance of all rules of nature, with an index of presiding spirits at once general, careless & desperately cheerful. There was something
actually rollicking about it, and there were even shabby people in it too
who ought to have added to its dispiriting effect but did not.[6]

Here the "defiant" scruffiness of the unconventional household probably
struck closer to the truth of being "desperately cheerful." Although she enjoyed their unconventional life, she at first remonstrated against what she
saw as her siblings' slide into lax and unseemly mannerisms, before realizing
that there was little she could do to change them.

Setting her earliest novel in London's Bloomsbury rather than in Tennessee barely disguised the Hodgson household to those who knew them and
identified several of the characters.[7] It was a place where "you shall be introduced to half-a-dozen people who toil not, neither do they spin successfully,
for their toiling and spinning seems to have little result, after all. You shall
see shabbiness and the spice of life hand-in-hand; and, I dare say, you will
find that the figurative dinner of herbs is not utterly destitute of a flavor of
piquancy. You shall see people who enjoy themselves in sheer defiance of circumstances, and who find a pathos in every-day events, which, in the camps
of the Philistines, mean nothing."[8] It appears eerily like the Bloomsbury
household later to be set up by the Stephen brothers and sisters of Virginia
Woolf after the death of their father Leslie Stephen.

Knoxville, like much of late-nineteenth-century America, was surprisingly
socially active during all seasons. Every winter there was a Snow Carnival,
for which carts, carriages, and farm animals were decorated like modern-day
floats and were paraded through the centre of the city by everyone from the
mayor to small farmers. In summer there were church socials and picnics.
The library published the titles of new acquisitions in the papers so that
residents could keep up with their reading. The Lamar House held balls
and wedding receptions, the local newspaper reported a boom in the building of "tasteful residences, from the unpretentious cottage to the showy
and expensive suburban palace" in the ten years following the war, and a
visitor to the city noted East Tennessee's pure air, "the men of this section
being generally the tallest and the best looking in the Union."[9] Even though
they may have been "a haven of talented misfits" occupying a ramshackle old
house, Frances and the Hodgson coterie were, for the most part, having a
fine time.[10] Herbert's friends Pleasant Fahnestock and Frank Bridges were
there so often they were nearly residents; the Hodgson cousin Fred Boond
also spent much of his free time there. Between them all they were able

to comprise a cheerful musical band, with Herbert and Frances playing the piano, Frances and Edith singing, Frank Bridges playing the flute, cousin Fred on the bass viol, and another friend, Charles Haynes, on the violin. They were all accomplished musicians with the possible exception of Pleasant, who toyed with the clarinet but really went round to court Edith. Interestingly, all of them were English, and they formed an English musical clique in the centre of Knoxville. Another source of society was St. John's Episcopal Church, which the Hodgsons joined. Largely pro-Union, it was also the church of many in the local expatriate English community.

Despite the seemingly free and easy social life, things were changing. Three of the Hodgsons—Herbert, Edith, and Edwina—were soon to marry, John was leading a questionable life, and Eliza ("Dear Mamma," as they always called her) was unwell. Early in their poorer Clinton Pike days, a Dr. Campbell had been summoned to Eliza's bedside. She was suffering only from a bad cold, but it marked the beginning of her decline. "He came home," his daughter recalled, "and told mother to take some food to that family."[11] Frances became a favourite with Mrs. Campbell and began spending a great deal of time at the Campbell home, befriending the young daughters Ada and Rosa, who trailed her around, listening to her tell stories and watching her write. By the time of the move to Vagabondia, the fifty-five-year-old Eliza's health had worsened, and on 17 March 1870, she died. The young people gathered around her grave at the Old Gray Cemetery in Knoxville were now completely orphaned, and Frances, as the oldest daughter, assumed an even greater responsibility for the family.

In her memoir, Frances recalled "hearing that 'Poor Papa' had died," an event for "which there was so little explanation that it was not terrible." When she was taken to see him for the last time on his deathbed "she was not frightened, and looked down with quiet interest and respect."[12] She left no written response to her mother's death. The young Hodgsons missed "Dear Mamma" terribly, and perhaps for that reason what had seemed light-hearted flirtations became serious alliances, and Vagabondia turned into a house of courtship. The same year that Eliza died, Herbert, now twenty-four, married Swan's nineteen-year-old sister Ann. Edith was by now "enchantingly pretty," and little Teddy was " a vigorous, handsome girl with a lively intelligence."[13] Frank Bridges, a painter and musician working with a local minister and living in a boarding house, found he had much in common with Teddy even though he was ten years her senior. Like the Hodgsons he was English, born six years before Frances, and later moved to Tennessee. On 8 January 1872, less than two years after Eliza's death, Frank and Teddy were married. Edith married Archer Pleasant Fahnestock about the same time, and both sisters had their first babies the following year—a daughter named Bertha for Teddy and Frank, a son named Archie for Edith and Pleasant. Herbert and Ann had their son, Edwin, about this time as well.

Frances's romantic friendship with Swan Burnett remained alive throughout all of this change. After beginning his medical school training in Cincinnati, he worked for a time as the superintendent of a military hospital in Knoxville, a job that kept him close to Frances and Vagabondia. He transferred to Bellevue Hospital College in New York City and received his M.D. degree there in 1870. Then he returned to Knoxville, rather than to New Market, to begin practising medicine. Certainly they were something of an established couple by now, although no promises had yet been made on either side. Like Dolly and her lover Griffith in *Dolly* and *Vagabondia*, Frances and Swan had been together for seven years, but both felt equal ambition for their careers. Frances particularly revelled in her freedom and seemed in no hurry to marry. Like Dolly, Frances "at twenty was pretty much what she had been at fifteen."[14] Unreliable as it often is to infer life from fiction, there is enough known of her relationship with her family and Swan to believe that in this first sustained story, worked on while she churned out shorter pieces such as "Ethel's Sir Lancelot" for magazines at ten or twenty dollars apiece, she borrowed heavily from her relationship with Swan.

From the first Swan was the more intense, the more seriously involved, of the two. Although sociable and friendly, he possessed less of Frances's cheerful gaiety. One morning, calling on her while she visited the Campbell house, he was led into the parlour by a servant and told that "Miss Fann" had gone out. Instead she was hiding behind the door and emerged, after he had left, "bubbling over with laughter." "Served him right to call before morning prayers," she asserted, but the truth was that she did not feel herself fit to be seen by a suitor: "Her cheeks were as rosy as a June peach and her dress hung every way on the bias," her friend Ada Campbell recalled. "Somehow, too, her shoes were not mates, and before she would let Dr. Bunett see her in this unconventional dress she would have gone up the chimney if there had been no other way out of sight, being proud and sensitive to a degree."[15] Frances enjoyed teasing, but not in an audacious or cruel fashion, so "her flirtations were of so frank and open a nature, that bewildered and fascinated though her victims might be, they must have been blind indeed to have been deceived." If *Dolly* is to be trusted as an autobiographical source, which it seems to be before it disintegrates into melodrama, we learn that while Frances cared deeply for Swan, "his long cherished love for the shabbily attired . . . dauntless young person . . . was the mainspring of his existence . . . and at this stage of his affection—after years of belief in that far off blissful future—to lose her would have brought him wreck and ruin."[16] This did not augur well for wedded bliss. Swan was as faithful to Frances as she was unwilling to commit to him, and so their "friendship" lingered on. In the meantime, they both had work to do in setting themselves up professionally. Still, Swan remembered these years in Vagabondia nostalgically. It was there that he learned the "old fashioned notions . . . the value of love, and faithfulness and unselfishness," and "extended experience has only taught me to value them still more highly."[17] Even with all the difficulty of those early days, he later stated that he would gladly return to them for the hope and confidence in the future that they held.

Frances had hit upon a literary formula and, in these first years, churned out a series of stories tailored to the women's magazine market. They always concerned romance and generally ended with imminent marriage. The heroine or hero usually needed to learn a lesson before the resolution could be reached. They suffered from pride and misunderstandings. Heroines followed a popular ladies' magazine model and were usually of the elegantly dressed, statuesque variety, but occasionally girls like Dolly slipped through, built in the Frances way: shorter, sturdier, with curlier hair. They were often of a moneyed class and lived in places she had not yet visited—wealthy estates or summer residences in Newport, Rhode Island. They shared exquisite taste in clothing even when their means were simple—a good thing, because the magazines included sewing and other needlework patterns in the issues for their readers of the middle and working classes. In short, a market existed, and she aimed to suit it.

Even so, she entered her name into the fray rather tentatively. Her first three *Godey's* stories used the pseudonym "The Second," chosen perhaps because it was with her second story for them that she first became published, perhaps because her second story appeared first. For her first *Peterson's* story, a melodramatic romance titled "Ethel's Sir Lancelot," set in a Pennsylvania mining town, she used the androgynous name F. Hodgson. Her first serial story, "Kathleen's Love-Story," published a number of times under several permutations of that title, came out in *Peterson's Monthly* from September through December 1870 simply as having been written by the author of "The Modern Sir Launcelot," apparently an erroneous version of her earlier title. The last instalment named her as Miss F. Hodgson.

At first she received similar payments from all the magazines, but after a few stories accepted by his magazine, Charles J. Peterson wrote her "a letter I could not easily forget. . . . He told me that my work was worth more to him than that of his other contributors, and that this being the case, he felt it only fair that he should pay more than he paid them. And he sent me a check which was almost double what I had received before."[18] She and Peterson would have their differences later as the publishers of her early stories began to capitalize on her fame, but even then she found him an "honorable and generous gentleman" who had protected her in her youthful innocence.

This was truly her apprenticeship. She strengthened her already considerable skills of dialogue, even though she could not resist the authorial intrusions of a nineteen-year-old in charge of her own story. She learned to conform to the subject restrictions of magazine publication, even though it often meant writing love stories more saccharine than she would have preferred. She wrote nearly non-stop, drawing on her English background and her American seasoning to create a style that appealed to a wide audience, recognizing that she was writing to an established pattern and knowing that her stories would not pass muster in publications of a higher calibre. She had no pretensions about this and wanted no one to "think that I considered the stories I then turned out as in any sense literature. I became known to an immense reading public who delighted in a [certain] type of publication."[19]

It wasn't until 1871, when she was nearly twenty-two and had been publishing for four years, that she trusted her talent enough to attempt something greater. She sent off a story called "The Woman Who Saved Me," a more accomplished story set in London, to *Scribner's Monthly*. Told in the first person by a woman who suffers from depression and listlessness, it differs from her usual stories by taking place within a marriage rather than during the courtship. Gervase Leith tells herself that she does not love her husband, "had never loved him, I told myself. It was not even love that had made us happy in the first months of our marriage. It had only been a weak mockery after all, and we had both learned the truth too late." On her doctor's advice, she goes to stay with a friend and her children at the seaside. She admires her friend's "magnificent children" but confesses that she has never loved children very much. A child of her own had died at birth, and "I was wondering vaguely if I were a wicked woman, and if my faded, empty life were my punishment. I do not think I had ever loved my baby or wept for it—Roger had ceased to love me long before its birth, and I had learned to know what a mistake I had made."[20] What unfolds is a psychological examination of marriage and postpartum depression, suspected and potential infidelity, quite unlike her earlier work and quite surprising for an unmarried writer with no children.

Scribner's Monthly magazine, to which she sent the story, was run by writer Josiah Gilbert Holland, who had for many years been the editor of one of the nation's most important newspapers, the *Springfield Republican*, which came out of Massachusetts. *Scribner's Monthly* began in 1870 as an offshoot of the book publisher Scribner and Company, and was to be "an illustrated magazine for the people." They hired the brilliant and adept Richard Watson Gilder as editor, and under his watch the magazine took off as a periodical that gave more established and respected monthlies like the *Atlantic Monthly* a run for their money. Unlike *Peterson's* and *Godey's*, *Scribner's Monthly* consciously supported the arts and sciences and the best in modern thinking. In the depths of the postwar Reconstruction era, both the monthly and the book publisher championed writers from the South and were firmly anti-slavery. Writing to a reader who complained that the magazine had run a "Life of Lincoln" in its pages, Gilder shot back that "The fact that the 'Century' publishes varying views from its contributors on these and other subjects does not imply that we have no mind of our own or no policy of our own." Indeed, what use was it to southern writers to be read only by other southern writers? The magazine offered a wide national audience, he continued, and "it is great use that a Northern periodical should be so hospitable to Southern writers and Southern opinion, and should insist upon giving a fair show to Southern views even when they were not altogether palatable to our Northern readers, among whom, of course, is our greatest audience."[21] They published the works of the African American leader Booker T. Washington, called for support and encouragement of black Americans, and attacked in print the lynchings that were all too common in those years.[22]

In this postwar climate, Knoxville was something of a southern anomaly. The Ku Klux Klan began 250 miles away in Pulaski in 1886, but in 1870 Knoxville itself was about 30 per cent black, with no record of any lynching ever having occurred there. Although the city was known as the most pro-Union southern city, it was also the centre of Confederate sympathy for that part of the state. Even before the war, a quarter of the black population had been free, some of them owning their own businesses; those who were slaves had been well-spoken house servants. It wasn't until the 1890s when Jim Crow laws became pervasive throughout America that racial segregation took root in Knoxville, and in Frances's time there were mixed-race neighbourhoods and businesses. Not only was Vagabondia probably located in one of these neighbourhoods—Mechanicville, made up of Welsh and African American ironworkers—but the house itself is likely to have been the one that later became the house of the president of Knoxville College, an all-black institution.[23]

Frances drew on postwar Knoxville in her 1899 novel *In Connection with the DeWilloughby Claim*:

Both armies having swept through it, Delisleville [Knoxville] wore in those days an aspect differing greatly from its old air of hospitable well-being and inconsequent good spirits and good cheer. Its broad verandahed houses had seen hard usage, its pavements were worn and broken, and in many streets tufted with weeds; its fences were dilapidated, its rich families had lost their possessions, and those who had not been driven away by their necessities were gazing aghast at a future to which it seemed impossible to adjust their ease-loving, slave-attended, luxurious habits of the past. Houses built of wood, after the Southern fashion, do not well withstand neglect and ill-fortune.[24]

It was a "hot little town left ruined and apathetic after the struggle of war." Into this sad place she inserted a character of hope and redemption, "Uncle" Matthew, a former slave so loyal and obsequious ("he was an obstinate and conservative old person [who] actually felt that to be 'a free nigger' was rather to drop in the social scale") that it pains the modern reader, but he is drawn firmly from the romantic Harriet Beecher Stowe model of *Uncle Tom's Cabin*. Because Uncle Matthew is such a sympathetic character whose acumen and persistence save the fortunes of the white people in the novel, it is clear that Frances was playing upon an antebellum wistfulness for an era before she arrived in America, writing the novel at a time of enormously popular minstrel shows and pre-war nostalgia. She recognized this, and in a moment of self-irony called him "an old black man—out of a story book."[25]

Knoxville could be a rough place but it wasn't entirely a literary backwater, although those who made their mark from that time tended to leave. Adolph Ochs, who went on to become the editor of the *New York Times*, was a Knoxville adolescent when Frances lived there. Before she arrived, it had also been the home of George Washington Harris, whose enormously popular "Sut Lovingood's Yarns" were considered a seminal and thoroughly American voice, influencing William Faulkner, Mark Twain, and Flannery O'Connor.[26] But for a mentor and promoter, Frances needed to look elsewhere.

Richard Gilder, who was to play a considerable part in Frances's life and in her development as a writer, was a fascinating man. His photographs show little change in his appearance during his adult life, with the exception of an enormous greying moustache. He had large, lustrous brown eyes, a slim figure, and a quick mind. His own poetry graced the pages of the magazine, alongside those of the finest poets of his time. Only twenty-six, and therefore just five years older than Frances, when he took on the editorship of *Scribner's Monthly*, he lived in a remodelled carriage-house and stable in lower Manhattan, near Union Square. There he and his wife, Helena, and their two children lived an artistic life surrounded by the most important people in arts and letters. Helena, herself a former art student who had studied in Europe and spoke four languages, was a friend of Henry James from his Newport days. The impressive first floor of the carriage-house, the "Studio," was a single airy room with an open fireplace and a bas-relief family portrait above it. A visitor to their home recalled his first visit there in 1883, when the other guests included the naturalist writer John Burroughs, the editor of *The Nation*, the sculptor Augustus Saint-Gaudens, the actor Joe Jefferson, Andrew Carnegie, and the English poet and essayist Matthew Arnold. At other times one might hear the opera singer Clara Louise Kellogg sing spirituals or see the famous actress Helen Modjeska.[27]

Gilder believed in the possibility that through the arts the American middle class could be lifted into a higher, better, and more just and ordered society.[28] A humanist, he moved towards agnosticism later in life. He was known for his combination of fast-paced editorial work and intense conversation, and his desire to bring "serenity and repose" into the world. He pulled no punches when he wrote and spoke to authors about their work, but his comments, even the negative ones, contained a kind and quick intelligence that elated them. One author wrote that "he could return rejected manuscripts in such a gentle and caressing way that the disappointed scribblers came to him from hundreds of miles away to thank him for his kindness and stay to dinner with him!"[29] While his work with the magazine and his championing of the real (as opposed to the popular) arts defined the future of *Scribner's Monthly* and its later incarnation *The Century*, his dedicated involvement with social issues such as tenement reform and work with a number of civic groups had lasting effects.

Frances's story received a brief but direct response from Gilder on 3 October 1871. "F. Hodgson, or Dr. Burnett: (which is the writer of it?)" he began. "The story of 'The Woman Who Saved Me' is declined on account of its length. It would make nearly 16 of our pages—which is too much for a 'short story,' and we don't want any more serials. Who are you? You write with a practiced hand—and we shall always be glad to hear from you. Stories should not be more than eight or ten pages in length."[30] They did publish the story two years later, but this initial contact left an impression on them both, and it was clear that he saw her as a writer to keep in mind.

Her timing could not have been better, for American magazines were in something of a predicament with regard to fiction. The readers of monthly magazines like *Scribner's* and *Peterson's* were mostly female, and publishers struggled to capture and maintain an audience. The best way to do this was through serials, which ensured that readers who did not subscribe to the

magazines stayed hooked from month to month. But in 1870, good American storywriters were in short supply, and those whose work was of a high
quality were already loyal to other publications such as the *Atlantic Monthly*.
Readers were used to British settings and accomplished work, so the most
prestigious magazines solved the problem of available fiction by reprinting
the work of British writers such as Dickens, Thackeray, Meredith, Bulwer-
Lytton, and Trollope. Even here, though, writers remained loyal to their first
American publisher, and it was often difficult to convince them to switch to
other magazines. Holland, the managing editor of *Scribner's*, declared in 1875
that as a loyal citizen he would publish only stories by American authors, but
this was bluster since he could not get the British work he wanted for his
new magazine.[31]

Into these editors' laps fell a young, and to them unknown, writer named
Fannie E. Hodgson. She lived in the South but wrote with ease and sureness
about English people and settings. She solved their problem of relying on
American authors, but at the same time she could offer readers the setting
and tone they had come to expect from the imported stories. Unfamiliar at
that time with the sentimental romances on which she had cut her authorial teeth, they saw her as someone who could step into the breach and offer
work of a higher quality than that of the other ladies' magazines. With this
encouragement, Frances tackled her work in a new way. She continued contributing to the Vagabondia household expenses, but she began to put aside
much of her income for another purpose: she had decided to go home to
England for an extended visit. Knoxville was already becoming rather too
small for her. "I've always wondered how FHB mixed with this disorderly,
sometimes violent place," a Knoxville journalist later remarked. "I think she
must have carried her own Secret Garden around with her."[32]

A steady stream of her stories appeared in 1871–72 in *Peterson's Magazine*
and in *Godey's*: "In Spite of Themselves," "Jarl's Daughter," "Sir Patrick's
Romance," "The Tragedy of a Quiet Life," "The New Governess," "The
Curate of St. Mary's," "Little Polly Lambert," and "Tom Halifax, M.D."
Some of these were revisions of stories she had scribbled in the ledger book.
("The Curate of St. Mary's," for instance, was much shortened from her
original, wordy, and seemingly endless version.) She practised writing in
southern regional dialects, based on the speech of people she met, and retold
in this way the story of Adam and Eve in "After Josh Billings," for her own
exercise. In her Islington Square days she had acquired an ear for accent and
dialect, when she and Edith leaned on their windowsill and listened to the
conversations of the children who occupied the back street forbidden to
the Hodgson children. She found them "a race more exciting to regard as

objects, because their customs and language were, as it were, exotic. 'Back Street children' *always* spoke dialect, and the adult members of their families almost invariably worked in the factories—often, indeed, the children worked there themselves. In that locality the atmosphere of the *foyer* was frequently of a lively nature, generally the heads of the families evinced a marked partiality for beer, and spent their leisure moments in consuming 'pots' of it at 'th' Public.'"[33]

Dialect writing was enormously popular in late-nineteenth-century America. Mark Twain had his own version of it in *The Adventures of Huckleberry Finn,* much as Dickens did in England with his Sam Weller in *The Posthumous Papers of the Pickwick Club* and in a whole host of his other novels. Paul Lawrence Dunbar, the African American poet, would find it hard to break away from the dialect poems that made him famous, and the enormously popular Indiana poet James Whitcomb Riley, author of "Little Orphant Annie," drew upon a Hoosier dialect for his work. As Frances worked to finance her return to Manchester, she composed her breakthrough story in the Lancashire dialect. "Surly Tim's Trouble" concerned a laconic factory worker named Tim Hibblethwaite who is finally persuaded to narrate his tragic history to the factory manager. Tim's wife and child have died, and it turns out that his marriage was not legal; her first husband, presumed dead, returns to claim her, with heartbreaking results. "Somehow," Frances said, "it so broke my heart as I wrote it, and I found myself sobbing and weeping, that I could not help thinking that at last I had written something I might offer to one of the higher-class magazines."[34]

Her instincts were correct. Encouraged by Gilder's letter about "The Woman Who Saved Me," she sent it off to *Scribner's.* "My Dear Miss Hodgson," Gilder wrote back to her on 23 February 1872, "Dr. Holland, and Dr. Holland's daughter and Dr. Holland's right-hand man (myself) have all wept sore over 'Surly Tim.' Hope to weep again over mss. from you. Very sincerely and tearfully, Watson Gilder." His letter "was all and more than I dared to hope. . . . If one's apprenticeship can ever be said to be ended, I think mine came to a close after the publication of the little sorrowful Lancashire story, 'Surly Tim's Trouble.'"[35]

CHAPTER 5

~

THE RELUCTANT
BRIDE ABROAD

1872–1876

IN THE SPRING OF 1872, Swan was just about the only one who couldn't muster much excitement for Frances's trip to England. Perhaps he suspected that she would stay away longer than she planned, and the truth was that once she left, she certainly seemed in no hurry to return to Knoxville or to take up married life. Or perhaps she lingered in England in the hope that Swan might change his mind in her absence. There is evidence that the financial pressures that necessitated her hard and relentless work, coupled with the loss of her mother, left Frances so physically and emotionally depleted that her family thought a sojourn among her Manchester relatives might allow her the rest and care she needed.

The fact was that she never had any particular desire to marry, a disinclination that hardened as she grew older. She could now support herself by her own hard work and aspired to what she saw as a more fulfilling and less confining life. For a woman who made her living writing stories that so often ended in marriage, she had no illusions about happily-ever-afters in real life. She adored the children of others and seemed to know just how to play with them, but she also knew first-hand through her mother's experiences what it was like to be a widowed mother. At twenty-two there seemed no reason to rush into a situation that might confine her just as the world's doors were edging open. She later described herself as "a woman who loathes marriage" and "holding as my most fixed creed that *not* to [be] married was Paradise," yet for all her independence she was a kindhearted woman who wanted to please and who was genuinely fond of the young doctor.[1] With her younger sisters marrying that winter, with a brother already married, she had given in to Swan and agreed to an engagement. Amid signs that

48

overwork was beginning to affect her health, this was her last chance to travel alone to England and to spend time with her friends and relatives from the past. Instead of the promised year's absence, it was to be nearly a year and a half before she returned to Knoxville, and her first novel to appear as a single volume would have its genesis not in Tennessee but in her Manchester childhood.

As a writer with a growing reputation in America, she could go back to Manchester in some triumph. In April her story "Little Polly Lambert," drafted first in her ledger book as "Little Polly Landsell," appeared in *Peterson's*. That same month her story "Tom Halifax, M.D.," in which a young doctor much like Swan attempts to set up a private practice, came out in *Godey's*. "Surly Tim's Trouble," which had brought tears to the eyes of Gilder and his colleagues, would appear in *Scribner's* in June, after she arrived in England, with "Miss Vernon's Choice" following it in July in *Peterson's*. Although the preparations for her trip were less complex than were those for the Hodgson family's emigration seven years earlier, there was still a lot to do: dressmaking—Edith and Teddy helped her to sew a new travel outfit—packing, and arrangements with publishers, for she would continue to be a working woman while away.

In the spring she set off gaily to New York, where she was to meet Gilder and Holland at last and see the Manhattan sights before crossing the Atlantic. Because of her accomplished literary voice, both men expected to meet a much older person who was "as sophisticated as brilliant women usually are," and they were stunned by the very young and unsophisticated woman who "in spite of a British accent looked unmistakably fresh from the small town of Knoxville, Tennessee. Her lack of worldly wisdom was so apparent that it won their paternal affection and Richard Watson Gilder appointed himself a tactful committee of one to advise her during her stay in the big, bad city of New York."[2] They quickly discovered that she acted exactly like the young person she was. Rather than waiting for Gilder to collect her at her hotel as arranged, she allowed herself to be swept off for an afternoon and evening of pleasure by a woman editor from one of the magazines to which she contributed. The worried Gilder made three visits to the hotel that day, but the unrepentant Frances did not roll in until after midnight, having had a fine time. It was her first freedom, and loosened from the responsibility of being the oldest daughter in a parentless household, she joyfully gave herself over to the companionship of another professional woman in the city that never seemed to sleep.

When she met Gilder at last, she was captivated by the "luring gleam in the extraordinary eyes." Barely older than she was, he seemed to exist on the same literary plane she did and "to render elate one's imagination with the ecstatic knowledge that here was one who *saw* at once in all things all that one had seen one's self in one's most enraptured moment of appreciation and comprehension."[3] This was the beginning of her most important literary partnership, in which the young editor taught her to control her sometimes unwieldy and repetitive prose, to prune and tighten. Five years later, when she was an established and successful novelist, she still wrote to him that "it would do your heart good to see me write & cut out & brook & groan & set up & lead myself around the room by the bang" as she struggled to keep her sprawling writing under control.[4]

In Manchester she stayed with her Boond cousins as well as with friends at Cheetham Hill, but she also made visits to other old friends. Her days combined social visits and tourism with her regular and necessary routine of writing, because her income depended on the stories she sent back. Nine of her stories appeared in *Peterson's*, *Harper's*, and *Scribner's* while she was gone. One of them, "One Day at Arle," which came out in September in *Scribner's*, may have been written before she left, but an important serial story called "Lindsay's Luck," culled from her ledger book and brought out as a serial in *Peterson's* during the months of October through December, must have been written in England. Gilder agreed to print "The Woman Who Saved Me," that first story she had sent him in 1871, if she made revisions. This she did, and in a letter to him just before her twenty-third birthday in November, she explained something of the circumstances of her life in England.

> If my time was at my own disposal of course I could do a great deal more but I have scarcely an hour to call my own. I have so many places to go to whether I feel like visiting or not. And then my friends are not used to me & wont let me work. They say I came here to get strong & they will make me go out in the daytime & wont let me sit up at night & they are so kind that I cannot be so ungrateful as to tell them it only makes me feel restless & dissatisfied. Of course when every one is so good to me I must be happy but you know I feel as if I was wasting time & I wish I was'nt & I am not nearly as well as I was even before I left the South. But just wait until I am settled & you shall see if I wont send you something respectable again. I say this you see because I don't want you to think I am lazy & indifferent.[5]

This is a first hint of the illnesses, often in the form of what her doctors termed "nervous exhaustion," that were to plague her for the rest of her life.

Frances's father, Edwin Hodgson. This is the only known picture of Frances's father; there seem to be no extant pictures of her mother.

Courtesy of Katherine P. Hodgson.

The Hodgson house on Cheetham Road in Manchester.

Courtesy of Penny Deupree.

"Frances as she appears in her new dress and Hat." This drawing, perhaps by her youngest sister Edwina, is from the ledger book containing Frances's earliest surviving stories. "Colonel Scarborough" is a character in one of the stories.

Frances Hodgson Burnett Collection (no. 6817), Clifton Waller Barrett Library of American Literature, Special Collections, University of Virginia Library.

"A Quiet Place." Probably a drawing of the house in Clinton Pike, Tennessee, from the ledger book.

Frances Hodgson Burnett Collection (no. 6817), Clifton Waller Barrett Library of American Literature, Special Collections, University of Virginia Library.

The log house in which the Hodgsons lived on their arrival in
New Market, Tennessee.

Courtesy of Penny Deupree.

The earliest known
photograph of Frances,
used on the cover of
Peterson's Magazine.

Engraved for The Book Buyer.

Engraving of Frances from a photograph, as published in *Book Buyer*.

Frances Hodgson Burnett Collection (no. 6817), Clifton Waller Barrett Library of
American Literature, Special Collections, University of Virginia Library.

Frances's husband, Swan Burnett,
during their Washington years.
Courtesy of Penny Deupree.

Richard Watson Gilder, Frances's
most important editor.
Library of Congress.

Mary Mapes Dodge, editor of
Saint Nicholas Magazine.

Courtesy of Robert M. Jackson.

Oil portrait of Frances as
a young woman.

Courtesy of Penny Deupree.

Kitty Hall, as she would have looked
when Frances first met her.

Courtesy of Hargrett Rare Book and
Manuscript Collection, University of
Georgia Libraries.

Gigi Hall.

Amherst College Archives and
Special Collections.

Daisy Hall.

Amherst College Archives and
Special Collections.

Nook Farm in Hartford, Connecticut, where Frances stayed with the
Stowe, Hooker, and Day families.

Harriet Beecher Stowe Center, Hartford, Conn.

All the cheer and good spirits she exhibited in company were matched by worry and the long hours she spent cramped at her desk. Stories themselves may simply have come to her, but the pressures of deadlines and ceaseless production began in her early twenties to come with a physical and mental cost. In midlife the antidote would be found in her gardens, but with this first trip to England she began a pattern of travel and escape, alternating with lengthy periods of bed rest, that would take a serious toll not only on her personal relations but on her emotional state.

The "places to go" included seeing her old teachers the Hadfield sisters and their father at Strawberry Hill. At Alice Hadfield's invitation, she stayed with them for several weeks, accepted as one of the family "and, though she wrote a great deal during her stay, was seldom absent from the family circle—entering into all its various arrangements—assisting the girls in making, repairing, and, even, getting up their dresses, which she did with a deft hand, and displaying a refined taste in all things relating to feminine adornment. She, likewise, took the initiative in getting up some private theatricals."[6] She made sightseeing trips to Chester, London, and Paris with her cousins. After visiting Chester in August, she wrote up her experiences there in the form of an article for the *Knoxville Journal.* Clearly she had enough local fame for east Tennesseans to take an interest in her travels abroad, especially when she used the opportunity to point out the differences between living in a youthful country and an ancient one. "To me, fresh from a land where cities spring up like mushrooms, and even the people don't live long enough to grow old (you should see the records in these English graveyards), it was like slipping back a century or so," she wrote. At one house they toured she was accosted on her way out by two children who wanted to know if the group would like to view the "old" dining room.

I turned to them at once, "What old dining room? How old is it? (That's always the first question.) Any thing less than 300 years old is regarded as unworthy of investigation. . . . "Don't know, mum, but it's the OLD dining room, mum, as Lord Derby was took out of mum, to be beheaded."

Of course an old dining room that anybody had been taken out of to be beheaded was a blessing to prowlers. . . . Confidentially, the old dining room was an excessively dingy, dilapidated and disreputable old dining room, with nothing in it, and which suggested to my mind the idea that Lord Derby must either have wanted little here below, or had been in extremely reduced circumstances when he was "took out" of it to be beheaded.[7]

The description of a run-down and empty old English house was a form of flattery to her American readers, who lived in "cities that spring up like mushrooms." She was already beginning to see herself as the mediator between two cultures.

Nor did she forget her friends. She was particularly fond of young Rosa Campbell, one of Dr. Campbell's daughters. The Campbells were now living in a fourteen-room house on Walnut and Oxford Streets in Knoxville, where the doctor reserved two rooms for his medical practice. Edith and Pleasant Fahnestock, now married, rented an apartment above the office rooms where Frances was a frequent visitor before making her English trip. She often met Swan there as well, spending what the Larews recalled as "sparking hours and Frances' everlasting teasing that made [Swan] roar with laughter."[8] There she played with the younger children, often taking Rosa upstairs when she cried, cuddling her, and offering lumps of sugar to soothe her. In September 1872, Frances was planning her trip to Paris, and from Balmoral Terrace in Manchester she wrote to Rosa of the gifts she intended to buy for her, among them a child's tea set and "a big wax doll that can open and shut its eyes, and has curls and wears blue shoes." They would name her Mademoiselle Fanchette, a French version of the name Frances.[9] She sent the child a Christmas card, and writing to "my darling little Rosie" again on New Year's Day of 1873, she confirmed that she had indeed bought the doll's tea set for her, but also indicated that she had been ill for some months but was now recovered.[10]

With her newfound health came a return to her characteristic playfulness. Early in 1873 she acted in a farce called *Betsy Baker* in which she and her friends portrayed characters such as Mr. Marmaduke Mouser, and at the end of it she sang "Little Bo Peep" while dressed in character. Around the same time she wrote a burlesque, *The Fool of the Family*, which they performed at the Hadfields' home at Strawberry Hill, in which she cheerfully played the part of the fool. This was playful stuff, however, and it was in her periodical writing that she made the greatest strides. She and Gilder were now corresponding regularly. Writing to thank him for the cheque for "The Woman Who Saved Me," she made it clear that his approval mattered to her a great deal: "It is nicer to know that than to have the hundred dollars, though a hundred dollars is a thing one can scarcely have any conscientious objections to." *Harper's* had taken her story "One Quiet Episode," assuring her that she had a brilliant future, but she still wanted Gilder to read and approve of it. She didn't mention a *Peterson's* story, "Dolores," which came out in January, perhaps relegating it to the moneymaking stories she churned out for that magazine. Two more, "Her Secret" and "Norah Ferguson's Story," came out during the summer. Although she had moved up the pay scale, and her reputation was rising, she told Gilder that "you are my only solid representation of the great guild of editors & writers I dont know any of the rest yet & I do know you so what you say seems real."[11]

In Paris she had herself fitted for a gorgeous wedding dress, which she arranged to be made up and shipped to Knoxville, evidence that despite Swan's fears, she fully intended to carry out her promise to marry him. Months before her return to Knoxville, she had calling cards for "Mrs. Swan M. Burnett" printed up. Saying goodbye to her family and friends, she boarded the steamer *Parthia*, arriving in New York on 7 September, where she stayed for a few days with Dr. Holland of *Scribner's* before continuing on to Tennessee. She arrived ahead of the dress, and as a lifelong lover of fashion and finery, she postponed the wedding as long as she possibly could, hoping for its arrival. Finally Swan put his foot down, and a quiet wedding took place in New Market, at the home of Swan's parents. The celebrated "Miss Fannie E. Hodgson" arrived in New Market quietly by train the night before, and Swan showed up the next morning. A group of Frances's friends and relatives came in on the next train, leading the locals to conclude that a marriage was taking place. Indeed it was.

"Obliged to wear a cream-colored brocade" dress she had bought in England, "and white apple-blossom, instead of white satin and tulle, and orange-blossom and jessamine," surrounded by her close friends and family—including Edith and Edwina, now both mothers—she and Swan exchanged vows in the Burnetts' candle-lit living room, and everyone adjourned to the dining room for supper. She laughed at the switch in dresses, describing it in July to a Manchester friend as "a blow actually aimed at the very foundation of society," but cheerfully acknowledged that Swan "was the author of all my woes."

> He modestly expressed it as his opinion that seven years was long enough to wait at once, and said he would wait afterwards: and this in the face of all my prayers, tears and agonised appeals. If he were delicate in health—just a trifle consumptive or so, or a little dubious about his liver—but words fail me! He is positively *aggressively* healthy, and is always confiding to me that he was never so well in his life as he has been since he was married. Men are so shallow—they have no idea of the solemnity of things! I am fully convinced that to day he does not know the vital importance of the difference between white satin and tulle, and cream-colored brocade. He thinks that one did quite as well as the other, and that neither could have much to do with the seriousness of the marriage ceremony.[12]

When the wedding dress finally arrived, it was nearly ruined by having been packed in tin foil that stained it. Fortunately for Frances, it was the custom at the time for a wedding dress to make more than a single appearance. She later wore it triumphantly to a Knoxville evening party, descending the stairway with Swan carrying the train, looking "very radiant and lovely" and "looking back over [her] shoulder . . . and laughing up into the face of [her] adoring husband."[13] Even so, some reluctance shows in the wedding's official records in that the marriage deed was not recorded until 1874, a full year after the wedding actually took place.

They settled into a house on Temperance Hill in Knoxville, next to the gas works, Swan returning to his struggling medical practice and Frances to her writing. Despite her reluctance, marriage agreed with them. Swan exuded a robust health that he had never shown before and delighted in confirming that since their marriage he was healthier than he had ever been in his life. She dropped the storybook name of Jerome that she used for him and began calling him Doro, a masculinized version of a name in Dickens's *David Copperfield* that referred to the rather naïve and ramshackle way they had embarked upon housekeeping. (Her sister Edith she called Trotwood, the name of Copperfield's aunt.)

Her followers were now numerous enough to enable her to publish another serial, "Theo," from September through December of that year in *Peterson's*. The story of a girl who was rescued from her predictably "shabby" home in an English coastal village by a wealthy London aunt, "Theo" begins as many in Frances's stable of stories did, in medias res with a striking immediacy of characters and situations. Clothes played a large role. Like many of the other stories, it has a slow build-up of romantic tension followed by a passionate burst of action and declaration that today seems over the top but then were typical of the love story genre at which she excelled. As her skills increased, she developed an embarrassment about this story and others of its kind written at this time.

Happy as they were together early in their marriage, it was clear now that Tennessee was too small a place to hold her ambitions. Her year and a half abroad, coupled with Swan's desire to improve in his profession by adding an eye and ear speciality, made them begin to look elsewhere to settle themselves. They thought of various American cities, but it was Europe that beckoned. Swan could get cutting-edge ocular training there, and although Frances's stories could be written anywhere, a change of scene and setting seemed crucial. They discussed their plans regularly, but when Frances became pregnant in 1874, she wrote to a Manchester friend that she could not face another summer of the Knoxville heat and was determined to leave, with or without Swan. As much as she had praised southern summers, this one's heat and humidity overwhelmed her. She spent her afternoons gasping for air, "lying on the bed in the loosest and thinnest of wrappers fanning with a palm leaf fan & panting & longing for rain." Unable to sleep or rest or work, she tried to persuade Swan to give her a

> six months leave of absence next year, & if he will, I intend to come to England. I wish his friends in Washington would make him consul to somewhere in Europe. I am tired of the South. . . . It is possible we may go to Washington this winter . . . and if so I am going to plunge into politics like the rest of the feminine Washingtonians, and be an active lobbyist and exert my influence on the affairs of the nation. I begin to think political life will suit me. Dont you think that I could do myself justice on civil right or protective Tariff. If I should ever distinguish myself, you can write a book entitled "Half-hours with immortal Females."[14]

The magazine stories continued to appear during these difficult months. *Peterson's* brought out "The Little Shop at Gowanham" in July, the same month that its rival *Scribner's* published "The Fire at Grantley Mills." Before her pregnancy, Frances's original plan had been to return to America and begin the novel that Gilder encouraged her to write. He thought that the best way would be to showcase it as a serial in *Scribner's*, and if it garnered sufficient reader interest they would bring it out afterwards as a book.

She knew exactly the story she wished to tell, based on a woman she had glimpsed in the back streets of Manchester when she was a girl, but much as this idea appealed to her, she was now unsure that first her pregnancy and later her maternal duties could allow her the time and the physical effort it would take to sustain a full-length novel. They determined to settle in France for a time in order to allow Swan to continue his schooling, but further medical study of course meant a suspension of his income, and for a while they saw no way to make it happen.

It was Charles Peterson who devised the plan that would make this possible. Advancing them the money for the sojourn, he told Frances to pay him back in stories that *Peterson's* could publish. This way Swan could study under the specialists in Paris, and Frances, without leaving her domestic duties, could support them while they lived in France. Their son Lionel was born at the Temperance Hill house on 20 September 1874. Within six months of his birth, the young family left not only Knoxville but also America, determined to make a new start in their professional lives.

Without thinking too hard about what it would mean to begin a novel, provide Peterson with the stories he required, and send stories to other magazines as well, they packed their bags and left for Paris in March 1875 with their six-month-old son. True to his word, Peterson published a steady stream of her stories that year, beginning in February—"After Thirty Years," "As Good as a Mile," "The Tide on the Moaning Bar," "Aunt Portia's Diamond," "Miss Jerningham's Version," and "The Men Who Love Elizabeth"— all of them knocked off for their financial rather than their literary value, some of them drafted earlier in her ledger book and some that she would later regret as critics looked back on them with disdain.

None of this would have worked without another kind of assistance. Priscilla, or Aunt Prissie—her last name is never given—was a former slave who accompanied them to France. She was always described in conventional Victorian racial terms as "a typical Southern mammy," wearing a bandanna, smoking a corncob pipe, and ruling the young household with stern and protective words shouted out in "a deep voice and a heart of gold."[15] Familiar as such a figure was in the South, she was an eye-catching rarity in Paris. Completely undaunted by the unfamiliar language, currency, or surroundings, she sallied forth to do the marketing and returned to cook the careful meals that sustained the young family. Her care and competence won the young couple's gratitude, but others saw her as a distinct oddity in France and England.

Frances's son Vivian later claimed that Prissie terrified the local children in France, and Henry Hadfield, who met her when the Burnetts passed through Manchester to and from their French sojourn, called her "an elderly nurse, who, if not entirely, was all *but* a thorough-bred nigger whose woolly head having become bleached by age, made her a first rate model for a study in black and white—and who was, moreover quite an original in her way."[16] Hadfield's reminiscences, designed to be entertaining, were less kind than those of a Mr. Fraice, who, with his wife, also met the entourage as they passed through Manchester. He recalled Prissie as being a grey-haired and quite light-skinned former slave who "was both devout and devoted" to the Burnett family.[17] Like Swan and other southerners, Frances, after more than a decade lived below the Mason-Dixon line, was quite accustomed to the ubiquitousness of African American servants and indeed could never have managed in Paris without Prissie. Nevertheless, she may have been showing off her Americanness to her Manchester family, with her southern husband and black servant in tow.

Frances and Swan thought that they had everything arranged. Frances was to write and thereby support them; Swan was to attend classes and prepare himself for greater success on their return; Prissie was to make all this possible by overseeing the household and caring for baby Lionel. In the intervals they would travel: England, France, the Netherlands, Germany, and Italy were all on the itinerary for this dream year. The money would be tight, but they would manage somehow. The entourage moved into a five-room apartment at 3, rue Paquet, in the eighth arrondissement, and Frances and Swan immediately set to work. Each morning he went off to his classes and she retired to her desk, with Prissie minding Lionel and seeing to the household.

The furnished flat had two bedrooms, a kitchen, living room, and dining room, occupied by three adults and a baby. Money was so tight that although Paris was a tempting city, "we are so poor as to be almost beyond temptation." She wrote to Edith that she only saw the outsides of the famous buildings and shops but that she did not want to complain about her husband or her poverty. "You must not think I begrudge my struggle," she assured her sister. "When I am the wife of the greatest ophthalmologist in two hemispheres, I shall forget my present troubles. . . . D is just as busy in his way as I am in mine—studying all morning, at the hospitals all evening and study again at night. D feels he is reaping great benefit from his stay here, and if he does, my end will be accomplished to a great extent." And later, "D. is getting along splendidly. He is drawing and painting eyes, and says he would not have missed these opportunities for anything. He has met so many celebrated men."[18]

The one thing they had not anticipated was what Frances referred to as a little "calamity": in September, six months after they left for Paris, she became pregnant again. To the unceasing work she now added physical exhaustion. Not only did she have to write constantly throughout this winter, but she made all the clothes for herself, Lionel, and Prissie. "I never worked so hard in all my life as I am doing this winter," she wrote to Edith.

> I have just made myself a black velvet hat, remade my black velvet basque, made Lionel two outdoor suits: one black velvet trimmed with white fur, the other gray and blue flannelette; made him two underdresses and a warm skirt and bodice; made Aunt Prissie a black cashmere dress and basque, and cleaned and entirely made over my black silk, which was as much trouble as ten dresses. We dine at six, and last night after dinner I made flannel underclothing, and the night before hemmed half-a-dozen large handkerchiefs.[19]

Swan's future success was assured by the important education he received in Paris, yet it was clear to everyone that it was Frances's efforts that had made it all possible. Hadfield stated that "she may be considered to have literarily . . . paddled her own canoe" and was explicit in declaring that "the whole of her travelling expenses were defrayed . . . by a goose quill . . . or, in other words, by the writings she produced during her peregrinations—and this, too, notwithstanding the time occupied in sightseeing, and giving birth to a child when in Paris."[20]

Although she continued to churn out the stories Peterson had contracted for ("Wanted—A Young Person," "Lisa's Little Story," and "My Cousin Katherine" appeared in his magazine in January, February, and March 1876), she reached a point of serious depression and exhaustion. Four weeks before her second child was born, she wrote the following poem and secreted it away among her private papers.

When I am dead & lie before you low
With folded hands & cheek & lip of snow,
As you stand looking downward
    Will you know
Why the end came & I wearied so?

I think you will remember as you gaze
Another look you saw in other days
A brighter look you used to love and praise.
    But will you know
Why the change came & why I wearied so?

Perhaps a hot, impassioned, useless tear
Will fall upon the face you once held dear
And you will utter words I cannot hear
    But will you know
Why the end came & why I wearied so?

I think you will remember something done
By the hands chilled to Death's responseless stone,
Something to give to thought a tenderer tone.
    But will you know
Why my heart failed and why I wearied so?

You cannot mourn me long—Why weep for Death?
Rather let Death weep for Life's laboring breath
And the sharp pains Life's labor ever hath!
    But will you know
What mine have been & why I wearied so?

The world *your* world will be before you yet—
E'en while my grave grass with Spring rain is wet
You will have found it easy to forget
 But will you know
Why my heart failed & why I wearied so?

But I—the Dead—shall lie so low—so low
And soft above me the Spring winds will blow
And Summer rose will pale to Winter snow
 And—No, you will not know
Why the end came & why I wearied so.[21]

Although not explicitly addressed to Swan, the poem carries clear resentment of the physical toll taken by her ceaseless work and advanced pregnancy that winter and spring, while he went off each day to his studies. She acknowledged that she wanted a rest and longed to "lay down de shovel an' de hoe, Hang up de fiddle and de bow"; she had "worked like a slave when I ought to have been resting," but every penny she earned went towards their living expenses and they barely scraped by. Her impending confinement would be expensive. Still, she did not regret the money they spent. "Three thousand dollars would certainly have bought a house in Knoxville," she wrote Edith in April, "but then, you see, I did not want a house in Knoxville; that is not what I have aimed at. I want my chestnuts off a higher bough." Her ambition for herself and Swan drove her on, and she vowed that "after all, I have not been beaten in this fight yet."[22]

Frances wanted a daughter, and she and Swan selected the name Vivien for the baby. However on 5 April 1876, after passing through "every conceivable agony," she gave birth to a second son whom they named Vivian, having been told that this was the masculine version of the name. As was customary at that time, she hired a nurse for two weeks after the birth, despite Prissie's presence. The new baby couldn't have been less like his brother. Vivian was a "sweet, gentle little thing, just nurses and sleeps and nestles and grows fat. . . . From his first hour, his actions seemed regulated by the peaceful resolve never to be in the way." The toddler Lionel was a rip-roaring little boy, "the roughest, biggest, tearingest rascal the family has ever known." They found him utterly delightful. He was active, playful, and sometimes so busily dirty that "I can only fold my hands resignedly and give him up as a bad job. . . . Sometimes I don't see *him* for weeks for all the dirt on him."[23] He pulled the legs off his toy lamb and scrubbed the floor with him. He stirred up the charcoal pile with a doll he named Gutter and subjected her to all sorts of abuse: dragged her about the flat by a string, cracked open her head, and filled it with smoke from Prissie's pipe. Edith reported that when her sister "wanted quiet for her writing Prissie would shout to Lionel, 'You come here! You keep away from yoh Ma, you little rascal, or Ah'll flay you alive!'"[24] With Swan, the sterner disciplinarian of the two, away each day, and Frances amused by her son's vagrancies, it fell to Prissie to keep some sort of domestic order with the children.

Frances's name received increased attention, even though she had yet to make her mark as a novelist. Just weeks after Vivian's birth, the *Literary World* referred to her as "one of the youngest of the contributors to *Scribner's Monthly*."[25] Although she had knocked out the required *Peterson's* stories during this winter and spring ("What Might Have Been Expected" appeared in May, "Merely an Episode" appeared in June, "My Dear Friend Barbara Sharpless" came out in August, and her second serial story, "Miss Crespigny's Absurd Flirtation," began appearing in September), she truly did want her "chestnuts off a higher bough." She had for some time wanted to begin a longer, more serious work that would show her increasing talents in a way that the made-to-order stories could not.

She had in mind a scene from her Islington Square days, when the Hodgson house backed onto a rougher neighbourhood populated by miners' and factory workers' families. She vividly recalled one evening when she sat in an upstairs window and watched a self-possessed young woman sitting with her friends by a lamppost in the square, knitting a sock. She was a factory girl of only about sixteen, but "somehow of a majestic mould," and somehow different from the others: "She had a clear, colourless face, deep, large grey eyes, slender but strong, straight black brows, and a rather square chin with a cleft in it. Her hair was dark and had a slight large wave, it was thick and drawn into a heavy knot on the nape of her neck, which was fine and full like a pillar, and held her head in a peculiar stately way."[26] The girl fascinated her because she seemed out of place—someone born out of her proper place in the world and destined to suffer because of it. One evening the girl again visited the square, and again was more reserved than her boisterous companions, when her drunken father appeared. Clearly he frightened the others, but the girl stared him down as he swore at her. Finally, still knitting, she turned away and walked home silently, without acknowledging him.

Frances never forgot this scene. Through the years of penning the stories of wealthy young people on the marriage market, or romantic girls living in shabby gentility, she knew the episode suggested something more solid, with its possibilities of a natural nobility relegated to the crudest social circumstances, told in part in the same dialect that had made "Surly Tim's Trouble" so popular. It was with this nascent novel that she began the kind of stories that would become her trademark: a sudden shift in social and personal condition, a crossing of class boundaries, the young person who remakes him or herself. She sent first chapters of the story to Gilder, and in August 1876 "That Lass o' Lowrie's," the book that brought her fame, began to appear on the pages of *Scribner's*. That same autumn the young family returned to America. It would be eleven years before Frances returned to Europe, but nevertheless she had been instilled with a lifelong wanderlust.

CHAPTER 6

~

PIRACY AND
A PLAY

1876–1878

FRANCES AND SWAN DECIDED that Knoxville was now too small to contain their ambitions, particularly after a year spent in one of the world's cultural centres. They determined to settle as soon as possible in Washington, D.C., once Swan could establish himself there in his profession. The city offered a great deal to a couple like Frances and Swan. Literature and science flourished there, with practitioners of both valued in literary societies and the four local universities. Especially after the lonely, hardworking year in Paris, the Burnetts looked forward to re-creating the Vagabondia of their Knoxville days among a new circle of friends and colleagues.

This was especially important to Frances because her own Hodgson family situation was changing. While she was in Paris, both of her sisters had given birth—Edith in January to a son she and Pleasant named Ernest, and Teddy to a son named Herbert. All three sisters had been pregnant with their second child, all boys, at the same time, but Frances had been without the support of her family when she gave birth to Vivian in April. Then in 1876, the same year Frances returned to New Market and Swan prepared for their reception in Washington, Edith and Pleasant and Teddy and Frank packed up their children and their belongings and headed west to California. It was to prove a tragic time for Edith, for a smallpox epidemic swept through San Francisco not long after their arrival. She and Pleasant sent their small older son back to his grandfather Benjamin Fahnestock in Tennessee for his own protection, keeping the infant Ernie with them. Both Pleasant and Ernie were swept up in the unforgiving epidemic: Pleasant died and the baby was scarred for life. This was the beginning of a series of personal heartbreaks for Frances's favourite sister.

Before leaving Europe in June 1876, Frances, Swan, Prissie, and the babies had stopped back in Manchester to pay a last visit to family and friends. Frances, in good spirits now that Vivian was born and with high expectations of Swan's career chances in a new place, began to gain a sense of herself as a writer with a growing reputation. With the serialized "Lass" now running to good reviews in *Scribner's*, Hadfield and his daughters introduced her to their friends as a novelist of repute, even though few in England had ever heard of *Scribner's Monthly* and the novel was not yet completed. Proud of her as the Hadfields were, Frances herself exhibited no signs of pride except in her young family. She "appeared to us pretty much of the same type as many thousands of young English wives and mothers, and more disposed to chat about her little family than any other topics," recalled Henry Hadfield's friend Fraice. He found her "a bright intelligent woman capable of noting types of character and ways of life, without betraying the process," and "a fond unpretentious wife of a husband eager to explore all the depths of physiology."[1] The young couple positively glowed with a sense of possibility: the children were healthy, and with Frances's first book soon to appear and Swan's medical career looking quite promising.

Before they could set up house in Washington, though, Swan had to make his way there alone and establish himself as an eye and ear doctor. Unlike the millionaires who had made their fortunes in western silver mines and erected mansions in Washington and nearby Georgetown, many inhabitants of the capital—including senators and congressmen who left their families back at home during the political season, as well as single men and women who worked for the federal government—found it necessary to live in boarding houses. They could have meals delivered to their rented rooms, or eat breakfast in coffee shops and dinner in any number of small restaurants. Lunchtime commonly found them at "dairy bars," where they could purchase drinks, eat sandwiches they carried in from home, and read the newspapers. This was the life Swan found himself forced to lead, for a boarding house was no place to settle a family, and he had no practice yet and knew no one in town who could help him. Frances drew upon his experiences there in her novel *In Connection with the DeWilloughby Claim*, in which a North Carolina judge elected to Congress finds himself living "in a back room in a boarding-house—a room which contained a folding bedstead and a stove."[2]

Frances, Lionel, and Vivian moved in with Swan's parents in New Market while Swan made his lonely and discouraging way through Washington. "We came back from Europe not only penniless but in debt, and I came to Washington without money or friends or even acquaintances to establish myself in my profession," he recalled. "As I look back at it now I dont see how I had the courage to attempt it. But I had determined that I would and I came. I wont tell you how I suffered and almost starved—of the dreary months of loneliness and despair, but still I would not give it up. Finally patients began to come in—very slowly—but they came and have continued to come in slowly increasing quantities all the time since."[3]

Back in New Market, Frances fared much better. The editors in the book-publishing arm of Scribner's watched "Lass" with great interest as it unfolded in the magazine. In October they wrote to "Mrs. Fanny Hodgson Burnett," the name she generally published under, to let her know that they would like to publish it in book form once it completed its serial run. Their terms were generous: they promised to bear all expenses, to "bring the book out in handsome style," and to give her royalties of 10 per cent of the retail price after the first thousand copies. Gilder himself offered to check the proof sheets. With the serial due to end the following May, the book could come out as a summer book. Frances sent the letter on to Swan in Washington and with this act appointed him her business manager. It is unclear whether, as a working writer with a toddler and infant to care for, she wished to leave such matters in her husband's hands, or whether Swan believed this to be more properly the responsibility of the man of the house. In any case, from this point on, and for some years, the non-editorial correspondence between her publishers and Frances was channelled through her husband, and not always in the friendliest manner.

In addition to writing the next instalments of "Lass," Frances's final episodes of "Miss Crespigny's Absurd Flirtation" appeared in the October and November issues of *Peterson's*, fulfilling at last her agreement with Charles Peterson for the Paris sojourn. One of several stories she wrote that were set in Paris, "Mère Giraud's Little Daughter," came out in the November issue of *Scribner's*. She had continued to correspond with Gilder while out of the country, sending him stories for the magazine and developing their mentor/ protégée relationship further. Now, inspired by the ease with which she had been able to write the higher-quality *That Lass o' Lowrie's*, she turned her hand to a piece that combined southern characters and a European setting. "Esmeralda," which would appear in the May issue of *Scribner's*, concerned a newly wealthy American family in Paris. The mother was determined to rise in the world and to become more cultured and worldly, while the father and daughter pined for home and the daughter for her uncultured but faithful lover. "I am more than glad that you liked 'Esmeralda,'" she wrote now to Gilder. "I was so much interested in it myself that it would have disappointed me awfully & have given me a sort of *mistaken* feeling if you had not. Thank you for the kind things you said. They help me to believe more in myself & when I can do that it makes such a difference. And there is no danger of my becoming [proud]. East Tennessee is a good place for ones modesty to thrive in."[4]

As Frances's writing matured, she no longer wanted to publish under the name of Fannie, associated in the public eye with her less mature stories. "I dont know why I have not done it before," she wrote to him. "I was never called Fannie until I came to America & I dont like it. It is too babyish for a woman & might mean any body. So if you please Frances Hodgson Burnett in future." At the same time she wanted to justify to him the sort of stories she continued to churn out for Peterson and others. "The fact is I work very hard but [just] now it is impossible that I should do the work I like best. I dont mean you know to urge that thread bare old plea 'I must live,' I should not consider that necessary or even desirable but then you see there are four of us now."[5] She didn't add that with Swan struggling to set himself up in Washington, she remained for the time being the breadwinner of the family, compelled continually to think up new characters and angles on the traditional romantic tale and on the working person's tragedy. Stories such as "The Fire at Grantley Mills" (*Scribner's*, July 1874) and "The Tide on the Moaning Bar" (*Peterson's*, July and August 1875), melodramas of industrial and maritime accidents, began to make their way into her repertoire, but for *Harper's* and the other magazines to which she contributed, standard romantic fare was in order. This unrelenting story production made her "feel like a species of shovel. I take & slice off some body almost every day. I wonder if it is quite fair." She ended her letter to Gilder rather enigmatically: "I suppose you know Dr. Burnett has been in Washington some time & intends remaining there."[6]

There is something odd about this letter, in its suggestion that the decision to move to Washington might have been Swan's alone, and its hint that she might decide to stay behind. Her well-known desire to move in wider circles makes it unlikely that she would have preferred to remain in the sleepy backwater of New Market, but clearly there were already a few cracks beginning to show in their young marriage. Only a week before she wrote this to Gilder, she wrote to Swan "because I know you will be blue." It is one of only a few surviving letters between them: "I am a better girl than you think & I wont be bad to you now you may be lonely & want comfort. I will work like a Trojan & help you until your good luck comes. It has been on its way so long it must come soon. . . . I have set my heart on your success in your own groove & I *know* it will come. Someday I shall drive the boys out in that pony carriage. *You* dont know yet how unbounded my faith in you is." She signed it "Your Little Wife."[7]

While Frances kept up her correspondence with Gilder and remained busy correcting the proofs and writing chapter titles, Swan kept up his with others at Scribner's, asking among other things that a dozen "presentation" copies be set aside for his wife, to be forwarded to Washington as soon as the book appeared. This was not normal practice, but they readily agreed. The novel about the proud pit girl speaking in a broad Lancashire dialect falling in love with a middle-class mine manager from the south of England was just the sort of fare audiences craved. Joan Lowrie is very American in some ways: proud and independent, with a strong sense of self. She does not take assistance lightly, and when at the end of the novel Derrick wishes to marry her, she is very English in her deep awareness of their class differences, deciding to bridge their cultural gap before she sees herself as a suitable wife to someone like him. It is Anice, the vicar's daughter, who helps her in more ways than one. Joan is presented as a masculine character—tall and majestic, she has the physical strength and stature of a man. She works at the mouth of the pit and shows no fear of her drunken and violent father. She has no mother. When a local girl named Liz returns to the village with an illegitimate baby, it is Joan who defends her to the local people and who takes her into her cottage, where the three share a chaste bed. Liz is flighty, so it falls to Joan to care for the child as well as work all day. When Dan Lowrie, Joan's father, threatens Derrick's life, she secretly follows the mine manager home at nights to protect him from danger. And near the end of the novel, after a mining accident, Joan and the more feminine curate deliberately named Grace go down into the mine to search for survivors, something the miners fear to do.

The novel concerns a spiritual awakening as well as a social and gendered one. Through Liz's baby, Joan becomes aware of her unsuspected maternal side. A picture of the crucifixion on Anice's wall causes Joan to read the Bible and attend church. She starts to help at Grace's night school and improves her own education. She begins to sew in the evenings. Once she realizes that she and Derrick are falling in love, she leaves town to avoid a socially inappropriate marriage. Again through Anice's help, she becomes the companion of a gentlewoman, and her conversion from rough masculinity to socially defined femininity is nearly complete.

Although there is something reminiscent of Elizabeth Gaskell's novel *Mary Barton*, in which a working-class girl is wooed by the wealthy son of a mine owner and only finds strength when she works to clear the name of a neighbour accused of the seducer's murder, Frances created in Joan a strong woman immune to traditional seduction and reluctant to marry into a rank above her. She was a new kind of heroine in the industrial novel, and for the first time in her writing career Frances began to worry about readers' reaction to her work.

> If you are sure it will be best all round leave out that final paragraph. Let me tell you it cost me a pang to write it—for me the book ended with Joan & Derrick in the garden but I felt as if I must drag in the rest & I will wager you all the immense profits the book will naturally bring me that if it is left out I shall be promptly sat upon by fifty thousand ghastly people who will ask me why I did not "do something" with Anice & also "if it isnt rather incomplete." The question suggests itself however as to whether I am writing for those people. I would rather not—but must I? Nevertheless if I may be pleased & write for people who will take a hint— leave it out. Sometimes I hate that girl too. She seems too Sunday schooly. She is not what I meant her to be but every body wont dislike her as much as you do. Thank you for saying I shall not make such a mistake again. I dont think I shall.[8]

Not surprisingly, Scribner's was anxious to sell the British rights to the story and so approached Frederick Warne, letting him know that they were "much interested in the success of the book."[9] Excited as she was about the book's coming appearance, Frances was just as anxious about its financial success. "In a few months I hope I shall have the satisfaction of knowing whether or not I can do work worth money," she wrote to Gilder from New Market on 8 March 1877. "Standing as I do upon the low level of those debased persons to whom the money must be the first object I am degradingly anxious to know that."[10]

She needn't have worried. The novel appeared to numerous and strong reviews, with one critic "prophecy[ing] a brilliant literary future for the author."[11] The *New York Herald* said that the "publication of a story like 'That Lass o' Lowrie's' is a red-letter in the world of literature," while the *Philadelphia Press* called it "the best original novel that has appeared in this country for many years." The *Boston Transcript* wrote that it knew "of no more powerful work from a woman's hand in the English language, not even excepting the best of George Eliot's." The *Hartford Courant* believed the "novel is one of the very best of recent fictions, and the novelist is hereafter a person of rank and consideration in letters."[12] By the end of the month, Scribner's was beginning its third printing of the book, and the English edition, enthusiastically published by F. Warne and Company, was brought out. With justifiable foreboding about her treatment in a world of tenuous transatlantic copyright, Scribner's wrote to Warne that he must treat her well or else they would not offer him her next book, "and she is considered by good judges as the 'Coming Woman' in literature."[13] Frances finally relaxed. She wrote to Gilder that "having read about fifteen reviews I sat down & gave a sigh of relief. The throwing up of hats I defer until the sale of the tenth thousand until then I can't afford it unless I could borrow a hat from some bloated aristocrat with two. . . . Doro alternately reads notices in a sonorous voice & snubs me to reduce me to submission but secretly he quails before the eagle eye of the 'Coming Woman.'"[14]

Perhaps the greatest evidence of *Lass*'s success in England came in November, when *Punch* began a serialized satire called "That Lass 'o Towery 's!" Mocking Joan's height and the Lancashire dialect of the mining families, the authors of the spoof explained their title "as a real specimen of dialect. They say that the story will justify the title, the heroine, as will be seen from the first chapter, being above the usual stature, towers above the others, and so is spoken of in the dialect of that particular county as a 'Towery lass.' The sentence, in full and plain English, read thus:—'That Lass who is so Towery (i.e. tall),' or 'That Lass who so Towery (or tall) is,' and rendered into Sangilshire language it becomes, as written, 'That Lass so Towery is,' or, as pronounced colloquially, 'That Lass 'o Towery 's.'"[15]

In April, the same month that *That Lass o' Lowrie's* appeared in book form, she and the boys were able to join Swan in Washington at last, moving first to 1104 F Street, then to M Street, then to 813 13th Street. She wasted no time in resuming her work but also in gathering a new group of friends around her. Julia Schayer, a journalist whose first husband was a German count and whose second husband was the recorder of deeds for the District of Columbia, came to call and found Frances wearily carrying the crying and irritable baby Vivian around the parlour. Herself the mother of a large family, she quickly struck up a sympathetic and long-lasting friendship with Frances. Schayer's was the first of a series of descriptions of Frances, "the Coming Woman," written about this time. Although some found her distant and quiet, and others lively and enthusiastic—depending on the mood in which they found her, Schayer saw her as a stout woman with a large forehead and nose, but with a pleasing mouth that was quick to smile and lovely eyes of indeterminate colour. "For the rest she is as one happens to find her— gay, amusing, fascinating, or reserved, distrait, even haughty, as the case may be."[16] Frances wrote Julia long playful letters, as in one from Rhode Island in which she purports to be struggling with Emerson, DeQuincy, and Browning as an antidote to her own intellectual frivolity, and another congratulating Julia on her recent inauguration story, which Frances found "so nice and niggery," a word she seems never to have used again in her life.[17]

As the author of a very popular book, Frances immediately found herself the object of great interest in Washington, and descriptions of her rivalled those she inserted in her own stories. One newspaper reporter marvelled that although she was a professional writer, "her graceful fingers show no traces of ink."

> Personally she is plump—almost too plump for her short stature. She wears her soft brown hair [it was actually auburn] braided behind and frizzed in front, to cover what she calls a horrid great forehead, which really is too square and too projecting for beauty. Her nose is good, though rather large; her jaw and mouth are firm, with pretty teeth and a cordial, charming smile, often breaking into a jolly laugh. Her eyes are large, intense, very expressive, of indefinite, ever-changing color, though ordinarily of a lustrous gray. She speaks frankly of her writings, enjoys her popularity as an author, and is greatly amused at the things said to her about them. She seems to have no jealousy or envy in her composition, to be wholly unconventional and in every way free and large.[18]

Frances told the interviewer that she loved going out in society and regretted that her work prevented her from being more socially active. This was true enough, but another side of the story, a familiar one from her days in Knoxville and Paris, was developing. It was tiring enough being the mother of small children, even with household help. Now that she was achieving some fame, it seems that the pressure on her to write increased rather than diminished, and she fell once again into exhaustion and depression.

It seems that Swan was behind the push. He was her biggest fan but also her harshest critic. He wanted her work to be the best it could be, and he read it all carefully, praising her to the skies when the writing merited praise, listening to her craft the characters and plots in the evenings as they sat together, yet also continually pushing her to succeed. "I wonder if it ever occurs to any one that it is possible that I should be tired," she wrote in a private piece called "A Real Record," which she put aside as she had done earlier with the Paris poem about her fatigue and despair. "I dont think it does, in even the faintest manner. 'How did you get on this morning? How much did you do? Is your story nearly finished? How much longer will it take you?' That is what they say to me. I am a kind of pen driving machine, warranted not to wear out, that is all."[19] She was so tired that her eyes were bloodshot and her hands trembled. As with her Paris poem, she thought of dying, and believed that no one—with the exception of her sister Edith— would care or remember her.

It is possible that the pressure came as much from herself as from any-one else, but there is no doubt that she keenly felt the weight of being con-stantly and firmly before the clamouring public's eye. With the success of *That Lass o' Lowrie's*, those who had published her work in the monthly mag-azines over the past nine years saw a goldmine in her past work. *Scribner's* tried to keep the line between legitimate and illegitimate republications clear by bringing out a handsome green and gilt volume called *Surly Tim and Other Stories* as soon as the success of *Lass* became clear. But in 1877, the same year as these two books appeared, three other books bearing her name were published, and in the following year four more—making an astound-ing nine books in publication in eighteen months—and only four of them authorized by her.

It was her own very prolific story writing that caused the problem, for there were now dozens, perhaps hundreds, of these early stories knocking around. Publishers like Peterson's jumped immediately on the bandwagon and brought out her earlier serials, fleshed out by the addition of a few other stories, as books. In September 1878, a year after *Lass's* success sparked the flood of unauthorized reprints, Swan was walking in downtown Wash-ington when he noticed they had printed yet another volume of her earlier stories and found that they were advertising the lot as "five new books by Mrs. Burnett."[20] Charles Peterson himself seems to have had little to do with this opportunism, but the book publishing side of the company, F. M. Lupton, leaped at the chance to cash in on her previous work. To "Theo," first sketched out in her ledger book, and later expanded into a *Peterson's* serial, they added—without indicating it on the cover, title page, or table of contents—two of her other magazine stories, "Wanted—A Young Person" (published by them in 1876) and "Miss Vernon's Choice" (published by them in 1872). Though they prefaced the book with an effusive encomium to her literary prowess ("Mrs. Frances Hodgson Burnett is one of the most charming among American writers. There is a crisp and breezy freshness about her delightful novelettes that is rarely found in contemporaneous fiction. . . . Of all Mrs. Burnett's romances and shorter stories those which first attracted public attention to her wonderful gifts are still her best. She has done more mature work, but never anything half so pleasing and enjoy-able."), the reappearance of these early works threatened to seriously dam-age her new reputation. "Theo" begins strongly enough but dissolves into romantic melodrama of the sort that she had now left far behind her—and the critics noticed. Indeed, with *Lass* now reaping strong reviews, and the new book *Haworth's* well under way, Frances was making a strong and viable bid to be considered a writer of industrial novels who followed in the footsteps of those such as Elizabeth Gaskell and Charles Dickens, and the reappearance of these less accomplished stories hurt her reputation.

Frances and Swan were alarmed as these other books appeared.[21] Indeed, there was a veritable tide of them, each one representing her writing-for-remuneration past, which she wished to move beyond: *Theo* and *Lindsay's Luck*; *A Quiet Life* (subtitled *A Pathetic Love Story*), which was published with the story "The Tide on the Moaning Bar"; *The Tide on the Moaning Bar*, published on its own as though it were a novel, and brought out without permission by her new English publisher, Frederick Warne; *Pretty Polly Pemberton*, a serial first published in 1876 by *Peterson's*; and *Dolly*, published by Porter and Coates of Philadelphia, which proved to be the reworking of her stories "Dorothea" and "Dolores." Five years later, in sending a copy of *Dolly* to a friend, she remarked that the book had been pirated and that it was "a very unripe little story but I was a very unripe little girl when I wrote it & it makes me feel queer to read it, in these my worldly & sophisticated days. But perhaps it will make you laugh or cry or something. It inclines me to do all three when I remember the queer inconsequent days in 'Vagabondia,' the real Dolly & Millie & Aimée & Grif & Phil [Frances and her siblings and Swan]."[22]

Scribner's countered this flood by adding *Earlier Stories, First Series* and *Earlier Stories, Second Series* in 1878, which contained the authorized versions of "Theo," "Lindsay's Luck," and others. Scribner's believed a matter of honour was involved; they would bring out the new, corrected editions—one of the grating problems with the unauthorized ones was that they were riddled with errors—and advised her and Swan to let things go at that. Frances found this hard to do, even though Peterson's sent her a dozen free copies of *Theo*. "It is a pathetic sort of thing to me now," she told Gilder. "It is such a nice idiotic sixteeny little thing. I did not know whether to laugh or cry last night when I went over it. I was a much nicer girl when I wrote that than I am now. Of course the Petersons have broken their promise to announce in the title page that it was a reprint & not a new book."[23]

It was Swan who proposed that Scribner's try to head off the piracy by publishing an authorized set of the stories. He assured them that he didn't presume to offer them publishing advice, "but it does seem that sooner or later every thing that Mrs. B. has written will be hunted up and printed."[24] Scribner's was delighted with the success of *Lass* and *Surly Tim* but had no particular desire to engage in a publishing war. Upon consideration, though, they decided the plan had some merit and went ahead with the two volumes of her *Earlier Stories*.

Although Scribner's preferred not to address head-on the unauthorized editions, Frances insisted that some sort of clarifying preface appear in each book. Even Swan, although angered at Peterson's mercenary presumption, felt that to insert such a preface would antagonize Peterson's and make a bad situation worse, because any repercussions would, by contract, fall in their laps and not in that of Scribner's. Scribner's reluctantly agreed to a more succinct version of the preface, and *Surly Tim and Other Stories*, published in October, therefore carried an author's note, written on 14 September 1877, declaring that "'That Lass o' Lowrie's' and the present volume are the only works issued under her name which have been prepared and corrected for publication in book form under her personal supervision." A year later, in the *Earlier Stories* series, she published a similar disclaimer. For years, ignoring the advice of her friends and family, she continued to respond in print to the often personal and unfounded stories printed about her.

It turned out that Frances's concerns about these unauthorized editions were justified. The *Literary World* praised *Dolly* but commented that "we can well understand why Mrs. Burnett might wish that her *Kathleen*, which first saw light, we believe, in *Peterson's Magazine*, should have been left there buried and forgotten, for, though in no way discreditable to her as the effort of a young writer, it is wholly lacking in the picturesque power which she has manifested in her later work."[25] *Theo* came in for harsher words from other critics, one of whom listed it among recent failures and said that "we cannot affirm with positive certainty that Mrs. Burnett has engaged in the speculative enterprise of selling chaff after wheat. The story, however, published under the title of 'Theo' (T. B. Peterson) bears all the marks of a tentative, crude essay, and is to 'That Lass o' Lowrie's' as a tyro's stiff, pale etching to the broad, glowing performance of an experienced hand."[26] Still, in all her discussions and interviews, she was careful to keep Charles Peterson personally clear of her complaints, knowing that he had been the first to recognize her talents and pay her accordingly, and he had gone on to make their Paris year possible. She owed to him her present success, "and I can never, never, cancel the debt of gratitude that I owe him."[27]

Swan echoed her words. In sending on the manuscript of Frances's latest story, "Smethurstses," to Charles Warren Stoddard of *Scribner's Magazine*, whom he had met while on a trip to New York, he added that "We have told [Peterson's] in language more choice and perhaps terse they [may] go to the Devil with their 500 dollars. Mrs. B. cannot sanction the publication of her earlier work. They will probably go ahead with the publication. If so I will inform you. In any thing you may say about the matter I hope you will say nothing disparaging about [Charles Peterson] for he is a perfect gentleman and has been wonderfully kind and considerate for us."[28]

It was Gilder who finally led her to understand that by not copyrighting the earlier stories, she shared some of the blame for the spate of unauthorized editions. She had been so incensed at their presumption that it had not occurred to her that she too might be at some fault, becoming so "savage & desperate & generally worried by the hopeless aspect of the thing . . . that Doro was afraid to come home & that he confided the fact to you in fear & trembling again," she wrote to her editor. "Am I in secret a virago & does Doro know it—& you too."[29]

Just as things seemed to get better, something else occurred to rouse her anger. No fewer than four dramatic versions of *Lass* appeared in London, none of them authorized by her. The most prominent of these was one by the well-known writer Charles Reade, known as a dramatist and theatre manager, as well as for being a novelist of much repute and a journalist. Among his best-known works are the novels *The Cloister and the Hearth*, about lunatic asylums, and *Griffith Gaunt*. In England, at least, his reputation far exceeded Frances's, but that did not prevent her from challenging him in the newspapers. Joseph Hatton, who in collaboration with Arthur Matthison dramatized the story in London, consulted with Reade so that the latter's version would only play outside the metropolis.

The problem lay, once again, in copyright. In America, novelists could reserve the dramatic rights to their own work, but this had to be done within a specified period of time after the initial publication. Even if this were done, however, it held no legal sway in Britain. British writers were no better off; they could not even reserve translation rights, and nothing had been resolved by the courts. "As the law now stands," a *New York Times* editorial complained on Frances's behalf, "a novelist has no legal means of preventing the robbery of his property for stage purposes except by dramatizing it himself, and copyrighting the play before he publishes the novel. If the latter is published first, the author cannot prevent any person from adapting it for the stage, even though he should himself dramatize it."[30]

Reade was adamant that he had done nothing wrong in not consulting Frances before producing his dramatic version of *Lass*. "There was no earthly reason why we should not do so. The authoress in her book has shown a natural and proper desire to retain *copyright* in both countries. But she has not printed one syllable to lead one to suppose she desired to retain *stage-right* in it. And, as it is not the habit of novelists, unless they are known dramatists, to dramatize their own works, she has left this entirely open, especially as the law of England gives no novelist *stage* rights in his work, but only copyright, or the right of printing and publishing."[31] To the Manchester *Examiner* Reade wrote on 15 September that in his interpretation, the

American phrase "all rights reserved" had nothing to do with dramatic rights. When she and Swan wrote to him incensed, he claimed he had legal right on his side; she claimed the moral right: "Standing on a good law written into smoke by legislative scribblers, Mrs. Burnett declined to deal with me, and demanded the withdrawal of her drama."[32] Her country of origin had not, so far, treated her well: Warne's had paid only twenty-five pounds each for the right to publish *Lass* and *Surly Tim and Other Stories*, and now her dramatic rights to the former seemed lost as well. Reade did offer a compromise. An American actress wished to put on his play *Liz*, his dramatic version of *Lass*, in the United States. Not only did he withdraw the play in Britain, but he offered payment to Frances for both versions.

Despite his proffered olive branch, the American papers were on Frances's side, and she flew into action to protect her intellectual property: not in court but by writing her own version of the play. Disgusted by Hatton, who claimed that no one would have known about her book had he not written his play, and annoyed by Reade's presumption, she knew she could do a better job: "I make Dan Lowrie talk Dan Lowrie, and Joan talk Joan, instead of drivelling about her broken heart as Hatton has her do. I am wild to finish it and have you compare the two. We have got it safe in America, at least, and Hatton's play shall *not* be played to spoil my reputation." Swan, awed by her drive and fury, cautioned her not to get too excited and suggested pounded ice for her headaches.[33] What angered her even more was the fact that Hatton stated on the script entered at Stationers' Hall that his and Matthison's play was "the only version of Mrs. Burnett's Novel authorised by the author. It cannot be performed without the express permission in writing of Joseph Hatton and Arthur Matthison or the Dramatic Authors' Society, London, to whom all applications should be made."[34] Not only had he stolen her work and claimed to have her permission to do so, but he did it badly. Unlike Frances's Joan, who was as strong as a man and carefully developed, his Liz simpered and whined her way through four tedious acts.

Her play, co-authored with Julian Magnus, was put on at the Booth Theatre for several weeks, starring the newcomer Marie Gordon and featuring original music. The production was underwritten by John T. Raymond, whose wife, Marie Gordon, wished to play Joan. Frances received only twenty-five dollars per performance, not surprising given that admission was only seventy-five cents for reserved seats, and general admission just twenty-five cents and five cents. The critics weren't always kind, either. One noted that Marie Gordon "labored hard [and] moved throughout the scenes in a dreamy and disagreeable manner, and apparently was unconscious of the demands of the part." They all praised William Davidge, who played Sammy Craddock, and particularly liked Florence Wood, a gamin actress who played the boy Jud.[35] The play had a short run, but something greater had happened: Frances discovered that she could write for the popular stage and that she loved the whole process of play production, including rehearsals, design, and mixing with theatre people, whose often unconventional lives widened her social and professional circles. On a weekend visit to the Petersons in Philadelphia while the play was in rehearsal in New York, she wrote back to Julia that "the other morning, as I was going over the additions I had made to Jud Bates' part (I have made him a clever London gamin) and we were bemoaning that the girl who has it is not clever enough for it, I said, without thinking, 'Oh, how I wish I could take it.' Mrs R. clutched me and almost shrieked, 'Oh,' she said, 'if you only would. I would give the *world* if you would. If you would only try it in some little town.' Of course, I told her it was impossible, but wouldn't it be a lark? However, I have a husband, also offspring, and consequently rather shall my right hand cleave to the roof of my mouth."[36] Having written *Pretty Polly Pemberton*, the story of a good girl who must overcome a bad reputation simply because she is an actress, Frances was well aware of the difference between writing for the stage and appearing on it.

Instead of attempting the stage, she threw herself back into working on her new novel, *Haworth's,* and found that it went better than ever. She wrote to Gilder that Swan was about to mail him the first part of the new book and that it was marvellous.

> After working & going through agonies untold & raving & tearing & hating myself & every word I ever wrote I have suddenly walked out into a cool place & begun to soar & have soared & soared until I dont think I shall ever return to earth again. How it happens how after loathing a thing & planning over it & writing every chapter of it over again & over again & over again, & slashing into it, & cutting out of it I can suddenly stand apart from it in cool blood & say "It is stunning!" I dont see. The room I have written it in has been a torture chamber & yet at Chapter 27 I am just tearing along & to my utter bewilderment I feel as if I had done something as far beyond the Lass as the Lass is beyond "Dolly." I actually do and it takes away my breath. . . . There is a dead man in it who is the most living creature I ever made. . . . Read for yourself. I want you to know each other though. Let me introduce you. Mr Richard Watson Gilder A dead man! —This is the Author of the New Day. I wish you had lived long enough to read it.

Her great effort over this book evidently took its toll on the family peace during the winter before its completion, for she told Gilder at that time that "Doro swears that after this book is finished I shall never write another," a comment that belies her earlier representation of him as her taskmaster.[37]

The struggles over copyright to her own work in England and America awakened in her a desire to protect her work and to outwit those who sought to cash in on her labour and hard-earned profits. Indeed, her work excited her just as much, needed just as much protection, and took just as much effort as the raising of her children. What remained to be seen was which would take precedence over the other—family or her expanding world.

CHAPTER 7

~

A CITY OF GROVES
AND BOWERS

1877–1880

IN THE 1870S WASHINGTON, D.C., was developing into one of the
most exciting American cities, with an autumn and winter season that
rivalled the famous London season of social and political affairs.
Although there was an established "society" disparagingly referred to as the
Antiques, the nouveaux riches and the up-and-coming flocked to Washington for the opportunities to hobnob with politicians and visiting European
diplomats, make a display through real estate, and try to move up the social
ladder, even when the ranks were carefully circumscribed by government
influence or family position. Rather than relying on manufacture and industry or finance for its economic base, the district depended on service industries and government for its livelihood.

Washington City, as it was then commonly called, offered an exciting
novelty and an atmosphere that was more relaxed than that of frantic New
York or caste-bound Philadelphia and Boston. Many of the buildings that
we think of today as defining the landscape of Washington were then still
under construction: the Capitol grounds were landscaped by Frederick Law
Olmsted, the designer of New York's Central Park, in the 1870s, and a park
system was later designed. The White House added a major extension. The
Washington Monument was under construction, and plans were laid for
a national zoo to remove the exhibition animals from the grounds of the
Smithsonian, where they were used as models for the taxidermists. Although
part of the city was built on treacherous malaria-ridden swampland, producing a deadly miasma that claimed a startling number of lives each year, the
city itself had a great natural beauty that led Frances to describe it later as
the "City of Groves and Bowers."[1]

Washington's workdays consisted of notoriously easy hours, and "the capital from the end of the 1870s to the turn of the century was more nearly a city of leisure than any other in America."[2] The men strolled into work at nine in the morning and left their government offices at four in the afternoon. On the avenues, Frances wrote in *Saint Nicholas*, the "carriages roll by one after another. Inside there are to be seen ladies in lovely hats and bonnets. There are mamas in brocades and velvets and furs, and there are pretty slim girls in silks and velvets and soft feathers. They are going to make calls, to attend musicales or receptions or special afternoon teas, where they will meet scores of other mamas and pretty girls, and will talk and drink chocolate and nibble cakes or listen to some music, and then return to the carriage and roll away to another party."[3] Frances, recovered from her over-work and prepartum depression, was destined to become one of the lions of the city, charming everyone with her wit and sense of fun, and leading the pack with her nearly ruinous love of fashion and home decoration. The only potential roadblock to the Burnetts' social success was their lack of pedigree. Her family connections were modest at best—even in Washington, a back-ground in trade was looked down upon—and although Swan came from an admired Tennessee family, he was from one of its poorer branches. Books such as the *Elite List* and the later *Etiquette of Social Life in Washington* showed newcomers the ropes and informed them who was in and who was out. Nevertheless, in Washington "any well-mannered white person, in short, who could afford servants and who meticulously followed the 'cast iron' rules about making calls could be a part or hover on the fringes of Society."[4]

In more ways than one, Washington in 1877 was what Vivian later de-scribed as southern, which he saw as meaning that it had "a free and kindly sense of hospitality," a lack of wealthy first citizens, and little of the stiff and formal sophistication found in Boston, Philadelphia, and New York.[5] One of the most racially progressive American cities in the Reconstruction years following the Civil War, it was on the other hand rapidly becoming one of the most segregated. Fully one-third of the city's population was black, and a segment of that population consisted of wealthy, light-skinned aristocrats who vacationed in fashionable Saratoga and owned mansions like their white counterparts but who nonetheless found themselves entirely excluded from social interactions with whites. They could be served in white bars, but not in restaurants or ice cream parlours; they could serve in gov-ernment—the famous abolitionist Frederick Douglass was the highest example of this—but increasingly lost the vote in the southern states.

The Burnetts lived in an integrated neighbourhood in Washington just as they had in Knoxville. In those days, Washington was a mix of "shabby cottages or tumble-down shanties side by side with the largest and most comfortable houses there were to be found in the city," Frances later wrote. "The house in which I lived then belonged to General Grant, it having been presented to him by some of his friends and admirers. At the corner of the same side of the street was a large brick house where General Garfield lived; opposite my house there was a small row of frame houses all occupied by colored people." The neighbourhood policeman was a black man named Niel, about whom her sons always spoke "reverentially as 'Mr. Niel.' . . . He even condescended to let them examine his club and I seem to have some recollection of their having discovered that it was true that he sometimes carried a pistol."[6]

Despite Niel's position of authority, Frances tended to view most black people in Washington as happy servants. According to her, in early spring "little black or yellow boys begin to appear with bunches of arbutus" to sell. As the weather warmed, "smart colored nurses begin to sit on the benches and talk to each other and watch their charges." In the hot summer, fruit and vegetable carts, "always driven by colored gentlemen," rolled down the streets, and her sons delighted in "a colored gentleman of the name of Johnson" who hawked watermelons. She assured her readers that the "only people one sees in rags or asking alms are occasional negroes; and they are very safe, and usually look rather as if their profession were a matter of preference. Of palpable, hopeless wretchedness one sees nothing."[7]

Like most Washingtonians, she was mistaken in this view. Lack of opportunity caused by racism meant that the majority of black citizens in Washington were mired in poverty, many of them occupying an intricate maze of tenements in alleyways invisible from the streets. Entire families lived in single rooms with no indoor plumbing. Black mortality rates were double that of whites. Whenever social reformers attempted to improve the dreadful conditions of the slums, they were met with disbelief that such places even existed. Frances, like others of her race, saw only the fact that at the annual Easter egg-rolling on the White House lawn, white children were joined by "some little black ones in a pleasing state of excitement," and that the "colored young ladies who preside in the nurseries . . . frequently know a great deal of the doings of the party-going world."[8] Like all Washingtonians, she employed black servants, including a houseman named Dan, probably the model for Uncle Matt from *In Connection with the DeWilloughby Claim* who immerses himself quickly in the Washington way of life and, like most servants, is able to hear more useful and private information than his employers imagine. Years later, back in Washington to visit friends, she was delighted by their "most perfect colored servants. There is something tender in their attention."[9]

Although the years 1876 to 1878 kept Frances on an emotional roller coaster, and despite the weariness and depression that often overcame her, she found herself living the life that suited her best. She was surrounded by a coterie of new friends, including Julia Schayer, a gentle schoolteacher named Euphemia Macfarlane (always called Effie), and her sisters Virginia Prall, Emma, and Rachel, who took care of their brother-in-law's four children; William Henry Dennis, always known as Will, a sedate young lawyer with a wonderful sense of humour; the sociable and handsome New England bachelor Charles Edward Rice, who sang beautifully, let the boys fall asleep on his lap, and carried them up to bed; an artist named Hiram Fischer; Thorvald Solberg, a Knoxville friend who now lived in a Washington boarding house and had shared his F Street lodgings with Swan when he first came up from Tennessee; Dave Hutchison, an intellectual who headed the Congressional Library and had outlined a reading programme for Frances; and many others with whom she could indulge her sense of fun. Swan participated enthusiastically in their lively evening gatherings.

Their sons were healthy, and Frances and Swan were enormously proud of them. When Gilder invited Frances to stay with him and his wife and their small son Rodman in New York, she replied that she should like so much to see Mrs. Gilder and give her some incidental information concerning "babies who could stand in corners at three months lift chairs & valises at seven & walk along the streets of London at nine. Facts of this kind are always interesting to the person who relates them."[10] She loved to parody the doting mother whose children were always superior to everyone else's, but her pride in Lionel and Vivian was real. "How is Rodman," she asked Gilder, whom Swan had seen in New York. "Doro told me he was beginning to try to pull up by a chair. I will not say anything about Lionel who walked alone round Russell Square when he was nine months old or about Vivian who followed his nurse upstairs at eight. Far be it from me to mention the subject."[11]

When she worked at her writing table, Lionel quietly lay underneath it on his back, which "in 'literary' houses we call 'being good' & it is the condition on which he is allowed to stay with me." But, she added, "somehow there is something sad in it to me."[12] She loved her time with the boys, reading what they called "po'tery," caring for them, and playing games. At the same time, she was a working woman who needed quiet and concentration each day as she shut the door to her den to work. Still, she knew which came first. When Lionel became ill for the first time and Vivian hurt himself by falling down the basement stairs, all her work was put aside as she nursed them back to health. Throughout the winter of 1877–78, her life combined working on the manuscript of what would be the new novel *Haworth's,* caring for her children, and pursuing a seemingly ceaseless round of social engagements. Everywhere she went she found herself admired by an adoring public, and those who knew someone who knew her rose in the public estimation. One of her lost gloves was put up at auction. At parties and teas, the tightly corseted little woman with the auburn hair and lively eyes always drew a crowd of admirers. "If I had time I could write a great deal about what I have been doing," she told Gilder. "I find myself obliged to go out very often & if I were to tell you what happens to me you would think my head was turned. I think so myself often enough. If I live a thousand years I shall never realize it. People are amazed that I dont seem to & that I take it so coolly but they wouldn't be if they knew me as well as I do. I have a very exciting time. I daresay if I stayed here long enough I might have a boiled senator for dinner every day . . . but I have to work like fury."[13]

Aside from Swan's, though, only Gilder's admiration held any value for her. "Praise me! Exalt me; say as much as you can. You have no need to be afraid. It is not fine speeches I want in the least. I have them by the hundred by the thousand by the million. I have had a whole winter of them. At last I know what it is to be (in the words of an ardent admirer) 'a roaring raging lion' & yet there has never been a time when all I hear said over & over again has given me a moments courage or inspiration. I never seem to believe it or realize it or something. But you are different. You no more realize your power over me than I realize mine over other people."[14] Complaining that she could get no quiet in order to write, she nonetheless finished the manuscript of *Haworth's* by spring and was so moved by its ending that she felt weak and shaky. Calling Swan up to her den, she read it to him and then collapsed in tears in his arms.

The spring was glorious, with the trees in full bloom and the new book at last finished. She and Swan and the boys moved into a splendid new house at 1215 I Street, bigger than the two-storey brick house they had first occupied on M Street, an "uncomfortable, inconvenient and insanitary house,"[15] or their next home at 813 13th Street, where they entertained their crowds of friends. In the roomy three-storey house, with its big windows, marble mantelpieces, two parlours divided by sliding doors, and first-floor nursery, the family began to be able to afford the decorative comforts Frances adored: lovely soft rugs and curtains, comfortable sofas and armchairs, and log fires. The gas-lit nursery was near Frances and Swan's bedroom. Each had an office in the house. Frances wrote in a den on the top storey, where a black fur rug stretched across the floor in front of a fireplace and a sofa sat beneath windows that looked out over treetops. The room was large enough for tables, chairs, a rolltop desk, and a sizable bookcase, and despite her warnings that the boys leave her in peace as she worked at the writing desk in the middle of the room, they often curled up in her lap as she sat in the armchair, or pretended to be invisible under the desk as she scratched away at her work with a heavy gold pen, the gift of an admirer.

Vivian treasured this room as a special and loving space, where she went to work immediately after breakfast each day, leaving instructions not to be disturbed. However, "there were discovered a thousand irresistible reasons why one or two pair of stout-calved, heavy-shoed little legs should trudge up the two flights of stairs and their owners knock on her door, the excuses running all the way from a cut finger or barked knee to the discovery of some pretty stone or leaf that should immediately be put in the 'treasure drawer.'"[16] As the boys grew older, they were able to play safely in the broad and empty street in front of the house, or run errands for Frances to Stuntz's emporium around the corner or to Page's grocery. James Garfield, not yet elected president, lived on the corner of 13th and I Streets, and his children played with the Burnett boys. The Franklin Public School, where both Lionel and Vivian would be educated, was less than a block away.

Swan's career also made steady progress. He joined the staff of George-town University's medical school in 1878 as lecturer of ophthalmology and otology, a year later establishing a graduate course there in those fields. He had a private practice as well as a hospital practice. By 1889 he would be on the consulting staff of three more hospitals, president of Washington's medical society, and a member of several others.[17] The family was, clearly, on its way to prosperity and professional and social position, and settled into what was their happiest and cosiest period together.

Frances held Tuesday "evenings" attended by some of the best-known Washingtonians who came to hear her talk. "Senators, Diplomats, Supreme Court Justices," according to her friend Elizabeth Elliot. "With one or a roomful she was just the same, laughing and making others laugh. . . . Grad-ually, one after another, the little groups gathered round the central figure, and always it was far into the night before the last few left the circle round the open fire."[18] She called her more intimate group of young friends her "blood relations," but even they felt they were invited to the at-homes more to fill the space than to be noticed.

The Tuesday evenings were even livelier than Elliot described. Frances's plan was to begin with a few young women in the afternoons, joined later by a few young men for an "Inferior dinner." As people wandered in later in the evening, she'd play on the piano "in a nice loud pounding way" some of the waltzes and quadrilles she was learning. If the mood moved them, people might jump up to dance; if not, they could instead drink punch and eat cake and play cards.

> Last Tuesday we tried the first & it was a Success indeed though we did not dance & had invited only one man besides the Inferior dinner party. After dinner the Extra Man arrived & we went up into the Den—A wood fire burned—Charles Rice immediately turned down the gas—a brunette girl sat in a big chair in one side of the hearth & a blonde girl in another— with the blue India shawl draped over the back of it. I took a footstool & a peacock feather screen—Doro took a footstool—Charlie [Rice] sat on the floor—the Extra Man sat next to the Brunette Girl. The Extra Man has eyes like a Gazelle—and things—he does not speak—he *looks* at you from under Eyelashes—it is not necessary for him to speak. He sings—like a Bulbul—in a firelight voice—& has a collection of Maddening firelight songs—not loud songs & not a loud voice—You know what his eyes mean when you hear his songs. "Dana" said Charlie with mellifluous abusiveness (They are old friends) "Go and sing—its all you're good for." The Extra man did not utter a word, he simply rose & went to the piano & sang song after song while we listened—& Mooned. A couple of Interlopers from the unaesthetic world outside came in & protested that we looked like a picture. Their corpses are buried under the back stairs. *Dont mention it.*
>
> It was the kind of evening you could not *plan*—it had to happen & I hope it will happen again. I am an aesthetic creature myself—aiming at the Cimabue Brown style you know.[19]

She even attended a séance in the spring of 1878, where she "was thumped by guitars and tambourines, had a guitar played in my lap with the string against my body, had soft strange hands laid in mine, & was visited by a friend who died in England four years ago. There was a lot of idiotic blatant humbug going on & some very nice queer things."[20]

Swan loved this life as much as Frances did. He could be charming and outgoing, yet didn't mind as she stepped into the limelight she loved. He indulged her desire to make a fine impression, though his tastes took him towards collecting Japanese art while Frances loved interior decoration and beautiful clothes. She still, at this point, sewed for herself and the boys, a habit she continued even when she could buy the best that Paris had to offer. Her parties required new frocks, and her male friends anticipated the dresses' appearance as cheerfully as did her female friends. As with the late-arriving wedding gown, Frances made a public showing with one new dress: "The advent of the gown made by Frances' own fair hand was heralded beforehand to Doro, Hutchison, and Solberg. At the appointed hour the sliding doors between the parlor and dining-room were rolled apart, to disclose to the audience that had been herded in the front room—Frances, in all the dainty glory of her newly finished toilette. She took the uproarious applause, bowing and smiling, and the gown was voted in every way a success."[21]

The most welcome visitor of all, however, was Gilder himself, who proposed to travel to Washington to go over the *Haworth's* manuscript with her and to visit the Burnetts. She offered him a room in their new house, or one in a boarding house across the street, but wherever he chose to stay, "our happiness will be complete."[22] She considered his coming to her an enormous compliment to her growth as a writer, and as always these days her letters to him fell into a teasing flirtation in ways that went beyond the usual mentor–protégée relationship. In writing to him about James Haworth, the protagonist of *Haworth's* who uncannily anticipates Henchard in Thomas Hardy's *The Mayor of Casterbridge* (serialized in 1886), she admitted that the awkward and rough Lancashire factory owner excited her somehow, that he "stirs me up & I have a kind of brutal delight in him. (Swear you will never tell any one I said that.)"[23] At the end of the summer she planned a trip to New York, hoping to spend part of the visit devoted "to forming your acquaintance & letting you form mine. Dont you think it will be nice to pretend that I never wrote anything at all & you are not an editorial person or at least that your editorialness has nothing to do with me. Let us pretend it & see how it goes?"[24]

Happily married and serious, Gilder apparently enjoyed these confessions and flirtations; he was enormously fond of her and read portions of her lively letters to Helena. He was the first editor to take a hands-on interest in her work, and although they probably had met only once, on her youthful visit to New York on the way to Manchester, their correspondence had now lasted for seven years. Things took an awkward turn, though, when she suggested that the illustrator of *Haworth's* model the face of the inventor Murdoch on Gilder himself. Murdoch was gaunt and dark and brooding and rather unhealthy, and not unnaturally Gilder took umbrage at the comparison, causing Frances to backtrack and apologize: "Of course I should not have been guilty of the impertinence of dragging you into the illustrations in my letter. I am afraid I led you to misunderstand me. I did not mean that Murdoch was *like* you. I only meant that a foundation of your color & outline would have been truer than the present pictures—since you are a dark & angular individual." She recognized that she had offended him, pointing out that "It would have been rather *strong* in me, would nt it, to have put

you in a story & asked you to sit for the illustrations. And No—*Mon ami*
I am *not* strong however guilelessly I may have expressed myself."[25] When
the first instalments, running in *Scribner's* in 1878–79, arrived at their house
in Washington, she was delighted, but Swan was even more so. "Doro is
reading it with rapture for the five hundredth time," she exclaimed. "With
you for a critic how nice to have Doro for a husband!"[26]

Much as Frances and Swan enjoyed the city life, Frances in particular
often found the Washington summers simply too hot for comfort and too
difficult for concentrated writing. Their growing financial ease allowed them
not only a new house and the ability to entertain friends but the opportunity to escape the steamy summer heat for the mountains. In the summer
of 1878, the family took off for North Carolina, where they spent the hot
months riding horses, writing, and going for walks. Logan House at the
Hickory Nut Gorge of Rutherford County (today known as the Pine Gables
Inn at Lake Lure) was a forty-year-old log structure that had just been ren-
ovated the previous year to add two more buildings. It was on the stagecoach
line, on a road used for more than a century by cattle drovers and other trav-
ellers, making it accessible for summer tourists desiring a mountain stay.
The mountains were bare and rocky, but the inn commanded an imposing
view. She boasted of riding more than 150 miles on horseback over mountains and across precipices, "over such roads as only the most vivid imagination could picture," but she also spent a great deal of time writing.[27] Across
the road from the main lodge was a detached rock mass, where Frances sat
to write in fine weather: the rocks are today known as "Esmeralda's Cabin"
after the play (based on her Paris story "Esmeralda") that she first worked on
there.[28]

She also engaged in a favourite pastime of people watching. Not content
just to "steal a slice" of those she encountered, she enjoyed meeting others
on her travels. In North Carolina she made friends with a former Civil War
colonel whom she considered one of her "'finds'—a hero a scholar a gentleman, in a mountain school house—a kind of religious fatalist devoting his
life to the people he lives among. Looks something like the late Prince Con-
sort, Colonel of Artillery in Confederacy—leg taken off by cannon ball."
She begged Gilder to send him a magazine subscription at her expense,
because he was "starved for books."[29] The trip home took six long days, with
them pausing in Virginia, giving her a chance to read Henry James along the
way. They would one day be neighbours in England, and she found his a
"neat imagination," his work orderly and tidy and presumably less "messy"
than her own—and less moving.

They returned to another Washington political "season," refreshed by their mountain summer. Lionel was now four years old, still in long curls and short pants, an active and somewhat moody little boy, and Vivian a more robust and rugged two-year-old. With young children very much part of her daily life, she began to write a few pieces for Scribner's new magazine for children, at the request of its editor, Mary Mapes Dodge. But these remained small sidepieces, very much the peripheral work of an author now clearly established as writing for an adult audience. Looming ahead of her was another battle on the copyright front, another new set of friends who would call her away from home, a Washington novel about a married woman teetering on the edge of adultery, and not surprisingly, a prolonged and silent lapse into exhaustion.

~

CHAPTER 8

IN THE COMPANY
OF WOMEN

1880–1884

EXCEPT FOR FRANCES'S VISITS to New York and Philadelphia,
her life remained largely a southern one. Washington life suited her,
and it certainly suited her family. With the beginning of 1879,
though, her trips up North became more frequent and more prolonged. The
southern summers, ever since her pregnancy with Lionel, proved oppressive;
she found it difficult to sleep and to work in the heat and humidity, especially as her health began to decline from more than ten years of non-stop
writing. Then too, there were attractions that the North offered besides the
weather. For the first time she began to associate with women who held
advanced social and intellectual ideas, women who wrote and edited, and
who regularly moved in the stimulating atmosphere of books and debates on
women's rights. Over the next few years she befriended several women
whose influence on her life and work was immense.

In early February she received an invitation from John Boyle O'Reilly,
president of Boston's Papyrus Club, asking her to be the guest of honour
at a dinner whose guests would include Mary Mapes Dodge and Louisa
May Alcott. This was altogether of a different order than the Washington
events, at which she needed only to "murmur gently 'Thanks. You are very
kind to say so.' 'You are very good' &c &c."[1] She was a big fish in the
rather small pond of Washington artistic life, even though luminaries such
as the celebrated actress Madame Modjeska regularly passed through town.
Frances felt honoured and excited by the Papyrus Club invitation; she had
"been sighing" to visit the American centre of learning for some time and
to meet the very people now planning to gather in her honour. Still, she
wrote to Gilder, "it startles me just at first to be brought before the world by

people who have entertained Longfellow and Holmes & other distinguished persons."[2]

She already had a great deal in common with both Dodge and Alcott, two of the most famous American women writing at that time. The forty-eight-year-old Dodge had grown up in New York in a family that associated with the most influential people of their day. She married young but at twenty-seven found herself a widow with two sons to support. She turned to writing, and in 1865, the year Frances arrived in America, Dodge published her second book, the enormously popular *Hans Brinker, or the Silver Skates*. She moved in the same literary circles as Gilder, and perhaps at his suggestion took on the editorship of the new children's magazine *Saint Nicholas* in 1873. Five years earlier she had edited *Hearth and Home* with Harriet Beecher Stowe, author of *Uncle Tom's Cabin*, and Donald Grant Mitchell.

Dodge naturally had an interest in Frances, who, although young enough at twenty-nine to be her daughter, was also the mother of two sons and supported, or helped to support, a family by her writing. Dodge persuaded Frances to write her first story for children, "Behind the White Brick," and published it in *Saint Nicholas* in January 1879. In it a little girl named Jem, frustrated when her aunt throws her book into the fire, falls asleep and discovers Santa Claus's workshop behind a chimney brick. It was a story originally written for a little girl, Birdie, she had known in Tennessee when she was first married; after she went to Paris with Swan and the baby Lionel, Birdie and her siblings began to publish a little paper, and Frances sent the story to them from London for their paper.[3] "The Proud Little Grain of Wheat" was a story she had invented for her sons "when they were mites in white frocks and entering into abstruse calculations as to the ingredients of cake wanted to know what flour was made of."[4] In it, two boisterous little boys named Lionel and Vivian "with strong little legs and big brown eyes, and their sailor hats set so far back on their heads that it was a wonder they stayed on" visit the country, much as they did in summers spent in New Market. A farmer, his black helper, the farmer's wife, and her black cook—some of them actual servants in the Burnett household—produce a cake that "nice little mamma" brings to them.[5]

When Frances accepted the Papyrus Club invitation, Dodge wrote to suggest that Frances join her in staying at the Revere House where the dinner would take place, as it "it will be 'handy' for unprotected females to step down stairs to the dining room."[6] Frances was lucky to have Dodge at her side, for at her other side was another woman writer who "scorns reputation and adulation" and "is also very severe on people who flirt. She says nothing would induce her to so far forget her womanhood as to flirt. She weighs four hundred pounds and pins three little yellow puffs on her bare scalp with hair pins, and I thought it very noble in her to say so. If we had more women like that there would be less flirting. Men would not be led astray as they are. She assured Mr. Peterson and myself that she wouldn't lay herself out to allure *any* man—not to save his life or her own—and it made me feel that I belonged to a sex of which I might be proud after all."[7]

Louisa May Alcott, although an unmarried woman without children, also had much in common with Frances. The daughter of the transcendentalist Bronson Alcott, she had grown up in the rarefied intellectual community of Concord, among such thinkers as Ralph Waldo Emerson, Margaret Fuller, and Henry David Thoreau. Like Frances, her first stories were written for money, and she churned out potboilers rather than romantic tales to help support her family because her father, for most of his life, was unable to provide for them. Also like Frances she tried her hand briefly at teaching before turning to her pen for her income. She shared Frances's growing difficulties with health, having contracted typhoid during her brief stint as a nurse during the Civil War. It was with some reluctance and scepticism that she turned to the autobiographical fiction that made her so famous, but when *Little Women* appeared in 1868–69, it made her name as a writer for young people. Her less well-known novel *Work* involved the exhaustion of a young woman who took a series of menial jobs in order to support her family. She created strong, independent female characters and shared her family's belief in social reform.

Through Dodge and others, Frances began to move in a more intellectually stimulating atmosphere. Dodge had a formidable intellect and a great knack for editing, convincing important writers like Alcott to try their hand at children's writing and hoping to elevate it to the status of important literature. Dodge was well connected, introducing Frances to William Gillette, with whom she would collaborate in a few years' time. Alcott too, having been educated largely at home by parents who were part of a utopian community of philosophers, knew the value of both hard work and rational and spiritual thought. It was perhaps through her that Frances began slowly to develop her own philosophy of spiritualism, which depended less on institutionalized religion than on the power of the human mind and a belief in metaphysical healing.

Meeting these two women was the beginning of a new direction in Frances's thinking, but the trip to Boston bore an uncomfortable resemblance to her first visit to New York in the spring of 1872, when she was nowhere to be found when Gilder called at her hotel. This time the lure was an afternoon visit to Concord to meet Emerson, proposed by a young Harvard professor. He assured her that they would return to Boston in plenty of time for the

banquet, but to their horror they discovered late in the afternoon that there
was no train to return them to Boston in time. Humiliatingly late, Frances
slipped into her seat next to O'Reilly, and managed to mumble her apolo-
gies to her host and offer her gratitude to the company. She wrote to
O'Reilly after her return home to apologize again, and while he cheerfully
agreed that she "behaved badly at the dinner—deliciously and exquisitely
badly," he also asked whether she knew "how you charmed everyone in
Boston, Mrs. Burnett? Oh, of course not; but you did."[8]

Back home, Swan continued to act as Frances's manager. Shortly before
she left for Boston, he wrote to Scribner's to ask for copyright clarifica-
tion. "Are you or we owners of the copyright?" he asked. "I should like for
you to consider the matter further as business men, with our mutual good
in view."[9] In May he was "preparing to bring suit against Mr. Maguire manager of Baldwin's Theatre in San Francisco for violation of the copyright of
'That Lass o' Lowrie's.'" Although in the next line he amended his words to
say that "it is a question as to whether Mrs. Burnett has the power to bring
suit," it is clear he viewed himself as an equal partner in her business life.
Convenient for her in some ways, the arrangement left her free to write and
to recover her flagging energy, but a proprietary tone was now slipping into
his dealings with her various publishers.

In what now was to become routine, Frances arranged to spend the
summer in Newport, Rhode Island, stopping on the way in New York to
visit Dodge. Swan joined her at the end of the summer on a brief trip across
the Canadian border. Her English publisher, Macmillan, discovered that the
way to secure the English copyright for a "foreign" author was to have the
author on the soil of a Commonwealth country on the day of publication. To avoid with *Haworth's* the problems they had encountered with *Lass*,
Frances and Swan spent 28 August in Canada, returning together to Washington. She repeated the trip alone the following April for the publication
of her new work *Louisiana*. When the finished books arrived in early September, she and Swan were delighted with their appearance and pleased
that her research of mines and mining while on trips to North Carolina and
Virginia had paid off. One Philadelphia reviewer declared himself quite
satisfied with the book but asked that she drop the dialect that so charmed
her other readers. "If she can, (& I don't see why a woman of genius cannot)," he wrote to *Scribner's Magazine* when he sent in two copies of his
review, "she should get out of Lancashire & its dialect, and give us an *American* story, but without any Yankee or nigger talk."[10] With comments like
this about who was American and who was not, who was English and who
was not, she ceased reading reviews.

On 11 April 1878, Frances had written to a friend, "I saw Mrs Hooker on Monday & she said I must pay a visit sometime to Nook Farm (I think she called it Nook Farm) & then I should see ever so many people."[11] New England clearly appealed to her, and she left the children with Swan while she visited Boston again, first in January 1880, making a quick visit to Nook Farm in Hartford, Connecticut, a place that so impressed her that she rejoiced when she received an invitation from Isabella Beecher Hooker to spend the summer. Nook Farm and its inhabitants were to form her second crucial New England influence—less so because of its internationally known residents Harriet Beecher Stowe and Mark Twain than for the nationally important figures of Isabella Hooker and William Gillette.

Nook Farm was the name of 140 acres of land purchased in 1853 by John Hooker, Isabella's lawyer husband, and his brother-in-law Francis Gillette. There they built a number of houses into which various of their friends and relatives moved, developing quickly into a warm and familial community of writers, professionals, and activists who spent nearly as much time in each others' homes as in their own. Although Frances had met Stowe— "Mrs. Beecher's Toe" as she playfully referred to her behind the scenes—it was Stowe's younger half-sister who brought Frances to the community. If Stowe, whom Abraham Lincoln was rumoured to refer to as the "little lady who started this big war," had rocked the world with her anti-slavery novel, Isabella Hooker had a more local but powerful reputation as an activist for women's rights.

A series of awakenings had carried Hooker into the crusade: her husband's reading to her from his legal texts, from the writings of John Stuart Mill, and from local cases in which two brilliant sisters were prevented from property ownership and the right to dispute their taxes had aroused her indignation, and the emerging suffragist movement headed by Elizabeth Cady Stanton and Victoria Woodhull had suggested an avenue for action. She organized the National Woman Suffrage Association convention held in Hartford in 1869 and presided over the Connecticut Woman Suffrage Association from 1871 to 1890. In 1883 she addressed the International Council of Women in Washington, D.C., telling them "that the sooner men understand [that women must be allowed to vote] . . . the sooner will this precious domestic tranquility be insured."[12] Quieter and more diplomatic than his beautiful and utterly determined wife, John Hooker supported her causes fully even when they led to an enormous rift within the Nook Farm community.[13]

Originally supporters of the Connecticut Woman Suffrage Association, Stowe and her sister Catharine quickly dissociated themselves from it in favour of a more domestic and less strident approach to women's issues.

There was no rupture among the sisters until Woodhull, who favoured easier divorce and free love along with the right to vote, took what seemed to them and others the outrageous step of publicly accusing their brother Henry Ward Beecher of having carried on an extramarital affair with a married woman. Woodhull, who had been married at only fourteen to a man who proved to be an alcoholic and gave birth to a retarded child, took "the radical position that marriage was sexual slavery, that wives were raped by their husbands, and that sexual relations ought to be regulated by love alone."[14] It was her way of calling attention to the inequities between men's and women's sexual lives, and she thought that by striking at the heart of a socially liberal yet also religious and acceptable community, she could force her point. Woodhull, the first woman to be nominated for the U.S. presidency, became an enormously successful stockbroker through her friendship with Vanderbilt, and moved to England in 1877 with her new husband Martin, where she continued her suffragist work, dying in Britain in 1927 as a respected social activist.

At Nook Farm, however, Woodhull's name was anathema to Stowe. In December 1872 she wrote to Frances's friend Mary Claflin that "no one could understand the secret of her influence over my poor sister—incredible infatuation continuing even now. I trust that God will in some way deliver her for she was and is a lovely good woman & before this witch took possession of her we were all so happy together."[15] Stowe herself made a disastrous attempt to address the sexual politics of marriage when she published in the *Atlantic* in January 1870 an account of Lord Byron's marriage. In "The True Story of Lady Byron's Life," she took up the cudgels for Lady Byron, a wronged woman who had revealed to Stowe (and others, as it turned out) in 1856 that Byron's incestuous affair with his half-sister Augusta Leigh was the reason behind their separation. Cast as a "cold and calculating wife" by the men who had written about the separation, Lady Byron kept an understandable silence that led to her vilification in print. The attempt to call attention to the sexual wrongs women endured backfired, and both Stowe and the *Atlantic* suffered in reputation and readership. It was, Stowe's biographer asserts, "a symptom of the polarization of literature along gender lines that was such a striking feature of the post-Civil War period."[16]

Frances was more concerned about her domestic arrangements than social issues as she prepared for her summer in Hartford. "I have a great deal of work to do this summer—a big book besides the play—and I regret to say I don't feel at all equal to my tasks," she wrote to Hooker on 25 May 1880. "I cannot remain in Washington where the heat is actually unbearable & it would be next to impossible to work at any ordinary place where I must live in a hotel, so Nook Farm seems a happy thought. I have been away from home so long however that Dr Burnett (who has a dreary summer before him) is desolate at the thought of my leaving him all alone again so soon." She therefore decided to remain in Washington with Swan until the end of June, even though "it is 94 in the shade today and we go to bed panting."[17] The play was the dramatization of her story "Esmeralda," which she was preparing for the stage with William Gillette, who had grown up on Nook Farm and was gaining recognition as an actor and playwright.[18] When she met him in Boston she felt sure they could work well together; even though she had some theatrical knowledge after putting on her version of *Lass*, she needed someone with more expertise to show her the ropes if she wanted serious theatrical success for her work. In the meantime, she needed to arrange things for Lionel and Vivian, at first planning to send them to Tennessee for the summer, and she wanted to spend some time with her increasingly lonely husband.

Aside from the heat, her need for a respite was very real. "About three months ago I seemed to arrive at my breakdown," she told Gilder in June. "My backbone disappeared and my brain and when I found they were really gone I missed them. Their defection seemed so curious that I began to try to account for it & finally rambled weakly round to the conclusion that it might be because I have written ten books in six years & done two or three other little things. . . . I have about three hundred pages of a book done and generally I dont seem to care about it. Theres a good deal of it in one place and another if I could find any brains and my wrists didnt seem to dangle so. I generally lie on my back and despise myself." She complained that her brains were "atrophied on the story side where they bulge out unnecessarily in a lop sided way."[19] While she used a light tone with Gilder, she confessed to Hooker, "I *must* get well—I have been miserable since I came home [from Boston] and I seem to lose all stability through the heat."[20]

The troublesome novel was *In Connection with the DeWilloughby Claim*, so reflective of Reconstruction (1865–77) and post-Reconstruction Washington, Virginia, and North Carolina, and it would not be completed until nearly twenty years later. She called it "an obstinate demon of a thing," and it was to remain a monkey on her back all those years, picked up and put down in frustration between other projects, and when finally it was published in 1899, it had the naïve and nostalgic aura of a long-gone era.[21] In the meantime, she chipped away at two projects reflecting her fascination with transatlantic pretensions and social mores: making the play *Esmeralda* and writing *A Fair Barbarian*, the latter about an elegant American who shakes up a small and narrow-minded English village by her refusal to respect their petty and restrictive codes of dress and behaviour.

As with London at the end of its social season, America's capital city emptied into the countryside when the members of Congress dispersed for the summer. The reasons for this had more to do with health than society. Aside from the heat, Washington in those days was a breeding ground for malaria, and it was considered prudent for those who could leave to do so. Leaving husbands like Swan behind to continue in their offices, wives like Frances regularly searched for cooler climes in New England or in the mountains of Virginia. Without family close by in suitably cool places— Edith, now a widow earning her living as a seamstress, was sharing a house in San Francisco with Teddy and Frank and their three children (another son, Frank, had been born in 1879), and Frank T. Jordan, whom Edith would soon marry—Frances relied on the invitations of new friends eager to open their homes to her, and on hotels along the Atlantic shore. Earlier that year she had visited Mary Bucklin Claflin, wife of William Claflin, the former governor of Massachusetts; Frances had undoubtedly met her on the Papyrus Club–Boston trip since Claflin was a supporter of the arts. Frances also counted Stowe among her acquaintances, but Stowe also was a regular visitor to Washington, D.C. Frances was glad to have "defied marital authority and left Washington to pine on its stem and the Government to languish on account of my absence" during that visit to Boston earlier in the year, and now she was relieved to arrive in Connecticut, along with "a faithful and reliable colored woman."[22]

At Nook Farm she divided her time between working on *A Fair Barbarian*, lying in a hammock and sitting in the sun while her redhead's fair skin freckled distressingly, participating in the social life of the community, and working on her play. She wrote to Gilder about *Esmeralda*'s prospects. She admitted she knew little about the business aspect of such an enterprise, "but I could put these people into positions & make them say things." She wanted to dramatize the story because, once again, her works were being adapted for the stage without her permission, and the only way to circumvent it was to produce her own versions of her work. "I will own to some qualms of course about stealing the Western dramatists thunder but then Doro says they are stealing mine. Would it be unfair in me do you think?" She had more confidence now that *A Fair Barbarian* seemed solid: "I set it up & walk around it & look at it & try to shake it to see if it will fall but it stands pretty strongly so far. When I have written the first few chapters I shall know."[23]

The closest friendship Frances formed at Nook Farm was not with Isabella Hooker but with Hooker's married daughter, Mary Hooker Burton, with whom she developed a playful relationship. Isabella Hooker's open letter to her daughter on women's suffrage, published in *Putnam's Magazine* in 1868, became something of a classic, pointing out that women who had raised large families to responsible adulthood surely knew enough to make political decisions. Burton developed an entirely jocular and teasing relationship with Frances, telling her "when you came to Nook Farm I never imagined that I should love you so much, as I do, sweet little woman." She declared that she had "been risking all future hope of your husband's regard by urging him to insist that you stay longer at Nook Farm. . . . I was crafty enough to put it as a necessity for your health & never intimated that the real reason was that I wanted another chance at your freckle lotion after I got home."[24] Frances remained at Nook Farm until nearly September, taking time out for a brief visit to New York. She wanted Gilder's opinion on *A Fair Barbarian* in order to decide whether to continue with it. He pronounced himself "so much charmed in fact that there presented to his mind the daring idea of republishing it in Scribners—beginning with the February number."[25] She returned to Nook Farm rejuvenated.

Frances gained new perspectives that summer. Even though Stowe and Twain were absent, she had the confidence of residing as close to their inner sanctums as possible, as a recognized writer among writers. Although not a campaigning feminist, she found her complicated feelings about domestic life ratified: women could be both devoted mothers and ambitious authors. They could stand for what they believed and expect the support of their husbands. In theory at least they could find a way to achieve what they wanted on both the family front and the public one. She worked some of this different kind of feminine view into her fiction beginning that summer. To her southern story *In Connection with the DeWilloughby Claim* she added the subplot of a New England town populated by a working class and a ruling class. The tragic subplot centred on a working-class girl who was deserted and left pregnant by her lover, and paralleled by a tale of the elite class, in which a nationally famous minister behaved similarly to a respectable girl. It is a wise and elderly New England "spinster" who recognizes what has happened and places blame where it belongs, bringing the man to a tortured confession and showing sympathy with the young woman. There are echoes of Stowe and Lady Byron in the unmarried but matriarchal figure, and in the back and forth settings of New England and the South.

Much greater evidence of Nook Farm's influence on her thinking and writing come in *Through One Administration*, in which she takes a hard look at Washington society and herself. By the next summer, when she paid another visit to Hartford, the story was well on its way to publication. The main character, Bertha, is given the name of Frances's niece; like Frances, she is girlish and flirtatious, with curling auburn hair and an active social life that has driven her to exhaustion and false gaiety. Bertha's best friend is a man, Arbuthnot, based on Frances's friend Charlie Rice; Will Dennis, who remained Frances's legal adviser throughout her life, supplied the original model for Bertha's distant cousin Tredennis. More tellingly, Bertha has married a man she doesn't love. Early on in the novel, Bertha's father worries that instead of marrying the man she loves deeply, she will marry the one who loves and pursues her.

In his biography of his mother, Vivian admits all these connections to his mother's life but is careful to say that "Bertha's situation, in the book, was entirely fictitious, but the manner in which she expressed herself about it was very much the Frances Hodgson Burnett of 1880." He readily admits that Bertha's weak and capricious husband was based on "the physical characteristics of Doro . . . [she] imagined a wretched soul to go with them, which she paraded through the book as Richard Amory."[26] Frances grappled in this novel with the fact that "she married the man who loved her" rather than following her own heart, that she gave in to her worries that he would do himself harm and fall into misery if she refused. As with Bertha, "her illusions concerning his passion for her soon died. She found out in two months that he would not have perished if she had discarded him."[27] Outwardly she sang the praises of her husband. Like Bertha, she loved her children. But she began to spend more and more time away from Washington, and it was as a married woman that she could do so without public censure. When, for example, a year later Gilder turned to his wife and asked, "See here, Helena, could I take this girl down to Long Beach and keep her all night? Would it be proper and all that sort of thing?" And Helena said, "Certainly it would. You couldn't do it if she was not married, but under the circumstances it is perfectly proper," it reflected the respectable freedoms allowed to married women but forbidden to single ones—for they did go, and Frances had a marvellous time.[28] Similarly, she could work with Gillette on her play, with no one thinking the worse of either of them.

What things were like in the privacy of 1215 I Street, Washington, is not clear. Swan remained attentive, writing to her publishers rather more often than seems appropriate, but otherwise moving ahead in his career and sharing their busy social life. Frances was "at home" on Tuesday afternoons, generally entertaining a crowd of visitors (Oscar Wilde famously came to see her, wearing knee breeches and silk stockings, and they spent the entire afternoon huddled in a corner, chatting animatedly, leaving her other guests to fend for themselves), hosting Sunday suppers, and entertaining, like Bertha Amory, a host of senators and politicians and smiling when Swan flirted with the female guests. Her name regularly appeared in the papers; one persistent rumour that autumn was that she was so ill she was writing a novel flat on her back in bed. "I am sorry to be obliged to contradict the statement of the newspapers," she wrote to a friend in Hartford that winter of 1880. "I hope you will gather yourself together & endeavor to bear up under the sad truth that I am not at the point of dissolution better than my friends do. They call to inquire with an air of cheerful resignation and after seeing me, go away with their countenances overspread with gloom. No! I am not ill—but I died some years ago deeply lamented by a large & admiring circle of acquaintance which has never recovered the shock."[29]

She published her first poem, "By the Sea, September 19, 1881," at the end of the year to critics' compliments, and her income increased. Visitors and reporters were charmed by her animated conversation delivered in rapid speech, with half-parted lips, darting eyes, and waving hands.[30] The house became a repository for their decorating whims. Swan began to collect antiques, building an important collection of Japanese art and artefacts. One afternoon, in looking around her den, Frances turned to Swan and said, "Oh Doro do go down town & get me a piano which he did most obediently & as by magic which was very nice in him & very satisfactory to me. He sent to Tennessee for his Grandmother's spinning wheel for me before I came home & it is such a dear little thing & stands in the other corner by the fire. He also found me an old fashioned brass handled escritoire which goes into another corner & altogether I am fonder of the Den than I ever was."[31] She bought her first full sets of china and silverware. All this came at a price, for she spent her money as rapidly as she earned it. In writing to Gilder about some revisions he requested in *A Fair Barbarian* before it went to press, she urged him to "let me know as soon as possible the decision about it as—the sole object of my existence now being to make money—I want to put it out at once in book form if the Magazine does not take it."[32]

The children too were an endless source of pleasure. She was a relaxed mother, allowing the boys to dig in the back garden with her silver serving spoons, tear up and down the street on their bicycles, and campaign so enthusiastically for their neighbour Garfield that his wife admitted that "her admiration is nearly all lost in sympathy for their afflicted mother, watching with terrified eyes from the third story windows."[33] The political enthusiasm of her boys and other children was so great that it prompted her to suggest a story called "How Lottie Elected the President" to Mary Mapes Dodge, and when Garfield won the election, they rode their bikes through the halls of the White House. In November Lionel appeared in a school play wearing a white satin page's costume that Frances had sewn for him, and "the sensation he created was as wild as even I could desire."

> He looked as if he had stepped out of some beautiful ancient picture. In response to the applause the curtain was drawn & this small lordly creature came out and received a bouquet & made the most superb bow— & if you never saw a peacock before my dear, you might have seen one then sitting on a front seat & trying to look as if she was his mother. Just imagine having to sit there & hear people saying "Oh! That beautiful boy! Who is that beautiful boy?" And being restrained by a sense of decency from springing up & replying wildly, "He's mine! He's Mine! My own-own-own! More mine than anything else I ever had or ever shall have!" You have no need to mention that I am a victim to this particular species of insanity but it is nevertheless a melancholy fact. I don't care an atom for what people say about me but my vanity about those boys is something simply disgusting.[34]

Frances began going more and more often to the North, either because of illness or inclination. When Swan's father suddenly died in February 1881, Swan made the trip to New Market by himself while Frances stayed at the Sturtevant House in New York, carrying the manuscript of *A Fair Barbarian* with her and trying to sort out its publication. Various publishers were vying for it, and *Scribner's*, which began serializing it in January, lost out to the less reputable James R. Osgood firm for the book publication. She remained for some weeks, even through illness. Gilder went to dine with her in a private hotel parlour while the *Fair Barbarian* negotiations were going on, thinking that there "we can be as animated as we like without attracting . . . attention and my scowls of fierce indignation when you venture a mild criticism."[35] The issue of criticism cropped up more and more in her dealings with Gilder from this time; he often demanded changes to the serial, sometimes of whole chapters added or omitted, which she found ruinous to the book when it appeared between two covers.

Personally, however, they remained the best of friends, and it was to Gilder that she turned when looking for a place to settle for the following summer while *Esmeralda* was in New York rehearsals and she was working on *Through One Administration*. She wanted a place close enough to Manhattan that Gillette, appearing on stage in *The Professor*, could dash out for the day to help with revisions and still get back to the city in time for his performances. She preferred Long Beach but couldn't afford the steep prices of its resorts. Gilder pulled some strings, and she settled in for the summer,

leaving Swan behind in Washington and sending the boys to their grandmother in Tennessee.

This summer of 1881 seems to have been a turning point for her, during
which she began to live a more solitary life, but one lived in the public eye. It
was in July that Gilder proposed to his wife Helena that he take Frances away
for the night, and the hotel they stayed at on Long Beach was the same one
she returned to later on. At that earlier stay, they wandered along the beach,
lunched on the piazza, talked for hours into the night. Frances sang songs to
him "and he said he was afraid to leave me for fear I would say something
interesting after he was gone and finally we retired, and as all our baggage
consisted of one small pocket-comb, we had to perform our toilet with it by
turns—he throwing it over my transom, and I returning it under his door."[36]

When Frances returned for the rest of the summer, staying in the room
Gilder had arranged, she found herself the subject of disapproving gossip
and "upon the whole regarded with suspicion." It wasn't helped by Gillette's
"dashing in two or three times a week demanding that I be produced upon
the spot & sending up his name written in the boldest characters & then
bearing me off on to the beach & talking to me in the most infuriated manner for an hour or two afterwards bolting back to New York." They all knew
that she was an author, which somehow lent her such a disreputable air that
even "a little beast of a girl" glared at her at meals. "I know that people think
I am disrespectable & sometimes when I think how entirely respectable &
comparatively moral I am I enjoy it," she told Gilder. "I dont of course mean
that I am so moral that it isnt any use but I am convinced that the general
impression is that I am a hardened thing. I sit at a little table all by myself
like an extremely bad little girl who is being very properly made an example
of & try to look worthy but the spectators think that is only my artfulness
& its a wonder that I am not cut off in the midst of my sins."[37]

That summer too she found herself attracted for the first time to other
men, not in a way that would lead to infidelity but in a schoolgirlish way,
as she expressed in a letter to Julia Schayer about the swimming instructor
("I never noticed a man's body before. I was always so actively employed
searching for their brains—but his—Mon dieu! Gott im Himmel! Santa
Maria—and things!"), a musician, and the bandleader. She claimed she wrote
home to tell "Doro and Charlie . . . they might fill my place with another
person of equal attractions if they could find her, and I was hopelessly
enslaved by a member of the band, but today I find I was mistaken in my
feelings, it is the leader who has enslaved me."[38]

While she was away, Edith, now married to Frank Jordan in California,
wrote to Swan to revive their friendship. He confessed to her that since

his return from Europe he'd had a difficult time settling into his career, but adding enigmatically that Frances's play had "cost her enough in various ways."[39] He may have referred to her continued illnesses—she was liable to catch any cold, earache, and headache that came near her—or to the fact that she was trying to write two novels and a play at the same time. She was burning her candle at both ends in her work and in her private life, and the breaking point came over her "most Washington of Washington stories," *Through One Administration*.[40] She was wild about the story, and although it contained a tragic love story ("I hate & detest love stories," she told Gilder, "but it seems that you must have their grinning sentimental skeletons to hang your respectable humanity & drapery upon"), it was much more an examination of the sometimes chilling political and societal modes of behaviour in the nation's capital.

She had cast aside *The DeWilloughby Claim* to work on the political novel, but although the writing went smoothly at the outset, she found herself bogged down by it and overwhelmed by her other commitments. The boys both became ill, and she carefully nursed them through measles and Lionel's complication of rheumatic fever. They were better now and were to spend the summer at New Market with Swan's mother, returning to Washington in September or October. She longed to spend the summer in Europe, where she had been invited by a friend as chaperone, and wrote to Louise Krutch, an old friend from Knoxville, that Swan was the reason she probably wouldn't be able to go. The letter was meant to be playful, but it opens a window onto some of the dynamics of their marriage.

If there is one character I am more admirably fitted to sustain than another, it is that of chaperone, and just think of my being robbed of such an opportunity to shine, by *a mere husband*. (Don't you think "a mere husband" is rather good? I hope Dr. Burnett will think so when I hand him my letter to read, with that air of large-eyed innocence and utter freedom from guile, which is my chiefest charm!) Imagine, my dear Louise, it is the man who, in a moment of temporary abstraction, I casually married who is the fell destroyer of all my little plans. Of course, bold and lawless creature though he is, he does not say that I shall not go. Animated by that craft and wiliness of which he is so thorough a master, he chooses the better part of assuming a gentle melancholy when referring to the subject, intimating that words cannot paint the desolation of a certain establishment when deprived of its crowning charm—the result of which Machiavellian aptness is that a general amnesty is proclaimed and he retires to his office with a smile of quiet intelligence gently playing upon his features.

With certainly not more than five or six exceptions, he is the cleverest person I was ever married to.[41]

Esmeralda opened in October. *A Fair Barbarian* was published as a book in both England and America, where it was compared, favourably, to Henry James's *Daisy Miller* (critics also noticed her "passion for describing beautiful dress, and the larger the wardrobe of her heroine the greater her delight").[42] Then, probably for money, she made a decision she would quickly regret: to allow Gilder, now promoted upon Dr. Holland's death to the editor of *The Century*, to begin the serial run of *Through One Administration* in November 1881, before she was anywhere near finishing the book. By the following spring, the book was still incomplete and was "progressing so slowly that I am in a constant state of anxiety lest the Magazine should gain on me & this anxiety reduces me to a condition the most unfavorable possible for work," she wrote to Mary Claflin. "It is only by sheer force of will that I keep the horrible thing going at all . . . if I required anything in the way of a warning never again to be betrayed into the folly of allowing an unfinished book to be presented to the public, I certainly have one."[43] She spent a portion of the summer back at Nook Farm, at Isabella Hooker's invitation, where they installed her and the manuscript in Charles Dudley Warner's study to work.

The real disadvantage of working at such a pace, without a clear idea of how the story would end but with deadlines hanging over her for a year, was that the book could not take a natural shape. These pressures and Gilder's insistence on certain changes led to a serialized novel that she found to be "a broken backed, ineffectual, incomplete aimless travesty of what would have been the best thing I ever did—If my friends of the Century had let me alone."[44] Although this would turn out to be one of her most respected novels after it appeared as a book, it wasn't always treated sympathetically as a serial, and somehow Hooker came to believe that Frances thought she too had spoken unkindly of her. Frances was quick to assure her that she could never believe such things had been said of her in Hartford. Critics could write what they pleased—when a work was published, criticism naturally followed—but "what *could* you say of me that was unkind. I have never hurt any one at Nook farm & no one has ever hurt me."[45]

It had been a difficult three years. Frances was more and more in the public eye, with her work and her private life fair game for journalists. They found *A Fair Barbarian* to be modelled on Burnett herself—a positive response, since the heroine is a forthright American—and in 1883 defended the married love triangle of *Through One Administration* in book form, even after the magazine received letters from shocked readers. Although the *Saturday*

Review, for example, found the novel weakly plotted, it found nothing "in the story which need raise a blush on the cheek of modesty." Indeed, it found the book "thoroughly an American novel because of the qualities of its workmanship. . . . Mrs. Burnett has apparently made up her mind to show the New World that she can not only write forcible dramatic tales of the familiar European kind, but can rival Mr. Henry James in his happiest mood of ingenious futility."[46] The subject matter might not have come to her before the widening perspectives offered during the last several years in the North and the increasing influence of the idea and possibility of female independence within the respectable framework of marriage and motherhood.

Whatever minor quibbles some critics might express, none of them could ignore Frances's work. The *Critic* used her picture as the cover of its "Holiday Number" that year, devoting a full article to explaining her appeal. Comparing her to Dickens in his sympathy for the lower classes, and Thackeray in his delineation of character, it declared that "Mrs. Burnett seems to have an intuitive perception of character, and what belongs to it. If we apprehend her personages, and I think we do clearly, it is not because she describes them to us, but because they reveal themselves to us in their actions." The strong women she created came in for particular praise, as did the play *Esmeralda*, which was an "unquestioned" success.[47]

The book done at last, she fell almost inevitably into a prolonged illness and didn't write again for several years. One could say that the protracted effort of writing a long novel about a loveless marriage held together primarily for the sake of the children brought her into this state. But it is probably just as true to say that she was, quite simply, worn out. When she finally took up her pen again, she would be catapulted into a fame she could never have imagined.

CHAPTER 9

~

FAUNTLEROY

1884–1887

L ATE IN 1884 FRANCES, who had been in Boston for some months, was so debilitated that she sent the boys back to school in Washington while she remained behind in rooms taken at the Vendôme Hotel, hoping to find someone to help cure what was by now full-blown nervous prostration—in modern terms, a nervous breakdown—complicated by anaemia. As soon as the last words of *Through One Administration* were written, she found herself not only unable to keep up the frantic work pace of the past ten years but unable to write at all. The family had spent the summer of 1883 at Camp Cottage in Lynn, Massachusetts, and Frances spent her days lying either in a hammock while the boys frolicked on the beach, or in her bed, with Vivian and Lionel under strict orders to keep quiet and not disturb her. They tried hard, but their natural enthusiasm burst out one day into a pillow fight, forcing Frances to get up and fling open the door. "Now, Dearest," Vivian chastised her, setting down a pillow, "if you are going to whip us, just put your little bare feet right on this." She kissed them and went back to bed.[1] Vivian, who found in college that he was often able to soothe people who weren't feeling well, recalled that summer when Frances was "so ill in Lynn, and I used to get up to try and comfort you— You remember—It has been a living thing in my brain ever since."[2] Back in Washington, she remained unwell throughout 1883 and 1884, despite restful summers in the North.

Beginning to lose faith in doctors, Frances visited a Boston metaphysical healer named Mrs. Newman, who specialized in the "Boston Mind Cure." Newman treated Louisa May Alcott as well as Frances, both of them suffering from nervous and physical exhaustion brought on by literary overwork.

Frances vowed that she benefited from the treatments, but although Alcott found "the experience of the sittings was pleasant and peculiar up to a certain number . . . they ceased to affect her," and she warned people "not to waste time and money on a system she believes to be of little or no value." The Cleveland journalist who compared the two authors chalked up their differing results to their differing temperaments: Frances "has in a very rare degree the inspirational temperament. She has something of the mystic in her disposition. She is poetic, impressionable, receptive. Miss Alcott, while imaginative and creative, has the practical rather than the romantic and poetic temperament."[3] It is perhaps for this reason that Alcott's 1886 novel *Jo's Boys* imagines the startling and troubling story of a little boy at Jo's school who loses his mind and becomes mentally retarded after his father pushes him to excel in advanced study. Full of pity, Jo and her husband raise the boy on fresh air and wholesome domestic and agricultural pursuits and discourage academic pressure on gifted children.

Frances, at least temporarily, found Newman's treatments so effective that she arranged to spend a month in Boston in 1885 under her care. She was even more amazed than Swan at her improvement, "because I know better than he does how great the change has been—I do not in the least understand how all this is accomplished but I know that if any one I love were very ill I should send them to Mrs. Newman at once."[4] In an effort to find another way of returning to health, she began to read a great deal of what today we call alternative medicine. She read Mary Baker Eddy's work but never, unlike Vivian, his wife, and his children, became a Christian Scientist. She preferred her readings in Hindu philosophy, yet never, despite her conviction of their efficacy, found lasting relief ("I believe in it! . . . But when it comes to myself, I can't perform it!").[5]

She had hoped for a quiet autumn in Boston, but her growing fame meant that she was constantly called on and invited out. Ordinarily she would have tried hard to keep to herself, but in December Maria S. Porter, a distant relative of the Stowes, introduced her to Gertrude Hall, a woman who would quite literally change her life. They agreed that their meeting was predestined, and from that day forward they "spent long periods together . . . morning, noon and night, in town, in the country, on the road, in England, Italy, France, Germany and Austria, Lionel and Vivian being with us—until time changed that." They were so immediately taken with each other—"old friends from the first moment"—that the next day Frances ordered a cab and carried Kitty, as she was always called, off to help with her Christmas shopping. She talked the whole time of Swan, Lionel, and Vivian and was relieved to find someone she could talk to about her family life rather than her profession.[6]

Kitty and her family filled a gap in Frances's life that she hadn't quite known existed. The three sisters, Gertrude, Grace, and Marguerite—known felicitously as Kitty, Gigi, and Daisy—were the young daughters of Dame Edna Hall, a former concert singer who now gave music lessons at their home at 206 Dartmouth Street in Boston. They were New Englanders; Edna was originally a Vermonter, her late husband from New Hampshire, and their daughters all born in Massachusetts. The Halls were the most comfortably accomplished women Frances had ever met. Kitty had been educated in Italy, spoke three languages fluently, and was about to publish her first book of poetry. Edna herself had been a gifted painter before settling on music, once submitting a painting to London's Royal Academy, and she passed her artistic gifts on to her other two daughters: Daisy became a noted contralto in New York, and Gigi an artist. Frances wrote to them all with ease and delight, telling Edna in 1886 that "Kitty writes to me that you say I am a little Pig—which will not surprise you, knowing all her bad qualities—particularly her envy and malice. These were bad enough when I only played brilliantly on the guitar and danced the cotillion in several foreign languages, but now that I play on the Bolero and dance the banjo—No I mean play on the banjo and dance the Bolero—(but the principle is the same) I know full well what I may expect in the way of being undermined. Let her beware lest I apply myself to the trombone and the Ophicleide, not to mention the tight rope."[7]

Frances had never met women like these before. Not society women, they were nonetheless well connected socially. Unlike the warm but charged atmosphere of Nook Farm, the Hall household was one in which intelligence and accomplishment had an easier, less religiously corseted air. As opposed to the more rigidly turned-out Washingtonian women, the Halls tied their hair back in careless knots, read to each other in the evenings, and strode through Boston in comfortable clothing. Europe was their second home, and they freely travelled back and forth between Boston and the Continent. They were like the younger sisters Frances had lost to California, only with the polish of education and cosmopolitanism. Frances fell completely under their spell, soaking up this air of easy, artistic intelligence. When she returned to Washington she took Kitty with her to attend the fetivities surrounding Grover Cleveland's inauguration.

The attraction worked both ways, with the Halls completely charmed by what they called Frances's sweetness and desire to turn "even the prosy things of life to favor and to prettiness." They saw a woman who was short in stature, with a large but splendid head, deep-set eyes, a long chiselled nose

(Frances herself said that she had a nose like a knife), and "Saxon coloring, coppery red hair and eyelashes like a fringe of light over dark blue eyes." She was a fascinating combination of the masculine and feminine: "her skull was a man's, and her charming hand, colored like a sea-shell, was the most feminine hand imaginable, was like the hand, almost, of a little girl. She elected to wear outwardly, if not to indulge, her feminine side and to keep as a dark secret the fact of her large brain, that capable organ privately very helpful." The so-called feminine side indulged itself with trinkets, hats, and clothes. Once, as a lark, they counted the dresses in her closet and found ninety.[8] More than these outward appearances, the things that the world saw and began to comment on in the press, they found a woman who was enormous fun, who laughed almost silently with dancing eyes, who made comments like "I should so like prunes, if they were different," and who "attracted men as moths, drawn to the dimmed flame of her orderly curled hair. This was for her a part of the regular comedy, or drama, of life." Vivian writes that this hair and her obsession with her appearance led a Boston friend, George Simmons, to nickname her Fluffy, and that she and all her close relatives and friends immediately and permanently adopted it for her.[9] She first used the name herself in an 1887 letter to Kitty Hall, thereafter signing the letters to her closest friends that way, and becoming Fluffy to her siblings and Aunt Fluffy to all her nieces and nephews.[10]

Her illnesses, and even the periods between them, were characterized by exhaustion exacerbated by insomnia and depression, what Kitty described as the "aftermath of neurasthenia," or nervous breakdown brought on by overwork and mental strain.[11] Others described it somewhat differently: "Like many creative people whose imagination works overtime, she was prone to a malady called 'temperament.' During spells of fatigue she brooded over imagined wrongs, and out of this tendency grew moments when she was overwhelmed by self-doubt and found herself unable to write. Any block to her work was so unusual as to be frightening. She did not at first recognize these moods as danger signals of exhaustion, but as soon as they affected her work she heeded the warning that a halt must be called."[12] It was noticed publicly as early as 1886, when *Fauntleroy* was still being serialized, when one magazine regretted that her writing "is a severe mental strain, and after finishing a novel Mrs. Burnett finds herself completely exhausted" by having thrown herself so fully into her characters.[13]

It was the Halls' sorrow that they had never known her in youthful health, for by thirty-five "she was like something mended that can never be used as if it had not been broken. She was not an invalid, nor even invalidish, but those who surrounded her fell as a matter of course into the way of guarding her, saving her from every effort, and this, never demanded or perhaps quite realized, became her habit, making her always rather like a Queen on her progresses. She was never allowed to carry anything more burdensome than a bunch of violets."[14]

Frances's prolonged absences from home put a strain on a marriage that she was clearly beginning to question. She and Swan grew further apart during the early 1880s, partly because she was gone so much and partly because their lives were moving in such different directions. Now that he had settled into Washington life, with at last a successful practice, steady publication in top journals, and the respect of his medical colleagues, Swan was happy to remain where he was. For Frances, though, the world was getting bigger, and it seemed to expand with each publishing success. Her close friends Julia and Effie were her Washington mainstays, but increasingly the women and men who interested and inspired her lived in Boston, New York, and Europe. Then too, now with more money coming in, she began to indulge her tastes and whims, while Swan moved towards the frugality that reflected his wartime upbringing and would mark his middle age.

Frances found Swan's lack of ambition for himself or for his children, even though he was a hard worker, terribly frustrating. "He has never assumed a mans responsibilities in his life," she told Vivian in 1900. "He has never had money for anything but his own self indulgence & it is not easy for me to forget that *everything* I have done he has actually claimed the credit for himself. My life has been a heavy burden to me—a burden of work & uncertainty & the responsibility of high ideals towards which I strained for you two boys. If I had been like him I should have let you live commonly & poorly & grow up at a disadvantage while I should have saved a comfortable income & lived at ease."[15] Although Kitty believed that the Burnetts' could "not be called an unhappy marriage," and without any sudden break "it tapered to an end," Frances struggled against it for years while Swan clung to the union, letting her have her way in most things.[16] He wrestled with what he had known all along: that Frances had enormous talent and ambition, that he owed her a great deal for supporting him as he established himself professionally, and that prolonged and perhaps permanent separations were inevitable.[17]

When the Halls came into the Burnetts' lives, the marriage was still a going concern run along fairly easy lines. Kitty marvelled at the Washington house, so much a reflection of Frances's taste and interests, with so many books required to appease her literary appetite that there were bookcases on the staircase landings as well as in the more customary places. Frances was known to extract a book on her way down to the dining room, only to be discovered an hour later, still reading on the stairs. She read voraciously, freely skipping over the parts she found boring, but able to recite long passages from the rest. Her favourite author, a taste acquired in her youth, was Thackeray. She loathed being disturbed while reading or writing, sacred activities for her, but in a sense she was always writing or telling stories. She tried out her work on all her family and friends, testing stories before committing them to large sheets of foolscap, reading them aloud to everyone in the evenings once she had put them down on paper. To the end of her life, it was known among all her friends that if one discovered her absolutely rapt in her reading, her face glowing with pleasure, chances were that she was reading one of her own books. Her boys, as was common with Victorians, had when they were small long flowing locks that she combed and curled in the mornings, keeping them still by telling them what she called their "hair-curling stories" or "hair-curling series."[18]

Lionel was moving towards a serious and handsome adolescence, whereas Vivian was tremendously outgoing. By now short-haired schoolchildren rather than long-haired toddlers, they spent many of their at-home hours in the kitchen with the African American cook and manservant, Carrie and Dan (used, like Frances's sons, in the *Saint Nicholas* story "The Proud Little Grain of Wheat"), helping with chores and talking election-year politics. Carrie and Dan were Republicans—the party of Abraham Lincoln—and one night Dan carried Vivian to a Republican torchlight parade. As a small boy, Vivian was a cuddler, whether curling up in bed with his sleeping mother, his arms around her neck, or snuggling up affectionately with Carrie. He befriended everyone, from the neighbours met at the summer cottages in Lynn and Long Island, to the man bringing groceries to the back door. Once when he was three, Frances saw him making off with a loaf of French bread from the dining room table. When she asked what he was doing, he told her that a "lady, f'ont door—want bread," and handed the loaf to a ragged young African American woman who had come to beg for food.[19] Like Lionel, he always called Frances "Dearest," a name others believed she foisted upon them but which, in fact, came completely from her sons. His open, sympathetic, and egalitarian ways were the basis for Cedric in *Little Lord Fauntleroy*, and she converted some of his actual experiences and conversations with the real local bootblack and grocer into the characters of Dick and Hobbs, and used his relationship with Carrie and Dan throughout the American section, even though they were never mentioned in the book or play. One of the unpublished sketches of her domestic life is called "The Hatchet," which detailed the "drama" that ensued when Lionel went to her and announced that he wanted a cent to buy a hatchet. The sketch went on for several pages in the roundabout way that children and their parents have when trying to reason with each other. The "maternal parent" points out, "You bought a shovel, a rake, a hoe and a pick yesterday. You don't care for them; you don't know where they are. Where are they?" and the child answers, "I don't know, but Miss Stuntz [the owner of a local toy shop] has got a little hatchet and I want to buy a little hatchet." She sends him to find the other toys, which he cannot do, and it ends, as expected, with Lionel admitting that he only wants the hatchet because his friend Johnny Clark has one, and his mother sending him out of her den and refusing to buy the toy.[20]

One morning after breakfast with Kitty in the I Street house, Frances began telling a story of an American boy who became an English lord to eight-year-old Vivian. He stood next to the table with wide-eyed attention, listening to her tale before leaving for school. This was the beginning of the end of Frances's long literary silence. She had written short pieces for children in *Saint Nicholas* but had never thought of attempting a full-length piece for them before this time. It seemed a good way to ease back into writing; after all, she told her sons stories all the time, and the enthusiasm at her daily reports from the Fauntleroy front urged her on. In the winter of 1885, after her return to Washington and while still unwell, she had begun to scribble at a story she was calling "Sara Crewe" but which she later expanded into *A Little Princess*. The *Fauntleroy* story unrolled easily, and as it moved towards its close she sold it to Mary Mapes Dodge as a serial. "I left his Lordship lying sweetly asleep on the rug before the library fire at Dorincourt Castle," she wrote to Dodge in the spring of 1885.

> I think I will send him to you. The one or two persons who have made his acquaintance so far seem to find him enchanting I think he is rather delightful myself. Such an innocent kindly quaint little fellow—with such simple childish courage & unconsciously natural generous instincts. I want the special charm to be the unconsciousness—he is such a child although he is such a little man. He is to be a "long little boy" and he goes very quickly. Already he had filled about a hundred pages of manuscript & he has many things to do. Since my health has been so much better I have been in the most amazing working order. I have not felt so since I was in my infancy. I work in a rush from nine until nearly five & then it is my body & not my mind that is tired. . . . I should not be surprised if he were very popular.[21]

This was to be a wild understatement, and Dodge sensed that this would be a very important story indeed. They hired the British-born Reginald Birch to illustrate it. The highest price *Saint Nicholas* offered writers was ten or twelve dollars per printed page or thousand words; she offered Frances more than twenty-five dollars a page and let her expand the story to 53,000 words, finding the story "so altogether charming that we shall not have the heart to 'cut' him appreciably. He is a child to love and remember all one's life."[22] The story began to appear in the November issue and was an immediate hit, and an unbelievable one when Scribner's in America and Frederick Warne in Britain published it as a book in 1886. In every generation or two there seems to be a book that captures the attention of adults and children alike, sparking a sort of marketing frenzy. *Robinson Crusoe* was such a book in Defoe's day. It was *Uncle Tom's Cabin* in Frances's childhood, with its plays, toys, and knickknacks. *Little Lord Fauntleroy* was the *Harry Potter* of its day. It sold hundreds of thousands of copies and went into multiple foreign-language translations. In a few years, after the book hit the stage, there would be no one from the smallest midwestern American town to the streets of Paris who had not heard of Cedric, and who did not know what he looked like, for Frances had sent Birch a photograph of Vivian dressed in a velvet suit and lace collar to give him some notion of how to present the small, street-wise New Yorker who played baseball and chatted with the local grocer, and then turned into an English lord. The costume was one he'd worn to sing in at a charity concert, "and it was so becoming to his plump young body that I wanted a picture of him in it."[23] This innocent action inspired thousands upon thousands of mothers to stitch, as Frances herself had done, similar costumes for their sons, topping off their hair with wide-brimmed hats and sending them out into the streets or before photographers in a craze that Frances never meant to initiate. It brought fame and fortune to his mother, but Vivian found it a lifelong embarrassment.

Fauntleroy had its detractors as well, and not always from boys compelled to wear the designated costume. As late as 1908, Mark Twain wrote to a friend, "I doubt if Mrs. Burnett knows whence came to her the suggestion to write 'Little Lord Fauntleroy,' but I know; it came to her from reading 'The Prince and the Pauper.' In all my life I have never originated an idea, and neither has she, nor anybody else."[24] This notion must have been re-inforced for him when the mother of Elsie Leslie, the child playing Cedric on the American stage, wrote to ask him if he'd sell the dramatic rights to *The Prince and the Pauper* for her daughter to perform.

More disturbing were damning articles in London's *Fortnightly Review* and the *St. James's Gazette* claiming that Frances had plagiarized outright a story called "Wilfred" by A. T. Winthrop. The *Fortnightly Review* lined up eigh-teen similarities in plot and language between the two works, and although there were certain similarities there was no smoking gun. They claimed that she had "calmly" done something similar earlier in her career by rewriting a story published by Ward, Lock, and Company and had apologized. In this new case, "Mrs. Burnett has been pressed to explain how it is that her book is almost identical with one written by a poor and obscure woman."[25] At first Frances ignored the claims, which came with the territory of success, but this was the beginning of a series of attacks on her in the press, and she wasn't always so reticent in defending herself. When she did respond to the plagiarism charge, the *Spectator* took her sharply to task for making "a reply which is in very bad taste, exceedingly contemptuous and angry, and not at all the kind of answer which those who are interested for her reputation could have desired."[26] As a writer in the *Saturday Review* put it, "Mrs. Burnett has only committed one offence against the minor reptiles of the press. She has succeeded."[27]

As the family fortunes rose, they were able to move again, this time to a "lovely sweet dear" of a leased house in the northwest of the city, at 1734 K Street. It had all the latest architectural embellishments: a fireplace in the hall, shelves above the mantels, stained glass in the windows, and inlaid floors. It seemed a perfect place to regain her health and try to write. The boys treated her like fragile royalty, kissing her "every five minutes" and reading jokes to her.[28] It seemed perfection, but she didn't stay there long enough to find out. Only months after moving in, she left Swan and the boys again and spent the entire autumn at the Halls' house in Boston.

Without her, the Washington house quickly became a dreary place, and the boys pined for her. In what would be a familiar plaint over the years, Vivian wrote to her that he was "expecting her down every sunday [*sic*] but I suppose you have to [*sic*] much to do, so don't come if you feel tired. There is nothing going on down here and *Oh how dreary it has become. . . .* I am counting the days till I shall see you again."[29] Lionel too felt lost without her, writing in October that "I feel very lonely without you and I hope you will be home soon." In what should have raised alarm bells for her, but did not, he added "I liked my foot-ball very much but I can not play it with very much breath."[30] She returned home for the winter, but by now she was spending as much time away from her family as she spent with them. They were thrilled to have her back and "are always trying to help me to get better and they take great care of me. They cover me up in bed at night & kiss me & turn out my gas and say 'Now be sure to sleep, Dearest.'" One night Vivian tried to perform the mind cure on her by lowering the light and holding her hand while she fell asleep, slowly inching his way out of the room on his hands and knees so as not to wake her.[31] He was devastated when Lionel burst into the house after an evening party, destroying his

careful nursing. They were now twelve and ten, and for the past five years—
half of their lives—they had known her only as an invalid unable to sleep
properly or to play with them, requiring the greatest care and solicitude
when she was at home.

She had periods of good health, improving after her mind cure sessions,
energized during the writing of *Fauntleroy*, but it was a slow recovery. Her
heart was with her sons even when she was apart from them, yet that very
love took on, when she wrote or spoke to young people, a sentimentalism
that is startling today and perhaps even in her own time. To one boy she
knew in Massachusetts she declared,

> If there is one thing I would like to be more than another it is a Fairy—
> because then I could give all the children everything they wish for. When
> Lionel and Vivian were very little I would . . . pretend to them that I was
> one. And when their toys were lost I found them. And when they were
> broken I mended them by pretend magic. And when they were hurt I gave
> them fairy kisses to make them well. And then they would laugh and say
> "Little Fairy-Mamma can do anything"—And I would answer "Yes truly—
> a kind of fairy—I am a Mamma fairy—All Mammas are fairies." And so
> when I went away from them . . . to write stories they used to say "She has
> gone to Fairy land." And even now they call my room Fairy land very
> often. But if Fairies ever *should* come in fashion again I shall immediately
> petition Congress to appoint me one.[32]

The fairy theme continued throughout her life, and in her work, beginning
in 1886 with the publication of part 1 of "The Story of Prince Fairyfoot" in
Saint Nicholas, and ended with Vivian's declaration after her death that "one
had merely to admit that she was partly a fairy."[33] Fairies had of course been
a staple of Victorian fantasy for adults and children alike, but over time she
came to use the term "fairy story" to mean other things: the imagination,
daydreams, pleasant desires, and hopes. At this stage of her life, it was a way
of offering affection and goodwill to children, a replacement at times for her
actual presence, of putting a good face on difficult things. As a hard-nosed
businesswoman always on top of her accounts and investments, she never
read newspapers, but she always responded to children's letters and "would
spend a long valuable forenoon building for a faraway small boy the fairy-
story of one of her long delightful letters."[34] But there's also a sense that
she used childhood fantasy as a bulwark against unpleasantness, as a way of
holding the difficulties of life at bay. She reflected this in her personal style,
in her refusal even in older age to dress in sombre colours or to give up soft,

youthful colours or the wearing of fashionable hats on her Titian hair.

The new house in Washington was ill-fated in more than one way. Except for finishing the short story of "Sara Crewe" and a few magazine pieces, her literary output consisted primarily of the republication of earlier works. *A Woman's Will; or Miss Defarge*, serialized in *Peterson's* in 1879, now came out as a whole in America in *Lippincott's* and in England was published by Frederick Warne. Scribner's republished *Surly Tim and Other Stories*. She published a great deal but wrote almost nothing new in the house, and then in March 1887, only a year after they moved in, the house caught fire. They didn't notice until a boy rang the doorbell to tell them that the attic was blazing. Frances was in bed, and when Swan raced up the stairs, she followed behind with an ineffectual pitcher of water. The fire trucks arrived, immediately dousing poor Swan with their hoses. Frances went immediately to her room, grabbed her "manuscript from the shelf, emptied the closet of my clothes, put them on the back of the first man who appeared who was not a fireman—the flames roared—the skylight fell with a smash—they would not let me stay long enough to get my shoes." She presented herself as a dainty island of calm, wearing a frilly blue nightdress with satin ribbons, a Japanese robe tossed over her, while "the servants went mad . . . the colored servants became at once raving maniacs," and everyone rushed her, barefoot, into the street.[35]

The fire seemed the final straw. Only two months later she packed up her sons and left Swan behind in Washington. In May she boarded the SS *Ems* with Kitty Hall and the boys and headed for London, taking a house on Weymouth Street, Portland Place, with Kitty and the boys. It was Queen Victoria's Jubilee, celebrating fifty years on the throne, and Frances blossomed with the return to her original home. Her health miraculously revived, and she shuttled herself and the younger Burnetts to tailors and dressmakers, holding Tuesday afternoon at-homes and remaking their lives into something entirely new. Only a couple of months earlier, in an interview with a reporter from the *Knoxville Daily Sentinel*, she had been asked, "And will you remain permanently in Washington?" Without a pause she replied, "This is my home. I hope to need no further change except in summer."[36] Two summers would pass before she set foot in Washington again.

CHAPTER 10

~

RETURN
TO EUROPE

1887–1888

THERE WAS NOTHING LIKE watching the royal family roll past, in all its imperial splendour, accompanied by the Royal Horse Guards band and international royalty to make Frances feel more English than she'd felt in years, and freer. London was in its spring glory, and she participated wholeheartedly. Her new friends courted her in the flower-filled Weymouth Street house off Portland Place. Daisy Hall was performing in London, and she and Kitty introduced the Burnetts to the Lankester family, who lived just around the corner. She particularly befriended one of the sons, Owen, a large, boyish, and jolly physician. On an outing to Madame Tussaud's Waxworks Museum she nearly fainted in the Chamber of Horrors. One member of the group she was with was the young Zionist writer Israel Zangwill, who treated her gently and grew to be one of her closest friends over the next several years. She admired his books *Ghetto Tragedies* and *The Master*, as well as his column "Without Prejudice," which appeared in the *Pall Mall Magazine*. The world, it seemed, had come to London, and Frances was part of it, honoured, visited, and celebrated.

In August, with the metropolis emptying and her doctor ordering her to spend time in the country, Frances moved with Lionel and Vivian—as well as her maid Millington, a Londoner who was very demure and respectful but found Frances "very unsophisticated in my dealings with what she called the 'lower classes'"—to Elm Farm, a working farm in Wangford, Suffolk.[1] After their city life, her sons found themselves out of doors most days, pitching hay and helping with the farm chores. There they "made hay and reaped and gleaned . . . vowed eternal friendship with the cow men and harvesters . . . spent rapturous hours tending sheep with the little shepherd, while he sang ancient Suffolk ballads about squires who loved milkmaids, and ploughmen who loved ladies; . . . became gloriously intimate with the small 'pig-minder' and his family . . . went 'rabbiting' with the farmer, and were so blissfully happy that when in the autumn we left Suffolk to go to Italy, they began their journey in silence, leaning back in their corners of the carriage, their arms folded, and tears in their eyes."[2]

As September faded into October, they left for Italy via Paris. Both boys had, of course, spent part of their early lives in that city, Lionel as a toddler and Vivian born there, and Frances wanted them exposed to the city's splendours as adolescents. Her plan for them was now fully formed. She believed that if they remained in Washington, with short trips to rural Virginia, North Carolina, and Tennessee, their development would be stunted despite summers on the eastern coasts of New England and New York. They would settle into Swan's complacency and never become the gentlemen she wished them to be. As a child she had watched her own family sink from the comfortably respectable middle class in Manchester, and now with money, drive, and reputation she was going to pull her own children out of the comfortable middle class she had achieved for them into something even greater. For that they needed Europe.

In late October they settled into Villa Trollope on the Piazza dell' Independenza, a pensione once owned by Anthony Trollope but now in the possession of a family called McNamee, friends of the extraordinarily connected Halls. "You will perceive that I am in Florence," she exulted to Owen Lankester, "that I occupy a suite of huge rooms just vacated by an English Countess—that I have a piazza of my own, big enough for a ball room and that I lean over massive balustrades of stone to look into a garden full of orange and lemon and magnolia and cypress trees, and oleanders, and roses, and oleafragrante, and fountains, and ancient medallions, and Russian boar hounds and servitors who say 'Buono [sic] giorno, Signora,' and who are called Lisa and Pasquale and Carlo and Vittorio and Luigi and Assunta, as if they were part of an opera."[3]

They settled into a more regular life now, after their five months of travels. When Kitty left for a month in Rome and a long visit to Naples with an old school friend, Frances replaced her with a hired companion, took a large furnished apartment that shared a courtyard with a Russian church, on the Lungarno Nuovo, began French and Italian lessons, and registered the boys at a French school run for forty years by a Monsieur DeManger, who "had prepared boys for colleges in England, in France, in Germany, and in America. It seemed a droll thing to go to Florence [that] one's boys might learn French, but I had heard such fine things of this old master's affectionate, strong generalship of his pupils, that I made this long journey and sent my boys to him."[4] An Englishman, Erroll Sherson, was also hired to tutor Lionel and Vivian, making the household a bustling and international one.

These were big changes to two boys accustomed to running the streets of Washington, and Lionel, in particular, baulked. He liked Washington and his friends, sometimes preferring to remain there even when Vivian went away with their mother. He was as warm and affectionate as Vivian to their mother, though less outgoing with strangers, something Frances found a bit "imperial," but it seems more likely the result of shyness and a difficulty with change.[5] Unlike Vivian and Frances, who were temperamentally simi-lar, he simply couldn't force himself to handle difficult situations. His love for his mother became an ache in her absence, and while she was away he often sank into depression and poor health. In Italy he found it nearly impossible to make himself go to the DeManger school with Vivian the first morning. "Poor darling Lionel could not. . . . He tried & tried but he could not."[6] The family found its rescue in the companion, Luisa (or Liza, or Lisa, depending on their moods) Chiellini, who quickly became the warm and indispensable centre of the ménage. Lovely, efficient, intelligent, and devoted to them all, she saw them through the next difficult years with an astound-ing affection. She handled the correspondence using a sometimes delicious English, coached Frances in her language study, and nursed them through their illnesses. Vivian adored her, but fourteen-year-old Lionel fell for her like a ton of bricks.

Frances settled into a routine of language study, writing, and social calls. She was surrounded by British and American expats and visitors who wasted no time in making her acquaintance. Like President Garfield in Washing-ton, British Prime Minister Gladstone and his wife became comfortable if temporary friends ("I find Prime Ministers agree with me," she told Kitty), alongside a variety of writers, artists, and musicians. The boys joined her on jaunts to the Duomo and the Piazza Santissima Annunziata. Excited and energized for weeks at a time, she returned to her work with a vigour that had eluded her for years. *Fauntleroy* went into its thirtieth printing that winter, and with the resuscitated "Sara Crewe, or What Happened at Miss Minchin's," now running in *Saint Nicholas,* she thought she might be able to sell it outright in the English fashion. In those days, publishing took the form of a series of steps, each of them generating income. Generally speak-ing, a long story would be serialized in a magazine, with the author paid by the page and working to deadlines. As with *Through One Administration,* this meant that a piece could be appearing monthly while the author strug-gled to keep up, often with no idea of what the next chapter would entail or how the story would end. After a serial run, with the public interest primed, the story often appeared between two covers as a novel, generating additional income, this time through royalties. In the American structure, the author allowed the book to be published in exchange for royalties; in the British, rights to the book could be sold outright to the publisher. As time passed, Frances was able to negotiate favourable royalty terms, but she resisted the modern system of taking an advance against future royalties, seeing that as ultimately less lucrative. *Saint Nicholas* bought the serial rights to "Sara Crewe" outright, but that gave the periodical no rights to the resulting book, which appeared at the end of 1888.

Much has been written about Burnett's use of colonialism in both versions of "Sara Crewe" and in *A Little Princess*, and there is no denying that in the very English setting of the story and the novel she relies on India as a backdrop of loss and imperial power, just as she did in her later Emily Fox-Seton stories. But it is worth noting that two of her best-known works containing Indian characters, *Sara Crewe* and its later revision into *A Little Princess*, and *The Secret Garden*, were written wholly in America; *The DeWilloughby Claim*, with its study of the South, on the other hand, was finally completed in England. Distance seemed to allow her to see the stories more clearly, and it is likely that she called upon her sentimental and privileged response to her black servants in America, and upon her interest in Hindu philosophy and art; like many British Victorians, she decorated her London houses with Indian artefacts.

Although Frances wrote the original "Sara Crewe" in her Washington house, it resonated with her own childhood, with the dead father, the child's slide into poverty, and her faculty for reading, storytelling, and pretending, all apparent in her 1893 memoir *The One I Knew the Best of All*. Many critics also rightly attribute its literary influence to Brontë's *Villette* and *Jane Eyre*, and like the start of Thackeray's *Vanity Fair* it takes place in a girls' boarding school. As in *The Secret Garden* later, the girl has lost her parents in India and finds herself an orphan in England. Written a few years after she temporarily abandoned *In Connection with the DeWilloughby Claim*, *Sara Crewe* takes up some of the issues that so weighed Frances down in the adult novel. Both orphan girls are adopted by single adult men they call Uncle Tom, and both families are assisted by men of colour who are so devoted to their masters that they leave their homes to serve them. Both servants are kind and maternal, creating domestic environments. The unnamed "Lascar" servant in "Sara Crewe" dresses her room, buys her warm and attractive clothing, and provides meals in a way that makes up for the absent parent. (He becomes Ram Dass in both the novel and play *A Little Princess*.)

Uncle Matt, the former slave in *De Willoughby*, behaves in exactly the same way. Both men are instrumental in putting the orphan in touch with the lost fortune, and with love. As a non-English-speaking foreigner, the Lascar is nearly silenced in "Sara Crewe," able to converse with no one except Mr. Carrisford (ironically—to modern readers at least—referred to throughout the story as "the Indian Gentleman," as opposed to the man from India), and it is Sara's ability to speak Hindi that draws them together. In *A Little Princess* he has a speaking role, just as Uncle Matt is given a great deal of dialogue in *De Willoughby*, all of it in dialect that is supposed to be amusing and endearing, but sets him aside from the white characters and is a constant reminder of his difference and his race. In *The Secret Garden* Martha Sowerby, Dickon's sister, speaks broad Yorkshire as well as "standard" English and serves the same function in that novel.

A look at the sixteen advertising pages at the back of the first American edition of *Sara Crewe* gives some cultural context for the story. All of the advertisements are for children's books published by Scribner's, and nearly all of them have to do with conquest: two pages of boys' books by G. A. Henty, including *Redskin and Cowboy*, *The Dash for Khartoum*, and *Held Fast for England*; Robert Leighton's *The Thirsty Sword: A Story of the Norse Invasion of Scotland*; Thomas Nelson's *Two Little Confederates*; Noah Brooks's *The Boy Settlers: A Story of Early Times in Kansas*, illustrated with a drawing of Plains Indians; *The Boys' Library of Legend and Chivalry*, as well as various travel books, English literature, fairy stories, and Frances's own books for children, including *Little Lord Fauntleroy*. She lived in a time steeped in colonialism, both at home and abroad. Tredennis in *Through One Administration* lives for years in a western fort and dies in a battle with Native Americans; African Americans walk through her American novels, and Indians and Anglo-Indians in her English ones. A casual look at the newspapers of her formative American years reveals the predominance of race and conquest, in reports of Indian "uprisings" and postwar civil rights. The question is therefore not why she used such characters but where, when, and how.

Both *De Willoughby* and *Sara Crewe* contain Frances's familiar theme of a fall in fortune, and the reversal of ill fortune through the agency of coloured servants. It is impossible to read either work without reflecting on Frances's own childhood fall in fortune after the death of her father, her slow reversal after arriving in the American South, the loss of her mother just as she was entering adulthood, and the taking on of adult responsibilities at a young age. She was obsessed with her public presentation, especially where it concerned privacy and morality, and the barbs that dug deepest were those suggesting that somehow she used her income to climb the social ladder. Like the orphaned, abandoned, and faithful characters she created, her claim to gentility was internal, manifested in the imaginative process, in a deep belief in ethical behaviour, and in a growing belief in a spiritual power that fed the life force.

Sara Crewe was the second children's book she'd written, and she followed it that same year with *Editha's Burglar*. Children's books came more easily to her, were often shorter than the long and difficult adult novels like *Haworth's*, and were just as lucrative. More importantly, she found them less physically taxing to write, and they could appear in all sorts of combinations. Both Scribner's in New York and Warne in London published *Sara Crewe, or What Happened at Miss Minchin's* as an individual book in 1888. Jordan Marsh published *Editha's Burglar: A Story for Children* in 1888. Then Warne republished *Sara Crewe* in the same volume as *Editha's Burglar*, that same year, at Frances's request: Scribner's offer for the first story alone was less than she wanted, so she wired them from London to ask "Cant you add Edith's Burgl/and offer more."[7] In January she accepted $3,000 from them for *Sara Crewe* alone, but it seems that Warne must have agreed to a similar request. Lippincott, too, republished her earlier *A Woman's Will; or Miss Defarge* in the same volume as Joseph Haberton's *Brueton's Bayou* that year, and Warne brought out *The Fortunes of Philippa Fairfax*, a work that bears all the immature hallmarks of her earlier, reworked, and unsophisticated stories. It was such a step back from her more recent, more accomplished work that it was never published in America, and even Warne, in calling it "a revised edition," acknowledged that it was "but slightly altered" from its original version.[8] This prolific publishing required a great deal of behind-the-scenes dickering among the various publishing houses, particularly as Frances had been rather careless, selling the Canadian rights to both Warne and Scribner's. Still, it meant that her work was constantly in press and her name constantly before the public. *Saint Nicholas* even ran an article titled "Dogs of Noted Americans," devoting nearly three pages to Frances's dogs. In addition to the dog she'd left behind in Manchester as a child, and the one that had adopted them in Clinton Pike, she had owned three others by 1888, including a chihuahua sent to her from Mexico, which she eventually gave away to a little girl, and a Japanese pug named Toto, with silky black and white fur and a curling tail. This dog became ill and died. At the time of the writing, she had for several years owned an English pug with the words "Monsieur le Marquis" engraved on his collar.[9] (There is even a story that she entered a cat named Dick in the first New York cat show some years later.)[10] She loved animals, stating once that "in my various incarnations I believe I have been all sorts of animals. . . . I am sure I have been a beast again and again.

I am such friends with them and I understand them so and they are so sure of it and are such friends with me. You should see their eyes when they look at me."[11]

Little Lord Fauntleroy had cemented her financial fortunes, and even though she had had the experience of pirated editions and unauthorized plays, she was blindsided by the news in 1887, as she sat happily with her family and new friends in Florence, that a man named E. V. Seebohm had "dramatized my charming book" and was about to produce it in London. She was sure that printing "all rights reserved" on the title page had protected her against such piracy and didn't hesitate to telegraph him to tell him so. Seebohm travelled to Florence to bargain with her, offering half the profits if she would sanction the play. She refused, telling Lankester that "she was engaged in fierce battle with him. A large young woman—possibly your size—is to play Cedric. Figuerez vous! Figurativi! (French and Italian *ensemble*. It is *so* difficult to speak English.)"[12] The temper she had exhibited against the pirated editions of her early works now flared once again. Hiring Kaye and Guedella, a London law firm recommended by Lankester, she and Luisa left Vivian and Lionel in Kitty's care and set out by train, only hours after Seebohm's departure, to do battle, taking pens and ink with them so that Frances could begin writing her own version of the play en route. By April 1888—the *Critic* reported that she locked "herself up in her lodgings [and] worked steadily for two weeks"—she was able to write to Kitty that the play was nearly finished, that auditions for children to play Cedric were beginning, and that she had arranged to have it produced at the Strand Theatre (the play would finally run at Terry's Theatre in London).[13] From her rented house at 12 Weymouth Street, she wrote to the boys that she loved their letter. "I am sure you are being sweet, good little men, and are trying to keep Aunt Kitty from feeling too lonely. She says you are very sweet, indeed," she told them. "I miss you all very much and I hope you will write to me as often as you can to comfort me, but if you cannot write two letters, you must always write one a week to Papa."[14]

As Frances well understood, the rules governing the adaptation of plays out of published—and copyrighted—books were lax, and laxly enforced. No author in England had yet succeeded in protecting his or her work from such dramatic pirating, but Kaye and Guedella argued that the Copyright Act asserted "no one shall multiply his book, or copies of his book." Because the play lifted passages directly from Burnett's novel, Seebohm had in effect "multiplied copies of parts of the novel."[15] As the case went to court, Seebohm's play hit the boards at the Prince of Wales Theatre on 23 February. It starred Annie Hughes as Cedric, beginning a tradition of girls playing this part; Vera Beringer starred in Frances's. Frances's version, now titled *The Real Little Lord Fauntleroy*, began its run as matinée performances at Terry's Theatre on 14 May. She wrote to Kitty in Florence that "the 'case' comes off today and, of course, I shall lose it, but it was considered best that I should make the protest." Two days before Frances's play was ready to open, the court handed down an injunction against Seebohm.[16]

Frances won not only a permanent victory for her play but for all British writers. No longer could dramatists adapt stories willy-nilly for the stage, as had been common practice. If her stock was high in London before this case, her victory and the play's success made it exceptional. The London *World* declared *The Real Little Lord Fauntleroy* "altogether superior to the pseudo-Fauntleroy at the Prince of Wales."[17] Frances joined actresses Madge Kendal and Vera Beringer on stage for curtain calls, and the "real" play toured England for almost two years, to almost unmixed approval. Lionel, Vivian, and Kitty joined Frances in London during the play's triumphant run. Her success was capped on 14 July when the Society of British Authors, thrilled by what her court challenge meant for the work of their members, honoured her at a banquet at Queen's Hall, inviting American authors as well as British, and presenting her with a diamond bracelet and ring. A partial list of the 150 guests gathered in her honour reads like a Who's Who of the arts: Oscar Wilde, Bret Harte, George Meredith, William Rossetti, Edmund Gosse, and Wilkie Collins were all there, and Wilde disappointed them by failing to "gyrate and have some species of aesthetic convulsion. . . . He bore himself like the ordinary nineteenth century civil man" and sent her his photograph the next day thanking her for being "a brilliant hostess."[18] Less than two weeks later she attended a dinner for the Incorporated Authors. "I am not an Incorporated Author myself as yet," she wrote to Nora Phillips, wife of the poet Stephen Phillips, "but I shall probably become one between the courses."[19]

Kitty and the boys were now with her in London at her rented house at 14 Park Square East, and after the excitement and separation she decided to take Lionel and Vivian on a summer holiday to a little farmhouse, Joss Farm, St. Peter, in Thanet, on the Kentish coast. She decorated it with red Turkish "cotton chair covers and white muslin curtains" and flowers. Except for the holidays spent at rented cottages in America, she had never yet had a garden of her own, and each morning at Joss Farm she stood "in the midst of that field with my arms full of poppies and looked at the sea of amazing scarlet blossoms on every side of me—and listened to the skylarks reeling about in the blueness overhead—I used to reel and sway a little myself."[20]

Finally, after sixteen months away from America, they returned. Frances sent the boys on to Washington, dispatching their trunks and money via her friend Effie Macfarlane, while she herself stayed at the Victoria Hotel in New York. She was anxious for them to keep up their studies and to attend the school where their favourite teacher, Miss Morgan, taught. "I hope you will do great credit to your English tutors [in London] . . . and speak French and Italian to your Papa all the time and that he thinks you are very nice boys." Not trusting the condition of the house in her absence, she sent instructions for Ida, the housekeeper and cook, "to have the house thoroughly cleaned from top to bottom," even if it meant hiring someone to help.[21]

Little Lord Fauntleroy was to open in Boston in early September, and Frances worried that they had started production without waiting for her, but when she arrived she found herself completely charmed by Elsie Leslie, who had played in Augustus Thomas's adaptation of *Editha's Burglar*. She settled into the Halls' Dartmouth Street house, where a letter from young Elsie was waiting for her. They had never met, and Frances promised to be at the opening, wearing a yellow brocade dress, and smiling. The boys were now back with Swan in Washington, but she assured Elsie that she had two sons who always called her "Dearest," just like Cedric in the play. The Boston production was as big a success as the London one, and "old and young alike went to it in droves to laugh and sigh and weep."[22] Oliver Wendell Holmes wrote to tell her that "this work of natural emotions with all its tears and heart-beats was like an angel's visit."[23]

There is always a place for stories about children who teach adults how to live. This was the charm of Burnett's play, and the source of its appeal to adults as well as to children. By making Cedric a forthright but polite American boy, she called upon her stable of "Americans abroad" characters, like Octavia in *A Fair Barbarian*. She delighted in showing English audiences that Americans were not as brash and rude as their stereotype. "American impudence. I've heard of it before. They call it precocity and freedom. Beastly impudent bad manners—that's what it is," Cedric's grandfather, the earl of Dorincourt scowls in act 2. She loved bringing American forthrightness like a breath of air into the stuffiness of English class-bound society, and the scene at the end in which Hobbs the grocer (who scoffs at all things to do with English aristocracy), Dick the shoeshine boy, Cedric, and the earl unmask the mother of the pretender to the title (unfortunately referred to as the daughter of a "Dago") is a miracle of cross-Atlantic unity. The heart-wrenching premise of the play, that in order to inherit the title Cedric must live separately from his "Dearest," sounds a poignant note from the pen of a woman who spent months each year away from her sons.

As with Birch and the novel, Frances gave the costume designers photographs of Vivian in his velvet suits, and the craze that began with the book was fanned into full flame with the success of the play. All across the country, boys who had escaped the lace collars the first time round found themselves forced into them now. They were not the most comfortable of costumes: Vivian's two suits, with their hand stitching, heavy linings, and substantial fabrics, sat uncomfortably on children used to freedom of movement. For ten years such Fauntleroy ephemera as miniature playing cards, chocolates, perfumes, statues, songs, and toys flooded the market. The androgyny of the Fauntleroy look, not helped by girls playing the boy on stage, caused boys dressed in the suits to be taunted on the streets. It was worse, apparently, in the smaller cities. One writer claimed that in

> Davenport, Iowa, in the year of the Burnett play's opening, an eight year old burned down his father's barn because he was compelled to dress up in Fauntleroy fashion. In Madison, Wisconsin, a kid with brick colored curls battled in vain to be severed from them. After he had been inserted forcibly into velvet jacket and pants, he walked up to a policeman in front of the principal hotel there and deliberately kicked the bluecoat in the shins to call attention to his plight. In Worcester, Massachusetts, another victim of the plague traded off an expensive Fauntleroy suit to passing gypsies for some old clothes bearing patches which the local sufferer considered admirable.[24]

As late as 1928, the costume was blamed for damaging the wool industry in favour of velvet.[25]

Apocryphal as some of these reports no doubt were, Frances found herself the victim of journalists eager to deflate the woman who had generated the latest craze. Newspapers and magazines began to spread gossip about her private life, her choice of clothing, and the behaviour of her children. Her habit of wearing loose tea gowns at home, especially while writing or unwell, somehow made its way into the press as an affinity for "Kate Greenaway dresses of vivid silk, belted under the arms with wide sashes." Vivian and Lionel were accused of throwing stones at cats, of posing preciously against mantels in their velvet suits at adult parties. She challenged the writers to travel to Washington, at her expense, to learn the truth and to leave her children alone. "Does it or does it not, matter in the least that a man or woman who has done honest and respectable work should on that account feel that his or her character, good taste, and good manners may be impugned at so much a line in any newspaper," she fired off in a letter to the *Critic*. "Does it not matter that such an individual cannot live a life so simple, so secluded, and so well-meaning as to escape the most grotesque misrepresentation?"[26]

As for the pain such an article brought to her children, she found this inexcusable: "I endeavor as far as possible to make up to my sons for the misfortunes I have inadvertently brought upon them by being their mother, but I find it difficult at times, as their own inoffensive young characters are impeached, and in the midst of their lessons and juvenile amusements they share the maternal ignominy, and appear . . . sometimes as odious little prigs, sometimes as violent little animals. I should like to spare them if I could."[27] Later, on 15 March 1889, the *New York Times* came to her defence, writing that she made "a very just complaint." The press believed that any sort of fame entitled it to write whatever it wished about successful writers, with their homes, families, and personal appearance all fair game. The paper saw the problem as one of convincing the press that the famous did not want the publicity, but "nevertheless the right of privacy with respect to what are properly private affairs is a real right."[28] Even the *Washington Post*, her local newspaper, repeated the New York rumours about her supposed eccentricity of dress, but praising the new house on Massachusetts Avenue, which they expected her to fill "with foreign bric-a-brac" and where she would "take her place again in the literary and social coteries."[29]

The real question is why journalists found her to be such a ready target for their barbs. Somehow she had acquired a reputation for eccentricity, and the enormous success of *Fauntleroy* made her appear fair game for the envious, the annoyed, and the misogynist. Time and again her income—and the fact that she spent it—emerges as almost criminal; New York emerges as a place too sophisticated for upstart women ("Mrs. Frances Hodgson Burnett is still a regarded figure in New York on account of her eccentricities of dress and behavior. Boston lionized her but the metropolis is inclined to find her amusing," wrote one); her penchant for lovely clothes gets exaggerated; her social life inflated. "I think someone must have been masquerading under my name," she decided in March. Her life in New York had been secluded, living quietly as she did with Luisa acting as her secretary, spending her days in rehearsals and her nights in a rented apartment. As for the accusation of divorce, the "member of my family who would be missing if it were true is at the present moment, I believe, reading in an adjoining room." They accused her of "being harsh to women," but on the contrary she was "continually surrounded by a number of the very dearest and kindest, and . . . all my business affairs being in women's hands." The hordes of young men surrounding her were twelve and fourteen; "they draw themselves up in battalions and form themselves into hollow squares, and I am rather popular with them." As for the Kate Greenaway dresses, "I do not own such a costume, and I am also not mad."[30] Nonetheless the rumours seemed to have a

life of their own, and in mid-April the *Critic*, like the *New York Times* earlier that year, came to her defence, calling such ungrounded accusations
"shameful." Acknowledging and concurring with Frances's decision not to
wait out the spate of unwanted and false publicity, they placed the blame on
the salacious public for trying to steal her good name and reputation.

Frances spent some time in Washington with Swan and the boys after her
Boston success, where she had earned $700 to $800 a week. The play had
closed only because the lease on the theatre was up and another production
had earlier contracted for its use. The publisher Samuel McClure offered her
$15,000 for the serial rights alone of whatever book she wrote next. A news-
paperman offered her $400 a month to let him come to see her once a week
and talk over a special section for children. Someone else proposed to give
her thousands of dollars to travel the world in a yacht, "to write letters from
strange lands for children."[31] With the play scheduled to open on Broadway,
at the Broadway Theatre, in mid-December, Frances moved on to the Grand
Hotel on 31st Street in Manhattan in November, then to an apartment on
52nd and Broadway, helping with rehearsals and coaching young Elsie and
Tommy Russell, who was to alternate with Elsie in Cedric's role. The producers tripped over themselves to offer her whatever she wanted during rehearsals, she told Kitty. "And your Fluffy listens and smiles and watches and
speculates—and believes nothing and nobody."[32] The play was destined to
run for an unheard-of twenty-three weeks.

Worried that Elsie might view Tommy as a rival, she took the child to
lunch "and as she was sitting on my knee afterwards she asked if she might
call me by some pretty little name instead of saying 'Mrs. Burnett,' and, after
searching her little mind for some time, I asked her how she would like
to call me what Vivian calls me, and so it was agreed upon, and she wrote
on a piece of paper, 'My own Dearest.'"[33] Those who most claimed the right
to call her by that name were in Washington, where over time they began to
come across these articles about their mother. In the meantime, she wrote
to them from New York to say that the play was a rousing success, and that
both she and Elsie had taken curtain calls. Mary Mapes Dodge, who was
serializing Frances's story "Little Saint Elizabeth" in *Saint Nicholas*, asked her
to write a brief sketch of Elsie for the magazine. Finding the girl "utterly un-
spoiled," Dodge declared the Fauntleroy play "great missionary work. . . . It
is one of the best and most wholesome influences of the day."[34]

Frances made an important alliance at this time when an enterprising
woman named Elisabeth Marbury, who, already doing very well as a dramatic rights agent, had heard that Frances had placed the play with Henry
French at the Broadway. Knowing that Frances had little experience with the

theatre, Marbury presented a letter of introduction to her from a mutual friend and found herself immediately invited to a rehearsal. She loved the play and Frances's work, and the two women became inseparable for two weeks. Eventually Marbury would take over many of the business aspects of the play. For months she travelled down to Washington every weekend to report on its progress, even when running a fever. She was to represent Frances for the rest of her life and went on to become one of the most powerful forces in the business, with offices in New York and London.[35]

By mid-December, Frances was back in Washington with her family but no more settled than she had been before. She suddenly bought "a lovely house for myself" at 1770 Massachusetts Avenue for $27,000, cash.[36] There was no mention of Swan, and the sale was in her name.[37] No matter where she lived, and how many houses she had, for the rest of her life this was the place she considered home. It had an astounding twenty-two rooms and two drawing rooms, and she had spent her spare time in New York buying furniture, carpets, and wallpaper. Yet at the same time, she wrote to a Manchester relative that she intended to take a house in London. Her ship had come in, which was a wonderful thing, because it gave her the strength she would need to face her *annus horribilis*.

CHAPTER II

⁓

LIONEL

1889–1890

THE YEAR 1889 OPENED PROMISINGLY. With Elisabeth Marbury to handle all her dramatic and theatre matters, Frances found that her finances and clout improved greatly. She signed a contract with Daniel Frohman of New York's Lyceum Theatre for a production of her play *Phyllis* (the dramatization of her book *The Fortunes of Philippa Fairfax*). Now pulling in as much as $1,800 in some weeks for her plays alone and another $15,000 a year for her books, she was feeling flush and optimistic. Even though children's stories were proving so lucrative for her, she embarked on a short adult romance, "The Pretty Sister of José," which would appear with other stories; one reviewer found it "dramatic, simple as nature is simple, with a charm of youth and fervor."[1] Except for *Little Lord Fauntleroy*, she hadn't written what she called a big book for some years, since *Through One Administration*, but the market in children's stories and in plays offered her a very good living indeed. One magazine estimated her annual income at $50,000 or $60,000 a year but added that "this money does not bring with it unalloyed happiness."[2]

She loved her new house, where Luisa Chiellini was acting as amanuensis as well as companion and nurse, and it was Luisa instead of Swan who handled the correspondence with Scribner's. As Frances went back and forth to New York, Vivian and Lionel took up new hobbies: printing stationery and business cards on their own press, and later in the year, electrical experiments that Luisa was sure would end in someone's electrocution. In late spring Frances, Vivian, and Luisa left for London, with the expectation of spending the summer in Sorrento, Italy.[3] Lionel chose to stay at home with Swan but went to see them off in New York. None of them knew that this would be the beginning of a slow but steady decline, tragic months of heartbreak made continually worse by the unrolling of the miles between them. In an unfortunate omen, one of the passengers jumped overboard on the third day out and was never found.

Things began happily enough. Lionel followed the baseball games of the Washingtons, sending the scores to his brother. When the city flooded in early June, he and a friend went out in the thick of it, taking off their shoes and socks and poling through the streets on a homemade raft. His friend Sam Hillier was a juvenile entrepreneur who had started out as a shoeshine boy in Toledo, Ohio, become a mascot for the local baseball team, and travelled to Washington. Sam had gone on his own to New York, where he had seen the play of *Fauntleroy*. Back in Washington, where he met Lionel, he heard about a boy who wrote and sold a little newspaper and helped him round up subscribers. Lionel asked his mother to contribute, and she was taken with the boy's drive, finding such boys the hope of the future, but she also used him to point out to Vivian the great advantages he and his brother had enjoyed. "Sam is the beginning of an energetic man with his mind all alive," she told him,

> And you are the beginning of another, I hope, and you have lived in an entirely different way. . . . Sam has watched base-ball games, I have no doubt; you have seen great cricket matches at Lord's. Sam has taken long tramps from one city to another to sell his papers; you have crossed the Atlantic in a big steamer year after year, and have been on familiar terms with sailors and engineers. Sam has sold papers at inaugurations; you have watched the kings and queens, and princes and princesses, and all the grand pageant of the Jubilee. Sam knows how to manage a boot-black business and understands the language of the boys who take care of themselves; you can speak French and understand Italian. . . . Between you two boys it appears to me you have a great part of the world and the most interesting sides of life to discuss and compare notes about. I really think, you know, that any one listening while you talked and told each other things might gain quite a respectable education. And think what one might gain from a number of boys all with different lives and different views.[4]

It wasn't long before things began to go wrong for all of them. She had a difficult time getting her new play, *Phyllis*, off the ground. She wrote to the "boys" from 44 Lexham Gardens that rehearsing the play was nearly impossible, "as I never was able to get the company together all at once," and things weren't made easier by trying to furnish the house. "When I was not at the theatre I was always driving about from place to place with Louisita, trying to make furniture men keep their promises, and decorators finish their work."[5] Still, her seemingly endless chain of successes gave her enough confidence in the play to invite many people, taking seats for Owen Lankester, Luisa Chiellini, and several other friends, and inviting others, including Henry James, to a play only a few nights before that, cheerfully signing her letters Fluffy, Fluffina, and Fluffine.[6] The play opened on 1 July to bad reviews. The actors didn't know their parts, the critics didn't find it convincing, and it died a quiet death. Either by providential intervention or simple coincidence, she had changed the nature of Phyllis's father's illness to be a non-fatal heart ailment rather than the fatal tuberculosis and death of the original novel, *The Fortunes of Philippa Fairfax*.

Frances always attempted to get as much use as possible out of her writings. The novel had been published only in England and was slim enough: it told the story of a London girl raised by her profligate but debonair father, who is encouraged by him to accept an invitation to stay at a wealthy relation's country home. There she falls in love with the heir, but he discovers that her father has told his debtors that the young man will marry Philippa. Furious at being used by what appears to be a schemer, he breaks off the engagement, and the wounded girl travels in Europe until kind friends arrange a reconciliation. It is a fairly thin story, but becomes even thinner in the play, in which new characters are introduced in a comic subplot and it is unclear how the various characters are related. The play rushes to a close, ties up too quickly and neatly, and is, on the whole, unsatisfying. The *Boston Traveller* found the failure of the play to be "of no especial importance, regarded as merely one play more or less; but regarded in the line of its author's exceptional career, it is a matter of some speculative interest."[7]

It is probable that the poor reviews (and the only surviving copy of the play) are based on the copyright performance, which often involved little more than having the actors sit in chairs on the stage and read their lines from the script. Frances and other dramatists had learned to write and produce a stage version of their own fiction quickly in order to preserve their dramatic rights to it. *The Spirit of the Times* made this distinction on 27 July 1889, when it took the *World* to task for mistaking "the copyright performance of Mrs. Burnett's new play, Phyllis, for a trial matinee and criticises it as a rough sketch, rather than a finished work. At least forty-five minutes should be cut out of the dialogue and the situations at the end of the second and third Acts should be remodelled." However, the *World* goes on to criticize Frances for writing the play at all: "She should let experienced dramatists do this sort of work for her while she writes more stories. It is quite as absurd for her to make her own plays as it would be for her to make her own dresses. They do not fit and what she saves in wages she loses in time." Evidently the critic did not realize that she had written the script for *Fauntleroy* herself and that it fitted very well. In any case, some critics knew quite well the difference between an English copyright performance and a polished play. The day before the play opened in London, the *Post* made clear that "the production here on Monday is simply a performance for the purpose of securing the English copyright. Mrs. Burnett declines to follow the usual custom of having the lines merely read from the stage; she prefers to pay the expenses herself of a finished performance."[8]

They had taken a house at 44 Lexham Gardens, a house in which she decorated at least one room with "flowery walls and hangings, lounging chairs, and fanciful light bits of furniture."[9] Vivian, who had been petted by all the adults on the ship, singing for them on their musical evenings, and had paid a visit to the Paris Exhibition, found himself bored and lonely in London. With no brother around and no country amusements, he wandered the streets and stared into shop windows while his mother worked. Lionel wrote of his exploits with his friends—crabbing on the beach and planning for the Fourth of July—but almost immediately an alarming tone, one that Frances tried to ignore, crept into his poorly spelled but beguiling letters. In late June, sandwiched in between his cheerful reports almost without punctuation, he told her that "on one or tow [*sic*] days I have had the blues and some times I do not feel quiet [*sic*] all right but the rest of the time I am enjoying myself I do not want you to worry about me and tell Vivian I often wish he were here because I know we would have a very nice time."[10] In July she responded once again in the *Saturday Review* to rumours about her private life, and it was less than a week later that the *Boston Traveller* reported on the failure of the London production of *Phyllis*, finding it a subject of "speculative interest." This time, the interest was positive, caring less about the play's failure than about the source of her obvious literary power.[11] In August her reworked version of *Dolly*, renamed *Vagabondia*, opened to good reviews. "We confess that we are not sorry to miss the storm and stress of her recent novels," wrote the *Critic*, "and that we think the drollery and overflowing good humor of 'Vagabondia' a fair exchange for them."[12]

Everyone decamped for the summer, and the Burnett family separated once again. Swan left for a conference in Berlin; Frances wrote to Lionel that "Papa is already on the Atlantic—I hope he is not ill."[13] Lionel, now left without father, mother, or brother, was installed in an Atlantic City boarding house, where he rode the carousels, swam, took photographs, and made new friends. Frances, Vivian, Luisa, and various servants set up housekeeping in an artists' colony in Surrey, in a cottage called Bellagio but nicknamed Dorincourt after Fauntleroy's ancestral home. Never a great horsewoman, she nonetheless wrote to one of her London friends, the writer Edmund Gosse, that she had bought a lively horse called Gordon, whose feats in the stable were so frightening that when she returned one day "from a long drive I found the head groom panting at the gate just on the point of dispatching four others on horseback to scour the country and the reception given to me by my family was such as revealed to me that they had spent the hours between seven & nine in discovering beauties in me such as are usually only inscribed upon the tomb."[14] She found Gordon a lovely and exciting horse, even though he was "considered extremely dangerous by prejudiced persons at the stables."[15]

Caught up in her country life, she neglected to write very often to her son in America, even though he kept up his end of the correspondence faithfully, reporting his growth and good health. "Dear Mamma," he wrote on 17 July, "I have not received a letter from you for a very long time but still I will write to you."[16] And a few days later, "Why don't you write to me is it that you have not time?"[17] Frances's excuse, in a letter that crossed his, was that rehearsing the play and decorating and furnishing the London house had kept her busy. As Frances raced around London and enjoyed the country air in Surrey, Lionel tried to build his strength by exercising. Always a healthy boy, he found that a bout with "grip" or influenza the previous summer, and its complications with malaria, still left him occasionally winded. He asked Swan to buy him a set of Indian clubs, and he worked out with them regularly. He made "quite a small army of friends" in Atlantic City and went boating, trying to keep up his spirits and reporting that he was now 5'3" and weighed 96 sturdy pounds.

What so distracted Frances that summer of 1889 was not a house but a man. She had met Stephen Townesend sometime in the past year or two when he was acting in a play directed by Comyns Carr at the Comedy Theatre, and he was probably one of the reasons she had been so eager to return to England. He had become a member of the Royal College of Surgeons in 1883 and a fellow in 1887, but he had made his first stage appearance in 1882 at the Crystal Palace. More than ten years her junior, he aroused in her the same sort of response she had had years earlier to the young Swan—he was someone she could rescue. Like Swan he was a doctor, encouraged in that profession by his family, and clearly with some talent in the field. He longed for the more glamorous world of the theatre, had had some amateur successes, with some fifty pieces in his repertoire, and in 1888 had published *A short account of the Amateur Dramatic Club of St. Bartholomew's Hospital,*

with a few hints to amateurs on the art of acting. Born in York, he came from
a clerical family; his father was the rector of the church St. Mary le Strand
in London, and his grandfather had been a canon at Durham cathedral.

The story goes that his family, wishing to send him away from such disreputable temptation, was about to ship him off to South Africa as a ship's
surgeon. "That a deep-seated and serious ambition should be thwarted,
and a life warped by being starved of the thing for which it hungered most,
was more than she could stand," and she swooped in to save him.[18] He loved
the theatre; she belonged to the London and New York theatrical worlds.
He was young and handsome; she was soon to turn forty and was married
in name only. It was probably Stephen she referred to several years later in
an essay she called "When He Decides," published in the book *Before He
Is Twenty*, about the questions that arise when parents bring up sons. In
her essay she counselled letting the boys follow their own professional bent
rather than having one imposed on them by parents who won't themselves
have to live with the consequences of a poor choice. She cites the example
of a boy who, from the start, wanted to become an actor but unfortunately
had parents who "were gentle people, whose lives had been extremely narrow,
though they had been spent in a great metropolis. . . . A strong-willed father
and a weak-willed, timid mother did their best to eradicate it. The father
sighed, reproached, satirized, and stormed; the mother wept. . . . The boy
was totally dependent, high-spirited, proud, and helpless. He had the artistic temperament, and was capable of the keenest suffering."[19] Soon Stephen,
who had already acquitted himself well in several roles, such as an old father
in *Sowing the Wind* by Grundy, was accompanying her not only about London but also to Dorincourt, where his manly ease in handling the intract-
able Gordon convinced her of the horse's good nature and of his own, an
error on both counts. Stephen did not "seem to have trouble with the darling brute when he is driving him, and we have been miles and miles. Come
to Dorincourt and you shall help us with our horse-breaking," she wrote
gaily to Owen Lankester.[20]

It was a terrible mistake. In August she had the horse hitched to a small
trap and set off to fetch Stephen from the London train. She was found
hours later in a ditch, unconscious, with Gordon standing next to the over-
turned vehicle. Stephen, as a doctor, had her carried back to Dorincourt,
where he and Luisa kept watch, convinced that she might die. During those
blank days she kept up a pathetic moan, crying "Oh dear, oh dear" so piti-
fully and constantly that Luisa knelt by her side repeating Vivian's and
Lionel's names distinctly, trying to force her to swallow liquids by saying
"Take this for Lionel. Drink this for Vivian."[21] She recalled only dreaming

that there was something her children wanted but she was unable to get it for them. She remained in a coma for three days and awoke to blinding headaches, unshakeable depression, and no memory of the intervening time. Recovery proved extremely slow and painful.

On the other side of the Atlantic, Lionel too began to sink, even before he heard about her accident. He enjoyed his months at Atlantic City, where making new friends and having daily amusements took his mind off his absent family, but while he was there Kate Brady, who with her sister Margaret was a close friend of the adult Burnetts, died. That saddened him a great deal, and he reported that "once in a while I get the blues, but I fight them off."[22] On the same day he wrote to Swan in London, where he was stopping after his Berlin conference to collect Vivian and carry him back first to New York and then to Washington, "I suppose momma will tell you about Aunt Kates [*sic*] death so I will not tell you about it except to say that of course you know of course that I feel badly."[23] She had been ill for some time and seemed to be better enough for Lionel's friend DeVin Finckel and Margaret Brady to leave her and go to visit him at the shore. They were only with him for a week when they were summoned back in time to be with her when she died.

The fourteen-year-old seesawed all that summer between being a boy and being a man. He had his photograph taken wearing standing collars for the first time; a family friend reported that he sprouted a moustache. He shot up several inches and gained another five pounds. At the same time he was a child struggling with loneliness and depression, and occasional spells of poor health, although he'd always been so strong in his younger days. He spent his fifteenth birthday in Atlantic City without family or old friends, while a huge storm raged, with winds of sixty-six miles an hour crashing against the boarding house windows and waves washing away a hundred feet of the iron pier. "Dear Mamma," he wrote, "Let me know when you are coming home I want you to come just as soon as you can because sometimes I get the blues so bad that I feel like having a good cry but I try to throw it off because I know that you do not want me to feel badly."[24] To make matters worse, rumours about his mother were spreading around Atlantic City. Mrs. Owens, the owner of the boarding house, tried to squelch them, but Lionel ran across their source himself in the *Ladies' Home Journal*:

Mrs. Frances Hodgson Burnett, although in receipt of the largest income now made by any woman in America, is by no means wealthy. She earns an average of forty thousand dollars a year by her pen, one item of which is five hundred a week from the Broadway Theater. But Mrs. Burnett has fads that are expensive. She is one of Worth's best customers, and his annual bill against her is something enormous. Besides her extravagant taste in dress, Mrs. Burnett has spent a prodigious amount of money in hospitalities here with the hope of making herself as great a social success in New York as she is in Washington. But the metropolis which bears the Atherton, the Wilcox and the Rives, never could be persuaded to take up Mrs. Burnett since her divorce. So she has shaken the dust of Fifth Avenue from her bronze heels, and returned to Washington with the disgusted intention of ending her days there.[25]

There was no question that Frances adored clothes and spent enormous amounts on them. Kitty Hall recalled a time when Frances, in bed with a bad cold, was reprimanded for the inadequacy of her lace-trimmed night-dress. Lampooning herself she sighed, "I know. I must have more lace on it."[26] She used the design house Worth as the ne plus ultra in her story "Louisiana," about a country girl whom a city woman on holiday dresses up to help her pass as a lady. Later that year, in Italy, where she visited the graves of Keats and Shelley, the small daughter of the cemetery's custodian mar-velled at Frances's "long black plush mantle, which was bordered with soft black fox fur, and which had very long sleeves of a heavy brocade that fell from my shoulders to the bottom of the cloak." (Kitty herself "wore a black cloth dress, which was trimmed with black and gold," but unlike Frances, who never wore them, had on earrings.)[27] There was no evidence for the other allegations: she was not divorced, she left New York after her play opened in order to be at home with her children, and she had done no shop-ping while she was there. Although she had responded to these and similar charges in March, there seemed no end to the press's harassment and rumours. Another article reported that when she returned to the States, she was to become the editor of the Sunday *World* in New York, at a salary of $5,000 to $6,000 a year.

Lionel, the young man, wanted to spring to her defence. "I should like to know the person that wrote that article," he fumed. "I would take great pleasure in punching their heads."[28] He had reason for his frustration. That summer a reporter claimed to have tracked him down at the seaside and to have interviewed him; according to his article, Lionel confessed that Frances had made him and Vivian dress up and pose, and that both of them "hated the Fauntleroy racket." Lionel would never have used disrespectful language about his mother, and Frances denounced the reporter as a "liar and a cad."[29]

Just a week later a much more disturbing piece of news reached the papers. The *New York Times* reported on Frances's accident, saying that she was seriously ill. Swan and Vivian, who were travelling home, knew nothing of it and couldn't be reached in any case. Lionel was so upset that he asked his friend DeVin to write to her. Before he could do that, however, the Burnetts' Washington friends swung into action. Luisa Chiellini cabled to Charles Rice that the situation wasn't as bad as the papers reported. He contacted Effie Macfarlane, who, as Frances's closest and most trustworthy Washington friend, and as a gentle schoolteacher and a sort of surrogate mother to the boys, immediately went to see Lionel in Washington and explained that his mother was all right. Lionel wrote bravely to Frances, telling her she "must not worry yourself about me because I am all right though I was frightened when I first heard about you in the papers of course they had to say you were a great deal worse than you really were."[30]

Back in England things weren't as good as Effie and Charles had presented them. Luisa wrote to Lionel, hoping to cheer him. "She is better, much better, darling, and we spoke about you, and she taked [sic] her medicine once for you, once for Vivian—and is going on so nicely that she will be very soon quite herself again. . . . You know my sweet darling that I will take good care of your sweet Mama & bring her back to you all as soon as I can."[31] She wrote to him fondly, partly out of genuine sentiment for the affection that had grown between them in Florence and in Washington, where she had joined the family for a time, and partly to distract him, and he treasured her attention. She reminded him how, when he came in late from Washington parties and his mother was asleep, he used to ask Luisa to tuck him into bed, kiss him good night, and stay with him until he drifted off. "Yes darling," Luisa wrote, "you are right I am and shall always be your own, own, own dear Luisa."[32] At the same time, she needed gently to level with him about his mother's health so that he wouldn't expect her to come home too soon.

Frances was not, in fact, well at all. She had suffered a serious concussion and was extraordinarily weak. Her head hurt so badly that she could scarcely lift it, and she fell into a depression and foreboding just as grave as Lionel's. "I am given to desperate little fits of depression," she wrote to Kitty months after the accident, when she could still only occasionally hold a pen. "Awful little fancies creep out of the corners sometimes and stare at me. They say, 'Suppose that awful blow stunned that vivid, vital part of her brain that made the stories.' It is so ghastly to think of."[33] The letters from her sons sustained her, and she kissed them repeatedly, but long travel was out of the question. Summer at Bellagio, Surrey, now faded into a chilly and bare autumn, and the decision was made to remove her to London, but she was still unable to shake off her weakness, pain, and foreboding, and her doctors recommended taking her to the south of France, Rome, and the Riviera by slow, easy stages so that the warmth and light might help her improve.

Lionel was doing no better. He asked her permission to sell his bicycle in order to buy materials for electrical experiments. "I do not ride it very much now because you know it made my head hurt when I rode it to [sic] fast. . . . I wish you would get Luisa to tell us when you are coming home. I don't want you to write me because it will make you sick and I dont want you to do anything that will not be good for you. I want you to come home soon dear because I feel lonely sometimes but I can look at your picture I have four pictures with you in them the little one with you alone the one with Luisa in it which was taken at Bells and the two that you sent me from Bellagio that makes four of my dear, sweet, darling mamma and three of my nice, sweet, dear darling Luisa."[34] Surrounded by her photographs, he felt that it might be as long as another year before he saw her again. In fact they had been apart since spring, and it was now Christmastime. In the new year, writing to assure her that he had got over a cold, he wrote his most alarming letter yet: "I dont have the blues as often as I used to now but still I sometimes have them when I think of my dear mamma. I have the funniest felling [sic] sometimes as if I were going to get all kinds of diseases and die and all that kind of thing and I ask so many questions but I am trying to conquer them and I think I am getting the better of them."[35] Frances tried to cheer him out of these moods in her letters, reminding him how healthy and strong he was as a child, and encouraging Vivian and Swan to help bolster his spirits, but somewhere in his fear and intuition he knew that something was very, very wrong.

In February he was ill enough for Swan to keep him at home for a week and consult the family doctor. By Valentine's Day he was well enough to go back to the Franklin School and take part in the celebrations, although he found himself still weak, but two days later he was back home in bed with a relapse of the flu. Vivian now worried about both his mother and his brother. In Paris, Frances too had taken to her bed again after her crossing from Dover, with fever and headaches. Vivian was convinced that Lionel's "attack of the grippe [was] brought on by his bad feelings as he calls them but it is really what I had, when I was in England year before last, in a worse form. The poor boy always thinks that he has got something the matter with him and he worries himself about it. I try to get all those silly things out of him but he seems to stick to them."[36] The two boys expanded their home printing business and wanted their mother to finance the $150 it would take to make a real go of it. This kept them excited and occupied, but by the end of the letter Lionel admitted that he could not shake the illness, despite the doctor's help, and that Swan once again was obliged to keep him home from school because "you know it takes an awful long time for it to get well."[37]

Now in Italy, Frances became anxious about Lionel's inability to shake his illness and his depression. Seemingly unaware of how the reports of her own illness upset them, she kept them abreast of her progress so that they would understand why she didn't come home. Still, each letter that made its way across the sea left a little more unhappiness in its wake. "Sweetheart dear, it will never do for my boy to be ill while I am away from him," she wrote to Lionel from Rome at the end of March. "I should be ill again myself. I thought my journey had done me so much good but when Papas letter told me my boy was not so well I was so troubled that I was dizzy for three hours and all my nice pink color that had come into my cheeks went away and left me looking quite different. It is because I am not with you that I am so troubled. I know you want me and I want my darling more than words could tell."[38] She booked passage for him and Lionel to come to her in June on the *Gascogne*, on which Vivian had travelled earlier, though neither of them could be sure Lionel would be well enough to travel by then.

It was about this time that Frances fell into the habit of "adopting" other children while she was absent from her own. In Rome she took up two "tiny pretty little beggar boys" who sang for tourists near her hotel. "Luisita talks Italian to them & she said the other day to the prettiest one 'Do you know why the blonde Signora gives you money. It is because she has two boys and they are so far away she cannot see them. They are in America. So she loves *bambini* like you.'"[39] Over time she would bring in sick children to stay in her London house, bring her nephews to stay with her and would educate them, and would help establish a club for boys in London. She saw these disadvantaged children as somehow substituting for her own, and she expected her own children, so far away, to respond with enthusiasm towards those they might well view as their substitutes and rivals. Frances in some way believed that lavishing attention and gifts on other children, then telling her own children about it, would make her sons feel closer to her rather than jealous or replaced.

It was a pipe dream. At the beginning of April Swan cabled Frances that Lionel's illness, whether or not brought on or worsened by his unshakeable blues, had been diagnosed as raging consumption or tuberculosis, for which there was no cure. She left immediately for Le Havre, and on Vivian's fourteenth birthday, 5 April, she sailed for America on the *Gascogne*. Lionel's pitiful letter admonishing her "to get well, and not to worry about me. I also want to see you very much, but don't start until you feel well" was written to her when she was nearly home and would not have prevented her sailing.[40]

She vowed aboard ship that Lionel would never learn that he was dying and that she would resist his death with all her strength. She was still very ill, and the captain did his best to ease her discomfort. Altogether it took her two weeks to get home, "and I walked into a bed-room in my house in Washington where a boy with eyes as dark as [an Italian's] lay waiting for me with cheeks and hands hot with fever."[41]

At the sight of his mother and Luisa, Lionel at first seemed to improve— enough for Frances to welcome a reporter into her home and talk about her work. The journalist found the house impressive, with its "open stairway, the large fireplace to the left, the beautiful stained-glass windows, the soft rugs upon the floor, and the rich simplicity of wall and furniture like the interior of an English country house."[42] She chatted animatedly about her plays of *Fauntleroy* and *Editha's Burglar*, and was in high spirits despite her injury and exhaustion. "If Lionel can only recover his health," she told him, "I shall be so happy."[43]

His remission proved temporary, and Frances soon began a frenzied, nomadic search for a cure. Despite her distrust of doctors, she took Lionel to see American specialists in Atlantic City and Philadelphia, but to no avail. Giving up on American doctors, she resolved to carry him to the best European spas. Taking a specialist with her, she bundled up her sick son and left with him and Luisa for Southampton, where Stephen Townesend and a nurse from St. Bartholomew's Hospital met them.

The first stop was a spa in Göbersdorf, in Silesia, where she wrote to Scribner that "the condition of my poor boy is so hopeless and sad a one" that she might never have the heart to return to America.[44] Later that month they moved on to the German spa town of Marienbad, where from the Goldener Falke on Stefan Strasse she wrote to Effie to "keep your eye on Vivvie . . . and make him take care of himself. I don't think I shall live to do for him as I do for Lionel if he gets ill."[45] Stephen withdrew to London and handled Frances's business affairs while Swan joined them for a time, bringing Vivian with him. When Swan left without Vivian—who would never come to like "Uncle Stephen"—Vivian fell into despair. "We have been so lonely without you," he wrote to his father, "and *I* have not known what to do." He looked forward to joining his father in September and returning to school, since he was unable to help in any way and was left to his own devices and thoughts too often.[46]

In her sketch "What Use Is a Poet?" Frances recalled a walk that she and Vivian took that spring in Europe, in which he wanted to know what the "use" of a poet was. He was a practical boy, accustomed to utilitarian activities like printing and electricity. Frances assured him that they lived in a wonderful age of invention, that telephones, among other things, made life easier. But gentle words could make harsh realities easier to understand. Referring to Lionel, she said,

Suppose I were to say to him, "Yes, you are very ill. You cannot use your cameras, or your engines, or your bicycle any more. You must lie still and take medicine and peptonoids all day and night. When you travel to different countries you will have a doctor and a trained nurse always with you, and your medicine-chest will be in the railway carriage. I shall spend a great deal of money for you, but I don't know when you will get well." That would be telling him the truth in ugly, hurting words. But if I kneel by him and comfort him, and say, "Yes, you are ill, darling boy, but it only makes us all feel how much we love you. And we only live to make the days go easily for you. Everything you like you shall have. The doctor and the nurse are as nice as they are clever. We will pretend you are the Prince Imperial, and we are your court and have to fly to do your bidding. You shall go to any country you like and that agrees with you, and every country shall give its very nicest things to help and amuse you." When I tell him the truth in that way he is soothed instead of hurt, and his illness even seems to have a pleasant side.[47]

She recounted a conversation she had had with former Prime Minister Gladstone about the education Vivian was receiving in Florence. He encouraged her to have Vivian select not only utilitarian subjects such as modern languages but to have him learn the classics "to make his mind beautiful and develop its poetic powers."[48] This was a philosophy she appreciated. To her, words had magical properties that could soothe and comfort.

Losing faith in the spas and preferring some stability during the oncoming autumn and winter months, Frances, Luisa, Stephen, and Lionel finally settled into a comfortable apartment at 16, rue Christophe Colombe in Paris. They hired a nurse and brought in a French doctor to attend Lionel, who by now was able to eat so little that he was wasting away, his eyes becoming large and luminous. When he was well enough, they took him for airings in the park, but on other less good days he stretched out on a sofa, and they tried to entertain him by reading or playing games or putting together toys with him. Stephen treated him lovingly and gently, and Luisa remained his unswerving sweetheart.

Whether by his preference or hers, Frances fell into the habit of treating him more and more like the small child he had been than the young man he was becoming. Taller than she, with a teenager's moustache and no doubt a changed voice, he nonetheless could not bear to be apart from her for more than a short time. Recalling happier days in Washington, when the boys used to break in on her work to offer treats they'd found in the garden, she began to keep what she called a "fairy box" for him, which she stocked with toys, withdrawing one from time to time to cheer him. She and Stephen called him Boykin, and he fell into a sweet sort of lethargy, as though his illness had accomplished an unconscious aim of bringing him together with his mother. In late October she wrote to Vivian that "he always wanted me to be near him but during the last four or five weeks it has seemed as if he could not bear me to be away from him for a moment. I sleep in the room opening into his and I ask the Nurse to call me in the night if he wants me & then I go & hold him in my arms & soothe him until he is quiet, because no one else can comfort him now. He likes Nurse and she is very sweet to him but it is always 'Mamma—Mamma—Mamma' he wants. I suppose that is just Nature crying out."[49]

It was heart-wrenching and wearing, but perhaps his desperation stemmed from Frances's curious behaviour: having publishing business with her London lawyer Guedella, she left Lionel in the care of Luisa and the nurse, and went to London with Stephen for more than two weeks at the beginning of October. She tried to make up for her actions by writing to him almost daily and sending gifts to Paris. "Every day I am going to add something to the 'Fairy Box' & we will have 'sprises all winter," she wrote from her house at 44 Lexham Gardens. "Uncle Stephen is going to write to you. Could Boykin write just about three words to Mamma just scribble them any way. Just say how Boy feels—that is all—I dont mean write a letter because that tires you." In a postscript she added that "the most important of business matters on which your mother came to London" would be prolonged, as one of the people she needed to see was out of town.[50] In the meantime, she explored possibilities for further beneficial travel for him, to Cannes and other places that she thought might do him good, when in fact he was too ill to be moved. She trawled the London shops to have special toys made for him. She had an unusual mechanical engine specially tooled for him, and looked for things that would occupy his mind and weren't too taxing. But she also went to the theatre and spent an unexpected weekend in Bournemouth with Stephen, who was so involved with meeting potential business partners for their play *Nixie* that had opened in London in April that they missed the last train back to London. "I had no nightgown & no anything but a comb I had asked Polly to put in because I thought I might want to comb my bangs. Stephen had to come & borrow it from me in the morning," she wrote chastely.[51] This so closely parallels her story of her earlier trip to the shore with Richard Gilder that it is not clear whether either version is true. Somehow she ignored this trip in a letter she later wrote, claiming that "we three people never left [Lionel] and never had one thought that was not of him."[52]

Her behaviour was baffling. Lionel had sunk into illness during her long absences from him, a situation made worse after her accident. She knew by now that Lionel was dying, knowledge she determinedly kept from him. After months of caring for him, she surely was exhausted, even with the help of a maid, a companion, a nurse, and Stephen. Even so, with his physical condition steadily declining, his moods so desperately needy, her love for him so apparent, it is hard to excuse her for what seems like temporary abandonment. In London she saw friends, waited for her business appointments, wrote to Lionel, and began paying visits to sick children at the Invalid Children Aid Association, giving them gifts in Lionel's name. On 11 October she wrote to him, "I can only write a little letter because it is so late I have been out all morning visiting the poor little sick children. I have made three poor little ones happy today."[53] Set to return to Paris on a Monday, she wrote that she had been delayed by one more day, but "Boy must not be fretted because there is another day between us. We will have lots of fun this winter. I am going to give tomorrow morning to paying a visit to some American shops in the city. Perhaps I may find some things for the Fairy Box."[54]

After his mother returned to Paris, Lionel panicked whenever she left the room. He was so weak that when they tried to make a picture book together she finally had to do all the cutting out and gluing, while he watched her peacefully. She was desperate to work; writing was her income, and this illness was tremendously expensive: the apartment and the London house had to be supported; salaries for Luisa, the nurse, and the French cook; doctors' bills to pay. He had so little appetite that they fed him dry champagne and whatever eggs and milk they could tempt him with. In order to write, she had a fire laid in one room, and tiptoed in before dawn each day, swaddled in dressing gowns, and wrote by candlelight until he woke. She kept up her correspondence with Vivian, assuring him that she loved him but that "nobody will ever know what Mamma suffers. It is too hard to bear. . . . I am very unhappy & I have a trouble that breaks down my strength."[55]

One long night made her both fearful and hopeful. In the morning Lionel felt better, insisting on walking to his mother's room and having breakfast with her in bed, and apologizing for having caused her to stay awake.

It seemed such a wonder beyond wonders to have him in my arms—his beautiful darling body all straight & unhurt & his sweetest face not really disfigured at all! Only think what it might have been! But I dont want to think. He was so dear when I first went to him. He was lying in bed apparently unconscious & I bent down & kissed him & said "Lionel your Dearest is here!" & he opened his eyes & after a seconds pause recognition came into them & he said in the tenderest apologetic little voice "My Sweet little darling!—You see I fell down!—And I dont know what to do!" & with the last word dropped off again to sleep or stupor. He was always clear in his mind when we roused him but until the night was past of course we could not know what might develope [*sic*] & when the morning found him in such a perfectly normal condition you may imagine what a load was removed from us. He was up & dressed all yesterday though of course lying on the sofa.[56]

He spent much of his time over the next weeks drifting in and out of sleep. In an unfinished and unpublished story called "His Friend," written a short time later, Frances described a dying boy and his mother. Speaking to a celebrated physician, the mother asks, "He will die?" and the doctor replies, "Yes, he will die." She wonders, "if a creature could be kept from fear—from the knowledge of what was coming—if he were watched, and spared all pain that science or thought could save him—if all about him were kept bright and no one wore a sad face . . . do you believe he might pass away and not know—fall asleep unconsciously on earth and awaken—if he did awaken—in that other country—not even knowing how it happened?"[57] Frances always believed that that was how it had happened.

Lionel slept all through the day on 7 December, insisting that he felt comfortable, just sleepy. When she kissed him good night he said, "God Bless Mammie." In the morning he gave a little cough, sighed, and was gone. Frances fell to her knees, sobbing, trying to put his arm around her neck. It slowly slipped off and lay still by his side. "I tried to carry you in my arms to the gates of Heaven, past Pain and Death," she wrote to him in a journal she kept in the terrible, distraught months that followed, "so that you would wake up to beautiful, strange surprise at your new, strong, happy body and the day that has no night, and the city whose gates are never closed."[58]

For her, for a long time, the gates shut down. She cabled Swan to let him know that their son had died, and she buried Lionel in a flurry of flowers in the St. Germain Cemetery, but she was never again the same.[59] "I appeared this, or I appeared that; I did this and I did that," she said to Kitty Hall about all her accomplishments and fame. "But all I ever *was* is the mother of two little boys."[60]

PART TWO

~

A Lady of Quality

CHAPTER 12

~

DRURY LANE

1891–1892

FOR MONTHS FRANCES WANDERED EUROPE like a ghost, attired in black dress, crepe veil, and bonnet. She thought incessantly of Lionel's body lying in St. Germain Cemetery, where to prevent the soil touching his casket she had the grave "walled and arched over and lined with flowers and green boughs."[1] Violets, the flowers he had always thought of as hers, covered his body. Kitty joined her in Paris and thought it best to take her away as soon as possible from the scene of her sorrow, so that shortly after his burial they travelled with Lionel's nurse to Italy, finally establishing themselves at the Hotel des Anglais in San Remo, a medieval city on the Italian Riviera especially appealing to the English because of its soft climate, stunning coastal views, and steep streets and alleys with houses perched on their edges. Artists particularly loved it and roamed the streets with their brushes and easels while the locals went about their picturesque lives. Violets, "Mamma's flowers," abounded, sold on the streets by vendors at a fraction of their cost in England or America, and Frances always wore a bunch tucked into her waist or bodice as she walked through San Remo with Kitty, submerged in her sadness.

During Lionel's last months in Paris she had bought a few ordinary notebooks, hoping to use them "to write something about him every day—about what he had said or done, or patiently suffered, so that it would be a sort of record after he was gone. But I could never write in it. He wanted me with him all the time, and I never left him except between eleven and twelve in the morning when I went to walk. When he was asleep at night I was too tired to do anything but go to bed myself."[2] Now she used the book, spilling into several notebooks over the next four years, as a repository for her grief, both as a journal and as a series of letters to her lost son about his life in the unknown beyond and about her "life, which is ended."[3] They make for heartbreaking reading. "Lionel is dead. Lionel is dead," she wrote in early March. "His beautiful four year old picture is always before me on my table as I try to write. What a wonderful, grave, baby face, and what great brown eyes looking far away with such solemn thoughts in them." And later, "My Pet! My Pet, I did my very best! I always feel as if I ought to implore his pardon because I let his life go—and yet I fought so hard to save it for him."[4]

Now, as she walked on the promenade at San Remo or sat in her rooms talking to Kitty, she recalled his younger life. She remembered his birth, a healthy baby placed by her side, a baby who was not a beauty but who grew into a handsome child with curling blond hair that darkened in his adolescence. She remembered him at fourteen months old, determined to toddle alongside her in the Parisian streets while she was pregnant with Vivian. She recalled how he'd always been "Mammie's Man" when he was small, and how in his illness she began calling him "Mammie's Boy" instead and using baby talk, regressing him in time and age as he grew weaker and weaker. She spoke of kneeling by him in Paris, telling him stories, and speaking in "negro dialect as if I was a fat, comfortable old darkey Aunty expounding her views about things good to eat. He put his arms round my neck—I was kneeling by his bed—and hugged me, laughing and saying 'Oh! my little Mammie, you are so 'musing.'"[5] She saw him now, in death, as being in perpetual young manhood, in a "youth that will never fade."[6] It seemed to her now that although he had been a healthy child—she always prided herself that neither he nor Vivian was ever ill—she should have noticed danger signs years earlier. Vivian's skin was rosy; Lionel's was ivory. "I suppose," she now thought, "that fine ivory tint was only a sign in Lionel that strong and splendid as he always was, there was really in his blood that deadly taint of the disease which killed him. . . . I shudder now when I remember how I used to say with such certainty, 'My two boys are never ill. There is one thing I need never fear when we are apart—that they will be ill.'"[7] She wrote again and again of her relief that he never knew he was dying, that although brokenhearted she always approached him in his illness with a smile on her face, even when she first entered his sickroom in Washington after her sudden return from Italy after her accident, in "a sort of Mother's Calvary."[8]

Reassured though Lionel had been by her constant presence during his illness, he sometimes missed his home. One afternoon she had found him crying because he missed his friend DeVin Finckel, and she could do little more than promise to send for him in a summer that she knew Lionel would never

see. It had taken enormous strength to appear cheerful and reassuring, yet
never did she seem to reproach herself for having been separated from him
in the first place. After Lionel's death, Frances wrote a long letter to DeVin
from San Remo. "Perhaps by this time Dr. Burnett has taken to your house
to read to you a long letter I wrote to him, giving all the details of the end,"
she told the young man. "I asked him to let Lionel's friends see it because
I am so broken that I cannot keep writing the story over and over. It would
seem like living it over again and indeed I am very much shattered. There
are not many days when I dare to let myself *speak* of him. But I want to tell
his DeVin that he died as softly as a child going to sleep. I do thank God for
that." She recalled that Lionel had expressed the wish that when he got well
they would buy his friend a beautiful dress suit and opera hat. In his honour, she told DeVin to go to a good tailor and get fitted for these items, as
her gift, and that she was also giving him a gold watch and fob chain that
had been Lionel's. In a strange remark to make to so young a person, she
ended by saying that "if I live and am well enough I think I shall bring
Lionel home in the Autumn. If I do not live I have left instructions that we
shall be taken home together. I know he would like to be in America, and
where he is I must be with him."[9]

How Swan felt when she took their son away we do not know because
so few letters between them remain. Except for his visit to them in Europe
as they moved from spa to spa seeking medical help, he never saw his older
son again. Nor do we know how he felt when on 7 December he received
her cable "announcing the death of their oldest son, Lionel, in Paris." The
Washington Post reported that Lionel "as his friends all here remember, was
one of the healthiest boys in Washington."[10] Swan remained in Washington
with Vivian during their mourning, and he and Frances wrote to each other.
At the end of the month she sent him a photograph of Lionel, taken from a
recent picture of her with her arms around their sons. Although three dozen
copies were made, she couldn't bear to send them to people "who would
only put them in albums or stick them about in no special place. You will
put this in a frame & keep it on your table I know." She was not in good
shape, and although she wanted to return to London from Italy, she told him
that everything from arranging a route to remaining calm seemed beyond
her power.

> I am ill and more than unhappy. I have a constant cough and I feel phys-
> ically depressed as well as mentally. I am specially unhappy just now
> because I feel as if I *cannot* go back any way but by Paris & Nurse & Kitty
> say I *must* not go—that I am not in the condition—to be able to bear it

& I should probably fall ill there. I dont know what to do. How can I go by and never see his grave. I have *never* knelt by it. They are rather disturbed about my cough but I dont care about it myself. I would rather it got worse than better. I should *like* to die just as Boy did. It would make me almost happy. All the rest were careful of themselves but I used to lay my head on his pillow & hold him in my arms & kneel & sit alone by him for hours. I am not the sort of person to have consumption but if one can get it as they say I have every reason for having it. I am not the least depressed about that. They say I can go over to Paris from London when I am a little better. But there are times when I feel I *cannot* go round by Milan & not see him. I suppose you will see that I am all broken up & emotionally worn out until I am hysterical. I suppose I am. I know I feel emotional.

Good by poor boy.[11]

So confused had she become during this time that she lost the entire month of March, sending Vivian a cheque for his birthday a month early. She also sent him a box of his and Lionel's things from Paris before she left for Italy, and although Swan wrote to say that they arrived, Vivian was more delinquent in responding, causing her to worry that in her desire "to contrive things to make you happy . . . sometimes I am afraid I may make you selfish."[12] He readily agreed with this and went on to tell her that he was falling in love again—even as a small child he had loved the young ladies, and loved being in love—but later shocked her by asking if he could sell Lionel's bicycle and pocket the proceeds. Horrified, she wrote back, "my dear Vivvie, you did not stop to think or you would not have said it. One cannot sell or barter the things that have belonged to one made sacred by love & death. That would be too mercantile. All that he used or owned is sacred to me. Do you know that was a thing I should never want anyone to know you had said. More than ever it made me feel I ought to be with you. Dont become too utilitarian. Be tender—be fine."[13]

All her thoughts were of Lionel during these months in Italy, and she threw herself into paying tribute to him in her writing, in philanthropy, and in paying what she saw as her debt to Stephen Townesend for his gentle care of Lionel during his illness. In only some of these did she succeed. She worked on the manuscripts of two books based on his death, "The Friend" and "In a Fair, Far Country," stories she had begun in Paris, writing in the pre-dawn hours before devoting her day to Lionel's care and amusement. Now that he had died, she wanted to use these stories to come to terms with her anguish and pay tribute to him, to offer relief to others who had been through similar experiences, and to work out her beliefs about God and the afterlife. Most of all, she wanted to talk to Lionel. She began reading the Book of Revelation and found some comfort in thinking of him as an angel who could guide her and Vivian. "I feel as if I were writing a letter to you— 'To Lionel, in the Fair, Far Country.' And it seems quite natural to ask you to do things for me. Will you watch over Vivvie and take care of him. I can give him the things of earth, and if he has an angel brother to stand by him, his life must be beautiful. He is so clever and bright and gay. He needs a hand to guide and hold him." At other times she cried out on paper: "Darling, come near to Mammie! Love Mammie! Tell her what to do."[14] She never finished these books even though she laboured over them for years.

It was at this time that she began to formulate a vision of the afterlife and wrestle with her religious belief. Calling him "my Boy Angel," she envisioned Lionel walking in the "Far Country" or "Golden City," surrounded by white light, matured and wise for having passed on, for "surely if there is a God, He must be tender and you are not afraid of him. On earth one thinks, 'How could one speak to God!' *You* know how to speak. You are a shining, radiant creature with bright, swift, white wings."[15] She believed he sent her dreams of the beautiful place he now occupied. She called on him to advise her, asking him to "bend before the White Throne and say for me, 'Great, dear Father, my mother asks . . . that there may never pass by her, unknown, one kind, helpful thing she might have done for one who needed. However a little thing it may be, do not let her miss it. Help her always to see and help her to do her work so that she may always be able to give.'"[16] At other times she felt much less confident in God's existence and mercy, seeing the "impassable barrier" between those who lived and those who died as reason for doubt. Her inability to see or hear Lionel raised these uncertainties: "If there is a God, surely—surely he would be merciful and let us hear one sound—see one glimmer of light." She was horrified in September to read in the newspaper of the torture and murder of a five-year-old child. "I laid down the paper and gasped out, 'Suffer little children to come unto me and forbid them not, for of such is the Kingdom of Heaven.' Where was God? Darling, if you know, try to tell me. I want so to believe."[17] In her darkest moments she sat alone and wrote to Lionel, blaming God for her unhappiness: "Either there is no God—or He is as poor and weak a mockery as we. He cannot—*cannot* help us. And He must suffer too—too—to see our pain—and know he is not Godlike in his Power."[18]

Before she left San Remo, she encountered a boy about Vivian's age who sang under the hotel windows for the coins the foreigners threw down to him. Like Vivian, he loved singing, and he held himself in the same way as her younger son when he performed. Day after day she was drawn to her balcony to listen to him and to toss down francs wrapped in paper. One day she and Kitty encountered him in the street and called him over to them. In her fluent Italian, Kitty chatted with him and discovered that his name was Giovanni Calcagni. She told him that Frances had a son who sang Italian songs in America, so that Giovanni's singing gave her pleasure. Frances's story "Giovanni and the Other" grew directly out of her own life at that time. In it Kitty went by her given name, Gertrude; Vivian and Lionel became Geof and Leo; Frances herself was a mother in full mourning. She may have given the real Giovanni Calcagni little more than her appreciation and her coins, but in the story she sets him up in a musical career after tracking down and empathizing with the mother of another boy who ruined his voice and later died. When she returned to 44 Lexham Gardens in the spring, she finished the story and threw herself into helping other children.

She found London now a bleak place, even when sitting in the lovely Japanese Room that Luisa had decorated for her during her recovery from the accident, so "dark and foggy and dreary outside that though it is afternoon I am obliged to have the gas lighted."[19] She came down with the flu and found her depression deepening as she lay ill, the tears "stream[ing] down my face just as they did at first."[20] Soon after her return to England, Henry James, at that time, as Kitty put it, someone "whom she would naturally meet with self-possession and reserve," although they socialized and she had read to him in her early London days, paid a condolence visit to her at the Lexham Gardens house.[21] As she told him the story of her loss, he listened with such quiet sympathy that she broke down completely, weeping uncontrollably.

The only way out was through hard work. She began to revisit the children's hospital that Owen Lankester had shown her, helping an increasing number of poor, invalid children, providing for their medical care, and carrying books, fruit, flowers, and warm clothing to them. To one, a girl with a spinal deformity, she gave a specially designed carriage so that she could be wheeled outdoors. She sent a sick boy to a seaside nursing home. She paid the cost of nursing at St. Monica's Hospital for others. As she did with them all, she showed Nellie James, the girl to whom she'd given the carriage, Lionel's picture and told her that these were gifts from him.[22] On Lionel's "first birthday in the Fair Country," 20 September, she gave money towards the care of a sick girl who was in great pain. She found a woman suffering from tuberculosis, whose husband was unable to find work and whose five children were hungry; she sent them money for food and paid their rent until the husband could find a job, and began canvassing contractors to see if any of them could employ him as a bricklayer.[23]

Her biggest project by far, however, was the Drury Lane Boys' Club. It had started in the streets of the West End, where children roamed the streets alongside, and invisible to, the theatre-going crowd. Three boys got together and formed a small club that met a few nights a week, using the cellar of one's house as a meeting place. The boy, Andrew Buckingham, convinced his mother to sell the mangle stored there to make space for them, which she gladly did. The boys made rules and collected a few games with their six-penny dues, organized a few outdoor sports, and soon found themselves overwhelmed by other boys who wanted to join. They approached a woman named Frances, called "the Good Angel," and through her help gained access to the parish room of a church in Russell Court; the rector agreed on the condition that someone older supervise them during their evenings, and they were lucky to find a young man named Carlos Wilson to step in.

All this had taken place three years before Frances's current return to London. She promised them before she went away that she would continue to take an interest in them, but time passed without the chance: she had been away from London with her two boys, and then she spent a year nursing Lionel. By the time she was fully settled there again, the club had swollen to seventy-five members, and young Wilson was searching unsuc-cessfully for a larger place. A former factory building on Kemble Street was available, but the agents turned them down flat when they realized the building would be overrun with what they thought of as a swarm of slum boys. Frances intervened, using her name and prestige to gain the building, and then became absorbed in its renovation.

It was a modest building, and she was at first at a loss as to what to do with it. The basement was cement, the ground floor had unplaned timber floor-ing, and the top floor, only gained by means of a ladder, was surrounded with a series of low windows. She couldn't use carpeting or finished wooden floor-ing, because the boys' hobnailed boots would ruin them. She couldn't use upholstered furniture for the same reason. Decorating was her other métier, however, and these were intriguing problems. The cellar, covered with lino-leum, became a gymnasium with climbing ropes and vaulting equipment. The ground floor became a games room. Resigning herself to linoleum for the top floor, she visited Shoolbred's department store and found a thick one with the pattern of an inlaid floor. After having a small staircase built, she turned the room into the Lionel Reading Room, stocking it with books rec-ommended by her friends (Vivian, once again, was remiss about providing his list) and supplied as a gift by her London publisher Frederick Warne, and with copies of the *Illustrated News*. Lionel's portrait, along with one of a young woman who had helped with the club before her own early death, hung on the walls.[24] She approached influential people and found willing donors, including the young Victoria Mary, duchess of Teck, soon to marry King George, who wrote that Frances's "charming & interesting letter touched me deeply, how you must have suffered losing your dear child & I can well understand now what an intense happiness it must be to you to try & relieve poor little London children" and promised to send gifts of books, toys, and clothes.[25]

The official opening, held in the evening on 27 February 1892, made Frances nearly as nervous as the opening of one of her plays. The member of Parliament for the district, the young son of the founder of the W. H. Smith bookshops and stationers, attended, alongside the now grown Andrew Buckingham, Carlos Wilson, the "Good Angel," and all seventy-five boys. After a meal in the games room, they climbed to Lionel's room, where Frances gave a little speech, declared the room open, and shook hands with them as they filed out, each carrying a copy of a letter she'd written to commemorate the occasion. Downstairs they regaled her with cockney songs, little speeches, and music played on the old piano. Those leaving the theatres were treated to the sight of Frances, her arms full of bouquets, bundled off in her brougham by seventy-five cheering boys.

She undertook her other major act of charity in Lionel's name, but in this case as an obligation to be discharged rather than as a simple gift. Stephen Townesend, whom she referred to as Uncle Stephen, that ambiguous term mothers sometimes use for their male friends, felt that his life had taken all the wrong turns and that "he had not been allowed to do the one thing he felt he could do."[26] Although he never wanted to be a doctor, he had shown great tenderness as a nurse and companion to Lionel in Paris, and the boy had responded lovingly to him. Frances found Stephen highly strung, excitable, and prone to moods and worry, but because he had provided such exquisite comfort to her son in his final months, Frances believed she had to do something to save him. The one thing she could do was to provide a start to his theatrical career. He was an unknown actor to whom no producer in his right mind would give a starring role, so she resolved to bestow it all upon him herself: the play, the role, and the theatre, in the process taking on the role of producer. This project kept her exhaustingly busy, a condition made worse in early October when she sprained her ankle during a rehearsal at the Strand Theatre. Stephen helped her to write the play, *The Showman's Daughter*, the tale of a working-class man who manages to acquire money to keep his daughter in boarding school and allow her to come home to a splendid house. In true Burnett fashion, the now-grown daughter arrives home only to believe that the father who greets her is a servant. The play harked back in some ways to her story "Louisiana," whose protagonist asks her father to pretend he is a servant when she brings home a stylish young man and woman she met at a North Carolina resort.

This was not the first time Stephen's name had appeared with hers on a playbill as co-author. *Nixie*, the play taken from her children's book *Editha's Burglar* and for which they had left Lionel in Paris in April 1890, was produced in London's Terry's Theatre as a series of morning and afternoon performances, having been written by "Mrs. Hodgson Burnett . . . and Mr. Stephen Townesend."[27] The actual play of *Editha's Burglar* as submitted to the Lord Chamberlain's office bore little resemblance to the book. In both, Editha is nicknamed Nixie and has an encounter with a burglar. But that nugget is all that remains of the original story, which opens unsurprisingly in a Paris *pension*, with a young woman who has eloped with a man who promises to marry her; she nurses him for several weeks after he is shot, as it turns out, by his wife. Rescued by an older friend who marries her, the woman becomes Nixie's mother, and the rest of the play involves the return and rejection of her would-be seducer.

The production of *The Showman's Daughter* was a much riskier undertaking, both because the public expected familiar names in starring roles and because, as she wrote to Kitty, "there is much jealousy and spite among professionals, and, of course, the actors will all hate him before he does the part, and be ready to poison him when he has succeeded. But you can imagine how many chance speeches from outsiders crush him, or rankle."[28] She hadn't intended him to star (he originally took the juvenile role), but the actor originally chosen for the part proved so inappropriate that she gave Stephen his chance, although under the pseudonym of her Washington friend and lawyer Will Dennis. She also handed over to him much of her business dealings and secretarial work, as she had earlier to Swan and Luisa. Still, she wrote to Vivian, she seemed to do more in the way of taking care of him than the other way round. Even this early on, the warning signs were evident in his personality, and she was frank about these even to Vivian, although she tried to excuse them. "He is so delicate and nervous and irritable, poor boy," she wrote to Vivian. "But I have to remember when he seems to be unreasonable, that he was never anything but *perfect* to Lionel, and that he was his comfort and strength and beloved to the last minute. However angry he makes me I must always remember that." Then she added the rather ominous words, "You see he is the only person with an Englishman's temper that I ever knew. There was one thing we never had at our house, and that was tempers. It makes a great difference in the atmosphere."[29]

Although on her forty-second birthday in November the *New York Times* reported that she had fully recovered her health after her accident and Lionel's death, and was back at work, it was a difficult time for her.[30] Stephen's moods and neediness wore her down, and back in Washington, Vivian too was suffering. He wrote to her of his loneliness and depression, and wanted her to come home, a not unreasonable desire since not only had his only brother died but he hadn't seen his mother in more than a year. The house felt empty without her, made more so because many things were still in storage. She wrote back to him of her own unhappiness, telling him that London had lost its charms for her, that she had suffered too much, that there was much there in the way of poverty and suffering, and that she only remained there because of the play, which promised to bring in lots of money. She told him how much she missed him but at the same time chastised him for not sending her a list of his books for the Lionel Room, telling him that she always wore a locket with Lionel's picture inside, which she showed to everyone she helped. Still, she was worried about him. "Darling, Darling," she ended, "if you can just keep up your spirits until I have done this work about the play and can come to you I shall try never to be separated from you again."[31]

A few weeks later she tried to explain to him why the work that kept her away from him was so important.

I encourage myself by remembering what a difference I have been able to make in my boys['] lives by doing things like this. Do you realize how different you would have been if I had not been determined to do the best for you and make you happy. . . . You would have lived in a small house & worn shabby clothes, & would have spent your summers & winters in Washington. You would not have traveled and seen new countries, you would not have learned French & Italian & had printing presses & interesting life full of pleasures & changes. I have always given you the very *best* of all things—& I want to be able to give you every chance to make your life all it can be. I love you with all my soul & my life. And I cannot endure it when I think you are low spirited. Dear, just keep bright for Mammas sake. Is there anything you would like to do. I am going to write to Papa to ask him to have the things brought from Houghtons & the house made quite comfortable for the winter. Everything must look cheerful & you and Papa must look cheerful too. I am going to write a page or so every few days to tell you how things are progressing and I shall send you an occasional cable. When I got yours the other night I quite broke down. I shall send you a cable today so that you will not have to wait for my letter. I need to be cheered up myself.[32]

To Kitty she revealed more worry about Vivian than she let on to him. She confessed in a letter that Vivian's situation was uncomfortably similar to that of Lionel two years before, that "Vivian has written me two low-spirited letters and they kept me awake all night. It seems he has fits of depression when he fancies all sorts of things are the matter with him. It distracts me so to hear it, because that was what Lionel did the winter before he began to be ill. I nearly went out of my mind the night after I got Vivian's last letter. I *cannot* bear it if he gets ill."[33] She felt, as always, pulled in several directions, between her child and her work, and now between her responsibilities to her son and to Stephen. Her intention was to discharge her psychological debt to Stephen, launch him on the stage, and then return to America. Even so, she made no argument for why these two responsibilities had to be fulfilled in different countries, and why the decision was not made in favour of her lonely and now only child.

One obvious explanation is that she and Stephen may well, by now, have been lovers for some time. She was reticent about their relationship in her letters, but it is probable that her trip to England the previous year while Lionel was ill was as much to spend some time alone with Stephen as to launch *Nixie*. Now that she had allowed him into such intimacy and felt responsible for his happiness, she needed to see it through. Indeed, her attempt to push his stage career met with success. He would tour Britain in the role of the earl of Dorincourt in *The Real Little Lord Fauntleroy* in 1893, and other producers picked him up for roles after that. In 1893 he played the earl of Arlington in *The Black Domino* at London's Adelphi Theatre, before being chosen by Comyns Carr for the part of the solicitor in *Sowing the Wind* that autumn. The following year he rejected an offer to play another part in that play when it toured the provinces, choosing instead to remain in London in the small part of David Garrick in *Dick Sheridan* in 1894. He followed it with a play called *Frou-Frou*, taking first the role of the baron, and later the leading role, to good reviews. One good thing led to another, and Comyns Carr again approached him, this time to produce *The New Woman*, but Stephen had already accepted a part in the London production of *The Gay Widow* at the Court Theatre and, afterwards, good roles in plays at the Garrick Theatre and the Comedy Theatre. As far as Stephen's career was concerned, Frances had achieved her goal.

In this respect he could appear to have been simply another beneficiary of her generosity, but it is much more likely that she felt deeply attached to him as the only person—aside from the now-departed Luisa and the nurse—who had been with her when Lionel was dying. This was a bond shared with no one in America, and she was still suffering her loss badly. Still, she missed her remaining son and her other home. In compensation she took in a sick boy whose symptoms resembled Lionel's—coughing, weakness, and night sweats—and whose parents couldn't afford his medical care. He recovered enough for her to send him to South Africa, where he fully recovered. A newspaper clipping she sent to Vivian from Southport, where *The Showman's Daughter* had another trial run before its London opening, referred to this boy, Cecil Crossland, as her son.[34]

As the year wound to a close, and with it the first anniversary of Lionel's death, she was "nearly [driven] wild by Vivian's woeful little letter" that informed her he had received none of her letters. She and Swan had written back and forth about their son, and she sent Swan a picture of Lionel's grave, which he had never seen. She also sent him early reviews of the play, which had been tried out in Worcester. But Vivian, understandably, took her silence not as a post office error but as her desire not to return to him. Stunned, she responded that she wanted badly to be home and that if he wanted to join her he had only to cable.[35]

She suffered through the Christmas season with London swamped in a black fog so dense and acrid that the street lamps stayed lit all day and no one ventured out into the streets without gasping. She sent Vivian a long article she wrote on the Drury Lane Boys' Club to print up as a pamphlet in his homegrown Moon Press publishing venture, in addition to its later and wider publication in *Scribner's Magazine* as "The Story of a Beautiful Thing" in June 1894. Finally, on 6 January 1892, the play opened in London to good reviews.

Just as she felt she had fulfilled all her promises and could break away, Queen Victoria's grandson the duke of Clarence died. The country went into mourning, and the theatres virtually closed down from lack of patronage. Her theatre was already off the beaten path, in a location that had required weeks of advertising before any audience noticed it. With the gaiety taken out of a city in mourning, the play died a sudden death, and "everything," she wrote to Vivian, "is gloom."[36] At last, after two years away, she packed her bags and returned to Washington.

CHAPTER 13

∽

"GREAT LONDON
ROARS BELOW"

1892–1894

FRANCES ARRIVED IN NEW YORK on 10 March 1892, on the steamship *Teutonic* out of Liverpool. Like many winter crossings, this had been a difficult one, and she spent most of the time in her steamer chair and stateroom suffering from seasickness. The reporters who met her on the wharf found her looking decidedly ill, and she dismissed them in order to take to her bed at the Brunswick Hotel, leaving the next day for Washington.

Two days later she was comfortably ensconced in the 1770 Massachusetts Avenue house, where she willingly chatted with a journalist. Always careful to control her public image as much as possible, she paid the highest compliments to her adopted nation. Asked what she thought of London as a place to live, she immediately replied that it was not a home but "simply a place to which one should go for the season. That over, it at once became melancholy in the extreme, resolving itself into a desert, in which the streets and parks were so deserted one could walk or drive for miles without encountering a familiar face. She could not imagine any one who could possibly get away remained there through the Winter." She admitted that except for the past year, when her illness and Lionel's death had caused her to lead a quiet life, she had a wide and lively London social circle. She hoped to finish a new book soon and stressed that it was not a children's book. Asked whether she found play writing more lucrative than books, she immediately said yes, despite her recent difficulties with *The Showman's Daughter*; the profits from a book like *Fauntleroy* stretched out over a longer period of time but "could not be compared with those from the play of the same name." And in a nod to American playgoers, she stated that they were much more imaginative and emotional than their English counterparts.[1] Back in the house she shared with Swan and Vivian, she wanted them to believe that she was home.

The questions of home and family had become vexing ones since Lionel's death. Somehow her marriage to Swan managed to limp along in a fashion, at least publicly, despite another lengthy separation. They were both lonely, but whether they missed each other was another matter. Vivian, now about to turn sixteen, was no longer the small boy he used to be. "He is sixteen and a man," she wrote to Lionel. "Lionel is sixteen—and an Angel. . . . You will be sixteen always—You are, Lionel—sixteen—though you have been gone nearly two years. In that time Vivian has grown and changed so. He is so sweet and dear—but he has lost that touch of being my baby still—which you kept somehow—though you were my Big Boy and so stately. —If he had only kept that it would have been such a comfort to me. But I feel so lonely—lonely—lonely."[2] She sat in her old den at the top of the house, remembering when her boys used to tiptoe up to disturb her writing, recalling her sad return to Washington from Italy, when she had persuaded Lionel to sit on her knee and rest just as he had as a small child, and felt empty.

The solution lay in her earliest family, with whom she'd stayed in touch all these years even though she had seen little or nothing of them. Like her, they had their share of marital difficulties. Herbert's first wife, Ann, Swan's sister, had died years before. Leaving their son Edwin to be brought up by the Burnetts until he was old enough to join his father later, Herbert had re-married and now lived in Norfolk, Virginia, where he and his wife, Medora, were busily filling their house with children. Including his son Edwin from his first marriage, he had nine, naming them after family members and friends: Edwin, Frances Burnett, Frank Bridges, Vivian Burnett, Herbert, as well as Harry, Lillian, Alfred Eldridge, and Albert Edwin (named after the Prince of Wales). John George had become the ne'er-do-well their mother feared he might: in Knoxville he found more pleasure in drinking than in holding a steady job, and his wife, a South Carolinian from the wrong side of the tracks, took their small son, Bert Cecil, and moved across town in disgust. Teddy and Edith and their families were now living in California's Santa Clara County after many years in San Francisco.

Teddy's family had gone into ranching and farming, but Edith was less settled. After the death of her husband Pleasant Fahnestock in the smallpox epidemic and the months spent nursing her baby, Ernest, back to health, she had married the Frank T. Jordan who had shared a house with her and the Bridges in San Francisco. They later moved to Oregon, and this marriage was a happy one. Edith gave birth to a daughter whom they also named

Edith, whose prettiness and talent delighted them. Then, when she was only six years old, the little girl died suddenly from a burst appendix shortly before Lionel's death. Hoping they could comfort each other, Frances sent for her favourite sister, "and Edith's visit never ended."[3] Joined by her husband Frank, who hoped to find clerical work in Washington, Edith became from then on, for all intents and purposes, her sister Fluffy's other half. Frances installed them in a nearby house, paid for Edith's son Archie to attend college in California, and funded her younger nephew Ernest, who had great inventive talent in engineering. "My dear Ernest," she wrote on her thickly black-bordered paper, enclosing a cheque for one hundred dollars and telling him she was also sending him a cable to let him know it was on its way, "I do not like people to have to waste time in waiting which they might spend in being happy or comfortable. I hope the watch and picture reached you several days ago and that your friends beautiful eyes are watching you this very hour."[4] Lionel was, as always, credited as the benefactor.

The list of those depending on her charity grew. To a local eighteen-year-old boy whose parents would not help him make his way in the world, she wrote an encouraging letter. He came to visit and to tell her, "You don't know what that letter has been to me, and what it will be always," while clinging to her hand. A young woman told her of a friend trying desperately to find work, living alone and friendless; through her Frances sent a letter and a hundred dollars, although she didn't even know the young woman's name. The woman wrote back a passionate letter, saying, "You have saved me, you have saved me."[5] She wrote all of these tales to Lionel, desperate to help others in order to assuage her own misery. "I was always pitiful and wished to be gentle and helpful, but since you went away my life seems to have turned all into one broad, deep channel," she told him. "Always, always I am thinking, 'It all needs help so much. What can I do? What wound can I heal? Whose tiredness may I give a little rest to—however little.'"[6] Not all her attempts to help were successful, and there were those who tried to take advantage of her. "How is one to know what is right?" she asked Lionel. "Sometimes I feel like a naked, new born child, thrown among howling wolves."[7] Her friend Delia T. Davis remarked that "scarcely ever does the post arrive . . . without bringing her letters from unknown friends in the most remote corners of the earth. These letters are from people whom the writer has practically aided through some quiet, unobtrusive channel, and Mrs. Burnett is never too busy . . . to turn aside her labors and respond to any sincere human voice."[8]

Now, with Edith and Frank close by, a husband and son at home, she was able to return to her writing. Her book of autobiographical sketches was published by Osgood, McIlvane in England, under the title *Children I Have Known*. The *Athenaeum* gave it a mixed review, acknowledging its probable success but wishing that "Mrs. Burnett will be on her guard against tendencies dangerously akin to gush and verbal redundancy."[9] Frances paid scant attention to this, for she was now already well into a project begun before she left England, *The One I Knew the Best of All*, the story of her own childhood in Manchester told as the development of a young, inquisitive mind. Describing herself throughout as the "Small Person," she began it too as a sketch but found "the writing of it the most interesting work I have ever done."[10]

Scribner's was anxious to publish *Giovanni*, which she was enlarging after its publication in England, and she wrote to them about *The One I Knew the Best of All*. She had read some of it to Swan, who believed it should be published first as a magazine serial and then as a separate book; she was not so sure. Although it was about a child's mind, she did not view it as a story for children, believing that "only mature and thinking people . . . will get the real flavor of the humor & pathos of it. It is not the story of a life but a sort of study—from the *inside* of a growing infant mind."[11] Somehow it didn't seem right for *Scribner's*, and she was more inclined to sell it to a Philadelphia magazine that approached her for an article on how she got started as a writer, claiming that "they received thirty letters a day inquiring or thirty letters a week. This sketch will tell them how it happened, because that happened to be one of the incidents—in fact I thought of leaving the Small Person at her first accepted manuscript because it seems a good rounding off point—or rather exit—from the small stage to the larger one."[12]

Modern critics have noted that this book follows a developing tradition of child psychology begun with Wordsworth and the other Romantic poets, and growing in force at the fin de siècle. Frances was anxious to show, in scenes such as that of "the secrétaire," in which she climbed her father's shelves in search of stories, or the hours spent at the Hadfields' school telling the story of Edith Somerville, that the child's mind craved invention and imaginative writing. Yet she was also telling the story of a very Victorian childhood in England, where life seemed to be one of restriction, of her ultimate arrival in America, and of her embarking on a career as a writer while working out her theories about childhood. She developed some of this thinking in an unpublished fragment called "The Child of This Century":

> With the discovery of the world moving power of electricity—almost as though the one discovery had some remote connection with the other— has come the realization of the truth that a human mind is a mind from

its first hours, that it is never inert, that the earlier it is filled with beauty of image and thought the better for its being. Books for childhood and early youth have become literature, pictures for their illustration have become art. It is part of the evolution of the race that the dawning power which is the most august wonder of the world, the hourly evolving and outreaching mentality of the young human thing, should be given as part of its every day existence the opportunity to live in familiar companionship with the great friends of the world. . . . Visionary though it may seem to some, my own belief would be that a child whose earliest consciousness of sound was a consciousness of musical rhythm in the words lulling him to sleep or peacefulness might be led into fair places because life had begun for him with harmony and mysteriously melodious things.[13]

She was visiting England regularly and for long enough to think a great deal about her early life there. Her avowal that London was unwelcoming and Washington home was undermined by the fact that she was spending longer and longer stretches of time in England, and less and less in America. More interestingly, although it made perfect sense that her story of a mind should conclude with the public success of its main character, the moment of that success was the demarcation between her childhood and her adulthood, between being a schoolgirl and a breadwinner. The book (and her childhood) came to an end when she was at an age not much greater than that at which her own child died. From her den she wrote to Lionel, "today I have been writing a chapter about my first memory of Death. —My last memory of Death is so different."[14]

Scribner's was wild to get the story, and sent one of its editors, Edward Burlingame, down to Washington to bargain with her when they discovered that *McClure's* had already made an offer. In the end, they gained the serial but on Frances's terms. Knowing her propensity to turn in longer work than expected, the magazine promised to let it overrun the proposed limits and to pay her for the additional work. Writing from his hotel room at the Shoreham in Washington, Burlingame told Mr. Scribner that he and Frances had come to an agreement: "$3,000 if the completed story remains within four instalments of 10,000 words or so each; $3750 if it goes further. Of course I discount the first possibility (though she recurs to it *as* a possibility, & says she has a definite plan which she shall not overrun), and look upon the agreement as virtually $3750 for a five-part serial." Even though the *McClure's* offer was higher, she preferred to work with Scribner's, "so we get the story; & at all events with the advantage of the most cordial feeling on her part."[15]

The serial was to be completed in six weeks, but her business dealings with Scribner's were not over. When the contracts for *Giovanni and the Other* arrived, she had second thoughts about the 12 per cent royalties they offered. Warne, her English publisher, gave her 15 per cent for the book; why should Scribner's not do the same? They protested and she capitulated, her joy in writing about the Small Person offering, for the moment, plenty of compensation. "She is behaving like a dear, but my interest in her has been so great that she has led me into indiscretions. I want to write about her all day & have been adding to the number of hours of work so recklessly that three days ago, having written steadily from nine o'clock in the morning until six at night with only about fifteen minutes for lunch, I rather went to pieces. *C'etait imbecile de ma part*! I ought have known I shall be more careful. I must go to the sea."[16]

Soon, in Washington's June heat, she wrote to Lionel that she was packing up her papers to move to Marshall Cottage in Swampscott, on the Massachusetts coast, for the summer. The last time she'd gone there she had stayed in the town of Nahant, preparing a place for the boys to join her for the summer; this was a bittersweet return, as she recalled their joy when they arrived a few days after her, full of tales of their journey and revelling in the orchards, flowers, hammock, and sea. She remembered that "as we walked under the trees I said, 'Do you like it, sweethearts? Are you happy?' And you danced and laughed and hugged me and kissed me and said, 'Yes, indeed, dearest. We are so happy as we can hold.'" Now, "it makes me so homesick to remember it—so homesick for my two little boys—my little lads."[17] Despite this she found the summer to be a joyful and productive one. She managed to finish *The One I Knew the Best of All*; she was certain that it was with Lionel's help and thought it "a very real & interesting thing. . . . I wonder if it is absurd to feel as pleased with ones own work as I am with this piece of mine."[18] In the summer's warmth, having in a sense revisited and reconstructed the path of her early years, she began to return to life.

Vivian, who was with her, had to amuse himself without a brother's companionship. "I have been doing absolutely nothing," he wrote to Swan. "I take pictures, walk on the sands and come back and take pictures again. At present that is all there is to do. I don't know intimately one girl or boy of my age in the place yet somehow or other I am not having such a miserable time."[19] Frances brought a guitar, and he had a banjo; when Kitty Hall arrived she gave him guitar lessons, and the three of them sat on the veranda in the evenings playing their instruments and singing. They went rowing and visited the towns of Marblehead and Gloucester. Swan, lonely in the deadness of the Washington summer, came for a visit, as did a Washington friend of Vivian's. As the summer wound down and the seasonal visitors returned to their homes, Frances and Vivian found it less lively. He returned to Washington, and she went to Boston to stay with the Halls, whose house contained "a continual atmosphere of transatlantic traffic at 206 Dartmouth Street. Somebody is always either being welcomed from London or said good bye to on his or her way there. Either Fluffy is emigrating with all her family, or just coming back, or Kitty is going to Fluffy, or Daisy is leaving or arriving or Hayden is leaving or the Bayleys are coming or some of the score of others who vibrate between the shores are on their way to one side or the other."[20]

One of those "vibrating between the shores" was Stephen Townesend, who saw her in Boston in September before sailing back to England from New York. *The Showman's Daughter* had been touring the English provinces all summer, but Stephen spent the summer of 1892 in America. It is not clear on what footing they stood with each other or with her friends, nor how often they saw each other. Because her home was technically with Swan and Vivian in Washington, she felt free to mention his visit to her son. It begins to appear that she had a "husband" on each shore. In Washington, Swan was once again handling her correspondence with her publishers, just as Stephen had in England. Most likely is that she and Swan had come to some sort of agreement in which they were publicly married and privately free. Swan, however, was increasingly lonely and wished for a real marriage, if not with her then with someone else. He would hang on to what he had with Frances for as long as possible, but there were indications, as she confessed later, that if this marriage could not be salvaged he wanted to marry again. Shortly after Stephen left for England, Frances went back to Swampscott to close the cottage and returned to Washington for the autumn and winter, where she busied herself with the demands of the new books, commissioned a portrait of Lionel by a young artist, and was cheered by the fact that *Dolly*, her old novel about her days in Vagabondia, was published by Warne in England in December, receiving rave reviews in *Punch* and elsewhere, regarded there as an entirely new book from her popular pen.[21]

The young artist she chose to paint Lionel was Harry Franklin Waltman, and her taking him on was another of her "fairy stories." Born in rural Ohio in 1871, he was orphaned at eleven and indentured for five years on his uncle's farm, spending only four months a year in school. At the end of that time he was presented with fifty dollars—ten dollars for each year of work— but somehow, despite knowing nothing whatsoever about art, he decided that he wanted to be a painter. Another Ohio native, the painter Simon Jerome Uhl, gave a local lecture on painting as he passed through on his way home to Washington, D.C. With only a few dollars in his pocket, young Waltman took a train east and on his first night showed up at Uhl's Washington studio. Uhl took pity on the boy and let him sleep in the studio and gave him lessons, but Waltman still needed to support himself. At first he went door to door asking for work so that he could "study art," which netted him little but suspicion. He finally took a job crushing rocks for roads, the only white person in the crew.

When Frances heard this story from Uhl, she immediately wrote a cheque for a hundred dollars to help support the boy. "Do not let him thank me," she told him. "If he is shy, it would only make him feel awkward. Do not let him feel that he must even write to me. Simply say to him that I am sailing for Europe in a few days, and this is to give him the chance to work at the thing he cares for so much."[22] Indeed she did go away for three years during Lionel's illness and after his death, and forgot about her kindness to Waltman; it was just another in her string of sympathetic philanthropies. When she returned to Washington, she attended an exhibition of the work of Washington artists and exclaimed over one of the paintings. Informed by one of the artists that it was done by her protégé, she had no idea whom he meant. "'Why!' said the artist, 'the young man you saved from despair three years ago. Don't you remember young Waltman?'" She immediately bought the painting, hanging it in the hallway of 1770 Massachusetts Avenue. Waltman, who went on to be a celebrated portrait and landscape painter, later wondered, "I knew nothing of Mrs. Burnett, nor she of me. Why did she do it? I only know that that $100 was worth more to me then than $50,000 in gold would be to-day. I lived upon it a whole year, and it put me on my feet."[23]

Still, late autumn was a difficult time for her, despite all the signs of improvement in her mood. She turned forty-three in November but paid scant attention to her own birthdays, especially now that they signalled the approach of the anniversary of Lionel's death. Three days after her birthday she wrote to him, "Soon, my Pet, you will have been away from earth two years. In ten days more will come that morning when I whispered in your ear, "Sleep well—wake up refreshed—God bless Boy."[24] She kept a copy of Tennyson's *In Memoriam* by her bedside, understanding his elegiac poems as she never had before. Even if she couldn't cope with her novel about Lionel's last months, her work seemed to flow more easily. In Swampscott she had wondered if he was "standing by me now and reading over my shoulder as I write? Read this—You have helped Mammie in the divinest way! It is better than anything else. To help me to work—to show me how, will be to help all those who read—because you give me such beautiful thoughts. I feel as if my mind had changed and grown since you have been helping me. It has. Once I used only to *feel* and *imagine*. Now I *think*. —I really believe I do, and that all my work will be of finer quality."[25] Her confidence, and that of Scribner's, in the new work was not misplaced. The first instalment of *The One I Knew the Best of All* appeared in January, and she was bombarded with letters from enthusiastic readers.

Her only excursion that fall was a short trip to Chicago—most likely to do with preparations for the upcoming World's Fair—and, always one to get the most mileage out of her published work, once again she was writing and recycling her children's stories into books now coming out at the rate of one a year. In 1891 she published *Little Saint Elizabeth*, with the lead story about a small girl whose ability to live fully was limited by a strict religious up-bringing; the others were "Little Prince Fairyfoot," "The Proud Little Grain of Wheat," and "Behind the White Brick," all of them *Saint Nicholas* re-treads. In 1892 *Giovanni and the Other* appeared, the autobiographical vol-ume about actual children she had known in Tennessee, England, and Italy, expanded from its earlier English version. *The One I Knew the Best of All* came out in early 1893 as a serial and late in the year as a book. Already she was at work on the stories that would appear as an 1894 American book *Piccino and Other Child Stories*, allowing a magazine called *Romance* to reprint her 1877 story "The Captain's Youngest" and then discovering that they had left off the final paragraphs. "I am an amiable little person and not in the least given to laying stress on myself," she fired off in a letter to the publisher, "but I can scarcely tell you how cross it made me when I saw my dear little story—old as it is—robbed of that last thought which seemed to me absolutely necessary to complete it."[26] These compilations served as Christmas books, reliable sellers when they appeared at the holiday gift-buying season, and an important source of income for her.

It may be this old story from *Peterson's* that inspired her to put together the *Piccino* book, and the volume itself seems to hold the germ of *The Secret Garden*, a book seventeen years and many experiences farther down the road. "Piccino" tells the story of a little Italian boy near San Remo who is taken from his peasant family by a spoiled Englishwoman but escapes her unwelcoming villa of perpetual baths and bland food to return home. "The Captain's Youngest" is about a boy named Lionel, born in India to a care-less family that leaves him to be raised by his ayah and an English servant; he later dies in London trying to save his eldest sister Rose from dishonour. The final story, "Little Betty's Kitten," told from the kitten's point of view, is about a little girl who befriends the creature and then is taken ill and dies. In assembling these stories in 1893 for a new book, she put together three stories about a child's return to a family home, English children in India, and sick children, two of whom died.

As spring approached, she kept more publicly busy than she had for several years. The Boston Press Club gave her a reception, one of her first public appearances since Lionel's death; similarly, she read to Washington's Literary Society. She engaged a French tutor and was asked to send a set of her books to the World's Fair in Chicago. The Columbian Exposition was to be a dazzling tribute to international progress and beauty, with white buildings housing exhibitions on agriculture, technology, art, and various countries, on the shores of Lake Michigan. The Woman's Building, under the direction of Bertha Potter Palmer, designed by a female architect, Sophia Hayden, and put together entirely by women, paid tribute to the achievements, public and domestic, of women. It was an attempt "to instruct men as to the work and importance of women" and featured conservative speakers and displays along with such feminist speakers as Elizabeth Cady Stanton, Jane Addams, and Susan B. Anthony.[27] The building included a large library display, with one case devoted to the forty-seven editions and translations of Stowe's *Uncle Tom's Cabin*, and a collection of the works of major women authors.[28]

As one of the world's most popular living women writers, Frances was asked to contribute a set of her works, but she did not take this as the honour it was doubtless intended to be but rather as one in a series of requests. Her apparent annoyance seemed to lie more in the fact of a building devoted to womanhood than with anything else. "Will you please send a complete set of my books to Miss Emily J. Wilkins 1709 Mass. Avenue Washington," she wrote to Scribner's. "It is in response to one of those endless demands that one should send some of oneself to some Womans Department of Something at the Worlds Fair. I have grown so tired of Woman with a capital W though I suppose it is the rankest heresy to say so. I dont want to be a Woman at all. I have begun to feel that I want to be something like this 'WOMAN.' Nevertheless if every body is sending books I must send mine."[29]

On display at the Exposition were *A Fair Barbarian*, both series of *Earlier Stories, Giovanni and the Other, Haworth's, Little Lord Fauntleroy, Little Saint Elizabeth, Louisiana, The Pretty Sister of José, Sara Crewe, Surly Tim and Other Stories, That Lass o' Lowrie's, Through One Administration*, and *Vagabondia*.[30] Despite her reservations about the woman issue, she couldn't ignore the fact that the whole world was flocking to the fair and that everyone was writing about it. Two years later she took it as her subject for another book, *Two Little Pilgrims' Progress*, which took its form and theme from Bunyan's story.

She was approached about contributing to a book of World's Fair stories in October 1894 by a Chicago writer named Eugene Field, and as so often happened with her, the story she planned to contribute, about orphaned twins who save their money and run off to the City Beautiful, grew too long for the volume and appeared as a book in its own right. The twins spend three days touring all the buildings, some of them more than once. The Woman's Building is never mentioned, but this now-forgotten story came in for high praise when it was published.

She was also embarking on more experimental and humorous writing in the form of letters in the style of Samuel Pepys and the *Tatler*, writings with an eighteenth-century flavour that were the result of a dare by a friend, who challenged her to write exactly as she talked. Frances "had a habit of half-finishing a sentence, skipping to the next and the next, then weaving back to finish, at least partly, the original thought she had in mind. One picked up her thoughts with careful concentration, as if they were dropped stitches." Some of her friends went so far as to call her "the Crimson Rambler," with good reason.[31] These unpublished pieces referring to an unidentified "Sir Anthony" give a sense of her rambling conversational style, in which she often allowed herself to run off on tangents.

I am now engaged in a most interesting and distracting occupation. I chance to know you have never engaged in it so I will tell you something of it in case it is a later experience. Stationed on this side of the Atlantic I am endeavoring to engage by proxy exactly the kind of furnished house I want for the season—or the summer—in or near London. Sir Anthony—poor dear—is good enough to do all such things as these for me. Can you imagine his responsibilities and his feeling of deep affection for me at times? I really try not to be vague and bewildering and feminine, but it really is difficult to exhibit an intelligent clearness and decision about places one has never seen, when one is at the mercy of steamer mail. And then, you know, I am that most touching of all spectacles—a Mayfair beggar. My tastes and my purse are totally incompatible. They had grounds for divorce years ago. Possessing an income of a certain number of thousands a year, my modest necessities could only be properly supplied by an *un*certain number of hundreds of thousands. It must simplify matters so to be a multi-millionaire.[32]

All this was based on a real endeavour: even before leaving Washington that spring of 1893, Frances was making plans to engage a summer home in the English countryside as well as a more permanent residence in London.

With spring's advent, Frances made plans to return to England with Edith, to spend the summer in the country and the social "season" in London, making no plans for a return to America. Vivian was now within a year or so of entering college, and with her sister by her side, Frances expected that her son would continue to spend his summers with her wherever she chose to live. Having Edith with her made a return to England truly feel like a return to home, and Edith arranged—much like Frances but for different reasons—to leave her husband in Washington while she ventured abroad to the country where she had grown up. On 16 May the two sisters set sail for England on *The Lahn*, intending a long stay.

They took a cottage, The Glade, at Long Ditton Hill in Surrey, near Hampton Court, for the summer. Vivian joined them later and spent the summer travelling around England at his mother's generous expense. Perhaps because she'd spent so much time away over the past several years, even though she had remained in Washington for a long stretch this time, this summer was the beginning of a five-year period of what modern parents would view as spoiling her son. Try as she might to keep him on a budget, her long-standing declaration of turning her sons into gentlemen had its obvious result: Vivian adored her but came to expect a life of privilege. Staying at the Kings Arms Hotel in Christchurch, he wrote to her in September in frustration that the trunk she'd sent on to him after his stay with her in Surrey had not yet caught up with him. "Having been invited out to garden parties teas and lunch innumerable I am forced rather to forgo these amusements or disgrace myself," he pouted. "These last two days I have disgraced myself and gone. Necessity has forced me to spend 11 shillings on a flannel shirt and belt so that I may look presentable at the garden party, or rather tennis party."[33] Two days later he received the trunk and a cheque from her, "neither of them a bit too soon." When his hotel bill fell due, he asked her to send him a blank cheque.

This summer Frances found herself with another charitable cause. A young Englishwoman living in Washington had been abused and deserted by her husband. Her mother-in-law, who took their children in, turned them against their mother, who had fallen deathly ill with pneumonia. Frances had tracked down the woman's son and persuaded him to cable his mother, an act that turned the tide for the woman and which Frances claimed had brought the woman back to life. Now in England, Frances contemplated bringing them together and sending them off to Scotland or Switzerland.[34]

By early autumn, with Owen Lankester's assistance, she had found a house: 63 Portland Place was an elegant, high-ceilinged, and impressive affair next to the Chinese embassy and a short walk to Regent's Park. With this house it became clear she had found the place that suited her station in life; far from being a "Mayfair beggar," her tastes and her purse were fully in alignment. She and Edith spent months furnishing and decorating it, a statement that this was to be her real home, and that London was in fact to be her primary residence for some time even though she would need to return to Washington for the winter. Before that, during the summer and autumn, she wrote a long article on *Fauntleroy's* genesis, "How Fauntleroy Really Occurred," exposing Vivian's role in that already maligned story just as he was preparing to go out into the world as a young man. Much as he loved her, he found it hard to forgive this slur on his manhood, which was destined to follow him to the end of his life. The piece appeared in the December 1893 issue of *Ladies' Home Journal* just as he, his mother, and aunt returned to Washington on the *Paris* out of Southampton, and he began to prepare for his university entrance exams. To his cousin Ernest in California she sent a different kind of remembrance: "You are my boy for always and you are going to be one of the men of the Twentieth Century. You are, my dear," she wrote to him to offer encouragement. "In 1994 someone will write a book with a little something like that, and Ernest Fahnestock will be in it."[35] His brother Archie was due to join his mother and stepfather in Washington, and Frances was already thinking how to prepare him professionally as well.

She spent an uneventful winter in Washington, and in May returned to England and the new house. She was relieved to get a cheque for more than two thousand dollars from Scribner's, since "I rather expect to find the new house at Portland Place waiting for me with open maw like a giant whose only diet is coin of the realm."[36] An unpublished piece written the previous summer showed how much London had replaced Washington as the home of her heart:

I wonder if entrance into Waterloo Station awakens in others the glow of emotion it arouses in me. Once in Waterloo Station—or in Paddington or Charing Cross for the matter of that—one is so wholly in England— in London. The smoke, the busy air of things, the guards opening and shutting with a bang the railway carriage doors, the porters in corduroy hurrying about with trucks loaded with luggage, the peculiar odor which it is my habit to call "the London smell" and which combines asphalt and dust dampened by water cars, and smoke and all sorts of things—somehow all seem to constitute a sort of welcome and congratulation on a voyage past and done with. At least, that is how they affect me. . . .

Now I love Trafalgar Square, especially when I am just fresh from New York—that great, splendid, paved space with its stone balustrades, its benches for tramps and tired passers by, its fountains where the children play, its statues and its Nelson column with Lord Nelson and the lions unmovedly presiding over splashing water, playing children, sleeping tramps, riots or socialistic meetings—and great London, always sweeping by night and day—night and day.

What a huge Leviathan of life it is—this London. How it toils and schemes, sobs and sighs, laughs and plots, sins and struggles, and is never at rest—its big pulse never ceasing its heavy throbs!

One hears it throbbing as soon as one sets foot in it. As I went up the steps of the hotel I was murmuring something to myself.

"What did you say?" Sir Anthony asked. "Beg pardon, I could not hear. There is such a row in this part of the town."

I laughed. "That was what I was thinking of," I said, "I was quoting unconsciously a line of a song I once heard about a little Roundhead Maid who said beside her window.

> She sits beside her window,
> Great London roars below."

"'Great London roars below' I was saying, but I did not know I spoke aloud."

"It *is* rather a roar," remarked Sir Anthony in his moderate British way which does not seize upon the figurative or romantic with eagerness, "Trafalgar Square does differ from Kensington."

"I like it," I answered. "At least, I like it today."[37]

No matter how much she loved America and required both countries, it was her native country that now came first in her allegiance.

CHAPTER 14

~

THE NEW WOMAN

1894–1896

FOR THE FIRST TIME IN YEARS, when she left Washington for London in May 1894, Frances did so with peace of mind. Edith and Frank were now installed in the Massachusetts Avenue house, watching over Vivian and her rooms, and she no longer had what she called "the old dismal going away." Their presence in Washington was particularly important to her now that Vivian needed to spend the summer studying and sitting for his entrance exams for Harvard. Sometimes prone to nervous excitement, he was more likely to remain relaxed in his aunt and uncle's reassuring presence. "We miss you so much dear mammy," Vivian wrote to his mother several weeks after her departure. "I don't know what we would do if it were'nt [*sic*] for Aunt Edith."[1] Swan too found them competent and calming, especially now that he had begun to have some sort of alarming but temporary spasms. But Frances wished Edith and Frank could accompany her to England as well as remain in America, awaiting her arrival on both sides of the Atlantic. "Thank you dears for all you are to me. You dont know how I value it & love you both. Your price is above rubies," she wrote to them from her hotel in New York as she prepared for her crossing.[2]

The Massachusetts Avenue family circle increased again when Edith's son Archie Fahnestock moved back East after completing his college studies in California. Vivian took to him immediately, finding him to be an impressive and graceful figure, well dressed and manly, even with an "intangible western atmosphere"; he decided that "altogether he is quite the boy I should like for my cousin."[3] Three and a half years after his older brother's death, Vivian now found Lionel's shoes beginning to be filled by Edith's two sons, and they were destined to be close for the rest of their lives. Once he had completed his exams and was waiting to hear the results, he took stock and decided that things were looking up: his mother was writing again, and publishers were wrangling over the rights to her children's stories. She had taken for the summer a vicarage covered with roses and vines in Haslemere, and she was happier now than she had been in years. This was a great relief to Vivian, who had longed for the clouds over her to lift and "for the day when [she] would enjoy things again."[4]

This ease lasted only three months. In mid-August the axe fell again when Frances received a telegram from Washington: Vivian had contracted typhoid fever and lay in bed near death. Typhoid, like malaria a scourge of early Washington, struck even the strongest. Those who were run-down seemed to fall prey to it in surprising numbers. With resignation rather than panic this time, and with an accepting numbness, Frances wrote to Zangwill and her other friends to break engagements, booked a ticket on the next ship for New York out of Liverpool, and faced what seemed inevitable with a fatalistic certainty that the Power was surely about to take from her the thing that mattered most.

Zangwill, writing back from the Isle of Wight where he was spending the summer working on a book, warned her that "whatever has happened, you best be strong and of good courage."[5] She took this advice to heart when she sat down to write to Lionel, just before she left England for Vivian's bedside.

> My darling! I thought this morning that you must be near me. I have been passing through such deep waters and suddenly early in the morning a strange hopefulness came to me—a sort of feeling that all this was noth-ing and that Outside there was Something that cared for me after all. I am going back to Vivian as I went back to you from Rome five years ago. . . . Darling, I have learned so well how to suffer. I wonder if you know if he is coming to you. If he is—well, you know—I don't. Only, my dearest, if that last moment comes to him as it came to you—stand close beside his bed and let him see you smiling, just as he used to when you were little fellows playing together. I am going to America in two days. Be near me, Boy darling. Help your own Mammie. I have loved you so, dearest.[6]

Several weeks before Vivian fell ill, Ida, Swan's cook, told Edith that she had seen Lionel sitting on the porch beside Vivian and took this as a omen of some kind. Frances was willing to believe this; "perhaps it is true that these people with negro blood see things we do not. One hears it said so. And I am always so glad when I am told anything that has any air of truth and makes the veil seem thinner."[7] Just before Frances arrived two weeks later in

New York harbour on the *Britannic* and made her way down to Washington by train, the doctors and nurses had given up hope. Vivian had lain in bed gasping and drenched with fever while they worked to save him.

By some miracle he survived. She found him pale, thin, and weak, but alive and on the mend. Even so, Vivian's near escape from death reopened her barely healed scars over Lionel's loss. As with all the events in her life, the reporters were there to publish her "delight" at Vivian's recovery, but they could not know just how ghastly the experience had been.[8] She thought she saw Lionel everywhere, in the faces of small boys on the streets in Washington, in a teenager she'd glimpsed at Waterloo Station before her return to America. Whenever this happened she was swept by a "wild, homesick longing" that wrenched her, even as she felt relief and joy at Vivian's narrow escape.[9] She sat in her old den and spread her manuscript of "His Friend" on her desk and tried to make sense of it all. She believed that had Vivian been meant to die, nothing the doctors could do would have saved him, that their "science and struggles were all superfluous." Where was the sense of dragging another helpless boy through this misery, she wondered? "I am a poor, mistaken, wretched thing, but it is only because I *do not* know."[10]

By late September he was well enough to go out on drives with his mother, but starting Harvard, which had offered him a place, seemed out of the question for the time being. Frances and Vivian thought he might be well enough to enroll later that autumn, although Swan thought it was too risky and preferred that he remain home some months longer to build up his strength. As a tentative step, Vivian and his mother travelled to Boston in October, staying with the Halls and meeting with university officials in Cambridge. They agreed that he could begin in November or December with a lightened academic load, as a freshman. Signs of his recovery came in the fact that she needed to scold him—as she would throughout his four years at the university—for his "selfishness" in some breach of social etiquette, for putting his own desires ahead of the promised visits, or bread-and-butter letters thanking his hosts, or other rituals expected of those of his class. "I do not think you are naturally selfish, Vivian but you have been put first so much all your life that you may be in danger of forgetting to put others first now that you have reached the age when your turn begins," she chided him. She reminded him again how carefully she'd worked to put him into the class of young men of breeding and privilege, and trusted that she could "leave the rest to you. I always have felt that I could leave things to your own honor & manliness when you once saw a point in the right light. You are never wrong. You are like a house built on a firm foundation & on the right plans."[11]

She remained in Boston near him during these first months, and they returned to Washington together for the Christmas holidays. She arranged to leave for London as soon as he went back to the university in January. Even then he fell short of her training by failing to write home that he'd arrived safely, only sending a note to Frank asking him for a favour. Frances decided to send him a copy of Lord Chesterfield's letters to his son and use them as a model for her own instructing letters, to help him to avoid "the mistakes it is so easy—and almost natural—for young creatures to make." Without irony, she added, "Darling, I never lecture or upbraid. I have too keen a sense of justice and also of *humor* to do either. I have just called your attention to this and as I believe in your character very much I shall not say more about it." She reminded him to write to his father once a week.[12]

With Vivian now well and set upon his path, Frances devised another educative plan, one that was both surprising and generous. Although Vivian had had every opportunity to gain polish and position, Edith's sons had not. Archie, who was now living in Washington, had rough edges that Frances felt needed smoothing. Unlike Vivian, who spoke with an Anglicized accent that his mother had drummed into him, Archie had a western twang, no exposure to "culture," and no real vocation. Frances said that she had "struck him dumb with joy & gratitude" by proposing to take him to London with her. Her plan was to send him to a business school, hire a tutor for him in French and other areas, and get him some unpaid experience in an English firm, which would generally fit him up for a more gentlemanly career in America. She wanted him to "learn the things which will fit him for business—to write and speak correctly, to bear himself well & to know the simpler rules of social life. He is so desperately humbly conscious and so determined to do his very best that I believe he will surprise his mother by what he will accomplish. To my mind it is the most interesting psychological experiment. . . . I am almost as happy as Archie in the thought of this. I believe I shall find comfort in him as a companion. He is such a good fellow & so faithful."[13] Like Eliza Doolittle entering Henry Higgins's house, he was kitted out with a new wardrobe and all the accoutrements Frances considered appropriate to a gentleman's life: a thick overcoat, suits and linen handkerchiefs, brushes, and a travelling rug, all to be carried in a new steamer trunk. And just as well, for when they boarded the ship their fellow passengers included a Vanderbilt and an Astor, and he quickly saw the company into which he might aspire to move.

It was one thing to look the part and quite another to become it. His Aunt Fluffy arranged for him to be tutored daily by Erroll Sherson in English, history, and French, which he studied hard despite his terrible pronunciation.

She also enrolled him in Sir Isaac Pitman's Metropolitan School to learn bookkeeping. He was determined to succeed out of sheer willpower and hard work. She found his mind "so singularly crude and not at all brilliant" but chalked this up to the fact that he had been "surrounded by and steeped in that besotted ignorance from his earliest childhood." She couldn't help comparing his upbringing and education to that of Vivian and Lionel and referred repeatedly over the coming years to the fact that her sons had been raised on a plan she devised for them and which cost her dearly in terms of her public image and private life. "You are a temple that I am building," she wrote to Vivian when she arrived in London. "I want to build it high and adorn it perfectly."[14] Archie was to find his transformation as difficult as Doolittle's but ultimately more lucrative than Vivian's: like his illustrious travelling companions, he too would die a millionaire in New York.

Despite her improved spirits, by the time she arrived back in London Frances's own economic situation worried her. As a writer whose financial success depended as much on the next publication and play as on the continued royalties from earlier ones, she began at this time to worry incessantly about money and was desperate to keep the publishing wheels turning. She spent her money as quickly as it came in, and sometimes before it came in, both to help others and to keep up her two enormous houses, whose voracious appetites required that they be furnished, heated, and staffed. She made ill-considered business and personal loans to those she foolishly trusted, and sometimes she found herself borrowing against her royalties or even, short of cash, stopping into her publishers' offices to ask for small loans to tide her over. She and Swan worked out a system of paying for Vivian's forthcoming university expenses, with Swan's contribution amounting to far less than hers and given with his explicit refusal to bail his son out should he follow the eternal pattern of young university students and get himself into debt. In America it was Swan, Vivian, Edith, and Frank who wrestled with the questions of finances, particularly in terms of living expenses; in England, Frances, Stephen, and Archie pored over her accounts and prospects to try to maximize her income and minimize her debt. At issue was Frances's ability to finance two enormous houses, support her son in an expensive university life, and pay for her own luxuries, all without any immediate income prospects on her part but with the reality of mounting expenses.

Clearly she was living beyond her means with no reliable source of income. It wasn't simply a matter of frivolous spending; she was now supporting the Washington house by herself, for Swan had moved out, at last, to a place of his own near Farragut Square. In that house she supported Edith and Frank, although Frank worked at a variety of "promising" jobs. She was supporting Archie in London, Vivian at Harvard, subsidizing Stephen by asking him to handle certain business matters for her and preparing to take one of her plays to Chicago, and offering help to various poor acquaintances. When Edward Burlingame of Scribner's arrived in London, she lost no time in contacting him—he commented that she found him out only hours after he checked into Brown's Hotel—and asking him to meet her on a matter of great importance. When he went to Portland Place, she at once proposed that Scribner's buy her nearly finished novel, *A Lady of Quality*, as a serial.

Although she began the novel in Washington, the Portland Place house inspired it, and she wrote most of the book in England. Frances referred to this house as a giant of a dwelling, even bigger than the one at 1770 Massachusetts Avenue in Washington. Her initial task had been to subdue its grandeur into something more comfortably livable, transforming its formal interior into gentler focal points of soft furnishings and utility, with fewer allusions to the aristocracy. "I want to use these big drawing rooms until they are so filled with the atmosphere of being lived and talked and thought in that they will no longer wear stately airs and graces and suggest that they are great & lofty & that they were built a century ago, have been inhabited by the characters in the stories of that celebrated author Debrett and have ceilings and & doors golden decorated by Adams," she told Vivian. "I have treated them from the first, in fact, in the most artful manner. I think they at first suspected disrespect on my part but now I think they are rather pleased with themselves & appreciate their own attractions." Their height and size must have caused visitors to feel that "each room represented journeys & perhaps awful perils. A discreet person would make his will before going from the front to the back drawing room."[15]

It was in some ways a terrifying house, bitterly cold in winter, full of long corridors upstairs and unwelcoming receiving rooms downstairs, and what seemed like miles of dark and terrifying cellars below stairs. Frances delighted in leading her guests into these depths in the evening by candlelight. "We went on and on and on, getting further and further underground. Over our heads was the dull, unceasing roar of the London streets," recalled her old Washington friend Elizabeth Elliot, who was visiting Frances at Portland Place.

At length our guide and her candle turned sharply to the right and round a corner. Then she opened the door of a little triangular closet, we all three squeezed into it, and she closed the door and blew out the candle. The darkness enveloped us like a solid wall. In the dense blackness Mrs. Burnett's hushed voice told of the midnight murder, of the strong woman carrying through the dark house the man's body to this tucked-away, forgotten closet. With her dramatic telling it seemed real and plausible enough; it was easy to fancy clutching hands or stabbing steel, and a relief when the candle again made a spot of light.[16]

Safe again in her cosy drawing rooms with their flowered wallpaper, pouffe chairs, and—in the best Victorian style—screens, palms, and Chesterfields, Frances found that this notion stayed with her and became the germ for *A Lady of Quality*, which would prove to be one of her most popular books and the first adult novel she'd completed since *Through One Administration* a dozen years earlier.

In some ways it was to be a seventeenth- and eighteenth-century period piece, "a story of the Spectator and Tatler times and . . . related exactly in the style of Richard Steele when he wrote in the character of Mr Isaac Bickerstaff."[17] She pinned nearly all her immediate prospects on this book, judging that its surprising style, character, and plot would prove popular and lucrative. Like her first letter to a publisher stating that her "object was remuneration," she counted on publishers vying for the rights to it and assumed that it would have a three-pronged success as a magazine serial, a novel, and a play, each providing a separate income.

After his meeting with Frances at Portland Place, Burlingame wrote to Charles Scribner that he

found her very interested about the new novel of which she has written you, which has grown out of the story—originally intended for three parts—of which she submitted a few pages to me some months ago (the masculine young woman of Queen Anne's time who used the language of her period). She tells me she wants "bids" (her own phrase) for both its serial & book publication, and wrote by the same mail to someone else in New York, who, however, cannot have it unless he make "an enormous offer,"—her heart seeming to be set on having it in our Magazine and having it illustrated by some of the well-known artists; finally making a play of it. She thinks it her greatest work, &c., & an entirely new start; & hints (as indeed the beginning promised) that it runs the proprieties and conventions very close, and is (as she called it yesterday) "virile."

Do not imagine from this unavoidable chaff that I am not taking & have not taken it seriously; on the contrary, I can see decided possibilities that she may have done a strong thing & still greater ones that she may have done a popular one.[18]

Although he mocked her hard sell, Burlingame and Frances got on well together—she thought he was "the most delightful American I know"—and they both wished publication to work out.[19] The problem was that she wanted nearly immediate publication and therefore almost immediate payment. *Scribner's*, like the other magazines she approached, had its publication schedule already arranged for the coming two years and certainly had no room in the near future for a serial as long as this one. The best they could do was offer to publish it in two years' time, or to bring it out as a book more immediately, skipping the serial and therefore, of course, the serial income, but offering an advance on royalties. She rejected this as too precarious; one might spend the advance but not be certain of earning it out. (Unlike today, the advance might have to be returned if not earned out in royalties.) Moreover, it could take quite a long time for the book to recoup its advance, leaving her nothing to live on while it did so. Clearly she didn't trust herself to put the money aside, so the negotiations with them and other publishers dragged on for months.

She gave the book the unwieldy title *A Lady of Quality (Being a most curious, hitherto unknown history, related by Mr Isaac Bickerstaff but not presented to the world of Fashion through the pages of "The Tatler," and now for the first time written down by Frances Hodgson Burnett)*. It was a literary conceit that wore somewhat thin, even though she felt she could easily imitate the style. Today the more sarcastic critics might refer to it as "seventeenth-century lite," with its repetition of words and phrases like "boon companions" and "'twas," and indeed some of her contemporary critics felt much the same, but its historical distance and gothic atmosphere allowed her to explore the question of what a woman was.

A Lady of Quality tells the story of a girl brought up as a boy. Her mother died in childbirth, having lost several infants and leaving behind three weak daughters. Sir Jeoffrey, Clorinda's father, hates all the daughters and his wife for being female, and never sets eyes on his youngest child until she is six years old. Reared as a sort of afterthought by the maids, footmen, and stable hands, she has a furious temper and an absolutely fearless demeanour. She can ride the fiercest horse in the stable and takes orders from no one. She first encounters her father when she discovers that he has taken a horse she believes to be hers out to ride. She strides through the house and attacks him with a whip, letting go a string of oaths that would embarrass a soldier. Sir Jeoffrey is delighted by this show of spirit and from that day forward

Frances in a studio pose.

Courtesy of Penny Deupree.

"Image of Eminent Women." A composite photograph of the most famous women writers of late-nineteenth-century America. Frances is on the far right.

Boston Athenaeum.

Lionel Burnett as an adolescent.

Courtesy of Penny Deupree.

Vivian Burnett in 1889, wearing
a Little Lord Fauntleroy outfit.
His curls have been shorn.

Courtesy of Penny Deupree.

Frances (standing) with her companion and language tutor, Luisa Chiellini.
Sophia Smith Collection, Smith College.

Elsie Leslie as Cedric in the play *Little Lord Fauntleroy*.
Courtesy of Penny Deupree.

Frances in Washington, D.C., in 1895. From a set of portraits photographed by Frances Johnson.

Reproduced by permission of The Huntington Library, San Marino, Calif.

Frances in 1895. From the same set of Frances Johnson photographs.

Reproduced by permission of The Huntington Library, San Marino, Calif.

Interior of the Burnetts' house at 1770 Massachusetts Avenue in
Washington, D.C. Note the portrait of Vivian in the centre.

Metropolitan Magazine, May 1898.

Stephen Townesend in one of his stage roles.

New York Journal and Advertiser,
25 March 1900.

Maytham Hall as it looked when Frances lived there.

Critic, March 1902.

makes her his constant companion. Until she is fifteen she wears breeches
and frock coats, and hunts, drinks, and carouses with her father's ne'er-
do-well companions—a sort of Tom Jones to her father's Squire Western.
It is on this fifteenth birthday that, inspired by a visit from the quak-
ing local curate bearing the message that she must mend her ways, she
announces her intention to change from male to female in order to marry
well. She leaves the room in breeches and reappears in sumptuous red velvet
and jewels, and coiled hair, the image of femininity. Frances found her
"thrilling."[20]

Frances may have claimed lack of interest in the "woman question" at the
time her books were solicited for the World's Fair Exposition in Chicago,
but this new novel and the resulting play were all about women and power,
in both the physical and social senses. She was seized by the creation of a
"grand lady who killed her lover & had him [buried] in the farthest wine
cellar in Portland Place." She was utterly absorbed by her new heroine,
Clorinda Wildairs, "a wonderful creature, born in 1660 the daughter of a
roystering drinking hunting gentleman of Quality and brought up among
his dogs & grooms & boon companions in a way that is the scandal of the
county but which makes such a picturesque story and explains in a way all
she does later. She is a beautiful virago renowned for her splendid build &
strength & nerves of steel."[21] Clorinda was many things Frances was not—
tall, physically strong, with knee-length black hair—but she shared Frances's
determination to remake herself and her future, her maternal instincts, and
her ability to keep potentially damning secrets.

A letter Frances wrote to her friend Zangwill makes clear that she saw
much of herself and her earlier writing in this character. "Clorinda is not at
all a new departure for me—notwithstanding a certain misleading gentleness of literary exterior I have presented to the world," she told him. "That
'Lass o' Lowrie's' was a Clorinda in disguise—so were Rachel Ffrench and
Christian Murdoch in 'Haworth's.' So was Bertha Amory, who laughed
and wore tinkling ornaments and brilliant symphonies in red when she was
passing through the gates of hell—so was little Sara Crewe when she starved
in her garret and was a princess disdaining speech. Oh, she is not a new
departure. She represents what I have cared for all my life."[22] If there's any
doubt that Clorinda represents aspects of her creator, it should be dispelled
by the fact that the novel opens on 24 November, Frances's birthday.

What seems like a fantastical story takes on more meaning when we recall that Frances herself left England as a child and arrived in America as a
budding writer at fifteen, with the determination to be paid for her work.
The question in the novel, however, is whether the newly feminine Clorinda

can wholly renounce her masculine ways or whether she will grow into an amalgam of the best of male and female. She now rides side-saddle but still breaks dangerous horses. She marries a much older man but keeps a private room for her writing. When her husband dies, she becomes engaged to the man who is her equal in height, strength of character, and natural gentility, and when her happiness is threatened by an earlier lover, she does what is necessary to protect her future.

As Frances wrote about Clorinda, she continued her habit of reading her latest work to her house guests and visitors over cigarettes in the evening. After one after-theatre supper at Portland Place for her widening circle of writer friends—where they dined on consommé, lobster mayonnaise, tongue in aspic, foie gras in aspic, cold game pie, amontillado jelly, crème Bavaroise, cakes, lemon cheesecakes, bonbons, salted almonds, stuffed olives, as well as sherry, burgundy, and champagne—most of the guests left around two in the morning, but Zangwill remained until three while she read a portion of Clorinda to him. He told her that she was "writing the book of [her] life— that it is so virile that it is amazing."[23] With such encouragement, her hopes were high that she could ride out this difficult financial period.

While she tried to work out her finances, with Stephen's help, Vivian continued to upset her with appeals for money to cover his burgeoning expenses and to buy new clothes, only months after beginning at college. His father had already refused him and scolded him for his extravagance, refusing "to give me a cent beyond the 500 that he has already."[24] She knew Swan's contribution was small—only fifty dollars a month, leaving the rest, including tuition and room and board, up to her—but "a faint little grin overspreads my countenance when I think what capital he will make of 'That boy of mine at college costs me a tremendous lot. I dont know how to stand it.'— It will be worth money to him. He can refuse to do anything on the plea of 'that boy of mine at Harvard.'"[25]

Swan may have been penurious, but he rightly believed that Frances spoiled their son. She had brought Vivian up expect that he had a certain place in the world, but now, at Harvard, he discovered that the things she'd led him to expect—like good clothes, food, music, college clubs, and reading materials—had to be held in check for lack of funds. She never thought she had brought him up to have unreasonable expectations, going so far as to declare that she believed "firmly in letting children develop naturally, that is, in interfering with them just as little as possible and allowing them to yield to their own inclinations, unless of course, these inclinations lead them to do things that are not good for them. I have no patience with the traditional fear on the part of parents of 'spoiling their children.' A child can't be spoiled."[26]

He was a nice young man who endeared himself to all his mother's friends, but he found watching the pennies a difficult lesson.

Finally feeling more secure about her income as the novel progressed, she was shaken in April when the writer Edmund Gosse wrote to congratulate her on the fine production of *Fauntleroy* that he had just seen in Paris. She sent Stephen to France immediately and discovered that she had indeed signed away some of the rights years before and had forgotten about it when the play was never produced. There was a tussle, but she was finally forced to settle and became more sanguine when the play promised to provide her a small but temporarily steady income. She was by this time in dire need of money, and nothing could be expected until *A Lady of Quality* was completed and *Two Little Pilgrims' Progress* began to turn a profit. "You have no idea how miserably poor I am just now," she told Vivian at Harvard, when he wrote to ask for money for singing lessons with Edna Hall. "During the last two months I have been wretched. I owe bills I cannot pay and it has never been so before and it makes my hair stand on end. I could not live and owe people money. I owe Mrs Hall some already for the pictures and I must not owe her any more until I can afford to pay it."[27]

He certainly expected her to bail him out, as she would soon have to do when his large end-of-the-year expenses became due, but by now her finances were in such disarray that she had only hopes to count on: "*If* the Chicago scheme succeeds,—*if* the Continental Fauntleroy brings in money worth counting—*if* I can finish Clorinda I need not be disturbed—but in the meantime it is awful."[28] Even her largely unsupervised housekeeper spent more than she should, and the food bills were mounting. More disturbingly, she had made a huge and mysterious loan of $25,000—in today's money, more than $525,000 or £300,000—to her Boston friend George Simmons, whom she had years before nicknamed "the Duke" because of his wife Mary's amusing love for the English aristocracy; he in turn had bestowed on her the enduring name Fluffy. Frances had become very close to Mary Simmons during the winter of 1885–86, which she had spent in Boston. Mary remembered with awe a ride into the country during which Frances told the story of Fauntleroy, which she was then writing, and another evening when Frances read to them from the manuscript of *DeWilloughby*. When Frances returned to Washington that winter, she gave Mary a book of handwritten poems, bound in violet velvet, and inscribed "à la duchesse."[29]

Simmons owned a clothing business, G. W. Simmons and Co., and had agreed to pay her quarterly interest on the loan and to pay off the principal in increments. She counted on the income from this loan to pay Vivian's college expenses and tuition, with enough left over to buy a country house, but getting him to pay was nearly impossible. With little income in sight, she chided Vivian to write back and account for his expenses like club memberships, concerts, and magazine subscriptions, and for whatever income Swan gave him.

At the end of September 1896, with no one in England or America able to publish the serial to suit her timetable, Stephen negotiated a deal with Scribner's for a $5,000 advance and 20 per cent royalties, and Warne contracted for the British edition. Even then she persisted in trying to place the story in a magazine. In late October Stephen wrote again to Scribner's on her behalf; she had read in a London newspaper that a new serial by Sir James Barrie (creator of Peter Pan) was to begin its run in their magazine sooner than expected, and she again offered them the serial rights to *A Lady of Quality* even though she had "some very tempting offers on both sides of the Atlantic."[30] They knew, of course, that she was becoming desperate and gently, over the next months, repeated their original offer until she finally signed and turned to other projects. With an impending income gap for the next few months, she began to adapt *A Lady of Quality* for the theatre, picked up the old manuscript of *In Connection with the DeWilloughby Claim* with an eye to finishing it, and embarked on a new housekeeping plan— discovering that by planning her own dinners and going to the shops herself in the morning, she could save more than seven pounds a week.

She became more and more dependent on Stephen's business acumen at this time. He helped her to calculate royalties and contracts, taxes (apparently without great success, for she was to appear on the delinquent tax lists of Washington several times in 1899 for her various properties there), and other expenses, and acted as her intermediary with publishers in America and England. He and Archie, whose progress was "really wonderful," huddled over her accounts and proposed contracts, calculating the income of each one.[31] "My condition as regards money has never been so serious in my life," she wrote to Vivian. "I came back to town to find scarcely anything in the bank, the rent due, the taxes sent in & divers innumerable small bills. I should have been in despair if it had not been for Stephen. I did not know he could be so nice. The touch of real anxiety seemed to bring out a new creature in him. He has managed for me, arranged things & seen people & persistently cheered me up & insisted that we could get through the time of difficulty and that once through I should be easier than ever. It is just the next two months that require maneuvering through. It is such a new experience for me."[32] She counted on the Duke's next interest payment to tide her over, but when that didn't materialize she began to suspect the truth: that he had lost her money, and with only $2,000 of it repaid she was about to take a loss of $23,000, an enormous sum. "It does drive me rather wild to think of the $25,000 which I had felt I always had to depend upon," she told Vivian. "It is a little hard."[33] She wrote plaintively to him about her money problems, ending with a lecture on the necessity of reining in his expenses, but Swan was less gentle. "Daddy gave me the same lecture," Vivian admitted. "He never in his life spoke so violently to me."[34]

Vivian was having a difficult time as well. At home for the Easter holiday during his freshman year, he had found the Massachusetts Avenue house almost too depressing for words, denuded of Swan's belongings, with many of Frances's furnishings still in storage, and Edith and Frank relegated to "the smallest part of a corner, and the rest empty." Swan's new house was large but barely furnished and "dismal, oh very dismal." He and Edith had a long talk that ended with them both in tears.[35] By the following January, when Frances had been away from Washington for a year, he wrote to her about the dire situation Edith and Frank found themselves in, how they were using just a few rooms in order to save on coal. He urged her to let the house to someone who could afford to keep it up and to instal his aunt and uncle elsewhere.

His mother had no faith in the American rental system. In England, land-lords could require their tenants to provide regular upkeep. Her Portland Place lease stipulated that she must maintain it and make decorating updates every two years. In America she would have to spend thousands preparing the house for tenants, then repair it again when they left. Vivian's words left her in despair. "I do not quite understand what you say about its being hard on Edith and Frank to live in the house. I should have imagined to be given a beautiful furnished house rent free could not be very hard on people who have no money to pay either for rent or to buy furniture," she wrote to him from London. "What *would* they do if they did not live there. I dont understand why the house should go to ruin if the furnace is not kept going. No furnace was kept going when it was vacant for—I think—two years before I bought it."[36] She wanted to provide for her sister, but just as importantly she needed to have the house watched over now that her husband no longer occupied it.

Swan may have moved out of the Massachusetts Avenue house, but he and Frances kept up the pretence that their marriage remained intact, even when both the *Washington Post* and the *New York Times* got wind of his move in September. With Frances in London, Swan was left to issue strong denials on his own. Calling the separation rumour "an old and threadbare one," he told reporters that it was only Frances's literary work in England and his medical practice in America that kept them apart. "I don't care particularly to talk about this story," he told the reporters who accosted him, "but since it has been given this much publicity, I can only say that it is a fake out of the whole cloth, and one that is an unwarrantable invasion of a man's family privacy."[37] Clearly frustrated by having to explain her absences, he would only say that he didn't know when her work would allow her to return, for "she has her work that she has to follow up abroad, just as I have to attend to mine here. That is all there is to the matter."[38]

Public interest in her life and work increased during these London years. At the end of 1895, London's Vagabonds Club, made up of literary men, fêted her, having decided "in solemn conclave that I am 'the Woman of the Moment.' It is very flattering, but it makes me feel rather shy. They say it is apropos of the new book—but though I know it is a fine little book, I don't feel as if it was big enough to entitle me to be the Woman of the Moment. I shall be the Woman of several moments when Clorinda and DeWilloughby are in the world, but just now I blush under the burden of such honors."[39] Zangwill saw the announcement of the forthcoming honour and sent her a note remarking that "this is indeed the new woman."[40]

The term "new woman" came into vogue in the 1890s to describe the numbers of women who challenged traditional gender roles and claimed more public lives for themselves. In England and America they left the farms and small towns for jobs in the big cities, professional ambition, and greater sexual freedom. Frances, at forty-six, was older than the young women whom the term generally covered, but in other ways she could serve as a model for them. She had forged an independent life for herself in literature and, although married, no longer seemed bound by marriage's traditional restraints. She was Victorian and rather too frivolous in dress, but in other ways she served as a plausible role model for women who aspired to what she had already accomplished.

She was so nervous about public speaking that she trembled for three weeks before the Vagabonds dinner. Then, with Zangwill seated next to her, when she rose to speak to the audience of four hundred, she suddenly "discovered a composure earthquakes would not have shaken. I realized that my little voice has quite a clear far reaching note and that without effort I could make everyone hear me."[41] Her speech attempted, in its casual and rather rambling way, to capture in her ordinary conversational style some of the issues that most interested the public about her life. She protested that she had "not the slightest objection to being either illogical or feminine. To be either is amusing and interesting in moments of idle leisure." More evasive was her attempt to clarify her national identity.

In answer to the reference to a general indefiniteness of opinion as to the country of my birth, and the doubts as to whether I am an Englishwoman or an American, I can only say that I do not wonder that such doubts exist. They have at times existed in my own mind. The truth is, however, that I was born in England—all my people were English—even to the third and fourth generation—but I have been the mother of two American sons. That seems to give a country a sort of claim upon a woman, doesn't it? And it seems, too, to give the woman a sort of claim in the Halls of Congress, but if I did it would be a large one. So, perhaps, it might be said that by my own birth I am an Englishwoman, but by the birth of my two boys I am an American.[42]

Stephen later tried to use her English residence and background to protect her copyright in Canada, but his assertion that "Mrs Burnett was born in England, of English parents, has an English house, and pays rates and taxes as an English citizen" did not convince Scribner's that she was not American and therefore had little say over cheap Canadian reprints of her work.[43] The speech was printed in *The Queen*, which reported that it was "greeted with prolonged cheering," and Vivian, to whom she sent it, pronounced himself delighted and swore that he "could have almost given it word for word before you said it, it is so much like you and the way you write."[44] Only seven months later she was honoured again, and again she returned to the question of gender. This time London's Authors' Club selected her to be the first woman for whom they ever hosted a dinner, and this time she gave her speech with confidence. "Dressed in masses of fluffy chiffon, and with a tall osprey rising from her fair hair," she delivered a talk about being a pioneer in a new country. "In the course of what occasionally appears to be a somewhat protracted existence, I have never yet discovered a good quality— or a bad one—which seemed to have a gender," she told the audience of men and women. "As to one's success in the work one does, surely that is not a question of gender either. The big world settles that." She went on to discuss the public response to Clorinda Wildairs, whose bad language and accidental killing of her former lover seemed "unprincipled" to those expecting another Fauntleroy.

I think it probable that—say a hundred years from now—a woman may stand as I do, in some such place as this, the guest of men who have done the work all the world has known and honored, and she will be the outcome of all the best and most logical thinking, of all the most reasonable and clear-brained men and women—women and men—of these seething years. She will have learned all the things I have not learned, and she will be a woman so much wiser and more stately of mind than I could ever hope to be—she will have so much more brain, so much more fine and clear a reason, that if we were compared we should scarcely seem to be creatures of the same race. And of this woman I say, "Good luck to her, great happiness, fair fortunes, and all the fullest joyousness of living; all kind fates attend her, all good things to her—and to the men who will be her friends."[45]

Virginia Woolf's book *A Room of One's Own*, based on lectures she gave in 1928 to the women at Newnham and Girton colleges, Cambridge, about the inequality of women's and men's education and the necessity of money and leisure to produce literature, would not appear for another thirty-three years. Burnett as a product of Victorian England and America knew better than most what it was like to be a poorly educated woman who needed a room of her own and a proper income in order to write. What is more, she had known since her youth the necessity of work at a time when there were few if any colleges for women, and few if any careers open to them either. She looked ahead to the Virginia Woolfs of the world, unborn or in their infancy, and both envied and saluted them. Clorinda was her Orlando.

The issue of gender stayed on Frances's mind throughout the winter and spring as she struggled to make the novel of *A Lady of Quality* into a play. With so much on her mind—two plays, two novels, and her financial woes—she finally took herself to a small apartment in Paris to work on the new play and the yet-unfinished *DeWilloughby Claim*. She was invited there to visit her friend the doctor Kenneth Campbell, introduced to her by Stephen, and his new wife Rosamond, whom she always referred to and thought of as "the fair Rosamond." Stephen planned to escort her and her maid Norris to Paris and leave her there, for "I cannot go careering about Europe with a male creature and no chaperone or policeman."[46] After leaving the Campbells, she and Norris settled into the Hôtel de Calais on the rue des Capucines, and while she worked on the novel Stephen, presumably staying with the Campbells, helped her with the play.

It was the old story of needing to secure the English dramatic rights to her own work before someone else did, particularly now that the book was out and her dramatic agent, Elisabeth Marbury, was being approached by a number of theatre managers who wanted to mount an American production of *A Lady of Quality*. Stephen was no dramatist, but he sat with a glue pot and almost literally cut and pasted scenes together from the novel, which she later endeavoured to put into a decent form. It was a recalcitrant beast, and over the months she found it difficult to incorporate the necessary background story into a coherent drama. Clorinda was inherently dramatic as a character, but there was so much to explain that Frances continually lost the dramatic cohesiveness and movement that a play needs. Act 3 was written over and over, and the strain shows somewhat in the final version. It was easy enough to open the play by showing the breeches-clad heroine fencing with the disreputable Sir John Oxon, whom later in life she would accidentally kill, but to have her age in the play, develop from a boyish girl into a strong-minded woman, bury a man in her cellar, and marry twice was almost more than could be done convincingly in five acts. Frances had a fierce devotion to Clorinda—she never had approved of the delicately feminine etching of her in the book's frontispiece—and worked hard to portray her masculine side. In the opening act she made the butler comment on the young Clorinda, "more boy than girl hath she been." When Clorinda goads Oxon into fencing with her, she calls "Come on then, Sir John—come on—and let me show you who is the better man of the two." The weak chaplain is derided by the company as "the only lady present," and later in the play she tells Oxon, "I have no women's virtues, but I have one that is sometimes—not always—a man's."[47]

An interview later that year in the English magazine the *Idler* pursued this question of the sexes with her. Frances had been known for ultra-feminine female characters, and now with this new book she produced someone quite new. It was, they noted, her first book in nearly ten years that wasn't primarily for children. She agreed but made it clear that this had only arisen out of the circumstances of her private life; since Lionel's death she had "not had the courage to look upon life with sufficient interest to build comedies and tragedies upon it." Her new interest had little to do with dividing the sexes. "The man and woman question has no interest for me," she told the interviewer.

"We are not to be divided into mere men and women; we are human beings who are part of each other. Each part should be as noble as the other, and the one who is the stronger should teach the other strength. To be a man's wife and the mother of human beings is a stately thing. Frequently it is not, but it should be. And to be a woman's husband and the father of human beings should be quite as stately a thing. When it is not it is rather disgraceful. . . ."

"Then I gather that your ideal woman must be a mother?"

"She must be a mother if she has children. . . . She must have the reason and sense of honor and justice which one expects from the ideal man."

Having written a book that both bowed to and called into question the proper role of women, she ended the interview with a statement that seems to have sprung from her lips without forethought. "It is my opinion," she told the interviewer, "that the ideal woman, among quite a number of other things, should be a 'perfect gentleman.'"[48]

CHAPTER 15

~

LADIES OF QUALITY

1896–1897

I‌T WASN'T JUST THE MILES between Swan and Frances that kept
the rumours flowing, for around this time people began to remark on
Stephen's presence in Frances's life. A Berlin theatre manager who produced *Fauntleroy* in Germany greeted both Frances and "Mr. Dennis" in
his telegram to her. Elisabeth Marbury easily interested Daniel Frohman of
the Lyceum Theatre in producing Frances's next play and suggested possible
actors. When major actors were named for the principal roles, Stephen
selected a part for himself. Frances told Vivian that she "really invented the
play about a year ago because it is one of [Stephen's] favorite acting periods & I thought there would be something good in it for him."[1] When the
play went to New York in January 1897, Stephen went too. Whatever their
private relationship, however, Frances made sure he had no legal claim on
her. On 2 January she made out her will, leaving to Edith and her husband
Frank T. Jordan two Washington building lots in Kalorama Heights, as well
as her clothes to Edith; to Effie she left $300 "to purchase some memento of
me." Everything else she left to Frank and to her lawyer Will Dennis, to hold
in trust, manage, and invest for Vivian. If Vivian predeceased her, everything
would go to Edith and Frank or their survivors.

Although she worried about Stephen's temper, his business talents delighted her. He was able to induce Frederick Warne, with whom he had
arranged the English publishing contract for *A Lady of Quality*, to increase
her royalties to 22.5 per cent. "He has interviewed the Warnes so often for me
and has studied my affairs in such a way that he understands the situation
between author & publisher as well as if he were an agent," she told Vivian.
"What he has done for me both in connection with the Continental playing

of Fauntleroy & my other business, an agent would charge me ten per cent for. He thinks the percentage system unfair to the author and I confess I agree with him entirely. A man writes a few letters & has a few interviews for you & then for all the years to come your work may have before it he must be paid ten per cent."[2] She didn't say whether she was paying Stephen for this intervention, but eventually he would prove even more costly, financially and emotionally, than any literary agent. Over the next five years the gossip about them would only increase as Frances embarked on momentous changes in her life and made new commitments to England, the country she now reclaimed as her own. Over those years she repeatedly defended and praised him publicly, as though garnering public approval for his work helped to pay off her debt to him for his kindness to Lionel. Their private life was another matter for he alternated between sweet helpfulness and irrational outbursts, which she tolerated partly out of need for someone to help her with business matters but mostly for Lionel's sake.

Vivian made plans to join her and Archie for the summer at Broomfields, near Frensham Pond and Moor, in Farnham, Surrey. She engaged a tutor for Archie and spent the summer writing the final chapters of *A Lady of Quality* and entertaining her guests. Daisy Hall visited, as did Zangwill, who so delighted them by playing with a grey kitten and dancing on the grass with it that they named it "Mrs. Zangwill."[3] When he left, he wished her "fine weather & cigarettes & peppermints *ad lib*," a reference to her habit of nibbling on soft peppermints while she smoked, addressing his letter to "Mrs Frances Clorinda Hodgson Burnett."[4] Beatrice Herford, whom Daisy Hall introduced to Frances in London, lived in England with her parson father, although her adored brother Oliver lived in Boston, and she stayed for the entire summer. Constance Fletcher, a writer friend who used the nom de plume George Fleming, also spent much of the summer there, collaborating with Frances on the play *The First Gentleman of Europe*, about an incident that took place during the youth of George IV.

The notion for this play first came to her in January 1895, when she began to worry that her public would think that now she wrote only for children. "Men & women will begin to think I have said my last word—And I have'nt! The Regent was not a nice person but in reading him—as I did a year ago for a purpose—I found that he was tragic though he did not know it and finally grew fat & wore stays and curled his hair. He was once a beautiful, fascinating ardent boy, but he was a prince in the midst of a leprous court," she had written to Burlingame at Scribner's, pitching this as a story idea. It had costume possibilities as a play, and with money in short supply, now seemed a good time to pursue it. Despite her passing notion of enrolling Vivian at Cambridge or Oxford for the academic year, he returned to Harvard in September, while she returned to Portland Place for the autumn and winter to finish the novel.

With spring of 1896, London came to life and her spirits rose at the sight of tulips and freshly painted doors. *A Lady of Quality* was released in both England and America in March, and Harold Warne wrote to her that "it takes all our energies to keep pace" with the demand for the book. The *Daily Telegraph* "gave her a whole column of applause." Henry James wrote to tell her that "so far from finding The Lady of Quality 'visionary'—I see her better than if *I* had made her. And what is better still, she sees me. She winks at me—distinctly. There—she has done it again! Don't whisk her away and slap her."[5] Not everyone was so positive about the novel. London's *Nineteenth Century* called it a strong book yet commented that "Mistress Clorinda was wise enough to be born as long ago as 1690," a rowdy time, "before which the aspirations of the most hysterical New Woman seem pale and attenuated."[6] The *Saturday Review* called it "the poorest and least worthy piece of work that has been offered to the public by an author of any reputation for many years," but Frances never read reviews unless a family member found a good one and passed it on to her.[7] However, the *New York World* gave it two columns, beginning a rush for the dramatic rights in America. Both Elisabeth Marbury and Charles Frohman, brother and business partner of Daniel Frohman, cabled to ask for a play to be made of it, without even reading the book. The copyright performance had been given in England on the same day the book appeared, so "thanks to Stephen I am safe—safe—safe. . . . No more Fauntleroy business arrangements for me!"[8] From worrying about Continental performances of her earlier work, she now embarked on two years of unflagging and draining devotion to not one play but two.

Vivian, who would spend the summer of 1896 with her in England and in touring Norway by boat at her expense, had little faith in plays and worried that she was staking too much on them, both physically and financially. He would prove to be at least partially correct, but for now his mother was riding high on their possibilities. Her hope that *The First Gentleman of Europe* and *A Lady of Quality* would spell success was even more important now that her financial situation was so dire. George Simmons, who still owed her $25,000, had his business taken over. The new company, Oak Hall, noticed in the accounts an entry stating that the business had loaned Frances $2,000 and a notation from Simmons that she would be repaying in January. They had in their possession a cheque for that amount endorsed by her. It seemed clear that Simmons had taken the money himself, using a cheque written to Frances years before when she'd borrowed money to make a final instalment on a monument for Lionel, which she had paid back. Now, already in fear of losing the larger sum, she had a false claim against her. She wrote to her Washington lawyer Will Dennis at once, but the deeper hurt came from having been taken advantage of. "I have paid $25,000 to learn that appalling business ignorance such as mine used to be is more useful to the astute man who bears himself like a gentleman than it is to myself." The situation, if it became public, would be even more humiliating than losing her nest egg. "Imagine your haughty Mammy figuring in the clothing stores account books as the debtor of the clothier," she wrote in horror to Vivian. "I keep repeating it to myself semi idiotically. Perhaps he has entered somewhere the whole 25,000 with interest."[9] A year later the situation would take an even sadder turn.

No one outside her immediate family and Stephen knew much of her financial situation, for on the surface life was full of gaiety as her already wide social circle grew. She sent notes inviting her friends to theatre parties and gatherings at Portland Place, and responded to a flurry of invitations. Among her newer friends were members of the nobility, and some of the invitations were for weekends at their country seats. In December she had been the guest of the earl of Crewe (formerly Lord Houghton and the lord lieutenant of Ireland) at his home, Fryston Hall, in Yorkshire. She had met him earlier at a lunch party given by Sir Walter Besant, and "before I knew who he was I was attracted by him. He is young and tall & beautiful and has a *lovable* sort of face and peculiarly beautiful clear eyes."[10] She told Kitty that "he is the most beautiful Earl in England. . . . It is not that he is tall and graceful and has a beautifully cut face and lovely eyes—it is something else—a sort of touching beautifulness in *himself*—something which makes you feel tender to him. You *know* that he is exquisite and lovable and perfect natured, and of finer clay than the rest of the world."[11] He was a widower and lived with his adolescent daughters and his sisters. At Fryston she found herself among a houseful of guests, including the writer Bret Harte and the member of Parliament for Ireland. When she returned to London she sent his daughters three of her books, and Crewe wrote back that he took "special pride in claiming Sara Crewe as a relation."[12] Her other new acquaintance was Lord Ronald Gower, introduced to her by Hamilton Aïdé and destined to be a close friend and travelling companion.

She and Henry James, too, extended their friendship in joking notes and social engagements. He often found hers rather lively for his more retired taste—"the kind of entertainment I like best is weak and lovely, lukewarm tea, administered, toward 6 o'clock or so, by the hand of genius—administered, of course, in Portland Place"—yet they occasionally met in London and in the country.[13] She offered to go to Manchester for the opening of his play *Guy Domville* in 1895 before its London appearance. Perhaps not realizing that she would be returning to her original home, he discouraged her by saying that he found the offer wonderfully gracious, but "Manchester is far and hideous," and the play would open at the Theatre Royal in London in only a week or so.[14] In retrospect he should have taken up her offer, for the play was disastrously received in London by a booing audience; Frances was horrified at the response and felt terrible for James, who immediately fell into a severe depression. She also became friendly with art historian Bernard Berenson and the writer Douglas Sladen. She was becoming cheerful enough to warn Vivian against taking himself and life too seriously, something she had done herself ever since she was a small child. She confessed to him that she was prone to "deep melancholy," particularly since she had been in England, where she had no close female friends.[15]

Vivian too was often prone to depression and seemed to become ill whenever he overworked himself. Aside from his demanding courses, he found himself fully embroiled in theatrical productions. That spring his college theatrical club put on a play he'd written called *Fool's Goal*, and the club travelled around New England giving performances. They were praised in the local papers everywhere they went, but Vivian found that much of this was because of his past: the headlines nearly always read that the original Little Lord Fauntleroy was now acting in a Harvard production. One paper devoted two and a half columns to him, so upsetting him that "my dagger was out of its sheath, but I could not find the man—else there would have been blood on my hands," he wrote to his mother. "The only thing you can do—in justice to me—to relieve me in some way of the awful burden of my early history is to spread it about that John Oxon [the slain man in *A Lady of Quality*] is drawn from *me* in my later years—That would give me a reputation with the ladies indeed enviable." He was cheered by his father's presence, for Swan went to visit him for the first time, enjoying the college life so much that "he became quite young and frisky."[16]

Now, in the spring and summer of 1896, she had to go full tilt if she were to write one play, revise another, and continue with *In Connection with the DeWilloughby Claim*, which Stephen was already trying to place as a magazine serial. She took for the summer a wisteria-covered cottage in Buckinghamshire, close to the Thames, where Vivian joined her in late June and stayed in England until taking up his Norway travels in August; Kitty Hall also visited. A greenhouse was fitted out as a work room for her, and there she spent weeks writing and rewriting the third act of *Clorinda* with Stephen until "I dream about it and waken feeling rather crazy."[17] Suddenly one day, "after weeks of delirium I sat down at my table in the greenhouse—

Beatrice curled up on a sofa near—and began to write like a steam engine—
and finished it before I got up. It is so weird how such things *will* do
themselves only when and how they like. But nothing ever tormented me
quite so much before. Usually my things behave rather well. When they are
stubborn they *kill* me."[18] During this difficult time she gave the speech at
the London Authors' Club, which took a great deal out of her despite her
growing ease in public speaking.

Frances was overstressed and overstretched, and not surprisingly became
ill again. More than nervous exhaustion, from which she had suffered earlier,
her illness this time was her heart: she began having a series of "heart failures." These seem to have consisted of palpitations, shortness of breath, and
extremely painful chest seizures. From his berth on the Cunard steamship
Etruria, taking him back to America, Vivian cautioned her to "be coura-
geous & hopeful—and dont worry or think too much—remember that you
must not go to work till your strength has well returned. Try to rest a while.
Dont let things bother you, for you have no need to struggle so hard as you
imagine. Remember that your son loves you—and will do anything to help
you and make things easy for you if you will only let him."[19]

This went on for months. Rather than go back to London at the end of
the summer, she spent September at Hunton Rectory in Maidstone, in Kent,
trying to recover, but instead she was made worse by worrying about money
and by surroundings. Rain poured without let-up, and she swore it was the
worst month of her life. Still careful not to touch the $5,000 advance from
Scribner's until *Lady* had earned it out, she knew that summer and early
autumn were poor times for children's book sales and that without those
sales she had little income. She put up Portland Place to let, and hoped to
find a tenant soon and be relieved of that expense. Her illness forced her
to put *DeWilloughby* aside, for she was now "worthlessly weak. I cannot bear
the tiniest effort or excitement. I can walk slowly on the lawn here and have
been driven out but my heart is weak beyond words & the least change in
my diet makes me ill."[20]

She was, indeed, dangerously ill; Vivian later said she was close to death.
Only frequent rests and doses of strychnine kept her going. Even in this
state she began meeting with the actress Eleanor Calhoun, who seemed a
perfect Clorinda and desperately wanted the role. Rather than take the time
she needed to recover, she was about to push herself even harder. Daniel
Frohman contracted for the play *First Gentleman of Europe*, and she needed
to go to New York. Despite everyone's concern, she made the crossing on 21
November, with Kitty Hall at her side on the *Campania*. Before leaving, she
responded to Douglas Sladen's request for information about her for a *Who's*

Who he was putting together on modern writers. "Even if I had a weeks strength & time to do it . . . the entries would look too uninterestingly scant," she warned him. "I was born in Cheetham Hall Manchester. Father & Mother Edwin & Eliza Hodgson. Educated at small private school kept by nobody in particular."

> Married: Swan Moses Burnett
> Career. None
> Academical Distinctions. None
> Publications—List at Warnes
> Recreations—None
> Clubs—None
> Address—63 Portland Place, London W. 1770 Mass. Avenue Washington
>   D.C. America.

You see this is too [probably] uninteresting.[21]

She arrived in New York harbour on 29 November, as always to a group of probing reporters, who wasted no time in publishing the fact that she "has recently been ill from an affection of the heart" after being away from America for two years.[22] Her relief at arriving didn't last long. Her dear friend Edna Hall, mother to Kitty, Gigi, and Daisy and surrogate mother and voice teacher to Vivian, died in Boston in early December, while Frances was in Manhattan working on *The First Gentleman of Europe*. She went immediately to Daisy, who now lived in New York, and saw her off on the train to Boston. Heartbroken that she couldn't help, she wrote to Kitty and Gigi and offered to go to them, but Kitty firmly told her to stay put; the fact was that another invalid wasn't needed just then, but Frances ached for them and encouraged Vivian, already there, to wait on them in her place.

She was to remain in America for fourteen months, so immediately overwhelmed by revisions, rehearsals, and trips back and forth between Washington and New York that she almost immediately cabled for Stephen to come to New York and help her, deciding that she was "neither strong enough nor masculine enough to fight the matter out." The "matter" was that Frohman wanted another actress to play Clorinda, whereas Frances was standing by Eleanor Calhoun. The part ultimately went to Julia Arthur, a Canadian-born actress whose real name was Ida Lewis. Although she had acquitted herself well in London as Ellen Terry's understudy, she was neither's first choice, and the play suffered for it. In the meantime, Frances "lived in an atmosphere of cablegrams in cypher—letters—problems & difficulties."[23]

Stephen, who had managed to let the Portland Place house, thus saving her three hundred pounds, came almost immediately, but other problems didn't settle themselves quite so easily. Vivian was to provide some music for *The First Gentleman*, now in rehearsals, and he failed to do so on time; her attempts to find a position for Archie, who had returned with her to America polished and educated and ready to work, were initially unsuccessful. This meant she was supporting the entire Fahnestock/Jordan family, since Frank lost his position, and Ernest still hadn't yet made his mark on engineering, although, as always, he had some interesting prospects.

Her financial worries turned to outrage when she tried to borrow against the equity in the Washington house, only to discover that the bank could not legally lend money to her without Swan's signature, even though the house was in her name and had been paid for by her alone; the District of Columbia required a husband's signature for such transactions. She was forced to turn to Scribner's for a thousand dollar loan, refusing to turn to her estranged husband. "As he has never had any connection whatever with anything I own and has conducted himself in such a manner that I should not think of approaching him, this is entirely out of the question," she wrote to Scribner. Marriage, which had seemed to offer professional and social insurance, was now becoming a legal and economic liability. So many of her friends believed her to be divorced already that she began to think seriously about severing the relationship officially. Then, on New Year's Eve, she suffered another heart seizure "after a too joyful day with Beatrice," but managed to take a train to New York only a day or two later.[24] However, with the play about to open and Stephen to take on some of the burden, nothing seemed to keep her down. Her friends commented that they hadn't seen her look so well in years.

Stephen's presence seemed to do wonders for her, although it grated on others. He sat in hotel rooms in New York and Washington helping her to revise scenes; he sat in theatres and helped her to rehearse the actors in *The First Gentleman*, since neither of them approved of the way the play was shaping up; he arranged to take *A Lady of Quality* to Detroit for its opening and fine-tuning the following spring. With *The First Gentleman* about to open, Frances believed that "Stephen & I have saved the play. . . . Stephen works, arranges, manages in a way which sets his price above rubies."[25] The play as originally written by Frances and Constance Fletcher back in England was full of flaws and wasn't helped by poor acting and insertions made by the directors. She and Stephen sat down one morning and "cut every sentence they managed to drag in the second act. He rehearsed it next morning & the changes were played at night."[26]

The play opened on 25 January, and the press noted that it was Frances's first original play in America, *Fauntleroy* having been adapted from the novel.[27] *Leslie's Weekly* and *Harper's Weekly* gave it full photo spreads, and the revisions clearly paid off. The *Critic* pronounced it "constructed with a keen sense of dramatic effect . . . and very well written," although they didn't find the acting as good as the writing.[28] The story of a well-born young scholar trying to make a literary living in London and a young prince, both in love with the same landlord's daughter, was a critical and popular success but, disappointingly, not a financial one. Frances believed that the problem stemmed from Constance Fletcher's insistence on settling for a lower royalty scale rather than holding out for something better, but whatever the reason, the beginning of March saw the run ended and a new play opening at the Lyceum. Stephen sailed for London to look for acting roles of his own, while Frances settled back in Washington to attend to her family and work on another book. With *A Lady of Quality* still to come to the stage, she felt she had a breather and good prospects, a belief supported in part by a reception given in her honour by the Twelfth Night Club in Manhattan early in the year.

The new book, *His Grace of Osmonde*, was a "prequel" to *A Lady of Quality*. The idea was not only to fill in the background of Clorinda's husband but also to have a tie-in book for the play shortly after it opened. By now it was clear that to sustain her monetary needs, she returned to proven successes, and much of her writing went over familiar territory. Written in the same style, and with the same period setting, *His Grace of Osmonde* was the story of the upbringing and marriage of the only man who was Clorinda's match. Stephen and Vivian both wanted her to take up *DeWilloughby* again, but instead she climbed up to her den at 1770 Massachusetts Avenue and threw herself into this book, enjoying the spring, the familiar characters, the care that her sister lavished on her, and her returning health. There she remained until early spring, when she and Swan, presumably separately, travelled to Cambridge to celebrate Vivian's twenty-first birthday and the opening of another of his student plays.

She greeted her son with a happy poem on the morning of the birthday:

My darling One and Twenty Boy,
Rise to your strong young feet
And Look upon the April blue
And feel how Life is Sweet.[29]

Thrilled that she would be there to witness his triumph, she reminded him once again that "I have worked hard and borne a great deal to make your life what it is—the life of a man who has had advantages and the surroundings & education of a gentleman. . . . I have been reviled and blackguarded *because* I *would* not let your life begin so. This fact has been cherished for twenty one years & held up as one of my chiefest & vilest infamies. But I have done what I meant to do—You stand at a disadvantage with no man or woman."[30] Reluctant to speak out against Swan to their son, this letter and others seem to refer directly to their different opinions on child-rearing. Swan remained convinced that what she viewed as lifting Vivian and Lionel into a sphere so different from their own middle-class backgrounds had in fact been spoiling them rotten, a view that the more unkind members of the press propagated during the *Fauntleroy* years, but she and Swan made a show of agreeing to disagree. When Vivian referred to "having two antagonistic homes" in Washington, she was quick to reassure him that he was mistaken.[31]

Frances was fierce in her belief that she had done the right thing about Vivian's upbringing. "You *began* equal. You have had books refined pleasures & companionship, travel and ease. It was I who fought against bitter opposition that you might have them—it was your Mammy who stood like a little tigress between you and an inevitably mean, undignified & ignobly starved youth. *Because* I fought for you you are a free man so to speak. I have paid for all I have made you & your life with much more than money— Money is the smallest part of it. I have paid with silent endurance of . . . falsehood & misrepresentation of every kind. I do not grudge them."[32] She reinforced this belief later in the year when she wrote to him on his summer holiday in Rhode Island that "the loveliness of things is having them when one wants them most and not waiting until one is tired of wishing for them. I have been epicurean about your life."[33]

The birthday visit was not a success. As she said later, "when I went to you there was no place for me. It had not once come into my mind that you would not have wanted me with all your heart and felt you could not let me be away on that one day."[34] He had indeed begged for her to be there. Frances and Swan seem to have agreed to meet on friendly terms for Vivian's birthday, but Vivian, as a typical young man with a full cadre of friends and events surrounding his birthday and his play, spent little time with his mother. She stayed out of his way for the first evening, not wanting to make him more nervous than he already seemed. When she returned to Washington, she was disappointed by the trip but heartened by the Washington spring.

Part of her optimism was her belief that she'd found a person who seemed to understand the psychological theory she'd been trying to formulate for years. A Dr. Gates was introduced to her by Charlie Rice, and she was fascinated by his research on the human brain, which seemed so consonant with her own ideas about what she called Brain Science: the notion that the human mind was the most potent force on earth, capable of limitless power that rivalled electricity, light, and sound. Her book *The One I Knew the Best of All* had been a study of the child's mind on its way to harnessing this force, "that the brain is the greatest Engine—the greatest Motor of any yet discovered."[35] Her disappointing experiments with séances and mental healing years before in Boston, and her journal entries on her attempts to come to terms with Lionel's death and the "Power," were all part of this.

She was also buoyed by Stephen's return to America to help with the rehearsals for *A Lady of Quality*, by signing a contract with Scribner's and Warne for *His Grace of Osmonde*, and by news of "the Duke," to whom she'd sent Vivian with a letter inquiring about the loan. He replied that he anticipated soon paying the back interest on the loan. On the strength of this and the new book, she borrowed a further $2,500 from Scribner's. All of these hopes would crumble by the end of the year.

The source of so many of her troubles was the play. As a novel *A Lady of Quality* had taken possession of her and, as she would say about much of her work, "wrote itself" quickly. As a play it was fraught with impediments. It took a year to write and just as long to rewrite it. No actress, other than Calhoun, met Frances's clear notion of Clorinda, and Julia Arthur seemed to sleepwalk through the rehearsals. In October, when it hit another snag, Stephen wrote to Burlingame about the delinquent *DeWilloughby* in a way that makes it seem there was a clubby masculinity about their relationship: "I regret to say that another trouble in regard to the play which Mrs Burnett *had* to be acquainted with has upset her work again. However I am sending her soothing telegrams at suitable intervals and hope she will quickly get in the right frame."[36] It seemed she was surrounded by men whose incomes depended on her work and moods.

Stephen left New York in early October to open the play in Detroit, using that venue to work out its kinks and prepare the cast for the New York premiere at the end of the year. Frances expected to join him there but instead received a telegram from him telling her not to bother; the theatre had burned to the ground, taking the sets and costumes with it. Surprisingly, she saw this as great publicity for the play. They could bring the cast back, rehearse somewhere while new costumes and sets were being made, and open to a crowd of sympathetic New Yorkers. In fact, the stage company itself felt indebted to Arthur's assistance after the fire, when she arranged to have them put on half salary until the play could open in New York; even Stephen signed this published letter of appreciation.[37] As the time drew near, he became less sanguine. Julia Arthur was "a mule" and a "bad rehearser";

she and the other actors walked so lifelessly through their roles that the play dragged on for nearly three hours. Vivian's songs never arrived, and Frances, seized by inspiration one day, raced into Effie Macfarlane's house and picked out a refrain that was in her head, wrote it out in letters rather than musical notes, and sent it to her musical brother Herbert, who "made a Hades of a drinking song of it."[38]

Trouble seemed to follow the play from Detroit to New York, however. Stephen was listed as a co-author with Frances and had an important acting part. Julia Arthur was managed by her brother, Arthur Lewis, and disagreements arose between the two couples. Frances had apparently made Stephen her stage director, and both Arthur and Lewis resented what they saw as his "unnecessary officious[ness] during the rehearsals . . . hinder[ing] them through the medium of many petty and allegedly vexatious meddlings."[39] A row ensued, with Stephen being ordered off the stage, Frances coming to his defence, and the entire play put in jeopardy. It was the sort of story that the press loved.

The play opened on 1 November, with Frances, Vivian, Herbert, Edith, and Frank in the audience; Stephen was on stage as the earl of Dunstanwolde, Clorinda's elderly first husband. The *New York Times* proclaimed it a triumph of "good and stirring acting," but in private Frances thought Arthur a disaster. When the Sunday *Herald* interviewed her, she refused to complain in print, but "to those who know me & the situation there is fine reading between the lines."[40] The play's critics offered differing opinions, some believing that Arthur offered only a "feeble suggestion of the masculine side of Clorinda's character," others stating that Arthur's strong acting saved the play, and a number of them pronouncing the play disappointing and slow. Even those who had seen dramatic possibility in the novel said that the play was too long and was "marred by a deal of crude workmanship."[41] Only one reviewer fully understood Frances and what this play meant to her, and her determination to find only the perfect actress for the part. "In this book she has sought to crystallize the spiritual essence of her whole life's thinking; to give matured and ripened expression to ideas which have been simmering in her brain since childhood," wrote the *Critic*, in words so clearly Frances's own that they must have come directly from her in an interview.[42] The fact was that the play was a hit, perhaps in part because she changed the ending of the play from that in the novel, in which the duke of Osmonde never learns that his beloved wife killed Oxon, to a more morally satisfying confession by Clorinda to her husband, who forgives her, even though "no large section of the public demands that art shall always be preaching sermons."[43]

She ended the year away from all matters theatrical, devoting herself only to social life in Washington, where "the atmosphere is heavy with *Débutantes* coming out teas." She planned a special Christmas party for Vivian and his friends, even inviting for the week Herbert's daughter Frances, "a young woman who does not appeal to me but she is very quiet & lady like in man- ner & plays quite well . . . but I do *not* think she is at all interesting."[44] *His Grace of Osmonde* was published in December, recognized by the press as well written but also as the remake that it was; Frances, however, never read the newspapers and could ignore such criticism.[45] Best of all, in her mind she was planning her return to England at the end of January. Eleanor Cal- houn was ready to meet her to mount the English production of *A Lady of Quality*, but for now Frances was doing nothing more than entertaining and enjoying the crush of people who came to her finely catered evenings. She blossomed in this social atmosphere, with one reporter remarking that "she is just as rosy and as young looking as she was fifteen years ago, with the same tawney [*sic*] hair and the same big baby-like eyes. In her house is the luxury that she loves."[46]

When she left with Edith for England on 29 January, she left behind, un- beknown to her friends or to Vivian, a petition for divorce to be filed by Will Dennis only when she was safely out of the country and away from the American press, which would assume that she was freeing herself from Swan in order to marry Stephen.

She had other plans: to find a place in the English countryside where she could write and make a garden. She was about to transform herself into a lady of quality.

CHAPTER 16

~

MAYTHAM HALL

1897–1900

THE PRESS COULD SPECULATE all it wanted, but the fact was that Frances and Swan had carefully orchestrated their divorce for some time. In a time when mutual desire to end a marriage did not constitute official grounds for divorce, the simplest charge was desertion and failure to provide, which required that one party have moved away from the other for two years. Because Frances owned the house at 1770 Massachusetts Avenue, Swan obligingly moved out into the house near Farragut Square during Vivian's second year at college. This meant that a divorce could be obtained just as Vivian was graduated and launched into the world. Everyone knew that "desertion" on Swan's part was ironic at best in that it was Frances who had in effect left him years before, but it shortened the process by allowing an uncontested divorce that left journalists little to speculate about.

With Frances out of the country, Swan and their friends in Washington circled the wagons to prevent gossip and refused to speak to reporters, even though the story made front-page news when it appeared in March 1898. The *Washington Post*, as their local newspaper, had known about the Burnetts' difficulty for years and laid much of the blame on Frances's "advanced ideas regarding the duties of a wife and the rights of women" and on Swan's sensitivity towards her fame and success, things that originally had made him proud. Now the newspapers inadvertently added insult to injury when one reported that "Dr. Francis Hodgson Burnett denies that he has separated from his wife, the authoress."[1] Both of them were much admired locally, Swan for his respected medical practice and publications, and Frances not only for her books but also for her "commanding presence and

202

personal magnetism." (In contrast, one cruel account said that Swan was "of less than ordinary stature and a cripple.")[2] The London correspondent to the normally more staid *New York Times* used the occasion to speculate on the reason that so many women writers seemed to divorce their husbands, finally deciding that it could be attributed to the fact that "in households where the wife is an author . . . she insists upon reading her manuscripts to her husband, and then when he has taken to drink divorces him."[3] Will Dennis kept the Burnetts' confidence, and when Swan was finally accosted outside his house he admitted that the divorce was by mutual consent before almost literally slamming the door on further discussion.[4]

Again and again, Frances's ideas on women were mentioned as contributing to the separation as well as to the public perception that their relations had been strained for years. Even when Vivian was in high school "there was domestic discord. Husband and wife were rarely if ever seen together, and conducted themselves toward each other only as acquaintances. While Mrs. Burnett never posed as a new woman, yet she entertained very advanced ideas as to the rights of women and the duties of a wife, which in no way accorded with those of her husband, and hence what was at first only a difference of opinion grew to be the cause of their final separation."[5] Everyone agreed, however, that the two of them had planned it carefully, with the papers prepared before she left and the grounds purely technical.

In fact, their differences and separate lives were so well known that many of their friends were stunned not by the news but by the fact that it hadn't taken place years before. Those who knew they were still married had encouraged them to make a legal break of it so that they could avoid the financial entanglements of a two-career couple as well as move on in their lives. Indeed, Vivian himself had told them that it would be much easier on him if they divorced instead of limping along in the married-but-not-married state they had occupied for so many years. Frances acknowledged this when she wrote to him at the end of February before the news hit the papers. "You may remember that some little time ago you said to me that if the separation between your father and myself were more complete the position would be easier for you," she reminded him. "I did not quite understand why it would be so but I had no doubt you had a practical reason, and what you inferred rather set me to thinking. For a number of years many of my friends have expressed themselves strongly on this subject and finally I have decided that they are right."[6] She phrased it as being merely a business matter to be sorted out.

The divorce went through quickly, and by May they were free of each other. The affidavit she left with Will Dennis and Swan's lack of contest were all that was needed under Washington law for the judge to dissolve the legal contract of their marriage. In the process he added something unexpected: the right of Frances to revert to her maiden name, which she found an impractical gift since the world now knew her professionally as Frances Hodgson Burnett.[7] Vivian believed it was Swan who acquiesced to his wife's desire for a divorce, but several years later Frances admitted to another, more charitable reason for the action. Swan, she knew, was a lonely man who wished to remarry and could never do so as long as she remained legally in the picture. Six years later he married Margaret Brady, a woman Vivian and Lionel had known as "Aunt Margaret" when they were children. The couple would have only two years of marriage before his sudden death in 1906.

For the time being, the speculation was on her remarriage, not Swan's, and newspapers erroneously but gleefully reported that the woman who eschewed marriage and lived a fiercely independent life devoted to art was about to marry a man ten years her junior. They asserted that she was "preparing a sequel for the divorce she recently obtained," but no one had any evidence for this other than what Frances and Stephen themselves had provided in their professional inseparability. For months she denied these rumours.

The fact was that she was very busy establishing a very different sort of relationship. For many summers she had taken houses in the country—ranging from the Massachusetts coast to Surrey and Kent in England—and now she wanted something more permanent. London she found dreary, oppressive, and expensive. After spending several weeks in Manchester helping their impoverished cousin Emma Daniels and her crippled son Willie by taking a house on St. Bees Street and refurbishing it as a boarding house for professional gentlemen, she and Edith went south again to look at a house that would become Frances's most cherished home—Maytham Hall, in Rolvenden, Kent. In the same letter in which she informed Vivian of the impending divorce, she described it as "a charming place with a nicely finished park and a beautiful old walled kitchen garden. The house is excellent, panelled square hall, library, billiard room, morning room, smoking room, drawing and dining rooms, seventeen or eighteen bedrooms, stables, two entrance lodges to the park, and a square tower on the roof from which one can see the English Channel."[8]

Today the house is very different—as Great Maytham Hall, it was rebuilt in 1909 on a design by the architect Sir Edwin Lutyens and is now broken into retirement apartments—but in those days it was a gabled and timbered hall surrounded rather too closely by hedges and used by its owner, Howard Parnell Edwards, for shooting. It had been in the Moneypenny family for generations, but over time they fell into financial difficulties, and mismanagement left them virtually bankrupt. When it partially burned in 1893, it was repaired in the Tudor style. Frances immediately saw the possibilities and, once the lease was signed, collaborated with the delighted head gardener, Bolton, to rip out the hedges, opening the view to the parks and lawns surrounding it, and to fill the place with masses of flowers, including a rose walk. There was already an old kitchen garden bearing "grapes, figs, nectarines, peaches, apples, pears, strawberries, raspberries, gooseberries, cherries, currants of all shades & splendid chestnuts & English walnut trees in the park."[9] For a woman whose name is now indelibly associated with gardens, this, surprisingly, was the first one she had ever made. Bolton sent hampers of flowers and vegetables to Portland Place while she supervised the removal of her furniture, and she and Edith put an army of local men to work moving furniture, arranging fixtures, and fitting carpets; they also brought in her housekeeper, Bright, the butler, and her maid from Portland Place. As she shuttled back and forth between London and Kent, she became happier and happier at the thought of making Maytham her permanent English home. "I have seen a great many places that interested me," she told Vivian, "but Maytham I love."[10]

This was also the first time she became part of an established community outside Washington. In the nearby villages of Tenterden, Cranbrook, and Rolvenden, the occupants of Maytham Hall, like the occupants of Hole Park, the other big house in the neighbourhood, were a source of income and business, and local residents were more than happy to have the unoccupied Hall let again. "No gardener or carpenter or farmer or keeper talks to you ten minutes without referring tenderly to 'old Colonel Moneypenny,'" the former owner. "I hope they will end by being as fond of me."[11] As she drove through the villages on her regular shopping expeditions, "the people touch their hats & I know almost every one is related to me by baker-age or brewer-age or black smith-age. Just you give me time to make them adore me."[12]

In fact, with the taking of the Hall, her life made another of its important shifts. She still—with reason—worried about money; she still kept her old friends; she still fell prey to overwork. But now she had the scope and freedom to let her natural generosity have full rein and to play a role for which she seemed destined by temperament. The local residents adored her, remembering her for decades afterwards as someone naturally kind and benevolent. Friends old and new surrounded her, and she threw herself into village and country life with enthusiastic freshness. Almost as soon as she arrived, some of her neighbours, including the earl of Cranbrook and the Sackville-Cresswells, as well as the less illustrious, began to call, and as she settled in she returned their visits. The one significant hold-out was the vicar, who refused at first to visit a woman living in sin with a man to whom she wasn't wed, even one who spent his weekdays in London.

She took it all very seriously. Never a regular church attender, she now unfailingly filled the Maytham Hall gentry's pew with her house guests and the servants' pew with her staff. She wished to make friends with the children in the Sunday school, who hushed themselves as she passed. She contributed to the charity bazaars. She made her house guests stuff Christmas stockings for the children and sang loudly at the Christmas dinners for the elderly. She was, indeed, a new woman.

Edith, too, won the heart of everyone who met her. When she sailed back to Washington with her husband and sons in November, she left a "trail of friends behind [her] everywhere."[13] Frances particularly loved reading her latest chapters to Edith "before the ink was really dry," knowing that "when Edith begins to make little squeals and chuckles, I know all is well."[14] Even the maids and housekeepers spoke about her wistfully after she was gone, with Bright telling Frances that the day Edith left "it was as if some one had been buried."[15] Frances accompanied her sister to the port and addressed a letter to her on board ship as soon as she returned home, and every few days afterwards for weeks. "It seemed so strange to dress for the dinner party on Tuesday night knowing there was no Edith in the Green Room and that there would be no Edith until next summer," she told her.

> You may be sure the whole household misses you every hour & no one could miss you as I do. But I know you will be glad when I tell you that I am *not* lonely in this big house at all. . . . The day you went of course I felt sad about losing you & as I drove home through the lovely goldening rain swept country I kept expecting that lonely horror you spoke of to descend upon me—but it did not descend. I wrote letters & went & talked with my darling Bolton about the Rose Garden & the 800 tulip & hyacinth, & crocus, & iris & snowdrop & anemone bulbs which have just arrived, and discussed the 1001 which are to arrive in a day or so more; we planned where he would plant more roses, & were interested almost to tears. Then quite late in the afternoon the dear little vicaress came & we talked & had tea in the Billiard Room by the fire, & in the evening I went to the party at Westwell. It was so nice.[16]

She was rarely alone in the house, with weekend parties, guests staying for weeks and even months at a stretch, and Stephen, of course, there several days a week. Kenneth Campbell came down for summer weekends and holidays over the next year, and his wife Rosamond remained at Maytham for months, helping Frances in the gardens. Madge (also called Maddie) Hepworth Dixon and her daughter Ella, whom Frances first met when Ella wrote an article about her—which Frances completely revised—also stayed for weeks. In the mornings Frances and Ella shut themselves up in separate rooms to write, "& in the afternoon we walk or drive or cycle. In the evening we sit & talk & laugh & laugh."[17] When there were large weekend parties, they sat after supper in the billiard room, and when the coaches were called to take the local guests home, "Barrett sets a small table with whisky & brandy & soda in the hall so that before the guests go out into the night they may fortify themselves. . . . One has a number of new things to learn in the country. Perry entertains the horses in the stables—& the coachmen sup in the Servants Hall."[18]

Sometimes so many people were there on the weekends that extra servants had to be called in and schedules for baths arranged. Even with seventeen bedrooms the house might fill. At Christmas, on a whim, everyone decided to dress in costume, raiding Frances's cupboards for fancy dress, causing so much hilarity in the evening that the housekeeper and servants were brought to admire them. "The rest of the night we devoted to revels," she told Edith. "We danced, we sang, we played ridiculous games, we did everything crazy & amusing you can imagine."[19] It was this revelry that inspired a number of friends to create a book for her, "Presented to our friend Mrs. Hodgson-Burnett, the 'High Priestess' of the 'Pink Lamp.'" Over three years, various visitors used it as a guest book, filling it with coloured pictures of their antics, lively dancing and tennis playing, caricatures and cartoons. "This is the strenuous life of Maytham Hall when we go down strictly for work," Poulteney Bigelow wrote under a colour drawing of a man and woman engaged in a fierce game of tennis. "I mean brain work—this picture tells how it *feels* to Poulteney Bigelow." Americans as well as English guests wandered through Maytham; Richard Watson Gilder signed the guest book in 1900, as did Helen and Arthur Scribner. Some composed music and penned the lyrics to "My Lady's Garden (at Maytham)," calling her the "Lady of the Kentish Weald":

> Stay there,—in your peaceful dreaming,
>   All the wealth of Time is yours!
> Heaven lies but in our seeming,
>   Life goes past, but Art endures!

As one guest wrote, Maytham became known more for its high jinks and wild times than for its sedate country life.

Henry James lived nearby in Rye in Lamb House where Frances sent him baskets of fruit. One day Frances, Rosamond, and Ella were wandering the streets of Rye—Frances had a passion for antique oak—when Rosamond boldly marched up to his door. He was out, but when the servant realized that they were with Frances, he insisted they tour the house. Later that afternoon they encountered James himself on a bicycle. Frances reported that he was so delighted to see her that he insisted they all turn back and spend the night with him.[20] They declined, but another day she encountered him again, whereupon he "seized upon us & made us go to lunch with him at his lovely house. It is so quaint & pretty & he is so lovable."[21] This might have been the luncheon at which he inexplicably left the table and was later seen pacing in his garden.[22] James was certainly the sort of person whose friendship Frances wanted to cultivate, and she recalled the kindness of his condolence visit to her in London after Lionel's death. That James reciprocated Frances's desire to form a closer tie is doubtful, despite the effusiveness of his letters to her and his unflagging pleasantness to her whenever they met. Always the epitome of thoughtfulness in his letters to her, he nonetheless accepted few of her invitations to Maytham. He admitted to his brother being somewhat disheartened by the fact that her books sold far more copies than his and, unbeknown to her, had years before written an anonymous and not particularly flattering review of her play *Esmeralda* in the *Pall Mall Gazette*.[23]

Even though Portland Place was not yet off her hands, throughout her first summer at Maytham Hall Frances revelled in the new house and in the forthcoming version of *A Lady of Quality* on the London stage. Eleanor Calhoun had now won the backers she needed, partly because Frances herself believed in her and took pity on her and wished for her to succeed. She was "so full of anxiety & heart wrung sympathy for her and have felt that after her two years struggle and anguish it would be so *hellish* if the play was taken from her that it has been almost more than I could bear. I know she has suffered tortures."[24] In fact, Frances was one of the few who had faith in her ability to carry off the role, and she carried the day. As they waited to arrange a theatre, Eleanor became a regular guest at Maytham. Frances insisted that in order to avoid the fate of *Phyllis*, the play was to have a prime West End location, and she was willing to nurture and rehearse her protégée while they waited. When she was in London, Eleanor engaged a fencing master in order to be able to carry off Clorinda's on-stage swordsmanship.

Frances was determined that Eleanor be as big a success in London as Julia Arthur had been briefly in America, though Julia had caused difficulties by leaving the play early for another part, despite its success and her contractual commitment. Ironically, Julia later had a change of heart and sued the Samuel French company for the right to act the role in theatres in other states. Frances always believed that the play, rather than Julia's innate talent, had made her successful in the role, for "she has not the brains or the temperament or the art to produce any effect unless she has a big part to uphold her. . . . She will be furious to find that after all her bribery & corruption of the past it *was* the 'Lady of Quality' & not Julia Arthur the world wanted."[25] With Eleanor she felt she had found the actress who could make the play the lasting success it deserved to be.

Calhoun, from Vidalia, California, was determined to succeed in England. In their Maytham Hall rehearsals, Eleanor's dashing manner filled Frances with courage and strength. In January Frances moved back to London, staying at Walsingham House, carrying along her servants, carriage, and horses—and Stephen—in order to work with her. One day she and Eleanor went to the wig maker's "to see Eleanor try on her Clorinda wigs and she is absolutely *beautiful* in them. I had really no idea that rouge & blue black hair could make her look so brilliant. She merely sweeps the Arthur person from the surface of the earth as far as looks go. Her wigs are so much more picturesque and she herself has such a dashing air & such a bearing. Even Stephen was impressed & owned that she was beautiful."[26]

It turned out that Vivian had been right to warn her not to put all her faith in plays. He was now working as a newspaperman in Denver, after spending the months after his graduation in a *Wanderjahr*, travelling in America and learning his trade. One day in his Denver office he saw a wire story pronouncing the play's success when it opened at the Comedy Theatre on 8 March 1899, but the *Washington Post* picked up the story and declared that "though the performance was a distinct success, the general opinion is that the play will not have a long run."[27] The English reviews were harsher, declaring that Clorinda was on stage entirely too long. "We pardon her in the novel, and might do so in the play if we saw and heard less of her," wrote the *Athenaeum*'s critic. "It is a matter for genuine regret that neither the dramatists nor the actress can see that we might have too much of a good thing."[28] As in New York, Frances laid the blame everywhere but on herself. She and Stephen had worked "like Trojans"; how could it be their fault? Instead, they had bad luck in the manager, Mulholland, who was suburban and not in with the West End crowd; the play opened during Lent, when people were denying themselves pleasures; "poor Eleanor so utterly fails to attract. . . . She does her best but she is not powerful enough and she is so curiously without magnetism" that she surely would never be offered another part. She claimed that Eleanor came to rehearsals without learning her lines, and "my reward for being faithful to a suffering creature has been that my work has been reviled, insulted & thrown into the gutter," she told Edith. "I wonder how long it will take my soul to recover."[29]

The fact was that she felt humiliated, for once again the press laid the fault at the playwright's door, just as they had with the Julia Arthur version in New York. Vivian had warned her against the play, and Stephen had cautioned her about putting Eleanor in the role and about hiring Mulholland. Others too had advised her against Eleanor. "I was told she was so unpopular that no play could stand up against," she wrote to Frank Jordan. "I was told that she was unpractical & unreliable & tiresome in rehearsal." In rehearsals she refused to accept criticism without argument and "annoyed & wore out the company by constantly ranting."[30] Frances passed notes to her during rehearsal, Stephen no doubt entered the fray, and although Frances claimed to pity Eleanor, the actress certainly felt hounded by the two authors. In May, when Stephen wrote to her to recover fifty pounds he had loaned to her, she not only wrote to Frances to ask her for the money in order to repay Stephen but wrote him a terse letter blaming the play's failure on Frances and Stephen and their script. The reviews bore out this opinion, complaining that she was on stage for too much of the play, "frequently with next to nothing to say. . . . Our dramatist might do worse than take a lesson in these things from Shakespeare."[31]

None of this would have mattered so very much to Frances if she hadn't thrown herself so completely into the novel and play for two years. The solution to bucking up the sagging attendance came in flooding the English, Canadian, and American markets with cheap editions of *A Lady of Quality* and *His Grace of Osmonde*, a tactic that worked. In North America, Scribner's put Julia Arthur's portrait on the frontispiece and pitched it as the "Julia Arthur edition." Within weeks, Warne had sold 40,000 copies of *Lady* and 29,000 of *His Grace*, and well over 75,000 copies of *Lady* seemed likely to sell in America. This helped make up for low revenues from the play but not for more shaking news early in the year: George Simmons committed suicide, leaving his debts unpaid. Frances could only hope now that some sealed documents he left behind would reveal an insurance policy covering his debts after his family was provided for and wrote urgently to Will Dennis to look into it, but in her heart she accepted the loss.

Her family members still needed her help. Frank had lost his job, and they all pinned their hopes on Ernest, who seemed about to land on his feet, with a laboratory and salary offered to him by a backer, but still he needed an increase in his allowance. Herbert wrote to her from Virginia to say that his son Alfred Eldridge was about to marry and go to Germany and to ask whether, if he paid his daughter Frances's passage, Fluffy "would pay her expenses while she lived there studying." Frances knew that this letter came at the instigation of Herbert's wife, Medora, and

it really did seem to me too much. If I had not been feeling so anxious about my affairs I should not have felt it so impossible if I believed the girl would *ever* do anything but dress herself & sit in a rocking chair. To my mind she shows no signs of particular talent & she is so vapid & utterly without character that to send her to Germany for study would be simply to saddle oneself with her for an unlimited visit to Europe. I helped Ernest because he had determination & genius. I helped Archie because I saw he would work after he was set on his feet, but Frances seems to me a sort of nullity. I am so sorry for poor Herbert's sake. If I had been able & she had been different I should have been glad to do it because I am fond of Herbert. But the blank truth was I had not the money to undertake it if I had wished to with all my soul.[32]

When Vivian left Harvard in June, she and Swan each pledged to him fifty dollars a month to sustain him on his six-month *Wanderjahr*, which took him out west to Chicago and Colorado, and helped support him while he worked.

The journalism job on the *Denver Republican* was an eye-opener and changed Vivian from a pampered college boy into a hardworking cub reporter. He walked miles in the snow at night to cover local stories, worked fifteen-hour days with only a half day or one day off each week, lived in a modest boarding house, and took his meals with grizzled newspapermen in front of whom he shed his posh accent. It was all he could do to get a few hours' sleep, let alone lead a more cultivated life. "Your asking me to keep a guard on my accent is a case in point," he wrote to his mother. "How can I, in the strenuous rush of the life I am living, stop to think if I say gläss or glâss—if I say I or oi. . . . You have drummed it in to me so often that I cannot help but remember."[33] He missed his parents, and when Swan paid him a long visit in August, he hoped that his mother would do the same towards the end of the year. He also knew of her financial troubles and begged her not to do the thing she was contemplating, selling the Washington house. It made no sense, he told her; it was something she owned free and clear, so she could make an income out of its rental if necessary and would always be sure that she had a home to go to if things became difficult. Furthermore, it was the nearest thing he had to a childhood home. She owned other property in Washington, a couple of plots of land that seemed in a fair way to appreciate in value now that the city was expanding, and he thought she might end up making a profit on those should she decide to sell them later on.

With the play limping along, Frances retired to Maytham to finish *In Connection with the DeWilloughby Claim*, which had itself been limping along for some twenty years. Now so dated that its story and setting evinced nostalgia, it was completed at the end of the summer. At Frances's initiative, Stephen haggled with Scribner's for a higher royalty—25 per cent—than they customarily gave her, and they in turn tried to convince her to shorten the title to something more manageable. She refused, suggesting in turn that they break it up into two lines. The book was published in November under its full title, which encouraged American reviews about "Mrs. Burnett's New Story—A Beautiful One with a Long Title." The press lauded her "spellbinding" return to the fiction of her earlier years and "her own people" of North Carolina, Virginia, and Washington but pronounced that "it is with some trepidation that we attack a book bearing so fearful a name."[34]

The irony of a woman now so immersed in her English life being lauded as returning to her American roots underscored the confusion in which the public held her national identity. "Even in the matter of nationality Mrs. Burnett is always something else, contradicting and at the same time including what you would define her," one frustrated interviewer wrote.

Assert that she is American, and she will cry out as if the notion were preposterous. Then when she has explained that she was born and educated in Manchester, England, not coming to this country till she was entering upon young-ladyhood, and following which she has lived always half of the time in England—when she has told you this, and, rather ashamed of your ignorance of facts concerning so eminent a woman, you say, apologetically, "I did not know before that you are English," she will again put your wits to rout, exclaiming: "But I am not English. I am both English and American. I am more of one until the other of me is denied, and then I'm that; and taken altogether, if I were not English, I should not be American; if not American, not English. In fine, I must be both or not at all."[35]

The gardens and people at Maytham Hall worked their magic on her that summer, taking the edge off her many disappointments. As it would for years, Maytham Hall soothed her as the place where she truly belonged. She set up an outdoor study, with a table and chair under the trees near the rose garden, and wrote each morning in the company of a robin that grew tame. She and Rosamond brought up two orphaned lambs on a bottle, and they followed her about and slept on her knee as she sang to them. Her visitors wandered through, playing tennis and croquet in the afternoons. Annie Russell, who had played Esmeralda so long before, came to visit, and when she left Frances wrote to her about a party she had for poor London children.

We danced around in rings and sang songs, we had the most lovely tea— all cakes & jam puffs & sweets. I took the party to my fairy Wood & to the Fairy tree & I sat with them in the Fairy Tree & told the story of the Christmas Cuckoo. We had races—& I went into the house & robbed my maid of splendid ribbons & bows she was saving for me—& I gave them for prizes. You never saw anything like the success of those ribbons. The great race of the afternoon was one I ran myself with a baby boy. He was an angel of form who was more sweet than words can paint. He had a darling little head all covered with short curls, & a darling little face with blue eyes like flowers & an utter heavenly unconsciousness that he was *not* one of the gentry which made one worship him. When the bigger ones raced & won prizes he wanted to race too & so I entered the lists with him for a chase from the slope to the Ha Ha. Never was there such a Homeric contest. The baby ran with chuckles & shrieks of joy & I tucked up my lace petticoats & careered after him—always a yard *after* him & uttering cries of despair because he ran so *very* fast I *never* could get near him. So adorable. I never loved any afternoon as much in my life.[36]

As summer slipped into autumn, she began to miss America and her family members and decided to return for a visit. Vivian, to whom two weeks off was only a dream, begged her to visit him in Denver. She at first planned to go, even buying a sealskin coat trimmed with ermine "because I wanted Viv's Mammy to be very smart as well as warm."[37] When she consulted her doctors, however, they decided that the altitude of the mile-high city was too great for her still weak heart. Vivian went from doctor to doctor, gathering assurances that she faced no danger, but her biggest fear was not death itself but that she might become a terrible burden to him, dead or alive, should something go wrong. He was heartbroken, pointing out that they had not seen each other for more than two years and he wanted to introduce her to Denver society. In the end she prevailed, and he went home to Washington for Christmas, glad afterwards to have done so, for it enabled him to take a much-needed break and see his relatives and friends in Washington and New York.

He looked forward to her making a long stay in America, where they could carry on a more rapid correspondence (it took a month to get a letter to her in England and receive a reply), and everyone rejoiced when she arrived in November on the *St. Paul.* They spent a happy Christmas and New Year's together, but she disappointed them by leaving in February, only a few months after her arrival. Just before Christmas she hinted to Kitty Hall that barely was she released from the burden created by trusting in Eleanor Calhoun when she was now called on to bear another. "Fluffy begins her century wound up in the web of having tried to help one person and borne the consequences, and in rejoicingly beginning to help another, which, in this case, will of course turn out *quite* differently," she told Kitty. "They always *are* quite different—when one begins, and it would be so impossible not to stretch out a hand. But we are what we are, and the kind of thing it is the law of one's nature to do one does in the face of the condign punishments which are inevitably inflicted as the reward of what we think are good deeds."[38]

She now believed that no good deed went unpunished, and following an evening reception she gave in the new year, she fell ill with a severe cold that threatened to become pneumonia. Nevertheless, on 28 February she boarded a steamer not for London but for Italy. Washington journalists reported that her departure "closes one of the most charming literary and social centers of the West End. This talented authoress, whose name is familiar among lovers of literature the world over, took passage by the Southern line of steamships for Genoa, where she will be joined by a party of friends who will accompany her up the Riviera, with the intention of stopping at the Island of Corsica, and in May returning to Maytham Hall, her beautiful country place near London."[39] Perhaps she deliberately misled the reporter, for although she did board a ship for Italy, it was not with a party of friends. Instead, she met Stephen in Genoa, by arrangement, and married him. It was one of the biggest mistakes of her life.

CHAPTER 17

❧

STEPHEN

1900–1902

FRANCES AND HER MAID THOMPSON arrived safely in Genoa, but their letters to Gibraltar had gone astray and Stephen was nowhere to be found. In 1900 women rarely travelled alone, and certainly Frances never travelled without at least her maid; for a trip like this to the Continent, a woman certainly needed a male escort. Stephen had tried to make things go smoothly, even arranging ahead of time for a courier to meet them at the boat and see them through customs, but nothing went as planned, and Frances and her maid "fought our way unaided through the chuckling Italians at the Custom House & finally [took] refuge in a hotel in the town aghast at the fact that we did not know where our escort was. It was rather awful. Poor Stephen had taken such pains."[1] He at first tried to bribe agents in Italy to find out when her steamer was due and ended by wiring their friend Hugh MacArthur in London for information and arriving after Frances. After the wedding they moved on to the little town of Pegli, where it poured with rain for days. It was not an auspicious beginning.

The marriage made news on both sides of the Atlantic, more discreetly as an announcement in the London papers, more sensationally in New York, where it was front-page news. Some papers professed that the two had met while collaborating on *A Lady of Quality*, when in fact they had known each for more than ten years. Others called him her private secretary, and although he handled many of her business matters, he was much more than that in her professional life. Many articles stressed the ten-year difference in their ages (she was now forty-five to his thirty-five), with one lurid account asserting that he was "young enough to be her son" and concocting a crazy biography of Frances, beginning with her growing up in Cornwall (not Lancashire) in rags and bare feet, where neighbours called her "the lit-tle girl of the mines." This fanciful biography then skipped Tennessee alto-gether, landing Frances in a Washington tenement; it also credited Lionel (not Vivian) with inspiring *Little Lord Fauntleroy*, then begging Frances to take him to London and Paris to escape the resulting publicity, and per-suading her to move to Maytham Hall and write another book, *The Lady of Quality*. One article described Stephen as having "the physique of the average English college-bred athlete. In his face was that which indicated the artistic spirit. Some women's ideal of a god." In a separate box were quoted "Some Passionate Utterances from Mrs. Burnett's Novels," all of them to do with love, all them taken out of context, and all meant to portray her as sensual and even erotic. The article also included a full spread of photo-graphs of her, Stephen, and Maytham Hall.[2] All accounts made much of the fact that Stephen was a Fellow of the Royal College of Surgeons, a member of the Inner Temple, and the son of a clergyman; only one account, to make it clear that Stephen had collaborated with her on several plays, corrected the more scandalous suggestion that Frances had run off with her private sec-retary. In any case, her marriage "directed the public anew to a figure upon which it has often before been riveted. . . . The authoress . . . has thus alloyed the fine gold of her literary fame with the notoriety of a divorce and mar-riage."[3] A joke began making the rounds: "I see that Mrs. Frances Hodgson Burnett has married her physician," it went. "It's cheaper, of course."[4]

The newly married couple spent much of the early spring enjoying the milder weather of Arenzano, near Genoa, before returning to Maytham. Frances worried about this return, partly because she didn't quite know what to do about the servants when combining households, partly because "I have always had some one to do these things—or some woman with me," an aversion to solitude that went back as far as her early Washington days, when she was rumoured to have "a rooted aversion to being alone, liking to have some one at hand to talk to even while she was dressing, and when confined to the house by indisposition, if only for a day, would dispatch a messenger posthaste to a friend to 'come and sit with her.'"[5] Mostly she worried because of Stephen himself.[6] He behaved sweetly in Italy, but she feared how he might behave once they made their home in Maytham. She missed having her protective relatives about her in case something went wrong.

At first the spring of 1900 went well. Despite the bad weather in Kent ("the English weather is diabolical," she wrote to Edith. "The Spring is full of loveliness but freezes your marrow"), all the previous year's hard work in the garden paid off with glorious flowers. She wrote long letters home, worry-ing about Frank who had now lost a bookkeeping job to "a man who went out of his mind" and offering to lend him money without interest to re-launch his business. In May, when British troops defeated the Boers in South Africa and all of England literally went wild in the streets, Frances and Stephen sobbed with joy and ran up the flag on their new pole as the church bells rang. They clattered into the village in their phaeton, pinning ribbons and bows on all the children and handing out Union Jacks. When Stephen gave the bell-ringers a sovereign to drink to Baden-Powell's health, Frances went to visit two old invalid cottagers, holding their hands and ordering in beef for them.[7] United by this frenzy of patriotism, they seemed the perfect English couple.

Only a few days later she began to reveal to her friends and relatives in America the truth of this terrifying and terrible relationship. She was convinced that had she been surrounded several years before by the friends who now surrounded her at Maytham, especially the male friends, she never would have married Stephen. His temper, which she had noted immediately when she first knew him, never improved. He still had bouts of jealous anger in which he berated and threatened her, followed by periods of calm. Now he began to make scenes in front of friends and servants, accusing her of the most egregious improprieties, screaming at her, and making threats. He had bullied and blackmailed her into marriage, and she feared that he was mad. She wanted various friends to understand the situation, in the event that Stephen should harm her.

It is even worse than I thought it would be. I am certain it is not sanity I have to deal with in this violent madly jealous and strangely spiteful & malignant nature. I never saw or heard of anything like it. It *could* not be a sane thing. It is too frantic & unreasoning. But for a cunning which—between bursts of envious rage & bursts of reproaches—always works & always has worked to gain some material advantage—I should be positively sure that in a few months the man would be in a mad house. My one forlorn hope was that when this marriage was a faced acknowledged fact I could at least have a kind of peace—But as the weeks pass even that seems out of the question. It is all so grotesquely hideous—it is like some wild nightmare which I surely *must* waken from presently. And if I had only known, a few years ago, certain English friends I know intimately now, it could all have been prevented. Two or three men of the world who are gentlemen would have known how to deal with threats & violence alternated by hysterics. Two or three women who are not defenceless because they have husbands & brothers who *are* gentlemen—could have made him realize all I have to bear & how they could have rescued me. But in those days I only knew them formally & as a woman living apart from her husband. I was so desirous of avoiding scenes and scandals that my one thought was to keep things quiet & try to reach some reasonable & dignified means of escape. But let me tell you something—if a man is sufficiently indecent & unscrupulous—if he will rave before your butler & makes scenes before your maid & if you are a woman who has horror of publicity such a man can gradually attain almost anything he has in view. I write these things to you because if this monstrous thing ends in tragedy I should like you to be one of those who know something of the truth.[8]

Stephen protested angrily that Frances did not love him yet did "all the things to make love impossible & respect out of the question & then pours forth frantic condemnation of the woman who does not love her husband." Although she had seen no reason to divorce Swan—a married woman was allowed certain professional and social freedoms with a man that a single woman was not—Stephen "never for an instant seems to recall the fact that I was dragged & threatened & blackmailed & forced into this marriage."[9] When she repeatedly refused to marry him, he threatened to go public with stories about their relationship, to tell people that she had pursued him from the moment she saw him and that he had been able to kiss her within only two weeks of meeting her, and to join up with Swan "in hounding me down."[10] When he began to accuse her of "vile" things, she retorted that she wished him to repeat them in front of her male friends, for they would knock him down.

She refused to be alone with him at Maytham Hall, keeping herself surrounded by protective friends. Rosamond Campbell was there as much as possible, and her husband, Kenneth, Stephen's physician colleague, spent as many weekends there as he could. Madge and Ella Hepworth Dixon stayed often, as did another friend, Hugh MacArthur. All of them understood the situation, and many of them had witnessed Stephen's outbursts. After calming down for a couple of days, he begged to be left alone with his wife, and the friends reluctantly left. Things were all right for a while, but as he worked on a speech he was to give to an antivivisectionist group, he once again grew increasingly excitable. After reading one of Rosamond's letters to her, he became so jealous of their friendship that he tried to end it. "*Why* was I not happy & was I not happy & Why did nt [*sic*] I love him? I lied & lied & lied until I was sick but it was of no use; he is like some spiteful hysterical woman. He *will work* up scenes. He *will* not let things alone— And then he always virtuously explains that I begin things—that he *loves* me & that if I chose I could lead him by a thread."[11] He tried to cut her off from her friends, and when she finally suggested that she call in her male friends—including Henry James (one can only imagine this encounter)—to have a word with him, he calmed down once again.

Kenneth Campbell confirmed Frances's assessment of the situation in August. Among those to whom she had written in America was her brother Herbert, who responded forcefully in her defence. She showed Kenneth the letter, and he was so impressed that he wrote to Herbert himself. "Your letter, written to your sister, has been read by me," he said. "I realise it has been written *by a man*, and I want you to know that there are at least two men in England who will see that your sister comes to no harm! Although 3,000 miles of ocean separate us, I salute you." He signed it "yours in fraternity."[12]

Her life may have been in some danger, but so was her property. Stephen constantly reminded her "that it *used* to be considered proper for a man to become possessor & dispenser of his wife's belongings when he married her. He has also sent me a couple of letters from his relatives in which they seem to have been led by him to dwell heavily upon our money stations— the impropriety of a woman *not* handing over her fortune to her husband. He has evidently been talking the matter over with them."[13] She warned her friends not to discuss these matters in their letters, particularly as he sometimes read her mail, especially when it was addressed to "Mrs. Stephen Townesend," which he mistook for his own name. Interestingly, she signed this letter "Frances Hodgson," a name she hadn't used since 1873. He made a list of demands: "It is my duty to end my acquaintance with all such people as he suspects of not admiring him . . . it is my duty to make my property over to him—to live alone at Maytham except when he wishes to bring down a hospital man or so—he is to be provided with enough to keep his chambers and spend as much time there as he likes [he still retained his rooms in the Inner Temple], it is my duty to work very hard & above all to *love* him very much & insist on his writing plays with me."[14] She confided to Ella that "she would have loved an unbusiness-like husband . . . who would have refrained from leading her to her desk at ten a.m. with: 'My dear, I think you said that you would finish Chapter Ten this morning!'"[15] She believed it would be better to close down Maytham entirely rather than accede to his demands, and she refused to keep her friends away. He went off to London, writing her daily love letters from his rooms, and she wondered how it would all end.

Often as she was interviewed, and close as she was to Edith, Kitty, Effie, and Vivian, Frances tended to remain silent on highly personal matters. Her planting of these letters with her friends and family members indicated just how serious her situation was and revealed also that her ten-year relationship with Stephen had been a tortured one. He had insinuated himself into her life and wanted to drain into himself everything she represented: fame, financial freedom, even power. His jealousy and mood swings followed those recognized today as patterns of abuse; whether or not he physically abused her, he certainly did so mentally by first expressing jealousy, escalating into fury, trying to keep her from all her friends, then recovering and expressing remorse. This cycle went on and even escalated over the years. She ignored it at first, chalking it up to "English tempers" and overlooking it on Lionel's behalf, but as time went on and he threatened to ruin her public reputation, she withdrew more into herself and tried to protect her good name.

What was his hold over her? Although she was careful to cover her tracks, Frances seems to have been a woman with a past, something even her descendants quietly acknowledged even though no names were attached to the accusation. Her reputation stood so firmly on books like *Little Lord Fauntleroy* that if she found herself defending *A Lady of Quality*, any insinuations, let alone proof, of former liaisons would have ruined her professionally. To be denounced as a married woman consorting with another man, and that man one who claimed to know something damaging about her past, would have sounded the death knell of her career.

She clearly became persuaded that only by agreeing to marry Stephen could she hope to preserve her livelihood and her good character. As this realization grew, so did her awareness that she now experienced moments of pure hatred for him. If marriage would calm and satisfy him, however, she could get on with her life. But it did not. His outbursts increased, and he began to write to those she most trusted and respected, accusing her of disgraceful things. Short of responding to those who received these letters, she could only acknowledge, then ignore, them. To Gilder she wrote in late summer that "Mr Townesend has written you revolting details. I want to write about the story." She was now working on a long novel about international marriage, tentatively titled either *Betty Vanderpoel, Duchess of Wereminster*, or *The Destiny of Bettina*, based in part on the now notorious marriages between English peers and wealthy Americans such as the Vanderbilts, and "the forming of . . . character by both continents," but in fact the book was becoming a chronicle of the sordidness of her own marriage.[16] Like *In Connection with the DeWilloughby Claim*, it was to have a long gestation, but for now it went along in a rush, serving an important therapeutic purpose. She worried about getting involved again in serializing an unfinished book but needed the distraction that hard work and deadlines could give her. When Gilder and Scribner's thought it best to wait until it was finished—they too remembered the agony of *Through One Administration*'s episodes appearing while the ink was still wet and the conclusion a mystery—she was relieved. In addition to her emotional trauma, she was now experiencing debilitating heart problems again.

The hardest part of it all was keeping Vivian in the dark. He was back in Washington, having been ill himself in Denver and now summoned back to help care for Swan, who was having medical problems of his own. He took up a job as a congressional reporter, with all eyes on him, the press as usual noting that "he looks plain and businesslike, and not at all as it would seem Little Lord Fauntleroy might look as a young man of twenty or thereabouts."[17] Edith of course knew all, and Frances counted on her to give Vivian a sanitized version that would both explain why they needed to remain apart and keep him from worrying about her. He knew only that her new marriage kept them apart and blamed Stephen, whom he did not like in any case, for it. "You must not say you feel separated from me," she wrote to him from Maytham Hall.

> Nothing can come between us if we do not intend that it shall be so. I am trying now not to be swamped by the waves of a weird fate. Dont say or do things which will help them to swamp one. Perhaps the time may come when I can talk freely to you. Just now it would only make matters worse. Remember that I love you—remember that I have always loved you & remember that the one thing which beyond & above all other things I did *not* want to do—was to marry. Remember too when you set out to be a general saviour & mad idealist there is a likelihood that you may find yourself dealing with quantities and qualities unknown to you. Sometimes I sit & laugh little ghastly laughs at what I *meant* to do & what was done to me—as the reward of Heaven.[18]

It didn't take much for Vivian to piece together some of what was going on and to feel the enormous frustration of staying away from his mother when, as a grown man, he ought to be there to protect her while she was "going through the torments of the damned."[19] Having to live with his father only made matters worse; Swan wanted to use the opportunity to malign his ex-wife, and Vivian refused to participate in these conversations, trying his best, as always, to walk the tightrope between two antagonistic but beloved parents. Frances had done her best over the years to say little against Swan to Vivian, but now this second marriage brought out all the anger and frustration against marriage itself. When rumours of her divorce from Swan first reached the newspapers, they quoted her as saying more than once, "I want to be as free as a wild bird. Free to go where I please and stay as long as I like. If people talk, it is they, not I, who am wicked."[20]

As Vivian guessed at part of the story, Frances felt able to let him know a bit more. "I know that you do not think the one maddening thing—that this marriage was a thing of choice, instead of being the thing of all others on earth I desired to escape from," she wrote to him from Maytham Hall. "I revolt against that more than against anything else. It makes me sick with rage & humiliation. Why in heavens name should I—free, able to support myself—with an enviable position, surrounded by friends, holding as my most fixed creed that *not* to be married was Paradise—why should *I* marry any man—& of all men one who was penniless, horrible in temper & more impudently tenacious & exacting than any creature ever beheld—besides, seeming at most times, not to have one taste or thought in common with me. . . . I cannot imagine myself ever *willingly* marrying any man."[21] Indeed, part of Stephen's argument for her divorce from Swan had been that she could live in perfect freedom, and learn to love him, with no further demand for marriage.

Mildly surprised at Swan's desire to disparage her to their son, she reiterated the importance of Vivian's fidelity to him. However, she made equally clear that Swan's penchant for exacting pity might wear Vivian down if he were not on his guard financially. She wanted to make some money available to him, which had to be kept out of Swan's knowledge and power, in a trust that would allow Vivian a small monthly allowance but that Swan couldn't touch if he discovered it. "He has never assumed a man's responsibility in his life," she reminded him. "He has never had money for anything but his own self-indulgence & it is not easy for me to forget that *everything* I have he has actually claimed the credit for himself. . . . I have never had a husband God knows. I have only had shackled to me two creatures who seem to me indescribable in words."[22] Professing this to be her darkest hour, she inevitably compared her two husbands—the American doctor who pushed her to marry him and the English doctor who later did the same—calling them her "various husbands . . . gentlemen singularly light & airy in their entire freedom from any shadow of responsibility in the amazing relation of marriage."[23]

In fact, Stephen gained none of the concessions he desired, for he neither acquired control over her money nor managed to separate her from her friends. Too embarrassed to separate from her husband only months after her much-publicized second marriage, and too afraid to be left alone with him, she decided that the best course of action was to bring Edith over to live with them, sublet Maytham Hall for a while, and go back to London.

In London, with the "season" almost in full swing, their relationship would be more public than in the country. Stephen promised to reform, an effort she believed Herculean as she observed his attempts to rein in his temper. She and Edith and Stephen moved into the vast and stately house of the Burgcleres on Charles Street, off Berkeley Square, and with Edith's calming presence things settled down, and they lived more amicably among old masters, Sheraton and Empire furniture, and crimson brocade. "I feel that it is almost indecent to be as fond of another persons house as I find I am of this. I shall leave it in April with my handkerchief pressed to my face when I get into the carriage just like a person entering a mourning coach to go to a funeral," she told Gilder.[24] They ate their meals in a small room, eschewing the grand dining room, and settled next to a big fire in the evenings. She had made her bed, so to speak, and was willing to lie in it if she could possibly do so.

With the move to London, Edith's presence, and Stephen's resolution to behave well, the winter of 1900–1901 actually proved a largely pleasant one. Suddenly so many friends, old and new, surrounded her that her Sunday afternoons at home became quite crowded with those who returned week after week. She developed a new passion for a pianola, an instrument with a keyboard, stops, and bellows that required almost no musical ability for it really played itself. She came from a musical family—Vivian sang and played the piano, as did she, her brothers had had a band in Knoxville, and Herbert had gone on to become an organ builder and piano tuner—and loved to have music around. Apparently her mirth at this instrument did not translate into great skill. A reporter who went to see them at the Charles Street house was let in by a serious liveried footman who conducted him to the music room, where Frances and Stephen were discovered "experimenting delightedly with a newly acquired pianola, drowning melody and harmony by the deep, unregulated 'tumm-tumm' of the bass, but contentedly congratulating themselves that they were making music. Mrs. Townesend is a better writer than musician."[25] The lightheartedness of this encounter suggested that matters were, for a while at least, improving.

That winter both Frances and Stephen settled down to work. Stephen wrote and published a novel, *A Thoroughbred Mongrel*, to solid reviews praising its "unusual . . . sympathetic charm" and its anti-vivisectionist and temperance messages, calling it "a tender, graceful, sunny little story . . . with an undertone of serious thought and of deep feeling."[26] For all his difficulties with adult humans, Stephen felt deep compassion for dogs and other animals and was an avid animal rights campaigner; his tenderness for Lionel during his long illness may reflect a general gentleness for the powerless.

A Thoroughbred Mongrel is compelling not just for its antivivisectionist message—a long passage is based on Stephen's own horrifying encounter with this practice in a physiology class at Edinburgh University in 1882, leading to his activism against the practice—but for the way it brings Frances's country house atmosphere to life. The novel enjoyed a surprising success, going into eight editions of a thousand each between 1900 and 1913. Because Stephen was a frequent speaker and participant at London Antivivisection Society meetings during those years, it is likely that the book was sold at the society's public demonstrations against the practice. This success gave him enough confidence to list literature first and medicine second on the 1901 census.

The story is based on an 1880s incident in which Frances was given a chihuahua puppy as a gift from Mexico, only to have it grow into a much bigger dog, evidently of another breed.[27] Stephen recounts the story through the voice of Hett, his Skye terrier, who was long an important member of their household. Set at Maytham, although the original episode took place years before she took that house, its human characters are Frances ("Mrs. Flufton Bennett," instead of Fluffy Burnett), Stephen, Kenneth Campbell ("Dr. Coghlan") and Rosamond just before their engagement, Archie, Vivian, Constance Fletcher ("Miss Fretcher"), and Eleanor Calhoun ("Miss Balhoon"). Even the faithful Barrett figures in the story, and one gets a real taste of their daily life. Frances has "dainty little feet" that "peeped forth in the neatest of shoes" and a rather formal manner of speech. Archie is brash and Californian, with a penchant for playing rather cruel tricks on the false chihuahua. Vivian makes a cameo appearance as a sixteen-year-old. Miss Balhoon "was a London actress of more or less repute" whose real talent was for sparking heated debates, and Constance Fletcher "had too much bark about her." They gather for breakfast, then Frances and Constance retire to their writing for the remainder of the morning while the others play tennis. Everyone smokes cigarettes on the terrace after lunch. There is cycling in the afternoon as well as walks and croquet, and in the evenings they have lively suppers with good food and wine, after which the men smoke and drink whisky while engaging in very relaxed and colloquial conversations about dogs, worrying about Mrs. Flufton Bennett's embarrassment when she learns that her prizewinning dog is a fraud.

Frances wrote the introduction to the little book, describing how Stephen bought Hett at the Lost Dogs' Home in Battersea in 1891, and how the terrier's habit of holding one ear up and one down made her seem serious and human. A full magazine layout of photographs of Maytham Hall taken a year after the book was published in 1901 features Hett following a corseted and parasol-carrying Fluffy around the grounds, and the novel is full of photographs and drawings of Hett as well.

The dog charmed everyone. When their friend David Murray obligingly carried her back to Stephen in London, he wrote Frances to tell her of the safe arrival of "the most fascinating little doggie ever travelled by rail. He [*sic*] really was delightfully companionable, standing on my knees with his nose & one eye out of the railway carriage window looking out for surprises as if he were on the board of directors. At Charing X he was only claimed by Mr. Townsend [*sic*], (looking more sunburnt even than I), some considerable demonstrations took place between them & we all separated."[28] She was a fixture both at the Inner Temple and at Frances's English houses, and the well-written little book shows another side to Stephen, one that is compassionate and witty. It is one of the few testaments to his personality that does not come through Frances's letters.

Frances worked at *Bettina,* as she was now calling her long new novel, for months and began a mystery story called "The Ban-Dog," inspired by the ghostly image of her dog Roy, the other Maytham dog, crossing the lawn in starlight, but another book about marriage suddenly swept over her. Clearly she was absorbed by the investigation of marriages between seeming opposite types. With *Bettina* it was the transatlantic aspect that intrigued her— she herself being described that year as "an unusual mixture of English and American characteristics. At times she is quite English, and then again quite American"—and in the new book it was the disparity between temperaments, rank and expectations.[29] On 11 January 1901 she scratched a few excited lines to Gilder, who had visited her the previous summer to beg for something for the magazine, to let him know that the muse had struck again. "I have laid aside the Ban-Dog story because another one sprang upon me. It may make two numbers & it is going so rapidly that I may send it to you in a weeks time. It is a study of such a nice good promising creature to whom almost ridiculous good fortune falls. She is a well enough born person who lives in a 'Bed-sitting room' in Mortimer Street & does peoples shopping and odd jobs for them. I am so interested & amused. It will be called 'The Making of a Marchioness' or 'Poor Emily Fox-Seton.'" On 5 February, only a few weeks later, she reported to him that the story was finished, and later commented that she'd done the whole thing—some two or three serial instalments—in only ten days, "with absolute enjoyment," despite her sorrow at the recent death of Queen Victoria. For Frances, as for so many others, it seemed "impossible to picture the Nineteenth Century without this woman."[30]

The Making of a Marchioness is an unflinching commentary on marriage.

Unlike the other single women at Mallowe, the country house that Emily
Fox-Seton visits, Emily is not angling for a husband. Her fears are of an old
age in which she will be unable to work rather than regret for a youth in
which she had not succeeded in the marriage market. Her appreciation of
her unanticipated good luck in marriage when Lord Walderhurst unexpectedly proposes to her and her growing affection for him lie in no small part
in the fact that she's been rescued from what Burnett repeatedly referred to
in her earliest stories as a "shabby genteel" life. But, much though she allows
the reader to rejoice in Emily's great good luck, Burnett pulls no punches
when she talks about the Victorian and Edwardian marriage state. The wedding does not come at the end of the novel; Walderhurst not only falls far
short of being a romantic hero but seems barely touched by human emotion. His coldness was completely unlike Stephen's histrionics, but in the
guise of a Cinderella tale Burnett produced an important statement on marriage in the beginning of the twentieth century.

In small ways she incorporated her own life, in the form of little jokes
and autobiographical vignettes, into the story. A Mrs. Maytham makes it
possible for Emily Fox-Seton to have what little independence she has, by
leaving her two hundred pounds to invest and sending her off to London to
run errands for the titled and privileged. The happy fêtes Frances held for
the village children went straight into the novel when Emily helps with a
similar one at Mallowe. She was particularly interested in the ways this story
was not an American one, and indeed one of her greatest strengths was
taking American perspectives on uniquely English characters and situations;
she saw Emily as "a person whom one loves & the mental attitude of the
story is of a simple realism, entirely English," she wrote to Gilder.

> When I wrote it I felt it to be an actual inspiration. I have never done any-
> thing better & more subtle—realism is always subtle—(no, not always,
> but frequently)—than that scene upon the heath. Walderhurst is *complete*
> in his moments there. He expresses quite simply an ingenuous, not unam-
> icable brutality—or rather unadornedness of phrase & statement entirely
> unconscious & unintentional of offence, which just this particular kind
> of man is capable of. An American could not do it. He would have too
> much imagination & emotion & sensitiveness. Every English man is not
> capable of it—no clever man of any nationality could be—but as a type
> Walderhurst & that scene as a type of what his type can feel & *not* feel—
> are like Rosetti's loom—but 'A dream, a delirium & a joy'. I love them.
> *Dont* tell me you dont know what they mean with their queer well bred,
> ill bred limitations & inarticulateness.[31]

What she wanted was two characters who were neither beautiful nor clever, who were not introspective, yet who nonetheless found a way of interacting that suited them without the least suggestion of romance.

So taken was she with this couple that she wrote a sequel to it that same year. The Osborns, the Walderhursts, and Lady Maria Bayne all reappear. The *Cornhill*, in which *Marchioness* was first serialized in conjunction with an agreement with the American magazine the *Century* (formerly *Scribner's*), was "very keen on having some more Marchioness if possible. . . . And there has begun to float vaguely in my mind a thing probably called 'The Methods of Lady Walderhurst.' You know things would inevitably happen to dear Emily when she became a Marchioness. Think of the fury of the heir presumptive & his family when Walderhurst married again. I am so fond of Emily Fox-Seton that I feel there is no knowing what she may do for me." The critics responded well, finding "every one of its figures is singularly real."[32] At the *Cornhill*'s request for more of Emily, she began *Methods*, realizing quickly that the two books ought to have been a single story, without a break. The books, enormously popular on their own, later appeared in a single American volume called simply *Emily Fox-Seton*, with illustrations of the major characters. Emily looks majestic, Alec Osborn suitably degenerate as he glances up from a whisky decanter; Hester, in her loose morning gown, seems weak-willed, and Lady Maria sternly stares out. There is, tellingly, no picture of Lord Walderhurst himself.

In March they moved back to Maytham during one of the coldest springs in recent memory, and Maytham, unoccupied all winter, was frigid. Stephen spent his weekdays at the Inner Temple, and Frances and Edith warmed themselves by uncovering the Maytham furniture, pushing it around into new arrangements, and watching the gardens burst into bloom. The head gardener, Bolton, "has been bringing rival gardeners in by back gates in swarms. He is a proud gardener & has attained a boastful chuckle 'There aint no sich beds nit in Rolvenden, nit in Tenterden, nit in the whole county' he says. ('Nit' seems to be Kentish for 'neither'.)"[33] She was delighted to discover that, having spent years denying she could write to order, in fact she could do just that, and turned out an article on the late queen, "One Woman of the Nineteenth Century." She didn't think the article profound, but it was appealing to the newspapers and magazines, and at a hundred dollars for a thousand words, it was a less taxing supplement to her income. Although an encomium to the late queen, it also made several incisive remarks about England, calling it "conservative, obstinate, pugnaciously self centred" and referring to "the ruling quality of the English nature—a certain uncontrollable desire to interfere, to claim, to persist."[34]

She was determined after her recent years on a financial roller coaster to lay up enough money to generate a steady $5,000 a year in income. She wanted to put aside $10,000 this year, and the proceeds from her American book sales alone seemed to guarantee this when her June statement from Scribner's showed she'd earned more than $5,000 for that period alone. Stephen, who was still acting as her intermediary, reluctantly informed them of his wife's decision to place *The Making of a Marchioness* with the publisher F. A. Stokes, rather than with Scribner's, which had expected it after publishing the serial version, and in England with Smith, Elder and Co. instead of F. A. Warne. Her decision was purely a business one, for she felt just as warmly towards Gilder as she always had but found the firm behind the times in matters of publicity. She had been shocked when she arrived in New York just before *DeWilloughby* appeared and "was met upon the wharf by three different reporters who inquired ingenuously if I had written anything lately or meant to in the near future."[35] Advertising was now the name of the game, and she wished to go with a newer publisher with more drive, a decision that caused the *Critic* to sniff that "in old times, an author stayed with one house; to-day he drops his line into new waters and whips all the streams that flow into the great ocean of popularity."[36]

The spring and summer seemed a final riot of sociability. In May the actors Cyril Maude and his wife, Winifred Emery, came with their talented children, who put on plays every evening. Pamela Maude recalled Frances as overweight and wearing a red wig (the latter was untrue, although she almost certainly now dyed her hair), and felt sorry for Stephen, who looked unhappy. She noticed that the married couple never spoke to each other. Frances took the girls to the ruins of Bodiam Castle, telling medieval stories as she drove a pony carriage. She and the children toured the castle as twelfth-century characters in ancient stories, imitating their speech, and were thrilled when Barrett provided not a simple lunch of sandwiches but "a fairy meal" under a tree and waited on them as though they were in the Maytham dining room. They planned two huge events. The first was a cricket tournament in July between Maytham (most of the team consisting of members of the Tatler's Club) and the village of Rolvenden. They had so many guests that some of them had to be put up in the Bull Inn in the village, and twenty-five others stayed in the house. Two weeks later she held a "village treat" for all the children of the parish, with both events coming off exquisitely, thanks in part to Stephen's planning and cooperation.

It seemed a happy time, as Charlotte Harwood, who arrived to do a spread on their life at the house, recalled. She found it a warm and comfortable house, even though it had none of the modern conveniences like electricity, a furnace, or telephone. The billiard room had been made over into a red sitting room, and music from the famed piano and pianola got even the staid neighbours up and dancing. Vivian, ill again from overwork, was visiting and slept upstairs while Stephen was in London working on a stage revival of *Fauntleroy* in which he was to play the old uncle. They put up a good front, for it seemed to Charlotte to be a peaceable and friendly house, surrounded by rose gardens and low hills, with the villagers "devoted to Mrs. Burnett" for her heartfelt and unpreachy kindnesses.[37] In Maytham, the servants' sympathy was fully with Frances. They saw Stephen as someone who only "came down from London for his money and then was off on his cob, back to the station and London. He thought more of his horse than his wife, they said."[38]

The one shadow over it all for Frances was Vivian's initial refusal to participate. In Europe for the summer with two friends, he decided to remain in Paris rather than give in to his mother's and aunt's entreaties to take part in the cricket match festivities or the treat. She and Edith planned to join him in France and travel back with him, and they had their hearts set on his seeing Maytham Hall for the first time. He refused to stay under the same roof as the man who made his mother's life so miserable, an attitude no doubt mixed with jealousy of the man who seemed to replace him. "Dear boy you must not talk of being your 'stepfather's guest,'" she admonished him. "You have no stepfather in the ordinary sense. Stephen is only Stephen to you & so long as he is perfectly nice the best thing you can do for me is to act as if nothing had really changed. You are only one of thousands of boys whose mothers have remarried—That is the only dignified position for us both to take while he acts as he has been doing for some time now. During this cricket week he has been faultless."[39] She and Edith met Vivian in London, and they travelled together to Belgium.

By the time Harwood's article appeared, the pleasant atmosphere she described was already outdated and all the participants gone. Presumably the house was shut for the autumn and winter for her customary season in London. Whatever happened that autumn has lapsed into oblivion, and there is a complete silence for several months. By the time we encounter Frances again, at the beginning of 1902, she had suffered a nearly complete physical and emotional collapse, and escorted by her Maytham servants the Barretts and Thompson, returned to New York. She could barely walk and moved with great pain. By April her health was so precarious that she entered a sanatorium in Fishkill Landing, New York. Gathering what was left of her shattered strength, she summoned Stephen to Fishkill and told him that their relationship must end. He returned to London immediately, and slowly but surely she recovered from what she considered to have been the nightmare of this marriage. This appears to have been the last time Frances and Stephen saw each other, and with this final meeting Stephen stepped out of her life and returned to his rooms in the Inner Temple, although he probably did not practise medicine. He had a wide circle of friends among the anti-vivisectionists and continued to work for the cause and to write.

CHAPTER 18

~

RECOVERY AND
NEW THOUGHTS

1902–1906

O N WEDNESDAY, 22 JUNE 1904, Frances, Edith and Frank, along with their travelling companion the London theatre director Robert A. Stanley and his wife, drove up to the gates of Maytham Hall after Frances's absence of more than two years. They arrived after a storybook trip from America, in which they visited the Azores, saw such beautiful children in Gibraltar that they gasped, journeyed from Florence to Venice to Milan and Como, and passed through "transcendent things & places—Alps & torrents & ravines & snows tinted pink & azure" on their way to Lucerne. They didn't stay long in a "New Yorky" Paris that Frances found "destroyed by automobiles," before crossing over to Dover. Two carriages met them at Cranbrook Station, and along the way old neighbours waited on the road to greet them. A banner reading "Welcome home to Maytham" hung from the Hall door, and at the gate the gatekeeper and his family gathered to receive them. As they halted the carriage to shake hands, the elderly female lodge keeper across the way waved her handkerchief and hallooed with delight. In the Hall itself, a cake reading "Welcome" was waiting, along with a snowdrift of messages. Outdoors, cascades of roses had obligingly blossomed.[1] Frances was home, relaxed and happy, and this time she was sole sovereign of the manor.

It couldn't have differed more from her arrival in New York two years earlier, where the press wasted no time in trying to pry out her motives for returning. They declared her second marriage already a failure, pronounced Stephen "an adventurer," and proclaimed that in less than two months after their wedding Stephen "began abusing her."[2] She tried to slip away from their notice and find an apartment to rent, with no luck, and was worn down even further; she finally settled into a portion of an unfashionable but comfortable house on West 44th Street, where Kitty and Gigi and Daisy Hall, now longtime residents of Manhattan, took their meals. Even in this retired location the gossipmongers found her and sent up messages to ask whether she was in America to seek a divorce. She sent down a terse note saying she was there only to work and to see friends, but this didn't satisfy them.[3] "I have been hounded by reporters & asked mad impudent questions but I have not glanced at a newspaper & can only guess vaguely at the vulgar *blague* they contain," she said, trying to remain philosophical and ride it out. "I have fortunately realized that I am only one of thousands who suffer from the same indecency and that the day after tomorrow I will not be worth the penny a line & some one else will take my place."[4]

For the time being it was more important to find some relief for her physical aches. She took her meals in her room and left only to see the doctor, who ordered massages that seemed to do some good. She hoped to recover enough to go somewhere warm—Florida or California—especially now that New York was a riot of building, jackhammering, and subway construction that turned the "streets into a squalid unpicturesque Pompeii." She needed peace and quiet, she needed to be able to get back to work, but right now she felt even worse than she had when she crept off the ship, when she was "distracted with pain."[5] She was seeing Dr. William Whitwell, the husband of an old friend, who diagnosed her as suffering from neuritis or nerve inflammation and decided after a few months of outpatient treatments to send her to his rest home, Riverview Sanitarium, in Fishkill Landing, near Newburgh, New York. There she received constant care for her physical deterioration, but her mind and spirits once again flourished. Although at first she walked with difficulty and had trouble with stairs, after six weeks at the sanatorium she was able to go for walks, had resumed writing, and was planning to move to an apartment at 71 Central Park West. New York became her home for the next two years, and it was the first time she had such an extended stay in the city where so many of her plays were produced, and where they generally received better reviews than did her London productions.

While his mother adjusted to life in the Northeast, Vivian was travelling again, in search of journalist fodder, in the South and West. He was in some ways acting as a roaming patrician journalist, staying with genteel families and carrying letters of introduction as he sought interesting stories, and in other ways as a penny-scraping entrepreneur, hoping to write his way to the West and supplement the allowance his mother gave him. He managed to publish a few articles from this trip, complementing them with photographs he took, and was particularly interested in the varieties of people he encountered. He sent letters to his mother in Fishkill as a sort of travelogue, because she had been unable to make her own long trip. In Charleston, South Carolina, that most southern of southern cities, he was astonished to find that "all the pre-[Civil] war feelings still exist here, like rotten stumps in a field, and twice today in the pulpit did I hear General Robert E. Lee lauded to the skies as a great hero. The people still sigh over the lost cause, and the white man still despises a nigger, while treating him with the greatest humanity and kindness. I am studying the negro question, and hope to be able to write an article on the position that the negro is to occupy in the future in the industrial south." At the same time, he stayed with a well-off mill owner and banker, and "found his a typical southern home," distinguished and refined, with love among the family members the ruling emotion.[6] In his Alabama hotel, scorpions ran under the beds, and in Phoenix, Arizona, he was disappointed not to have heard "a pistol shot since I came here, nor seen a drunken cowboy—Even the saloons have a respectable outward appearance." He was delighted by San Francisco, though surprised at the way they spurned eastern pretensions to superiority in favour of their own genuinely impressive culture. "I must confess that it appeals to me," he told his mother. "There is so much freedom about it."[7] He found Chinatown intriguing for all the reasons that tourists and outsiders generally assigned to it: "the beauty of it lies in the fact that the Chinese are the most uncommunicative people in the world. No one really knows about them. Their home life is absolutely a closed book to the outside world of white people [and] they look down upon us."[8] His interest in Asia and its peoples began with Swan, who had an enviable collection of Japanese art and artifacts, and several years later he chose Asia for an extended grand tour, spending months in China and Japan.

Despite her time in the south—in Tennessee, Virginia, and North Carolina—and a trip to Chicago, Frances had not seen much of America apart from Washington, New York, and Boston. She knew the Alps but not the Berkshires or the Green Mountains or the Rockies, and now when she longed to travel, she feared to do so because of her fragile health. Vivian was her eyes and ears for the time being, no more so than when he made a visit to Edwina's ranch in Santa Clara County in California, sending Edith a long account of his meeting with the sister who had never returned to the East.

By summer Frances found herself so much recovered that she left Whitwell's sanatorium and took a house with Edith in East Hampton, New York, a picturesque artists' colony near the ocean. (She liked East Hampton so much that they settled, the following summer of 1903, at Dune Crest.)

Archie and Ernest and Frank visited, as did her old friend Effie Macfarlane from Washington, and she stayed there for some months before settling into a house at 44 West 87th Street in Manhattan. For months she was in a flurry of moving, as furnishings from Washington were shipped up to her by the vanload, and she could never remember whether the papers or books or pictures she wanted were in Washington, New York, or Kent. "I have as perhaps you know vibrated for many years between the two continents—which is a complicated thing," she told a friend who asked her to locate a letter sent to her from James Whitcomb Riley, author of *Little Orphant Annie*. "What is most necessary to one is always in Kent if one is in New York & in New York if one is in Kent."[9] As things settled down, Vivian decided to move to New York too, living a rather nomadic life for a year or so with his cousin Ernest and several friends before settling into an apartment with Ernest on West End Avenue—inadvisedly taking with him some of his mother's best furnishings—"roughing it" in a bachelor apartment with a woman to cook and clean for them, and working for *McClure's Magazine*. Always having an affinity for the sea, he encouraged his mother's summers on Long Island and for several years proposed plans for her that would allow him to have access to sailing and tennis at the local country club while she would have an American home convenient to the publishing and theatre capital Manhattan.

Despite her illnesses, now including a bad back and osteoporosis, Frances spent these two American years in a whirlwind of activity. She wrote *In the Closed Room*, a story about a girl who sees what others do not, befriending a little girl who has died—"not a ghost but that which is most real." She got the idea for this book when she saw a "lonely little child playing in front of a boarded-up house on West 74th Street, New York, opposite the place in which she lived." She wrote to Vivian that the new story was "The New Thing again and when I read it to Edith I found its effect to be—well, what I think it will be on all who read it. The thrill of things occult can be best felt, it seems to me, when they occur in the midst of quite simply mundane affairs, and occur quite simply as part of them. Then they become real."[10]

McClure wanted it for his magazine, and it was published later as a British book in 1904 and an American one in 1905. She took great care in expanding "Sara Crewe" into a longer novel, and in this followed her habit of presenting individual works sometimes in four forms: a short story, a longer serial, a novel, and a play. In this case she had already rewritten "Sara Crewe" into the play *A Little Princess*, which when originally titled *A Little Unfairy Princess* appeared in London's Shaftesbury Theatre in December 1902, and ran as an enormously successful series of matinees in the Criterion

Theatre in New York. The new play of *A Little Princess* was produced in London's Avenue Theatre by Robert Stanley in September 1902 during this American sojourn and incorporated a number of changes, including the addition of three Indian men, assistants to Ram Dass, who now had a major speaking role, and several additional schoolchildren. Once again, a play she'd seen succeed in New York met with much less favour in London, but it ran there again only a few months later at Terry's in January 1903, at the same time that Buffalo Bill's Wild West Show was in town. Scribner's encouraged her to take the scenes and characters that she had added to make the play long enough and enfold them into a novel called *A Little Princess*. She found this idea for a novelization a less simple proposition than Edward Burlingame did, for "it would not be possible to patch with any dignity or harmony. An entirely new web must be woven about the thread of the present story."[11] Nevertheless the idea appealed to her, especially if she could write a new introduction explaining that not all characters in a story initially make themselves known to an author. She also believed that the book would have a new generation of readers since its first appearance in 1887. She resuscitated her story "The Pretty Sister of José" and reworked it into a play that met with only moderate success in London and New York at the end of 1903, and then extracted a portion of *In Connection with the DeWilloughby Claim* and made it into a play called *That Man and I* that ran at the Savoy Theatre in 1904, produced again by Robert Stanley who came over from London especially to help direct it.

Not since before her marriage to Stephen had she been so productive and her work so well received, even though, except for *In the Closed Room*, none of these was an entirely original work. For the time being, "tender sentiment" was still in vogue, and critics called *That Man and I* "vibrant with feeling and so surcharged with genuine heart interest that it can hardly fail to make an appeal to those who may yet be stirred by tender sentiment."[12] *The Pretty Sister of José*, starring Maude Adams, netted her a decent income, and she hoped to earn even more from *A Little Princess* when it was published. She appeared relaxed and cheerful when she talked to the press now; her smiles revealed "the best natured, pleasantest face in the world that looks at you with merry blue eyes," an indication that many of her troubles were behind her. Calling herself "a prophet of happiness," she claimed that it was not a compliment to the "Supreme Being who put us here to go through life sad and miserable." Whether said for public consumption or an indication of her own lifted spirits, there was no doubt that for her, life had taken a better path in recent times. Her only disappointment was in the plays: not in the writing, which she now enjoyed because she had no collaborators, but in the disjuncture between what one has imagined and the realization of them on the stage.[13] She ceased attending opening nights for fear of disappointment, but that didn't keep her from declaring that she wouldn't be surprised if she eventually dramatized all of her stories.

She spent the winter and spring before her return to Maytham Hall in Asheville, North Carolina, with Edith, the Stanleys, and the Maytham servants Tom, Mary, and Herbert Barrett, and her Maytham maid Thompson, all of whom had taken so well to America that they refused an offer to be sent back early. North Carolina was the setting for *That Man and I*, so her arrival there at the same time that the play was meeting with success seemed auspicious. She settled into Sunnicrest, a cottage built and furnished by Vanderbilt and surrounded by scenic mountains. It was one of a series of cottages on an estate of more than three thousand acres, extending as far as Vanderbilt's private hunting lodge atop Mount Pisgah, and she was so impressed by it that she was tempted for a short time to purchase one for herself. She found herself immediately the centre of attention when the widow of former Governor and Senator Vance, a woman she'd known in Washington, came to call. Within days she was swamped with invitations from all the local and vacationing socialites, dignitaries, and their friends, and wondered "if there is a corner where [I] could go in which [I] would not find scores of lovely people waiting with their arms open! Sure and thats my good luck and I ought to be grateful for it and grateful I am for all the kindness it means."[14] To keep her precious writing mornings free, she refused all luncheon invitations and once again set up "at-home" afternoons.

Her head was full of new plays at this time, few of which reached fruition. Foremost among them was one reminiscent of *A Lady of Quality*, about a Lady Judith—tentatively titled "Lady Judith" or "Judy O'Hara"—the only child of the earl of Clanfergus, "who has ruined himself for the Stuart cause" and hidden himself away in "an old half ruined castle in a wild part of Ireland." Judy grows up in rags but makes a joke of it, speaking in an Irish lilt and having adventures. Frances finished the play in North Carolina and hoped to see it staged in the coming year. She was also working on a book of children's stories, a project that nearly got her into plagiarism trouble. She recalled a book of stories she had loved as a child, the one she received as a prize, and had searched for it for years to no avail. She proposed to retell the stories in a new book, explaining that they were versions of what she'd lost, but as soon as she published one of them, "The Story of Prince Fairyfoot," a reader pointed out that the book was *Granny's Wonderful Chair* and "no doubt felt wronged and robbed" when she saw it retold and altered.[15] Although a less-than-generous critic added this "plagiarism" to her list of failings, Frances was in fact delighted to have recovered something so important to her, writing a new introduction to the book and publishing it under the correct author's name, Frances Browne. Vivian oversaw the publication at McClure's and even designed a poster to advertise it, to promising advance sales. Shortly afterwards Frances found a copy in a London second-hand bookshop, carrying it with her everywhere she travelled. Whether as a nod to the book or an appropriation from it, at the opening of the revised play *A Little Princess*, Sara gathers the children around her and tells one of Browne's stories.

Now in 1904, it was a dream come true when she found herself at Maytham Hall once again, for with Stephen gone, "the black poisonous clouds have been blown away & left only pure sky."[16] As before, an endless stream of guests—Maddie and Ella Hepworth Dixon, Lord Ronald Gower and his adopted son Frank Hird, Lady Maitland, Kenneth Campbell, who had taken up motorcycling, reeked of petrol, and spent all his time in the garage with a valet who not only shared his hobby but could "be invited up from the Servants Hall to read you what he calls 'An 'oroscope'" (Frances's said "the most brilliant work of my life is now to be done")—made their way to the house, but this time they found a completely different atmosphere.[17] "The wonder of how all the past tragedy has settled into nothingness is to me a marvel beyond words," she exulted to Vivian. "The hideous physical suffering has gone. 'The Pain' is actually no more. And all the threats & oaths of vengeance are as if they had never been. Can you believe it. I cannot. All that remains is a strange unreasonable depression that wakens me every morning & comes upon me in the day at times. I suppose it is like the ache of a healing wound. It will be gone in time. . . . Now the nightmare is dispelled for ever. Oh! thank God, Vivvie. It does not seem possible that such good is true—And yet it is. Maytham is a different place. And since these troubles have melted—other fairy things will come."[18] The memory of Stephen had exacerbated what had been a lifelong struggle with depression. Kitty recalled that often, before Frances sat down to fill the pages of foolscap with her strong handwriting every morning, she confessed, "I am so low in my little mind."[19] With Stephen gone, her wish was to stay at Maytham for ever, a wish that seemed possible if she could only continue to earn enough to live on and to put aside, even though she did not own the Hall.

As always, at the crux of her current financial difficulty was the fact of having so many houses. The house on Madison Avenue needed to be let or it would become an albatross like Portland Place. A housekeeper, Miss Kellam, was installed in it and a real estate agent retained, but nothing seemed to move it. Vivian blamed Miss Kellam and distrusted her; Edith wrote him long letters about what he could take from it for his new apartment and what he must leave behind so that the place could show well, and Miss Kellam quietly put up with the hordes of young men Vivian let live in the house. Frances and Edith tried to sort it all out from Maytham, trusting the house-keeper and thrilled when Vivian managed to let it and crushed when the renter backed out, but through it all Frances forged ahead with her plays and *A Little Princess* and was happy to be home again.

Slowly things began to change. The vicar and his wife, whose children had grown up, decided to leave Rolvenden for Twickenham and wrote to say goodbye.[20] *A Little Princess* was turning out to be longer than anticipated and might be too late for a Christmas serial. She also had hopes for it, since she thought it would be "a nice detail-y book. . . . Children love detail. The garret and Melchisedec & Becky & Ermengarde are *so* nice. And Sara stand-ing on the old table with her head & body out of the skylight watching the clouds making islands & lakes at sunset & feeling as if she could climb up purple piles of cloud hills & gaze out upon primrose seas—ought to give you a quite queer uplifted feeling."[21]

Bettina still hovered in the wings, unfinished. Frances's friend Cyril Maude, with whom she hoped to place *Glenpeffer* (the working title of the play adapted from *The Making of a Marchioness*), wrote to decline it on the grounds that the public wanted comedy just now. She pinned her hopes on Elisabeth Marbury, who was currently in Paris with her lover Elsie de Wolfe, and would soon be in London and would let her know about placing *The Pretty Sister of José* in a London theatre.

She was drawn back into her early American life when on 12 November she received the dismal news of her brother John's death from spinal menin-gitis in a Knoxville hospital. She hadn't heard from him in years but had occasionally sent him money until they eventually lost touch. In 1898 he was listed in Knoxville as a jeweller—the profession Herbert had begun with—working in a shop of his own on the commercial street of North Gay, but not at the profitable end. That didn't last long, and he moved every year, finally ending up in the Bowery. It was no secret to her or to those who knew him in Tennessee that he drank heavily and was reduced to doing odd jobs when he worked at all and living in a sort of shack.[22] "Evidently poor long lost intemperate John had died without any one to bury him," she told Vivian. "I had not heard of him for years but it was a shock." She had Will Dennis verify the report and sent money to have him buried in her mother's grave at the Old Gray Cemetery, but without a new marker, even though a double burial in a single grave was a rare thing.

Always called on to help her siblings and their children, she also loaned money to Teddy in California, never demanding and rarely receiving the promised interest payments on it. Then more money requests to Aunt Fluffy came from Herbert's daughter Frances, now staying in New York. Exasperated by the financial demands made on her from all sides, Frances owned that she was "beginning to resent the cheerful promptness of the demands made & the sense of severely cold disapproval arroused [*sic*] when I *cannot* do what is asked. I have given away about seventy five per cent of all I have worked for & wholly realize that those to whom I have given it regard me with chill but stern disfavor." [23] Still, she felt obliged to help her relations, or at least those she found deserving. Vivian too was making his share of requests. He asked his mother to contribute to a publishing venture of his own, as well as to *McClure's Magazine*, by supplying a certain number of children's stories, to which she emphatically replied that she could never write fiction on demand.

The relationship between them remained stronger than ever, however. At twenty-eight Vivian felt he had no real family of his own. Even his father had remarried earlier that year, and although Vivian certainly wished him well, he was still hurting from the long separation from his mother while he was in Denver, and from a more general loneliness. Frances's long sojourn in New York reminded Vivian how pleasant it was to have easy access to her company, and now he searched for ways to fulfil both their needs. His present plan, one that he pushed in every letter, was for her to buy a house in Great Neck, on Long Island. Why, he asked her, did she not think of such a residence as a good place for her Madison Avenue furniture when that house was let? The expense of that would be far less than simply storing the furniture, and it would give them both a house in a desirable location. Much as she liked the notion of such a house, she reminded him that "I cannot afford to remove my belongings to Great Neck, give the wear and tear to them & pay a rent merely so that you can spend the summer there with a gay party of your friends. If I could afford it nothing would delight me more but I *cannot*." [24] At the end of the year, feeling that she couldn't get any of her projects and plans off the ground and worried that if she remained in Maytham Hall for the winter nothing would get accomplished, she made the sudden decision to go to New York for the winter. Since she still held the lease, she lent Maytham Hall back to the owner, Howard Parnell Edwards, and booked passage for Edith, Frank, and herself on the *Cedric* for 21 December 1904. She took pencils and the manuscript of *Bettina* and set sail. She hated winter crossings, always rougher than those in milder seasons, but she hoped to move things along by being on the spot. It turned out that her reluctance was warranted, for no sooner had the ship pulled away from London than they found themselves utterly fogged in and unable to move for days. At first Frances kept to her stateroom, but when she discovered that steerage was filled with poor immigrant families—Russian Jews, Italians, and Poles—whose 150 children would have no Christmas, she bestirred herself. Creeping along decks where it was impossible to see more than a few feet ahead, she approached all the first-class passengers, asking them each for a penny for the children. No one knew who she was, "but nobody gave her a penny. Some gave her sovereigns, some half sovereigns, some dollars or two dollars, or even again sumptuous five-dollar bills, some gave half-crowns or florins, and children proudly forced upon her sixpences or shillings. She asked stewards, she asked officers, she let nobody escape, and it was apparent that nobody wished to elude her. Everybody was interested as well as amused, and every one was kind." She even invaded the men's smoking room. When the money was distributed after Christmas dinner, she realized that the beneficiaries seemed to believe it to be some sort of American Christmas custom, and fathers repeatedly pushed their children back to the head of the queue, pretending not to have received anything yet.[25] She made little headway during this New York winter, but when she returned to Maytham in May, taking Edith and Frank back with her, she was now working on a new book, one she thought would change people's lives.

Professing that *The Dawn of a To-morrow* "is turning out so weird I do not know what to make of it," she used it to gather thoughts about religion, God, death, and the afterlife that she had been formulating even before Lionel's death. More parable than fiction, it describes a wealthy man suffering from depression who has decided to end his life in a London boarding house. He gets lost in a terrible fog on his way back from buying a gun at a pawnshop and meets a ragged street girl named Glad, who takes him back to her lodgings and introduces him to a thief who is actually a frustrated inventor, a betrayed girl who has been forced into prostitution, and an elderly reformed music hall barfly. The older woman lives in a glow of conversion and tells them stories of hope and redemption. Her creed is that one can speak directly to God, that God is kind and merciful rather than vengeful and cruel. This belief is a sore point with her curate, out to reform the rough inhabitants of the ironically named Apple Blossom Court. When a drunken young woman is run over by a cart in the street just outside the window, they carry her into the old woman's room, where the old woman, in a refiguring of the Lazarus story, tells the younger one that there is no death—only a blessed and happy new life—and the young woman dies in a moment of peaceful revelation, leaving behind a baby. The would-be suicide is moved to reconsider his life and, revealing himself to be the wealthy Sir Oliver Holt, promises to aid them in what they most desire:

a warm room for Glad, where she and the poor prostitute can have enough to eat and care for the baby, and patronage for the thief.

Frances protested to Burlingame that the story "has not written itself rapidly because it has written itself strangely in spite of me & I have argued with myself saying continually 'No. I cant say what I think of that—The time is not ripe enough. . . . Out of all the propositions & arguments of the New Thought the things said in this story are what *I believe*."[26] Although she specifically discussed the "New Thought" in connection with this story, the public came wrongly to believe that she was a Christian Scientist and "brought to her a marvellous response of gratitude for the help it gave to despairing souls."[27] Happy to have eased any human pain, she nonetheless refused when someone suggested that she write about Christian Science and its founder Mary Baker Eddy. In the first place, she said, she didn't believe that the public was really ready for such a piece and that therefore no magazine would publish it, but "secondly, such an article could only come convincingly from a person who had long known Mrs. Eddy as a friend and had personally watched the development and effect of her work. Though I have been for years deeply interested in her thought and believe its principle, even while I cannot demonstrate it as others do, I have known very few Christian Scientists—only two—more than slightly. I could not say 'I know' this or that, because I know nothing personally, but while I could not call myself a Christian Scientist, I believe in its principle because it is the exposition of the pure Christ-spirit applied to the needs of today."[28]

New Thought was a spiritual movement that was gaining in popularity in America at that time, even though it had its roots in the mid-nineteenth century with thinkers such as Emanuel Swedenborg, Ralph Waldo Emerson, and the magnificently named Phineas Parkhurst Quimby. Henry James's brother, the Harvard professor William James, was also associated with New Thought, which had certain affinities with Christian Science. Its basis was in the link between spiritualism and the physical world, the power of belief and the power of the human mind. Both were metaphysical in nature and allowed for new interpretations of the Bible.[29] Frances's fictionalized formulation of her "new thought" planted the seed that would influence her writing for years.

Her long struggle with the God who had allowed her son to die had taken place on paper as well as in her mind's conversation, through the pages of the journal she addressed to Lionel for four years. Church itself and institutionalized doctrine were more of the order of social requirement. She had attended church in her early Washington days, and only sporadically after that, until the noblesse oblige of being the occupant of Maytham Hall led her cheerfully to the twelfth-century pews of the church in Rolvenden, perhaps spurred into it by the vicar's initial refusal to call on her before she married Stephen. *The Dawn of a To-morrow* made clear her belief that people needed no intermediaries between themselves and the "Power." When Holt asks Glad if their thought is a kind of religion, she replies, "It's cheerfler. . . . There's no 'ell fire in it. An' there ain't no blime laid on Godamighty."[30] More than four years later, when the story became a successful play (it was later made into a film by Paramount), Frances made headlines around the United States when she declared that not only she did not believe in hell but that such a notion was "worse than archaic, it's rococo."[31]

Her beliefs influenced those of the rest of her family. Vivian did in fact become a Christian Scientist, and when Frances later worked on the play of *The Dawn of a To-morrow*, she wrote to her nephew Archie to say how pleased she was that he was "ready to receive this new thinking. . . . Good is stronger than evil, love is stronger than hate to a mind cleared of *all* darkness and smallness. Nothing is impossible because it is God's self."[32] Refusing to give her belief a name, she confessed that the story's original title had been "A Splendid Day" and was intended for a Christmas story. It pitted modern man's headlong rush into business and unhappiness against what some called her "childlike confidence in the safety of happiness, in the wisdom of turning a bright light upon shadows, so that they fade into nothingness."[33]

Clearly this book marked a shift in her approach to life, one that could come only after her experiences with loss and ill-treatment. Just as *The Making of a Marchioness* would not have been written had she not been through two failed marriages, *The Dawn of a To-morrow* arose from her coming to terms with unhappiness and depression. The New Thought that favoured hope over resignation and goodness over evil grew out of an emotional strength only possible now that grief and threats were behind her. It was also reflected in her children's stories. She wrote two during the winter of 1906: *The Troubles of Queen Silver-Bell* and *Racketty-Packetty House*. Along with *A Little Princess*, which had finally been completed and published the year before, the fairy tale genre was a new and idealistic direction for her, influenced by her life at Maytham Hall.

She appears as both narrator and subject in *The Troubles of Queen Silver-Bell*, although the fairy queen tells the actual stories. Perhaps too sentimental for modern taste, the story is an example of the popular and whimsical children's fare published in magazines like *Saint Nicholas* and in the illustrated books at the beginning of the twentieth century. In its introduction, the queen says she has taught people to write books, among them "*quite* a

Respectable Person [who] sits in a garden full of roses and any number of birds call on her and she writes books for a living, and she learned it all from me. She was apprenticed to me the minute she was born and with my help she has made quite a decent living and earned any number of all sorts of flowers." Later she mentions Frances's donkey, Amoret, who comes when she calls to her, and declares that she "would be as intimate as that with a Disrespectable Person."[34] Frances captures here exactly the three things she believes about herself: that her ability to write is a "fairy" gift; that she has a special way with animals; and most importantly, that these things make the head of Maytham Hall a respectable person, no matter what the rumours might be.

Frances was able to cultivate new friendships at Maytham as well as relax in her old ones. Among them was that of Laurence Alma Tadema, daughter of the Royal Academy painter Sir Lawrence Alma Tadema. Twenty years Frances's junior, Laurence was thirty-five to Frances's fifty-five, and she saw in Frances something of a mother figure. Her own mother had died when Laurence was only three, and even in adulthood she felt the loss, writing in one particularly touching poem, "Yet was I made by that untimely loss a child forever."[35] Laurence was renovating a cottage at Wittersham, not far from Maytham, and Edith and Frances adopted her into their family circle. "Do come play with us here," Frances wrote to her. "My sister and I are always doing up houses in America or England. It is our little monomania as well as our Fate. We are hugely clever—really."[36] On rainy spring days the three women sat together sewing and altering dresses. Later in life Laurence recalled Frances as "a great-hearted Englishwoman" who shared her home "royally and joyfully with her friends" and as an "inspiring presence" with an "inextinguishable spirit of delight that desired for each and all a perpetual earthly paradise."[37]

Frances and Edith decided to spend the following winter of 1905–6 in New York, leaving Frank behind to watch over Maytham, and while there she wrote to Laurence about the new children's stories she was working on and the particular pleasure over *Racketty-Packetty House* that kept her giggling as she wrote. "It was such a love—about a shabby old dolls house pushed into an unfashionable neighbourhood behind a door, and a grand new one swaggering in the West End of the nursery and my affection for the cheerful disrespectable old dolls in the shabby house became a passion before I had done with them. They didn't care a hang for anything and they had more fun than anyone."[38] Part of her purpose in these new stories was to rectify the grimly moralistic stories of her childhood, told without joy and depicted in hideous colours, whose "recollection . . . makes me shudder now. Those were the days when 'prig' education was the child idea."[39] These new stories were lavishly and cheerfully illustrated and calculated to give children joy.

It was during this New York winter, however, that another door to her past closed when Swan suddenly died. Vivian stopped to see his mother and aunt at their house on West 75th Street on his way to Washington, but Frances was in bed ill and Edith kept the news from her until she was better. "I wish I could have *seen* you and held you in my arms a few minutes to try to comfort you," Frances wrote to him as soon as she found out what had happened. "Oh, it must be peace now—And if souls do meet each other who would meet him first but Lionel." The passing years had given her perspective on their ill-matched union. "Perhaps he knows all the things I wanted him to know but could never tell him. Peace be with him—Love be with him—God be with him. My darling, darling one I send you all my heart of love and sympathy & understanding of your feeling. When you are alone with him kiss him once on his cheek for me. He may know what it means."[40] It was Ida, their Washington cook who had been Vivian's friend and who had remained to work for Swan all those years, for whom Frances felt the most when she heard the news. Going to Washington in April, she saw Ida twice and was pleased to see that she looked not a day older, "and indeed I was so glad to have seen her." Ida stopped to give her flowers from Swan and Vivian's garden, and "made me feel as if we were all of one blood."[41]

Only months after Swan's death, another calamity struck her family when the famous San Francisco earthquake of 1906 occurred. Collections to aid the victims were taken up, but Frances's first concern was for her own relatives in California. Things had just begun to look up for the perennially cash-strapped Bridges when the earthquake destroyed a windmill Frances had given them as well as their stable and buggy. Edwina, out in Santa Clara County, could receive no letters or telegrams from the city and wrote to Edith that she worried about her son Francis and his wife and baby. "It breaks ones heart to think of them," Frances sighed. "Just when they were beginning to hope again."[42]

Perhaps as a result of worrying about her family, Frances's health took a turn for the worse. Again in pain and exhausted, after a number of treatments in Washington she finally checked in to another sanatorium, this one run by a Dr. Fry. He and another specialist tried to locate the source of the pain in her back and pelvis, decided it might be in the ligaments, and ordered her into bed, bound into uncomfortable corsets, and massaged at regular intervals. Although she did not mention it at the time, during her difficult period with Stephen she had begun to add weight to her already plump frame, no doubt increasing pressure to her already stressed back;

photographs of her reveal her developing the curved back that often accompanies osteoporosis, emphasized by her famously grand head, the reddish hair now growing grey, and topped by her elaborate hats. (One of Herbert's grandchildren recalled Aunt Fluffy asking if she would like to see her hats, and opening drawer after drawer of enormous and elaborate chapeaux.) Nor were many of the posed photographs taken from then on particularly flattering; she fared much better in casual pictures. Her favourite photo shows her seated on a bench, one hand at her throat, looking out of a window; she wears no hat, her dress is a simple gathered one, and a long gold and turquoise lorgnette hangs from a chain round her neck.

Particularly horrifying to her were the drawings that magazines made from photographs, such as the one in *Munsey's* adapted from a picture Vivian sent to the magazine without her permission. She instructed him to "refrain in future from turning an honest penny with the aid of your mothers beauty & Munseys—or any other—magazine. Never have I seen anything as monstrous as the thing Munsey 'drew from' your picture of me—and I have seen some monstrous things in my time. . . . How a person with a nose as sharp as a knife can be transformed into one possessing a feature whose bulbousness could only be acquired by a protracted course of strong water I do not know. . . . You *must* destroy that negative."[43] She often did not photograph well and became increasingly reluctant to interrupt her work to sit in a photographer's studio, where "there are a thousand chances to one that some monster would be the result and I will *not* have pictures circulated representing me in criminal moments. My criminal moments are when a camera is glaring at me."[44]

Although she was nearly at the point of losing all faith in doctors, she went along with Fry's treatment for some weeks and found that if nothing else, the enforced rest gave her some relief. It meant, though, yet another delay in her work on *Bettina,* and she began to think the unthinkable—that if she couldn't manage to work she might have to give up Maytham altogether. "The pain has done it. Six years of torture has made my courage waver."[45] It had been six years since she married Stephen and six years since she began Bettina's still unfinished story, a story that so closely paralleled the dynamics of her marriage to Stephen that it must have been her way of writing him out of her life. It reveals much of what she went through in this marriage.

She had already written to Gilder in August 1900 that the book was based on the famous international marriages of heiresses like Consuelo Vanderbilt, and that it threw together the sister of an heiress whose "marriage is one of those Early English ones made when 'bad lots' were sent out to New York. . . .

The story makes a leap of ten years after this & then the Bettina child having grown up & advanced with her rapidly advancing country goes to Stornham to find poor Rosalie the faded, broken spirited mother of a family, bullied out of her money & the power to do anything but submit. Bettina has grown into a nice, long limbed handsome young woman with a brilliant incisive tongue & the power to speak truths concerning well born bad manners, impudence & imposition. I have not quite got her yet but I think she is a personage. She is really the heroine of the story." There was also to be a much-maligned but honourable man, "an ill used duke [who] will be a tremendously good sort. I believe he will end by vigorously thrashing Nigel Anstruthers & the event will be one which will cause every readers soul to exult."[46] If no man was ready at that time to step forward and thrash Stephen, Frances willed it to happen on the pages of her novel.

She used the book to praise all that was good about America and Americans: energy; a knack for commerce, whether in millionaires or in newsboys like the one Lionel had befriended so many years before; a belief that one could rise through the caste system over the generations by working hard; a sense of being responsible for earning one's own living. Bettina Vanderpoel and her brother-in-law are opposites in many ways. Bettina has a head for business, having learned it at her father's knee. She is level-headed and refuses to rise to emotional bait. Nigel Anstruthers, the faded nobleman, has a terrific temper and finds his weapons in propagating gossip, innuendo, and lack of emotional control. Once again Frances used her characters to thwart expected gender roles.

The parallels to Stephen are obvious. Anstruthers demands control of his wife's fortune and has "a great deal to say on the subject of wifely duty. It was part of her duty as a wife to be entirely satisfied with his society, and to be completely happy in the pleasure it afforded her. It was her wifely duty not to talk about her own family and palpitatingly expect letters by every American mail." Like Stephen, he believes that American women "had no conception of wifely duties and affection."[47] Frances's letters to Gilder during her marriage were veiled, but because Stephen had already written to him "revolting details," she could be sure that he would be able to read between the lines: "You stimulate me because you understand no one is so stimulating as an imaginative, intellectual American. He *sees* things. Thank you for our letter," she told him. "This story has become very vivid to me. I feel that it will be strong & that it will also deal with subtleties extremely interesting to Americans—perhaps especially at this period. Circumstances have been working up to a certain need of expression for the last twenty years. I may be able to express [them] because I have *lived* on both sides of the Atlantic & have been thinking so hard & fast on each continent. And, as you kindly say I am given to balancing the scales of justice." Proof that Frances had finally resolved the issue of her nationality and come down on the side of America comes not just in her fiction but also in her own life. When she and Edith crossed from England to America on the *Minneapolis* in December 1905, the ship's manifest listed them both as U.S. citizens, but whether she actually had become naturalized at that time is not clear.

She made Bettina as physically different from herself as she could, more on the Clorinda model of black hair, slenderness, and height, as well as giving her inherited wealth, but otherwise they were the same: "She is the New American woman—whose wealth has given her both worlds & whose American brain & initiative have absorbed & taken possession of both."[48] Stornham village is clearly Rolvenden, and Frances is the woman from America who puts the house and garden to rights, befriends the villagers, tends to the needs of the poor, attends church services and garden parties, and eases her way into everyone's heart. In this context it is the Englishman who is the outsider. Rosalie, the weak sister beaten down by her husband, Anstruthers, is what Frances refused to become.

Her letters over the nearly seven years that it took her to write the novel reveal her struggle with it, beginning with the fact that it was turning into a very long novel rather than a short story. Her original idea had been to make it into a play—an astonishing notion since of course it would have meant putting part of her life directly upon the stage—but Gilder, in a visit to Maytham in 1900, had asked her to write it as a serial for the *Century*. She expected to do so quickly, but as the first winter of writing dragged on, and Stephen's behaviour worsened, she found herself unable to make progress. She wrote the early portion describing Anstruthers's cruelty to Rosalie—he struck her and caused her to give birth to a deformed child—but then Frances, just before moving into the Berkeley Square house with Edith, had a heart seizure. In February she laid the work aside in order to write *The Making of a Marchioness*, based on "an incident which had occurred at Maytham [which] had suggested a short story I thought I should never write" she told Vivian, another story about a loveless marriage.[49]

In August 1904, after her return to Maytham Hall, Vivian had written in exasperation, "What have you done with Bettina. For heaven's sake finish it. Stokes was after me over the 'phone the other day. Is it such a Herculean labor to get the thing into shape?"[50] Apparently it was. Pleading poverty, she had plunged into getting the plays *The Pretty Sister of José* and *That Man and I* produced, and to writing *A Little Princess*, but she tried to take it up again on the steamer when she returned to New York that December.

In the summer of 1906, she sat in the rose garden at Maytham with Rosamond Campbell, rearranging chapters, and found that she had finally written enough to send off to be typewritten. In one of the stranger developments of her writing career, she had no memory of having written so much and was amazed when she took it out and saw the pages stack up. This was confusing, but another development was more worrisome: apparently Stephen, when he was trying to get a book of his own published, had contracted with Stokes on Frances's behalf for two books after *Marchioness*, but it was Frances's understanding that Stokes was contractually obliged to publish *The Shuttle*, as *Bettina* was now called. "When I had inquired by Mr Townesend *why* there was mention of a second novel he said that it was merely to make clear the fact that the Marchioness books did not take the place of Bettina which was to be the long novel. I am afraid I cannot persuade myself that he did not understand the situation. [Stephen] was too shrewd for that and Mr Stokes too frank & straightforward," she told Vivian. "In view of the fact that his little book was in Mr Stokes hands he wished to make himself of importance to him & engaged me to anything Mr Stokes asked knowing that he could make it impossible for me to ask questions or doubt his wisdom in the matter without realizing that there would ensue the usual costermonger scene in which obscene language was poured forth in tones expressly raised to reach the Servants Hall."[51] The book was already appearing as a serial in America, but now she found herself stymied and disheartened, without a clue as to how to end the story. Worried that Maytham Hall might well have to be given up—not by her choice but because the owner, Edwards, was now thinking seriously of selling it—she let it back to him for the month of January and took off for Montreux, on Lake Geneva, with Lord Ronald Gower, Frank Hird, and a lively older woman named Josephine Brown, taking *Bettina* with her.

She had been friendly with Gower ever since her first visit to his country seat. Frank, his adopted son, saw Josephine as a mother substitute and was charmed by her ability to climb mountains and tramp across the countryside for hours at a time. Frances had only recently met her in London and was just as admiring of her, if less energetic herself, and found her "the very sweetest & kindest & most dear person one could possibly know."[52] They passed hours in watching the young people on their toboggans, luges, sledges, and skates. They spent their mornings on their own but met for lunch each day, returning afterwards to Frances's salon to chat while she and Frank smoked. They met again for tea, rummaged through the local shops, listened to music, then dressed for dinner.

Even though Frances was having such a good time, she simply couldn't push *The Shuttle* to its end. It was growing longer and longer, and she felt that a serial would cramp all that she had to say. Although she complained that she had no "fire," once she opened the floodgates of this difficult episode in her life, mere magazine instalments were insufficient to contain it. After slow, careful development of the novel, in late May it suddenly rushed to a close in a melodramatic fury of attempted rape—what she called Anstruthers's "unholy love"—a violent beating, and his subsequent death from a stroke.[53]

Telling Gilder that "cut down to bare incident it might be made like a thing in a newspaper—which is why it is powerful & realistic," she finally succeeded in killing Stephen off. For the frail Rosalie, divorce was out of the question, just as it was for Frances herself. As Anstruthers knew, "there was not much limit to the evidence a man could bring if he was experienced enough to be circumstantial, and knew whom he was dealing with. The very fact that the little fool could be made to appear to have been so sly and sanctimonious would stir the gall of any jury of men."[54] All letters between Stephen and Frances vanished after he gave them to a friend at the end of his life, but the novel tells Frances's side of the story. In the novel, although the evil Anstruthers dies, Bettina finds her soulmate in the impoverished but manly Lord Mount Dunstan, whose estate is near Stornham. In real life, it was ironic that a woman who made her living writing about lovers who find joy in each other never met the man she could love in this way. Yet *The Shuttle* signals a more explicit feminism, as Frances confronted social double standards and a legal system that did not necessarily support women. The novel was to prove the financial success she needed: both Heinemann in England and Stokes in America published it in the autumn of 1907, when she was again in New York, and Stokes printed fifty thousand copies of the first edition.

This good news was offset by the distressing fact that her house on West 87th Street in Manhattan had been burgled. Over a period of six months, more than $14,000 worth of silver had been stolen, piece by piece. It had been locked up in a safe, and the house was in the care of her butler, George Francis, but whenever she stopped in at the house, she noticed that things had gone missing. Most of them were quite old, collected over the years in England, some of the pieces gifts from friends. Much of it had belonged to aristocratic families and bore their crests. By the time she contacted the police, hardly anything was left, and they all concluded that it was an inside job and the silver unlikely to be recovered. George Francis, whom she had trusted, rather disingenuously declared that the robberies must have taken place while he was sleeping in the attic.[55]

Happy though the novel's success made her, she had another heartbreak to face, one that she tried to face stoically although it meant the end of an era. It had seen the worst of times and the best of times, but those times were about to be over. Maytham Hall was about to be sold.

CHAPTER 19

~

THE END
OF AN ERA

1907–1911

AT THE END OF 1906 EDITH, as they packed for an American sojourn, wrote to Laurence Alma Tadema, "have you heard the good news—that Maytham is to remain furnished and we may be back again summer after next. We are all so happy over the thought that we do not have to tear down our beloved Castle before we leave. Sister was so happy over it that she seemed like another creature when I left her Tuesday last in London."[1] The Hall had been in the Moneypenny family for hundreds of years, but now Edwards vacillated about hanging on to a place he rarely used, even though it was profitably leased out to someone responsible for all upkeep and repairs, and even though he retained access to it for hunting. In 1904 he had offered Frances the chance to rent it by the year, rather than for a longer term, which suited her. With so much time spent in New York, she knew she could plan to be away yet always have the opportunity to return. She rarely wintered there anyway, preferring to be in London or New York during the cold weather. This new arrangement pleased everyone, particularly when Frances had the option of letting it for the months when she was away; it was Edwards himself who took it for the month she spent in Montreux. However, in 1906 he began to think seriously of selling the place. He lived with his family at Novingdon Manor near Brighton, which his children preferred as being livelier than Rolvenden. They wanted him to sell Maytham and use the money to make improvements to Novingdon. He remained fond of Maytham, however, and he and Frances worked out an arrangement whereby he could rent her furniture during the months or years when she was away, saving the expense of her storing it and giving her a bit of profit.

She despaired at the thought of completely losing Maytham, "the one place which has given me the atmosphere I like & feel at home in—but I do not let myself think about it except to say to myself obstinately that I shall find myself somewhere presently which will be even larger, more picturesque & more lovable. One can only live by taking that tone. The person who declaims about 'dear old days' & 'never again, alas never again' is paving for himself a way down a steep hill in to seas of misery—nice Early Victorian sentimental misery. Perhaps it is rather to my advantage that I never had any 'dear old days'. There has never been one thing I wanted back again but two lovely little boy things with sturdy legs & sailor hats, & rushes and hugs & kissings. But I do not let myself think about that either."[2] A couple of buyers looked at the Hall but nothing came of it, yet by the end of the year she began to realize that it was likely the place would finally sell. She herself could not afford to buy it, just as she could not afford the Berkeley Square house when it was offered to her. In fact, she was able to live as grandly as she did precisely because she could afford to rent houses that she couldn't afford to buy. She still clung to the one house she did own, the Massachusetts Avenue house in Washington—partly at Vivian's reasonable argument that she should always have a home to go to should she fall on hard times—but Maytham was the home of her heart.

The most reasonable plan seemed to be Vivian's after all: to buy or build a house in New York on the water, within a reasonable commuting distance of Manhattan. She wanted to be closer to Vivian, who had now shaken off his more selfish immaturity and grown into a responsible and caring manhood. Edith too wanted to be near her sons, and worried especially about Archie, who had recently married an interior designer, Annie Prall, a niece of Effie Macfarlane. Annie was a talented but highly-strung woman with a temper, and neither she nor Archie had much to live on, though Annie was later given the commission of decorating Frances's house. Frances tried to convince Edith that if they were in love, things might work out well for them. "God bless us all say I," she decided, but she was to find down the road, in a very public and upsetting way, that Edith's concerns had merit after all.[3] For the time being, Annie and Edith got along well and "amuse[d] themselves immensely together" when they got together at the young couple's modest flat on 155th Street.[4]

Vivian himself already had a small house in Queens, at that time a more countrified area than it is today. While his mother remained in England, he began house-hunting for a place she could rent on Long Island for a year or so while she figured out what to do. He found a place for her in Port Washington, but she worried his taste might not match her requirements. "Is the

Port Washington house on the water so that you could sail?" she asked him. "Is it decently furnished? Is it in a green place & has it any trees? Is the little town pretty? Is one obliged to see it or is it behind one at a little distance? Is it away from marshes where mosquitoes breed? Has it the right exposure. Do you *really* think it is desirable—not merely a thing one would be putting up with."[5] She took the house beginning in April, and Vivian spent delightful summer weekends sailing, playing tennis, and driving her new car. Privately, she thought the house "cramped and hideous" but made the most of it until moving into a much more satisfactory house in Sands Point for the winter.[6]

The problem was, of course, that nothing could compare to Maytham. She not only regretted the loss of the house and the grounds but despaired of certain aspects of American life, particularly in the matter of getting satisfactory servants, which she thought might "be the impossible barrier in the way of my buying a place in America."[7] She confessed to Laurence that her heart broke at being away from Maytham and living in the little Long Island house, but "I refuse to let myself be homesick for England but in a locked back cupboard of my mind I beat my breast and slowly tear pieces of my hair out. England my soul requires. I think of buying a little place here for Vivian and placing him softly on it with Edith and Frank to take care of him when I run over to my native land for run over I must. Oh, it does complicate things to have your Only Child earning his living in a land which is *not* ones native one."[8] She had returned to Maytham for only six weeks after her trip to Montreux, and when she sailed for America late in March, the Maytham servants were bereft and pooled together to buy her a gift. "We one & all are taking the liberty to wish you health wealth & *every* happiness and a very pleasant voyage," they wrote in a note of farewell. "We all hope to have the Pleasure of Serving you again at dear Old Maytham." It was signed by "your Faithfull Servants," George Millum, Harry Millum, Emily Coombers, David Piper, Emily Judge, Mary Barrett, Herbert Barrett, and Tom Barrett.[9] The Maytham servants hoped, like Frances, that she would return to live in the Hall.

One of the things that occupied her during that spring on Long Island was a new play. When *The Dawn of a To-morrow* was so successfully published, the actress Eleanor Robson had contacted Frances to ask her to consider making a play of it, with Robson to play the part of Glad. Frances at first refused, saying that she didn't want to commercialize a story that had such religious importance. "My feeling about a dramatization of Glad is that nothing earthly would induce me to do it if the play could not be made to produce the effect of the story. If that could not be done, to dramatize it at all would be vulgar sacrilege," she told Robson. "The effect of the story has been an extraordinary thing. The letters I receive & the things I hear have a tone of intensity beyond words. You can see what a mistake it would be to shock the people who so love the thing by destroying an ideal. The *real* thing might be achieved by two people who had the same point of view— an actress who could embody the thought itself as it was dreamed by the creator of it. Ever since I saw your Mary Ann I have felt that I should like to write something for you. I hope this may be the something."[10] They decided to try working on it during those American months, then present the script to Elisabeth Marbury to place in a theatre.

Robson seemed to be a good choice for Glad. She enjoyed great success on the stage, playing parts that Israel Zangwill and George Bernard Shaw, among others, wrote for her. Although younger than Frances, she had a certain similarity to her, having been born in England and moved to America when she was young; like Frances, she retained something of her English accent and made her own way in the world. She also suffered from difficulties with "nerves." Her mother had been on the English stage before taking her career to America after her husband's death; Eleanor left England at seven years old and spent the next ten years in a convent school. When she emerged, she announced that she wanted to act and was given her chance more as a way of humouring her than from any expectation that she might succeed. She proved to be a natural in that she could absorb lines, her voice and diction carried well, and she could hold audiences by her presence.

Eleanor, like so many others, found Frances to be a sweet woman, "totally different from anyone that I had known or worked with before," who was open to all suggestions and willing to give her best shot to writing and rewriting the play. "She was quite plump, rather a squatty little figure, with a mop of red hair going gray," the actress recalled. Like others, she was struck by Frances's conversational habit of leaving sentences unfinished, then circling back to them later; it was she who said that "one picked up her thoughts with careful concentration, as if they were dropped stitches."[11]

She and Frances set out to transform *Dawn* from a parable without a plot into a play. This involved changing Glad from a twelve-year-old into an older girl with a love interest named Dandy, downplaying the older Bet's part, and adding a second Oliver Holt, the jaded nephew of Sir Oliver. "I am happy to say that the more I work at the play the more interested I become & the more I see you in it," she told Eleanor, as she scribbled away at the new scenes. "You know you have very wonderful eyes—thinking eyes—on the stage. This young savage is possessed each moment with strange dawning thoughts—vague wonders she must follow. She doubts, she hopes—she fears, she is [alarmed] and compelled—she disbelieves—she believes—she is passionately uplifted. Interesting things for a person with wonderful eyes to do."[12]

After spending five weeks in Washington, in June 1908 Frances purchased a plot of land in the Plandome area of Manhasset, Long Island, and hired an architect to design her new American house. Her American lawyer Will Dennis warned her of a recent ruling that seemed to forbid aliens, or those married to aliens, from buying property in America, and worried about her citizenship status and her connection to Stephen. If she ran into difficulties, one thought was that Frank Jordan could be named the owner, or that the property could be acquired by some sort of trust. His concern seems to indicate that she may not have taken out citizenship until this time.[13] When she returned to Maytham in August 1908, it was to remove her belongings and make room for a new owner.

This latest return to Europe involved another of Frances's quests for health, and she planned to go to a sanatorium in Frankfurt, travelling on the SS *Zeeland* with Kitty and Gigi Hall. Their sister Daisy had been ill and was now recovering from an operation. The day before they were to sail to Antwerp they decided they couldn't bear to leave her behind. They rushed to Frances's Manhattan hotel to cancel the trip and were delighted when Frances thought for a moment and then asked, "Why doesn't Daisy come too?" Daisy "gaily pitched her things into a trunk," and the next morning the four women, accompanied of course by Frances's maid, boarded the ship.[14] Frances apparently paid Daisy's way and went even further by giving her own stateroom to Gigi and Kitty, and sharing another one with Daisy. Calling it "a divine voyage," they had the time of their lives, pampering Daisy until she glowed with health and happiness.[15] The only odd moment on the trip was when Frances noticed Gigi scribbling in her deck chair and asked if she was writing a story. Startled, Gigi said yes, and Frances replied rather imperially but encouragingly that she was sure she could do it well. It turned out that Gigi was financing her trip with an epistolary serial, "The Letters of G.G.," that was to begin its run in the *American Magazine* in a few months. Kitty had told Frances of it the year before but somehow Frances had forgotten.[16] Kitty was by now herself an accomplished poet and novelist, "identified in literature with work which is essentially artistic," one magazine noted, but its writer was even more struck with Kitty's photograph, which showed her to be a beauty.[17]

A planned visit to Dr. Lampé's sanatorium turned out to be more of a comedy than a cure. As Kitty and Gigi took off on their own travels, Frances checked into her room, but Daisy could only find one down the road, in a lovely convent. The younger woman was now well enough to handle all

their plans and finances—their hotel at Majence mystifyingly sent the bill
to "Herr Hall and family"—and loved being in charge. Frances quickly discovered that no one at Lampé's spoke English, and the doctor's English was
so precarious that it wasn't clear what regimen had been prescribed for her.
She sat at the dining table with other patients who spoke neither English nor
German, with an attendant assigned to each table to make sure that no one
strayed from the particular diet assigned to her. Frances was put on a strict
weight loss diet that consisted of a boiled egg and cup of weak tea for breakfast, a thin slice or two of dry boiled meat or fish and a small slice of dry
bread for lunch and supper, with a peach or plum between meals. Deciding
that the secret to weight loss was to go without any foods one liked to eat,
she naturally began to lose weight and to feel better, and expected to return
home "nothing but a willowy spin a voice and a lovely disposition."[18] The
doctor decided that her problem was nerves and put her on a daily regimen
of regular baths, electric baths, rest, and "every third morning there is fric-
tion with brandy . . . blown out of a cone onto ones pain places."[19] When
another English-speaking patient unexpectedly arrived, Frances nearly fell
into her arms: it turned out to be Lady Alma Tadema, Laurence's step-
mother. She was also visited by Elisabeth Marbury, with her life partner Elsie
de Wolfe. They showed up in a $4,000 Packard limousine and offered to
have another one shipped to London if Frances wanted to buy it. She left for
England in much better spirits, a bit lighter in heart and in body, ready to
face the task of leaving Maytham.

When Frances left Lampé's sanatorium, she went not to Maytham but to
Bonchurch, near Ventnor, on the Isle of Wight. Eleanor Robson had suffered a near nervous breakdown, and her Harley Street doctor sent her there
to recover in a well-known nursing home run by a Scottish doctor. Her main
problem, along with the exhaustion of overwork, was that she faced a cross-
roads in her life: whether or not to accept the marriage offer of August Belmont and give up her acting career just as she was becoming famous. She
cried non-stop for three days and nights, and was down to a mere ninety-six
pounds. When Frances arrived she was doing better, and the two of them
set to work on the play before Eleanor's planned return to America in September. When Eleanor set sail, Frances planned to go to London for a few
days and then off to Tavistock, in Devon, for a long visit to a friend before
facing the dismantling of Maytham.

The ground was broken for her new house at Plandome on 2 September,
and although it felt odd to her to be in England in the late summer without
living at Maytham with crowds of guests, she threw herself into working on
the building plans by letter with Vivian, who was in charge, into developing

the play, and into trying to stick to Dr. Lampé's diet. The new house, at first to be called Fairseat, gave her particular pleasure not because she desired to build but because she viewed it as her legacy to her son. "Just think, Vivvie that Sunday morning you were longing & dreaming of a sheer chance of that place & now it is bought & you are likely to spend your life on it!" she wrote to him from Brown's Hotel in London. "I am so glad for you. It is so wonderful to have the thing you dream of—so early in life. That is as it should be. That makes it worth while to be alive. When I was your age I was struggling with all my strength to earn a living for myself & children—& weights were hung on my neck & feet & hands. Joy, joy to think my only child will *begin* with all the most necessary things."[20] This, and the hoped-for success of his *Children's Magazine*, made her feel that he was settled in life, lacking only a family of his own.

Meanwhile, plans continued for the new play. Elisabeth Marbury, who had a London office as well as a New York one, met with her at Brown's to discuss developments. Marbury was certain it would be a great play and was anxious that it "should be perfectly cast." Eleanor Robson's precarious health worried them both, and Frances's experiences with Julia Arthur and Eleanor Calhoun prevented her from placing too great a faith in her latest leading lady's enthusiasm. There were too many other things to sort out at the same time: the building of the new house, the sale of Maytham, and her own refusal to think too hard about how she felt about leaving not just the Hall but England itself. She certainly intended to continue spending long stretches of time there, but as she confessed to Edith, "it was *living* at Maytham which meant England to me, in a way." In any case, living there as she was now, going from place to place, from hotel to hotel and friend to friend, made her realize that "being in England without a house of ones own is very different from being here with Maytham."[21]

The sale was pending although not completed, but Frances found it best to assume finality and went ahead with removal plans. She would have to sort through all the furnishings of the Hall—the old oak she had so passionately collected, the beds, the china and glassware—and arrange for Harrods to store what she wished to send to Plandome until the new house was ready to receive it. Edwards was at first solicitous of her feelings, sending her a brace of pheasants and keeping her abreast of the sale, but in the end he felt so anxious that the sale go through that he defaulted on his promise to give her six weeks' notice, once the sale was final, to remove her things. When news finally came that Maytham was officially sold, things happened so quickly that she had no time to indulge her feelings. With no time to adver-tise the sale of her own Maytham furnishings, she followed Edwards's advice and put the estate sale into the hands of Hamptons, the estate agents who had arranged the sale of the house. Her beloved butler Barrett helped her plan everything.

She moved in with Rosamond at nearby Wittersham, and the two women, along with Mary Barrett, rode over to Maytham on "a radiant Autumn day & the place looked so beautiful that I could hardly endure it," and despite her cheerfulness to Vivian, she poured out her heart to Edith.

> That place *belongs* to me—It is the only place I ever felt was *home*—except 1770 [her Washington, D.C., house] during that last summer when we were there together. But Maytham is *real* home. It seemed a sort of out-rage that I was not living there. It seemed so what one needed—that sense of being able to go out of one big room into another—to go down corri-dors into room after room—to go upstairs & walk about & upstairs again & walk about. . . . I went about the place as if I were walking in a dream and as if it *could* not be possible that it could be taken from me. If I would have allowed myself I should have been very unhappy—I was not *happy* of course—but I hold myself together by recalling the days when I had felt that perhaps it would be better for me to go somewhere else where there were no dark memories. . . . Millions of money spent on a place in America would never give me what I felt that I *walked into* when I went out upon the terrace at Maytham.[22]

On Monday and Tuesday, 24 and 25 October, Frances saw her expensive belongings, except for the ones ready to be shipped to America, knocked down for the sum of £530. Her physical pain was back, but otherwise she was glad that "the whole sad & tiresome business is over."[23] She turned her attention to Plandome, where Vivian's taste seemed at times alarming; he had, for instance, arranged for busts to be placed on plinths between the living room and dining room. Before setting sail, she made another round of visits to friends, had some medical bath treatments in London, and at the beginning of November received the following encouraging cable from Elisabeth Marbury: "Everything ready to start rehearsals & produce play with Miss Robson before January. Reply by wire immediately shall I accept payments."[24] She was already beginning her new tomorrow, one in which Maytham would be transformed into a literary classic.

She sailed back to New York at the beginning of December, staying in Flushing, Queens, while her new house was being built, and throwing her-self into the revisions and rehearsals for the play during the snowy winter. What is surprising is not only the extent to which she worked so closely with the actors and directors during these months, writing entirely new scenes and revising old ones, but that apparently everyone found it perfectly acceptable for her to give acting instructions. "I wanted to ask you not to move as you say 'Well—I aint druw [threw] me on the street yet'—The significance seemed rather lost & the words not clearly heard—If you move make sure the audience *quite* hears. I do trust the changes I send you will fit in well," she instructed Eleanor.[25] By letter, telephone, and in the theatre she passed on lines, most of them in response to requests by the director and others. She was pushing herself hard and, before the play went on, suffered another of her "heart failures," which alarmed her because she hadn't had one for two or three years. Confined to bed, she continued to write there; except for this interlude, and one in which heavy snow made it impossible to get into Manhattan, she attended all rehearsals.

Before opening in New York, the play had its trial run on 18 December in Norfolk, Virginia, a location perhaps chosen because Frances could spend time there with Herbert and his family. Local reporters called it "another play of slum life," one in a series of recent morality plays such as *The Regeneration, Salvation Nell*, and *The Easiest Way*.[26] A number of theatre managers, including Daniel Frohman, showed up to check its progress.[27] They worked out some of the kinks, tried the play out again in New Haven, Connecticut, and then opened it in New York's Lyceum Theatre on 28 January 1909. The play was well-enough received, but not everyone was easy with Frances's religious message. It was the "New Thought mixed with fantasy [and] served in [the] guise of melodrama" to some; to others, it was one of "the cults of the Faith Cure, Mind Cure, Rest Cure or the theology that has Mrs. Eddy as its oracle and guide." Despite its "too transparent artificiality"—the doctor hands Sir Oliver a Bible just before he goes out to buy his pistol—some found it "restful and uplifting" and approved of Eleanor Robson's fine performance.[28]

Frances was unapologetic about her message, even going so far as to condone stage censors to discourage the production of overly depressing plays such as *Camille* that made torment look picturesque.[29] Calling her ideas in the play and the book the "beautiful thought," she defined them as having to do with optimism, happiness, sacrifice for others, and a search for beauty. "We are to-day mysteriously conscious of this strange magic in the air that we will call the beautiful thought. It has so revitalized and stirred our souls that there has been in its most recent evolution a magnetic force that seems to me must almost stir the dead in their graves," she announced. "We have a new knowledge of love, a new conception of hope, new unwritten laws of conscience and mutual helpfulness that it is no longer possible to escape, and which we are consequently in constant effort to explain."[30]

It was easy to see how this "new" thinking and her new play, as well as the loss of Maytham Hall and its gardens, led directly to her next book, *The Secret Garden.* Convinced that "we want plays to-day that have in them some big moment of beauty . . . plays that are written with the same reverence of spirit, with the same sacred allegiance to the beautiful thought with which an artist alone sees and describes," she sat down to write the longer story for which she was contracted by Stokes.[31] The New Thought, or in Frances's words, the "beautiful thought," was everywhere and was the perfect repository for her long-developing ideas. When she had informed Edward Burlingame four years before, while discussing the serial of *Dawn,* that "out of all the propositions & arguments of the New Thought the things said in this story are what *I believe,*" she articulated something that was to stay with her for the rest of her life.[32] She made these beliefs clear in her growing distrust of medical doctors and of the public and commercial worship of science, although she found many scientific discoveries thrilling—she particularly loved electricity, the telephone, and automobiles—and supported her inventor nephew. However, she believed that there were "discoveries in literature . . . that have a far greater significance to the happiness of men and women than any scientific discovery can give them."[33]

It is no coincidence that major characters in both *The Dawn of a To-morrow* and *The Secret Garden* are doctors unable to cure their patients' largely mental illnesses and that it is a doctor in the play version of *Dawn* who offers a Bible as the ultimate cure. She had toyed with mediums recommended to her by good friends, and "once or twice she took part in 'slate writing' demonstrations, but she always came away disheartened and disgusted, describing what she saw as 'trumpery exhibitions,'" Vivian recalled. "But for all that she was disappointed in her search for definite proof, she could not down a feeling that there might be something in it all," as her ghost story *In the Closed Room* shows.[34] At this point in her life—she was now nearly sixty years old—"beautiful thought" came much closer to expressing her beliefs. She wrote to her nephew Archie, "You are *ready* to receive this new thinking. Let nothing cloud your view of it. The great truth is the foundation of all these beliefs, whatsoever they call themselves. All philosophers have taught them, but it has seemed to remain to this age to apply them on a practical working basis to every day life." The tenets were simple: "Good is stronger than evil, love is stronger than hate to a mind cleared of *all* darkness and smallness. Nothing is impossible because it is God's self."[35]

They had arrived in Manhasset, Long Island, in May, hoping that their presence would hurry along the cheerfully slow workmen. "Let no one speak to me again of the pleasure of building one's own house," she wrote to Ella

and Maddie Hepworth Dixon in June 1909.[36] She moved into her new house
at Plandome in September, quickly arranging a den where she could write.
As with the Washington house, her study was at the top of the house, overlooking trees and gardens. It was a new beginning for her but also an ending, for just as she was settling in, her old friend, ally, and mentor Richard
Watson Gilder died, breaking yet another link with her past.

Plandome was built with airy rooms and a conservatory filled with palm
trees, where she also set up a writing table. Two years later she sent an article on the new house to her Manchester cousin, Emma Daniels. Written
and with photography by Jeannette Cascaden Klauder, a young friend of
Ernest's, it described the new house as spacious and relaxed, even though
small by Frances's Maytham standards. She was still calling it Fairseat, after
an English village, a name that was dropped after a time; she later named
it Maytham, a name that didn't last either. Frances's only complaint about
the article was that it described the dining room furniture as old English oak
when in fact she had bought it all in Venice. But much of the other furniture, as well as her pewter, was Elizabethan.[37] Planning for the gardens
and work on them had begun before the house was completed, and later a
balustrade was added that allowed her to walk down to the sea on an outdoor staircase. It was in this new American house that she finished her most
famous, and most English, book.

One of the greatest mysteries about the writing of *The Secret Garden* is
that there is so little record of it. Her experiences in writing her other books
reel out through long letters to her family, but now that she was living with
or near them all, there was no need to write to them. Apparently it "wrote
itself" relatively quickly, for April 1910 found her and Edith in Manchester
and Liverpool because *Dawn* was to open that spring in England, with
Gertrude Elliott taking over from the now-married Eleanor Robson, and the
book was either finished or nearly so at that time. Although disappointed
that Eleanor was out of the play, Frances sighed, "Far be it from me, however, to suggest that any girl should not marry a nice millionaire. I 'ave not
a 'art of stone, even though my play is stopped at the height of its career and
I lose a couple of hundred pounds a week."[38] Once again her English jinx
with plays kicked in: the play had barely opened when King Edward VII
died and the country went into mourning. "The streets have not a gleam
of color in them," she wrote to Vivian. "*Every*body is in black."[39] The play
had been a great popular success, if not a great critical one, and the public
support seemed so great that the managers decided to ride it out. Like everyone else in the country, Edith and Frances were forced into black clothing
and watched the funeral procession from the Park Lane house of Francis

Shackleton, brother of the South Pole explorer, along with a depressed Lord Ronald Gower, Frank Hird, and Josephine Brown. Gower and the king had been schoolboys together, and though they were not close friends, Gower felt death closing in. Shackleton, so friendly at that time, had a very shady history. Run out of Ireland for his suspected part in the theft of the Irish crown jewels, he went on trial in 1913 for swindling a widow of her life savings. Josephine was forced to testify against him, put repeatedly on the witness stand as though she were the criminal and not he; he was ultimately sentenced, along with his lawyer, to nearly five years' hard labour.

Mistress Mary, as Frances was still calling the new book, was to be serialized in the new *American Magazine*, and she was delighted that an American publication was to have it first. Furthermore, "this is the first instance I have ever known of a childs story being published in an adults magazine."[40] On 9 October 1910, she wrote to her English publisher, William Heinemann, that the story was finished, and only a month later it began its serial run.

> With regard to the Secret Garden do you realize that it is not a novel, but a childs story though it is gravely beginning life as an important illustrated serial in a magazine for adults. . . . It is an innocent thriller of a story to which grown ups listen spell bound to my keen delight. Ella Hepworth Dixon said it was a sort of childrens Jane Eyre. I love it myself. There is a long deserted garden in it whose locked door is hidden by ivy and whose key has been buried for ten years. It contains also a sort of Faun who charms wild creatures and tame ones and there is a moorland cottage woman who is a sort of Madonna with twelve children—a warm bosomed, sane, wise, simple Mother thing. You only see her for a moment at the end of the book but she is the chief figure in it really. "Mother" baking and washing in her cottage on the Yorkshire Moor makes all things happen merely because she is. There is a house on the edge of the moor (delightful thought) and a hundred rooms nearly all locked up—and a tiresome cry rather like the wind heard far off down mysterious corridors. And in the hidden garden—which I adore—many strange and lovely quite natural human things happen. Oh, I know quite well that it is one of my best finds.[41]

Although the novel takes place in Yorkshire, the inspiration for the garden came from Maytham Hall. She wrote to Ella Hepworth Dixon after its publication that "it was our Rose Garden as it would have been locked up for years and years and years—and some hungry children had found it. You cannot think how everyone loves that story. People write to me with a sort of passion of it."[42] Her writing of bringing this garden to life coincided with a spate of letters on gardens and gardening that continued until the end of her life.

There is a ream of critical material on *The Secret Garden*, all of it analysing the novel. Some call it the greatest examination of nervous breakdown ever written; some refer to its message as "garden religion"; some call it, like *Dawn of a To-morrow*, an exemplum or religious fable; others view it as a story of sexual awakening. It falls squarely in Frances's tradition of outsiders entering England, as in her novels *A Woman's Will* (published in America as *Miss Defarge*), *Little Lord Fauntleroy*, *A Little Princess*, *The Shuttle*, and the next novel she would write, *T. Tembarom*, but it also falls into her newer "message" books like *The Dawn of a To-morrow*, which was recommended to readers from pulpits all over America. What Frances herself thought of it, other than what she said in a few scraps in letters written to friends, and how she created it, will probably never be known for various reasons. Clearly she read portions of it to her friends and relations in the evenings after a day's writing, sitting in her comfortable large armchair, wearing a lorgnette and smoking cigarettes as she read out all the voices in a manner reminiscent of Dickens's readings; there is every reason to assume this happened as it did with her other books. And of course she wouldn't have written letters to them about it since they were in the house with her. There they first learned of Mistress Mary, the girl who leaves India for a mansion on the moors, comes back to health, and teaches her invalid cousin to heal himself in the garden, under the tutelage of Dickon, a boy at one with nature.

In its own time the novel met with mixed reviews. One dismissed it as a "'new-thought' story, oversentimental and dealing almost wholly with abnormal people." The *Nation* was more positive, calling it a "charming story, fantastic, perhaps, but full of sweet admonition," and *Bookman* found it "more than a mere story of children; underlying it there is a deep vein of symbolism. But regarded purely as romance, it is an exceedingly pretty tale." No one spotted it as the enduring classic it would become, and certainly no one set it above her other books such as *Fauntleroy*.[43]

However the critics responded, one thing about the book is clear: it is the resurrection of Lionel, the boy who rises from his sickbed to cure himself with the aid of belief and nature. The book moves from winter through spring and into summer, just as the children in the book move into health. She had been unable over the years to write the story of Lionel's death in "A Fair, Far Country" and now, looking at the loss of her beloved home, Frances was able to preserve all that was so special about it in the story of a large-eyed, sickly teenaged boy who gets up and walks. Standing tall and straight at the end of the novel, Lionel in the form of Colin shows just how beautiful the far country is. It seems likely that as she took her last look at Maytham, the stories of her two great losses came together through the hope expressed in *Dawn*.

With the play of *Dawn* on hold, Frances and Edith decided to head for the Continent. Gower, Hird, and Brown went with them as far as Lake Garda, between Milan and Venice, and the other women continued to the Dolomites, in the Italian Alps. They hoped to make a tour of castles but instead found themselves trapped in a second-rate inn with forty other guests when torrential rains and landslides struck the region so badly that the roads were blocked. When they were finally able to leave, they travelled through northeastern Italy and part of Austria before doubling back through Switzerland, Italy, and France, reaching London at the end of June and prepared to sail back to America.

This trip marked a new era in her life, one in which she was solvent and financially comfortable, and would remain so. Not exactly wealthy, she could now do and see and buy pretty much anything she desired. Royalties came in regularly from all her books, and when one of her plays was being produced she netted another $1,000 to $1,500 a week (in the autumn of 1910, when *Dawn* had been running for two seasons and showed no signs of stopping, she was reported to be receiving royalties from it of $1,000 to $2,000 a week). When her latest royalty cheque came in for *A Lady of Quality* and seemed to be too small, she shot off an angry letter in October 1910 complaining about its size. She was chagrined when reminded that Stephen, as co-author of the play, was entitled to a share, and so tendered a contrite apology: "Incredible as it may seem I had absolutely forgotten that Mr. Townesend claims half the returns. He has so entirely passed out of my existence that the whole matter was blotted from my memory. I am sorry to have troubled you."[44] Not counting the income from the serialized version, *The Shuttle* had reputedly earned her another $50,000 so far. How many other women, one magazine asked, "are capable of holding the public attention and interest for more than thirty years, and of earning, single-handed and by sheer power of brain, far over a hundred thousand dollars, as Mrs. Burnett has lately done, in less than two years?"[45]

Now, forty years after she first began publishing stories, the press was as interested as ever in her opinions ranging from religion ("'What?' shrieked Mrs. Burnett in her really exquisite voice, her beautiful eyes opened wide. 'What? Do you mean to tell me you believe in a devil? Hell?'"), to the occult ("I believe our big creative powers of things intellectual are the powers that come from without. That is the real manifestation of the psychic. It is not a blurred, reddish haired woman, who has been sick a great deal and suffered much, who writes my stories, but the power from without. I am convinced of that because am I not the only one out of the five little red-headed children that came to my mother who can write stories"), to women's issues. When asked if she believed women ought to smoke cigarettes, she answered, "Now how can I answer that? . . . all my friends know I smoke them myself."[46]

With this financial cushion beneath her, and no husband to interfere, Frances felt more in control of her life than she had for years. She was never against marriage for other people. In fact, she declared that now, in the twentieth century, "there has never been a time when so many women married their ideal mates. There has never been a time when so many unions were so happy. Women to-day are freer than ever before from the awful necessity of acquiring the first man in sight."[47] When her books involved marriages now, they were often about strong women finding their equals. In 1909 she, along with other major writers, signed a petition by the National American Woman Suffrage Association supporting a constitutional amendment granting women the right to vote. As the women's suffrage movement gained force in New York and rallies were held in Manhattan in 1910, the Equal Suffrage League received a message from Frances saying "she was also a suffragist."[48] In her later years, when asked to join in marches, she agreed, but when her poor health kept her in bed she sent in donations and added her name to lists of supporters of the cause.

Safely ensconced in Plandome, she published *The Secret Garden* and watched the letters of praise come in from readers. An old man wrote to say how it affected him. A girl wrote from a New Orleans hospital that she read the latest instalment in the middle of the night and "resolved to tell the doctor when daylight came that she was going to be well—that she was well and was going home at once to her own garden. She did it, too. I have found a friend of hers who tells me she is at home, a normal creature."[49] The critics were kind, but there was no sense that she had written a masterpiece. Even though she declared this to be her favourite book and received letters for years afterwards about it, she always felt that her "great American novel" was *In Connection with the DeWilloughby Claim*, an adult book that took her so many years to write and garnered more critical praise in her lifetime.

There are additional reasons for the frustrating lack of Frances's own words on this book, some of them upsetting and one utterly tragic. Although she settled well into Plandome, everyone noticed that "from this time on she was never thoroughly well, and any real exertion tired her."[50] She went occasionally to the theatre with friends, but her social life and extraneous activities were curtailed. More frustratingly for biographers, five years after her death Vivian donated a portrait of his mother, photographs, and all her notes about *The Secret Garden* to a public school for the deaf in lower Manhattan. Frances had spoken there once to the students, and Vivian wanted them to have a memento of her visit and goodwill.[51] Unfortunately, they completely disappeared from the school's archives, perhaps almost as quickly as they were given. The only other record of the book's creation lies in her little story *My Robin*, which tells of the actual robin who visited her regularly as she wrote outdoors in her garden at Maytham Hall.

The other reason she wrote so little about the book immediately after its publication in 1911 is more horrifying. On the morning of 13 July 1911, just weeks before the book was published, Edith's husband Frank took Frances's car from Plandome, where the couple was now living, to the suburb of Port Washington. With him were Edith Johnstone, the sister of a printing company clerk, her sister Mildred, and their nieces, a six-year-old and a four-year-old. Frances planned to go with them but was detained at home. Edith Johnstone sat in the front, next to Frank, who was a good driver.

Mill Neck Road, which ran east to west, and also contained trolley tracks, met the Plandome road in a sort of V, with trees in the centre at the apex. It was a highway well known to be dangerous, so much so that a sign warned all vehicles to slow and sound their whistles before proceeding through the intersection. Frank and his passengers never heard this whistle. Approaching them from the other direction was a slow, clumsy, and heaving construction vehicle, moving at only four miles an hour. Seeing nothing and hearing no whistle, Frank speeded up a bit in order to top the hill. The construction vehicle caught it squarely in the middle, throwing the children and Mildred Johnstone out of the back of the car. Mildred injured her back and broke several ribs. She survived but the doctors feared a spinal injury. The little girls sustained only broken limbs. Frank and Edith Johnstone fell out of the car, which then fell on top of them. It rolled over and over, pushing them seventy feet along the roadbed. Frank, whose body was completely mangled, died there. Johnstone was dead by the time the ambulance reached the hospital.[52]

It was Vivian who received the telephone call about the accident, and he drove immediately to the hospital from Plandome. Frances was probably at home, but Edith was in Manhattan shopping. No one could locate her, and she read the news in the evening paper on her way home. She had now lost two husbands and a child. Any good news about her sister's latest book arrived in a house of utter, black misery.

CHAPTER 20

~

AT HOME
AND ABROAD

1911–1918

THREE MONTHS BEFORE FRANK'S DEATH, Frances and Edith returned from a winter sojourn in the place that would prove to be their steady winter home—Bermuda. They had gone hoping for a reprieve from the harsh weather that aggravated their combined aches and pains; Frances was now sixty-one and Edith nearly sixty, and both suffered from a variety of joint and digestive problems. At first they stayed at the Princess Hotel in Hamilton. With its swimming pool, tennis courts, and "weekly hop," it was the destination of flocks of New Yorkers: the list of steamer passengers arriving between December and March or April included many of the society names from New York and Washington.

Within weeks they were so smitten with the island's weather and ambience that Frances took a bungalow for them at Clifton Heights, in Bailey's Bay, a house that was said to have been paid for by the proceeds of *My Robin*, her little book about the friendly bird that was her companion in the Maytham rose garden.[1] There too she immediately set about creating a garden, one that swiftly became the talk of the island. The visit was such a success that they returned the following winter, in December 1911. Edith was a special favourite there, partly because people kept mistaking her for her famous sister. Even in England, those who first met the sisters assumed that the lovely Edith must be the well-known author, rather than the plumper and somewhat plainer woman who accompanied her. Frances was always amused when this happened. From now on the two sisters would be all in all to each other as they shuttled between Plandome and Bermuda, each of them vying to care for the other.

Bermuda was the playground of English and American socialites, officials, and artists. It had such a booming social life that even from Bailey's Bay the two found themselves in constant demand at dinners, concerts, teas, tennis parties, costume balls, and gardening shows. Frances hired a gardener named Riley, "a young colored man of intelligence & a tremendous worker," and between them they created a show-stopping garden within just a year or two.[2] Bermudans tended to start gardens slowly, from slips, and let nature take its course. Frances brought in plants, as well as bulbs and seeds, and set about furiously landscaping and pruning. She grew calla lilies, poppies, bluets, gladiolas, violets, and daisies, but as in England and America, roses were her favourites; some swore that she had seven hundred varieties, ranging from gigantic white blossoms to pink ones the size of a fingernail. She held them back by disbudding until she was ready for them to burst into simultaneous bloom. Her garden was so stunning that carriages and cars of tourists stopped in their tracks to peer over her white wall and exclaim "with choruses of delight."[3] By the time she'd been there several years, her roses were so famous that although she sent Riley with them to the annual flower show, she refused to enter them for a prize because she thought it would be unfair to the other entrants. Even so, he came back with a special award.

Her letters to Vivian in these years take on the aspect of one horticulturist writing to another. She makes no references to famous garden-makers like Gertrude Jekyll, but she owned serious books on the subject and sent instructions to her Plandome gardener and her equally possessed son that prove her expertise. "I want Watts to border *all* the herbaceous beds with white phlox Drummondi & to sow that entire curve by the rhododendron & azalea bed with nasturtium seed," she instructed Vivian from Bermuda. "Nasturtiums thrive in poor soil so let us give them a chance. Let Watts take up the platzcodin roots from there & put them in some better places. You might like a few for your own garden. Do nasturtiums grow from seed planted out of doors? I think they do but if they dont please order some seedlings from your seed man. . . . Get me some seedlings of Aritotis Grandis for the empty spaces—also lobelia ageratum & white candy tuft for bordering the fountain. Be sure to have that fringed & starred annual phlox sown thick round the beds of the Secret Garden."[4] In the frigid and snowy Plandome winters, Vivian snuggled up in an armchair with the next spring's seed catalogues before sending them on to her by the weekly steamer mail.

When Frances and Edith returned to Long Island after the winter of 1912, Vivian was building a house of his own on her property at Plandome, and Frances was well into a new novel. The most popular character in *The Shuttle* had been a young American typewriter salesman named G. Selden, modelled partly on Archie who had once held a similar job, and Frances longed to build a novel around him and the adventures of an honest slangy young American abroad. The result was *T. Tembarom*, about a young man orphaned and made homeless as a boy. He is finding his way in the Manhattan newspaper world when he discovers that he is sole heir to an enormous fortune and country estate in Lancashire. He has a bit of the Fauntleroy straightforwardness, but at twenty-five he is no child. In fact, he is one of the most beguiling characters she ever invented, with his exclamations of "Hully gee!" and his belief that Little Ann from Manchester, whom he adores, is a "beaut from Beautville." Frances made his lower Manhattan boarding house seem far preferable to the caste-bound Temple Barholm he inherits and makes it clear that he comes from a place where hard work and honesty trump centuries of pedigreed snobbery. She wanted to create someone who "was not a virtuous hero but a creature born straight & sane & who therefore did through natural instinct the human—the straight—the square thing. The theory is that when Man does not thwart the First Intention he is like that—& those who dont are *not* in the minority."[5] Critics caught on to her intentions immediately, finding it "the most delightful and entertaining of fairy tales," and agreeing that the "aristocratic owners of large estates to whom she presents us are not immersed in either vice or politics, but are highly respectable and unspeakably dull."[6] Indeed, the modern reader is led, erroneously, to believe that its Dickensian characters and obvious intrigue mean a predictable ending. Frances recognized the danger and thwarted all those expectations, deciding to build towards melodrama and then subvert it. It is a modern story, her first real twentieth-century one.

She sent the first chapters to Robert Underwood Johnson, her serial editor at the *Century*, and asked him, "Are you anxious—as a serial reader should be—to get to Temple Barholm & see what will happen there? Are you thrilled when you find yourself face to face with the man who cannot remember? Are you fond of Tembarom at once? Do you want to hug serious minded Little Ann, Manchester accent & all? . . . If so you have got what you wanted for the people who are willing to wait from one month to another for a story."[7] Her instincts were correct—the book would prove enormously popular, although its name has faded away today—and her usual warning about length was also correct. She wrote on a big scale, with chapter after chapter necessary to build character and atmosphere, bemoaning the page limitations of serials and restoring the cuts in the final book, which turned out to be one of her longest as well as an homage to the vibrancy of New York, including its working-class, Jewish, and African American inhabitants.

It was also New York that saw the production of her final play, *Racketty-Packetty House*, taken from her *Saint Nicholas* story and little book about the inhabitants of a London doll's house. Newspapers in early 1913 made much of the fact that Frances had a real doll's house in her living room, hidden inside a Jacobean cabinet that opened to reveal four rooms. "My doll's house has a writing-desk with a telephone on it, a vacuum-cleaner, a carpet-sweeper, a footman in livery, a perfectly good grandpapa and grandmamma, a litter of kittens and a collie dog, besides all the other unnecessaries," she wrote in an article titled "My Toy Cupboard." It was also inhabited by a family of Japanese dolls in "dazzling kimonos," as well as "a tiny and perfectly attired nursery-maid wheeling a tiny white perambulator, with a baby just the right size in it; a bath fitted up most satisfactorily with another baby; a piece of pink soap, a sponge, and a towel on a rack."[8] When she got it to Plandome, she doubled its size, papered its walls, and added another family, complete with servants and pets. She felt that children who visited the house deserved to be entertained just as much as their parents, and she happily threw herself down on the floor and played with young visitors for hours. When the play of *Racketty-Packetty House* was produced in 1912, it was the "first play for children to be given in a real Children's Theater and enacted chiefly by real children."[9] It was her final play, and a decided hit.

Even in Bermuda, as well as in New York, Frances found herself constantly besieged by health problems. On one particularly harrowing evening in Clifton Heights, she was in such agony from abdominal pain that she "could scarcely stand & had to clench my teeth to hide my feelings from Edith who was in a frame of mind which might have ended in her felling me with a blow & sitting on me to prevent my going" to an important government dinner party at which Frances was the guest of honour.[10] She found that she spent more and more time in bed, and caught every passing cold and digestive problem. Annoyed with herself, and hoping to get out of herself, she decided in the summer of 1913 that Edith was now emotionally steady enough to be left behind, so she planned a long sojourn through Austria and Hungary with Kitty and Gigi Hall, hoping that by travelling as slowly and whimsically as they pleased she would shed any nervous disorders. It was "to be a quiet search for the vitality which had sunk into some strange depths."[11] Vivian was in New York, and Ernest and Archie were now both married, with small sons, and living happy suburban lives near Plandome. Frances warned her son that Edith was left to him as a sacred trust, to be kept calm and unburdened by unnecessary work. Generous as always, she decided that the perfect plan was for Edith to keep a room at Archie and Annie's house, subsidized, of course, by their Aunt Fluffy, where Edith could play the doting grandmother to Ernest and Abby's baby Ken, and a good mother-in-law to Archie's Annie if she got lonely while Frances was away. It proved to be a serious miscalculation.

At the end of July, Frances and her maid Kirby boarded the *Kaiser Franz Joseph I*, headed for Trieste, leaving Edith at Plandome with their old friend Effie Macfarlane from Washington. Charlie Rice, wearing a dapper white summer suit, showed up to see them off, and when they went on board they found their staterooms filled with fruits, flowers, and cakes. The ship held a mixed bag of passengers, from a boorish nouveau riche couple in the next rooms who kept trying to get to Frances through Kirby, to the delightful *Harper's Bazar* editor Elizabeth Jordan, who would prove to be the most intimate friend of Frances's later years. It was a fitting send-off for what was to be her last trip to Europe.

She swung between good health and bad throughout the months away, and the bad health set in almost immediately when she and others suffered from what was apparently food poisoning on board ship, which served the same eggs, butter, and meats all the way from New York to Algiers to Trieste. Kitty quickly turned from guest to nursemaid, hovering by Frances's bedside in Austria rather than spending her days in the art galleries she so loved. This illness made Frances furious. "Through half my life I have been building up with medicines to the place where I could begin to force myself on again by sheer furious iron & steel *will* power," she grumbled. "I am not going to do it again. I dont care for anything but for peace & to get well—to feel like a human being—to act without medicine—to step without forcing myself—to learn how to stop thinking & carrying the world I did not make. I have been slower in gaining strength than I ever was before. I am as weak yet as a baby but I have no pain & I am beginning to believe I shall in time [be] *really* well again—but patched."[12]

It was Kitty who so patiently did most of the patching, though she longed to be out on the streets and had a book of her own to shepherd through the publishing process with Henry Holt. She slept uncomplainingly in Frances's room, getting up in the night, boiling water for the powdered Nestlé's Food that she found Frances could keep down, and going for walks with Gigi when Frances shooed them off to get some fresh air. In some ways it is easy to see Frances's difficulties from a modern perspective: she was overweight and a smoker (having, ironically, taken up the habit in early adulthood when a doctor suggested it might help her neuralgia); she used to be a walker and cyclist but was now more sedentary; and her diet suffered from a dislike of green vegetables. Frances wanted only what seemed normal to younger people who had never been ill: calm nerves, good appetite and digestion, no more back pain, and uninterrupted nights of peaceful sleep. When she offered her latest complaint to her osteopath, Cornelia Walker, the response was to "gaze at me with a stony eye, say nothing was the matter & advise one to 'get out on the earth.' It was like a certain form of Christian Science," which Frances found very amusing in that her own professions in books like *The Secret Garden* were being thrown back at her.

This trip was designed to be free of cares or even of itineraries, and they were to wander where they pleased and stay as long as they wished whenever they found a place they liked. When Frances was well, the long trip was a delight, and in her convalescent stages she happily read and marvelled at the scenery. She always had an affinity for mountains, which is why she repeatedly headed for the Alps. The minarets seen across the Danube from her rooms in Budapest thrilled her. Her penchant for picture postcards began on this trip, and she used them to share with those at home the sights and people she encountered. She counted on the recipients to share them among each other, but Edith made sure that the "pass-around" letters and the postcards came back to her in the end. Frances sent a long pass-around letter to Herbert from Vienna, making sure to spend several teasing pages on the Austrian crown jewels "for the sole benefit of persons of flighty mind such as Dora & Frances."[13]

One day, as she sat at her desk in Vienna, Gigi walked in from a visit to the national gallery and dropped a postcard in front of her. "Did you ever see anything like that?" she asked, causing Frances to catch her breath. It was a portrait of the fifteen-year-old Prince Ruprecht of Pfalz, who had lived in the early seventeenth century and was the spitting image of Lionel; in fact "he was so like Lionel that it brought ones heart into ones mouth. The head—the eyebrows—the shape of the face—the eyelids—the eyes were Lionels very own. . . . It gave me strange things to think of when I found myself looking at my own boys face in a picture painted three hundred years ago. What did Prince Ruprecht do? I must find out. Did he come back—and what for?" She carried her sons' pictures with her wherever she travelled, and this portrait seemed another resurrection of her own lost boy, who had had his own, and sometimes troubling, imperial mien. She found the word "occult," which reporters constantly brought up to her, to be merely "the unknown of to-day [which would be] the certain knowledge of to-morrow," but coincidences like this gave her pause.[14] This moment, in conjunction with the world unrest about to explode so close to where she now sat, planted the seed for her next novel, *The Lost Prince*.

In Munich she had more fun than she'd had in years, when their hotel turned out to be one of the central locations for Carnival. The hotel owner persuaded her and Kitty to take a corner table and watch the festivities, even though they had no male companion. Throughout the evening men approached them, kissing their hands and begging them to dance, but Kitty properly rebuffed them. Streamers hung from the walls, bands played, people darted in from the streets in fancy dress costumes and tossed balloons across the ballroom. They had a fabulous time, a frivolous interlude during a period in which "she was most of the time wretchedly ill." Even then, Kitty found that Frances only remembered, or cared to talk about, "the beauty and the good of those painful days."[15]

Although the three women spent much of their time in traditional tourist pursuits, the events and sights that impressed them the most had to do with modern technology. From the train to Budapest they saw a zeppelin, gliding its silent, silver way across the sky, and they watched breathlessly, not knowing what it was. An air show in Austria enthralled them, as the trick pilot Pégoud executed plunges, barrel rolls, and somersaults in his Blériot monoplane. In Vienna they became addicted to Kinos, or newsreel cinemas. All hotels had a projection room, and at first Frances wasn't interested when Kitty suggested they go down in the evening. Once there she found herself spellbound, calling the moving pictures "one of the wonders of the world as Aviation is." They were able to see the latest news in this way—a good thing since she didn't like to read newspapers—and now the whole world opened up. "We have seen battles with thousands of soldiers in them & processions & functions of great cities with apparently hundreds of thousands of people—we have seen heroines of plays galloping over miles & miles of veldt in South Africa, & lions prowling about in jungles—and the arena filled with thousands & thousands of maddened leaping struggling Pompeians on the day of the eruption which destroyed them," she wrote home. "We never wanted to go away. I think we rather like the silly things the best. We laughed & rejoiced. If we had seen the same thing in a play we should have been bored to death. We have given much time & argument to trying to explain what exactly the fascination is."[16]

During this extended trip, she was approached with the first contracts for films of her works, and she knew it was time to educate herself about this new medium. Stopping in London on the way back to America, she met both with her British solicitor Barrett and with a friend of a new travelling companion, Mrs. Ver Beck, who was knowledgeable about the cinema. Frances had first met Mrs. Ver Beck in Bermuda and asked that she join her in Europe when Kitty needed to see friends in Italy and Gigi was called back to New York for her job. The timing was perfect, for Mr. Barrett presented her with a Kinemacolor offer for *Fauntleroy* when she arrived, telling her that the film would run for years and the royalties would simply roll in. Jeanette Gilder, sister of Frances's late editor, had put together the deal guaranteeing a minimum of $8,000 for the first two years. At nearly the same time, offers appeared for films of *The Pretty Sister of José* and *A Lady of Quality*. She accepted them all, correctly anticipating that film rights would end up being a new and reliable source of income for her.

In her 1913 Christmas letter to Vivian, Frances eerily predicted "that 1914 must be full of new & strange & beautiful hopes & fulfilments for you. All the things you need most come marching toward you in battalions."[17] Among her wishes for him in the coming year were health, professional prosperity, and most of all, a wife. He was so unhappy that he threatened to advertise for a wife if he continued to fail to find one at parties and dances, his usual social venues. However, his mother's wish for him, along with the battalions, would come true. When she and Kitty pulled into New York harbour on 4 May 1914 on the steamship *Minnewaska*, they had been away for ten months and Vivian was there on the dock to greet them.

Only two weeks later she got word of Stephen Townesend's death in England of pneumonia, closing another chapter of her life. Stephen probably gave up the stage as early as the beginning of their marriage, although he retained his membership of the Green Room club. Instead, he had thrown himself into writing, drawing upon his medical and antivivisection experiences to write the articles "Katherine O'Neill," "A Leaf from a Hospital Daybook," "Peep-Show Vivisection," and in 1912, the novel *Dr. Tuppy*. He was no recluse, and held membership in the Authors' Club, remained an activist, and was admired by those who shared his beliefs. When in London he stayed at his Inner Temple rooms, but also lived in Colney Heath, Saint Albans, where he spent his final days at his home, Coursers. Rising from what proved to be his deathbed in Colney Heath in 1914 to berate a group of foxhunters who had chased that unfortunate animal onto the property, he probably exacerbated an already serious illness. He died soon after, and his old friend Owen Lankester signed his death certificate.[18]

His relatives knew that he was a proud man and mistakenly believed for years after his death that he had always refused to accept Frances's money.[19] This may have been only one of the misunderstandings about this complicated man, and his last novel, *Dr. Tuppy*, published in London by Hodder and Stoughton in 1912, offers some possible insights into his life. Charles Tuppy, a medical resident in London, is a misfit. Short and near-sighted, he is gullible, naïve, and the perfect butt for the jokes and pranks of his colleagues at the hospital. He is the son of an opinionated and rude clergyman in Covent Garden, who forced Tuppy into the medical profession when he

would have preferred music. A friend comments, "Of course he never should
have gone in for Medicine. He's not fitted for it mentally or physically. He's
a born Musician and wanted to take up the Piano professionally, but Canon
Tuppy wouldn't hear of it."[20]

Charles Tuppy is adopted as a boy by a compassionate elderly aunt who
wished to save him from his father's moods but who is fanatically devoted
to the antivivisection cause. They share a house with four dogs, all rescued
from the same Home for Lost Dogs in Battersea as was the "thoroughbred
mongrel"; indeed, that Skye terrier, now elderly and renamed, appears in the
book. Tuppy agrees with the cause's tenets but wonders if he is not being
hypocritical by opposing animal torture yet eating meat. Stephen himself in
his later years altered his position on vivisection. While still opposing it, he
nevertheless wrote to the *Times* in 1907 that "in view of the evidence tendered
before the present Royal Commission I now admit (in contradiction to the
opinion expressed [in 'Peep-Show Vivisection']) that, during the final period
of the narcosis, morphia may be regarded as equivalent to a true anaesthetic
if given in a lethal dose."[21]

The novel revolves around the cruel tricks the other young doctors play
on Tuppy, and his romance with a young nurse named Bella Jessop. All comes
right in the end, and the wise aunt arranges that the young couple build
and manage a convalescent home for children on five hundred acres in the
countryside. When a stuffy clergyman offers his services as chaplain, Tuppy
for once stands up for himself. "Our patients," he informs him, "will be the
children of the slums, and whether their parents are Christians, Jews, Turks,
Infidels or heretics they will be equally welcome." The inscription on the
wall over the mantelpiece reads,

> There is is so much bad in the best of us,
> And so much good in the worst of us,
> That it ill behoves any of us
> To find fault with the rest of us.[22]

Several years after Stephen's death, Frances wrote to Rosamond about
that time she had spent with Stephen in a way that showed how she had
dehumanized her second husband: "You [Rosamond] belong to the strange
days at lovely and beloved Maytham, which would have been so perfect but
for one incomprehensible, weirdly evil thing. I never could understand it—
no one understood it—it did not understand itself. Poor thing—poor thing,
it was only made. It could not have been that bad. Do you know, I do not
believe people are ever really *bad*. I believe they are mad! some strange thing

has gone crudely wrong with their brain cells. I wonder what brought that thing suddenly back to me? I never think of it. Poor thing—poor thing! God pity and help it, wherever it is!"[23] The war that would cut down a generation of young European men, signalled by that fatal shot in Sarajevo, was only three months away. By the end of the year, Vivian would marry and the world would be plunged into horror. Even sooner than that, Frances would be plunged into her own battle, less bloody but on her home field, when her family would be dragged into a public and nasty lawsuit that would last exactly as long as the Great War.

In Plandome during her absence, all had seemed to be tranquil. Edith didn't "see how it would be possible for a mother to have more devotion shown her."[24] She spent Christmas Eve and morning with Archie, Annie, and their son Francis, who wanted his granny with him. The rest of the day she spent with Ernest and Abby and baby Kenneth, whom she similarly adored. She wondered what Frances's plans were, for her sister now spoke of returning home for a quick visit and taking Edith with her to Bermuda for the remainder of the winter. Frances's lengthy descriptions of the winter wardrobe she had had made in Austria certainly suggested otherwise, so Edith put off looking for tenants for Plandome. Vivian, however, took up an offer to rent his Plandome house for two years and moved into a Manhattan apartment. Still, with a room in Archie's house, Edith felt secure and comfortable enough.

The first hints that things were not going to plan had surfaced late in 1913, when Edith wrote to tell Frances that Annie had said unspeakable things to her, felt that she was underfoot and interfering, and made it clear that the arrangement was not working and she wanted Edith out of the house. Gentle Edith was stunned and wrote to Frances in Munich, who felt it as "an indescribable shock." She cautioned Edith to make sure of the source of the information, saying that they had both admired Annie's "spirit & sense of justice & honor." However, she completely believed Edith and even felt that she'd had a premonition that something was wrong. "Do you know what I believe?" she asked. "I believe Frank came & told me that you were unhappy. You see there was no reason that I should have felt it myself— I was sure I had left everything so safe for you & that you would really have all you liked best—a darling room of your own in a darling house with the children who delighted in you & whom you had such fun with—And suddenly one day something said to me 'She is not happy—She feels lonely— She misses Frank & you too much. That place is not the place for her in the least.'" She made it clear that it was for Edith's sake that Frances supported that house, using money she would have preferred for herself and Vivian. She assured Edith that together they could turn their backs on this difficulty, "blot it out," and face the new year of 1914.[25] Edith moved back into Plandome and hoped for her sister's return, keeping up with other members of the family by passing on the travel letters, and buying copies of *T. Tembarom* for their sister Edwina and brother Herbert for Christmas.

Edith had not, however, made it up or mistaken Annie's message. Archie confessed it all and said that it made him ill. Edith thought "it all seems the most dishonorable thing I ever heard of for Annie was first so nice to me as could be to my face, while she was saying all kinds of things behind my back."[26] Among those things, she claimed that Frances hadn't taken Edith with her to Europe because she was tired of her and wanted to get away from her. Ernest and Abby tried to make up for it by stopping by to see her every evening, and a miserable Archie was caught between his mother and his wife. Edith finally escaped to Bermuda for the winter, taking with her their friends the Morans, who paid rent for their portion of Clifton Heights, even though the servants had been given the season off and they all had to take their meals elsewhere. Edith was happier there, but she fell ill in the aftermath of the betrayal.

The story would have ended there except for one thing: Frances, a tiger where her family was concerned, later wrote to Annie's sister and pulled no punches.

You and your family have known me intimately for nearly forty years. That has given you time enough to be quite sure as to whether I am a liar, a slanderer, an ill-bred meddler with other people's business, a hysteromaniac, or a woman given to evil tempers. You might call in your family and will reflect for ten minutes before you decide. . . .

That there may be no mistake sentimentally regarding their marriage[,] it may be as well for us all to remember that she was a woman of 35 [when they married in 1906] and had known poverty all her life. Archie is not an ardent person. It was Annie herself who told us—quite archly—that when Archie told her he could not marry her because he could not support any woman, she courageously replied: "You are afraid. I am not." . . .

When Archie, in common with thousands of other decent men, lost his work we saw that a task lay before us. Don't make the blunder to say we took it up for Archie. We were obliged to do so because of Annie. Archie, had he been unmarried, could have stayed at my house and have been cheered and encouraged until his luck turned.[27]

She went on to point out that had she not intervened, the couple would have starved. When Annie later suffered a haemorrhage, a doctor refused to go and see her until Frances guaranteed to pay his bill; he ordered her into a sanatorium, which Frances again paid for. "My servants, my belongings, my limousine, were placed at Annie's disposal," she wrote. "If a German soldier, fresh from Belgian atrocities, were bleeding to death in anguish at my door I suppose I should go and help him." Even though she made it clear that although neither she nor Edith had been pleased about the "unalluring" marriage, they decided to live and let live. If they had not stood by the couple, "they would have taken the bread line—if either of them had been ill an ambulance would have taken them to some city hospital. The rest of us would have gone on undisturbed in an unquarrelsome way, caring for and interested in each other. No talking, no vilifying of each other to the servants and wash-women. You see what a mistake it was not to have taken the stand that when Annie married Archie she did not marry his family." Frances pointed out that Archie pulled his weight, scrubbing floors and washing the dishes even while he searched for work. She made her point clear at the end of the letter: "I am sorry to be obliged to terminate our acquaintance. I will ask you not to reply. Several copies of this letter will be made. I decline to discuss the situation, but if any one is really concerned they can read your letter and mine."

Annie interpreted the letter to say that she was "a liar, a slanderer, an ill-bred meddler, given to attacks of hysteria, without self-control or good breeding; a shrew and brawler of doubtful character and antecedents; quarrelsome, unmaidenly and designing, ungrateful, and subject to brain storms." Edith, safely out of the fray in Bermuda, wrote to Frances to express her over-whelmed gratitude: "Thank you a thousand times for Annie's letter & your loyalty to me. There never was such a sister before."[28] Frances was just glad that Edith had been protected, and worried about Edith's health, recommending that she visit an osteopath. Clearly Edith's well-being was the reason Frances returned home sooner than planned, in May 1914, even before all this blew up and although her intention was to return to Europe after a summer in Bermuda. "Oh darling girl. I do hope you will get well. Now that Annie has failed me I feel as if I must never let you out of my sight again," she told Edith. "I would never have left you if I had dreamed of such a possibility."[29] They may have thought a crisis had been averted and that life would return to normal. It did not. In February 1916, long after Frances's letter was written, Annie, still furious about it, sued Frances for libel, asking for damages of $50,000.

For the time being, however, life settled into normality. Frances and Edith went to Bermuda for six or seven weeks in May, where she began work on her new book, *The Lost Prince*, and were met at the dock in New York by a joyous Vivian who announced that he'd at last found "the one." She was Constance Buel, the twenty-one-year-old daughter of Clarence Clough Buel, assistant editor of the *Century*. She shared all Vivian's joys: music, sailing, domesticity, and children. They planned a simple November wedding in the Buels' Manhattan apartment. Frances was, of course, thrilled, and wrote to Kitty and Gigi that "she is a *pet*—and a little duck and a little dear, and Vivian is the most fortunate and the most radiantly happy boy on this earth."[30] She was happy not only for Vivian but also for herself in that she claimed his marriage would give her more emotional freedom; perhaps she could stop worrying about his low spirits and exhaustion. "When my Only Child is a married person I shall feel that I can wander with a wholly free conscience because I shall not feel like a Deserting Pelican who ought to be at home pecking strips out of herself to feed her young," she wrote to her new friend Elizabeth Jordan. "My young will be happily pecking strips out of his own chest—the darling thing!"[31] She had, of course, wandered for years—and Vivian was now thirty-eight years old.

Her professional life was looking up as well, for the film contracts were coming to fruition. On 22 June 1914, the British film version of *Little Lord Fauntleroy*—the Mary Pickford Hollywood version would come later—made its New York screen debut at the Lyric Theater. In true Frances fashion, she made a "fairy story" of it, taking the hundred seats the producer had offered her for the first performance, a benefit for the Newsboys' Fund, and instead of distributing them among her friends made a children's party of it. With Frances as hostess, the dozens of boys arrived half an hour before the curtain went up and waited in great excitement. Although she had been told that there would be a few "novelties" in the production, neither she nor the children were quite prepared for the fact that the director decided to kill off each of the heirs to Dorincourt, one at a time, in florid details of hunting accidents and delirium tremens. By the third miserable death, one of Frances's small guests cried out, "I don't like this play! If I knew this play was going to be this kind of play I wouldn't have come to this play. I want to go home." With that he bolted up the aisle in tears, and most of the other children followed suit. Frances could only herd the wailing children out of the theatre in dismay.[32]

Up until now, Plandome had been planned as more of a pied-à-terre than a permanent home for her—she freely admitted having "gypsy and vagabond tendencies" and had hoped to return to her European travels.[33] The coming of the war in August 1914 changed everything. "Even *I* read the papers yesterday," she confessed to Elizabeth when war was declared. "As a result I have been trying to call you up both at your house & at your office to say that I am sure you ought not to go abroad just as the entire continent of Europe plunges into war! Surely you will not go. . . . An English friend said in a letter I received this morning 'We are very near civil war here.'"[34] Vivian was exhausted by attending to the duties of his job and trying to keep his venture of the *Children's Magazine*, with his mother as the nominal head, afloat, and Frances persuaded him to take a year off to travel after his wedding in November. Europe was naturally out of the question, so she financed a honeymoon tour to Asia. He had inherited his father's love of Asian art and culture, and the year was to be a Grand Tour, taking the newlyweds to Panama, California, Hawaii, Australia, Japan, Korea, and China. It was the trip of a lifetime, taken on a variety of vessels, some less seaworthy than others. In many of the places, introductions to resident Westerners had been arranged, and Vivian found that even so far from home his mother's reputation preceded him. More than once people had the impression that it was the famous author and not her son who would appear, and the truth disappointed entire classrooms of children who had prepared essays on *Little Lord Fauntleroy*.

In California he made one of the most satisfying visits when he and Constance went to Sunnyvale, in Santa Clara County, to visit his widowed Aunt Edwina, who had been ill. Frances had sent her money to do up her house, ordering her to indulge in new wallpapers and to knock down a wall to give her living room more space. On a beautiful warm Sunday, with the air filled with the scent of almond trees, her son Herbert and daughter Bertha—both of them named for her oldest brother—met Vivian and Constance in town in a six-cylinder car and drove them out to the ranch. Vivian "found Aunt Edwina in her comfortable chair, in the cosy front room, warming her toes at the wood fire. She looked wonderfully red cheeked, bright eyed and cheerful. Except for her stiff hands she bore not a trace of her illness—and it was hard to believe she had been through so much. She seems to have lost none of her capacity for joking and laughter—and she talked a blue streak all the time."[35] She longed to have her sisters visit; she hadn't seen Frances since their Knoxville days, even though they corresponded, and Edith had never gone back after her return East. Although somewhat crippled, Teddy took the young couple all over the farm, telling of her plans for its improvements and showing off newly planted trees. They sat down to eat with ten at the table and "made merry in fine style."[36]

Vivian may have been away from the war for a year as he travelled, but the next four years filled his mother with what Vivian called a "suspense and anguish that stirred her to the very depths."[37] She feared for her English

friends as well as for the world in general, for "nothing can undo the tragedy," as she wrote to Josephine. "The world will have to begin again."[38] An
actor friend wrote to her of his experiences in a London zeppelin raid and
"brought home the horror to me as it had never been brought home before."[39]
She finished *The Lost Prince* during the early months of the war, and it began
its serial run followed by a book edition in 1915. Although taking place primarily in pre-war London, the rather military story of how the descendants
of the lost prince of Samavia were reinstated on the throne after a bloody
civil war was no doubt influenced by what she heard of anarchy in Eastern
Europe. She also drew on what she'd heard of Eleanor Calhoun's new life
as the Princess Lazarovich-Hrebelianovich and the dedication to the Serbian
cause that she shared with her husband, the prince of Serbia. The ending of
the book is predictable, but critics found that the enjoyment of the story's
unravelling more than made up for that, "for the fascination of the story lies
in the exquisite style, and the romantic, idealistic spirit with which it is instinct. It is said that certain aspects of the ancient history of dauntless little
Serbia gave the author her first idea for this romance. . . . this book should
provide a welcome opportunity of escaping for a time from the problems
and difficulties, the bloodshed and horror, of the actual world about us."[40]

Unable to travel, and in need of distraction, she spent time dramatizing
T. Tembarom. She claimed that "there are several managers who want it, but
so far I have not seen the man who is T.T. I have been to several theatres to
see actors thought possible, but to me they were not probable."[41] The play
was never produced, but one advantage to not being able to go abroad was
that she was able to spend more time with her sister and brother. Herbert, "a
nice, adorably amiable, more than middle-aged Englishman [who] believed
himself to be entirely Americanized, but . . . reminded one of an English
schoolboy of mid-Victorian type," joined them in Plandome for an extended
visit.[42] He had no head for business but could play most musical instruments, compose music, write, and paint. He made his living in Virginia as
an organ builder, and his large family adored him, his children speaking of
him "as if he had wings."[43] The minute he got to Long Island he began pulling things apart and putting them back together as if new, in a "passion for
creation . . . that expresses itself in making things come alive again & in con-
quering difficulties. He is tremendously clever & so lovable & sweet."[44] When
her piano was out of tune, he completely dismantled and repaired it. He
shopped with her for a new cabinet to house her "Enchanted Coach," Louis
XIV glass, and old silver, and entertained her guests at dinner with his tale
of a visit to a strange house in the Dismal Swamp of North Carolina, a story
Frances later used as the basis for one of her "Romantick Lady" articles in

Good Housekeeping. She planned a trip to Norfolk, Virginia, to stay with his family ("Herbert's four sons have sworn that I must come and play with them"), and indeed visited more than once.[45] Herbert later gently reminded her of her promise to invite Medora and Frances to stay with her at Plandome.[46] He returned with them for a long visit in November.

It was the demands of her family in Virginia, New York, California, and Manchester that made her unable to contribute as much to the war effort as she wished. As a famous person of presumed wealth, all sorts of groups appealed to her for funds. She gave money in smaller amounts to nearly all legitimate causes but found she had to explain what might seem like parsimony. In October 1915, she begged an acquaintance to

> please *do* understand that I do not carry mere single persons I carry whole families and they are on both sides of the Atlantic. I have been a fortunate woman but I am far from a rich one absolutely because I have *always* done this thing & also because there seems to be no charity or kindly plan of help on earth which does not—as it sometimes seems— appeal to me. . . .
>
> During this last year I am sure you know the *unendingness* & dire necessitousness of the claims one has been forced by ones very soul to try to meet. When the whole world lies shattered & bleeding & homeless & starving what can one do but ones very utmost. I have done that God knows. And apart from the outside needs I have had special serious duties which must be attended to. I have relatives in England who would *starve* if I did not care for them. And just now one shudders to think of the condition a score of ones nearest friends may be in before long. And then one must make another effort. I am feeling the terror of things especially this morning as I have just received a letter from a friend in London who depicts the horror of the last Zeppelin raid & the devastation it wrought. It brings the ghastliness to ones very door. If these raids cannot be put an end to—and how *can* they?—the most wonderful ancient city in the world will be in ruins & ones friends will be homeless if they are not murdered. I am heart wrung. God help us all.[47]

She involved herself in the war effort, sending "books and sentiments and autographs to California for a sale for the Belgians. There is but one thought in all the world—indeed there is room left for no other. How can one say, 'I wish you a Merry Christmas'?—one must say, 'Peace, peace upon earth, and good will to men.'"[48] She befriended a variety of soldiers, meeting with them when she could and writing to them regularly. Her letters to the friends she'd left behind in England are painful reading, for while she sat safely in Plandome, she knew that "there must be many a darkened home in little Tavistock and in big, silent Dartmoor," as she told Josephine.[49] And to Ella she wrote that "surely, England is a different world now—a different soul—a soul seeing into deep places."[50] A sign of her increasing involvement with political issues was her agreement to participate in New York's suffrage parade on 23 October 1915, an event that attracted between 33,000 and 40,000 marchers. Frances was among those who were in cars at the rear of the marchers. "I dont believe that my presence would either be observed or missed," she told a friend, "but as I never do anything but sign papers & subscribe what trifling sums I can afford I feel that I ought to do this."[51]

The sinking of the *Lusitania* brought the war closer to home, and she decided to give up trips to Bermuda as well as voyages to Europe. She accompanied Herbert to Virginia when he returned home and had "a delightful time." Of his nine children, four sons and two daughters were still in the Norfolk area, and she found the boys "such good fun and we simply *larked* together." She also wanted to do something special for his wife, Medora, and "did several Magics while I was there. The chief one was transforming Dora's little beaten down back yard into a formal garden full to bursting with flowers. I made it a formal garden because the family wash has to be hung out weekly & paths were required. It was landscape gardening with a view to laundry. It was *such* a success."[52] Either during this visit or a later one they made another excursion to the Dismal Swamp just for her.

In August she and Edith visited friends at New Windsor-on-Hudson, near Newburgh, New York, about an hour and a half away from Manhattan, and they took a three-week motoring trip through the Berkshire Mountains of Massachusetts. Well travelled though she was, the Berkshires were a revelation to her. She had had no notion of their lush beauty, so accessible by car from New York. Her trip gave her "a new America which is at once beautiful & astonishing."[53]

It was well that she felt rested and surrounded by friends, for the next two years were to bring upsets and sorrows. In February 1916, the dreaded lawsuit actually became reality. Frances's attorneys were served with a summons, and the letter she wrote to Annie's sister, as a document in the case, became public and was printed in all the New York papers. Saying that Annie was "flayed in the best of English," they analysed Frances's words and intentions. Frances moved into the Devon Hotel in midtown Manhattan for her depositions and cross-examination, and on the witness stand she explained her motives for writing the letter. It was Emma Knorr, Annie's sister, who was the source of information on the initial attack on Edith; it was her letter that

Frances had cautioned Edith from accepting as fact without proof. Frances testified that when she realized how miserable Edith had become over the affair and that she was unable to defend herself, she decided, "Now I will come in. I shall end this matter. And so the letter was sent."[54]

Almost inevitably the tension of the situation caused tension between the two sisters. Edith quietly testified in court, in a response to a question by the prosecution, that "Fluffy always says I write so badly," and Frances was stunned by "a sense of utter helplessness" at the fact that a single chance remark could be construed into a consistent character flaw. Already crushed by the public nature of the case, she now felt that those closest to her were turning the tables against her with hearsay. Fayal Clarke of the *Century* apparently "thought" he had said something; another "believed" those might have been his words; in the testimony "I realized that if not only an enemy accused me of saying things I have never uttered but any nearest & dearest insisted that I had said something I was sure I had not . . . what defense had I or what hope had anybody? What *could* one do to protect oneself?" She wrote to Edith from her hotel room to beg her pardon for anything she might have said in anger after Edith's remark and to ask that their love for each other keep them united.[55]

Things quietened down for several months and Frances took up a new book, *The White People*, a ghost story that haunted her just as much as it did the child in the story. She dedicated the book to Lionel and made the connection clear through a portrait of a grown man who knows he is going to die soon, calls his mother "Dearest," and tries to convince her that death is a passage to a lovely place but not an end. In it she used the verse from Isaiah that she had wanted to have printed on the programme to *Dawn of a Tomorrow*: "Behold the former things are come to pass and new things do I declare; before they spring forth I tell you of them."[56] The book's message was that death took one to a beautiful place that one need not fear, another take on the "Fair, Far Country." She carried her work with her in the spring of 1916 when she and Edith returned to Bermuda, which now seemed safe to voyage to. Even there they were affected by the war, and her letters passed through the censors' hands. She was saddened by the news of Sir Ronald Gower's death, who had been shocked and broken by the loss of all his money as a result of the actions of a friend, and by the death of her old Washington friend Charlie Rice.

As if to make up for all these exits from life, Frances became a grandmother in mid-August when Constance gave birth to Verity, a baby who seemed "to have been born by Magic so quietly & beautifully it appeared & so wonderfully well & radiant is its lovely little mother. I have now invented the relationship of Fairy Grandmother. The Fairy Godmother will pale by comparison."[57] She had indeed been formed for grandmotherhood even more than for motherhood. This was the fairy story she had wished for Vivian, and she threw herself into the new role with joy.

Perhaps this newness inspired her in another way, for once again, while visiting her friends the Royces at New-Windsor-on-Hudson, she heard of a nearby farm for sale—and bought it, all 219 acres with a thirteen-room farmhouse. The farm was a much bigger venture than any garden she had ever created. She had it sown with rye to preserve the soil and made plans, one of which was to use it to house visiting writers, but in fact it was more often occupied by house-sitters or those who paid nominal rent. She counted on a promised road to be built around Storm King Mountain to make the place easily accessible by car from Manhattan, where, on another sudden whim, she took an apartment. Now, in her sixty-seventh year, she had five homes: Plandome, Bermuda, New Windsor, Manhattan, and 1770 Massachusetts Avenue in Washington, as well as some investment properties in that city. There seemed something unquenchable about her house-making desires. In April 1918, however, she finally broke the last link with her Washington past by selling her house there. (Unoccupied for years, it was large enough for the new owner to remodel it, as an investment, into a house with seventeen rooms and seven bathrooms.)

Such extravagance was sharply curtailed at the beginning of 1917, when Herbert died on 8 January. All of Norfolk mourned the passing of "one of the finest minds in this community . . . a man of gracious presence and strong personality."[58] Medora adopted a deep, black mourning that reminded her grandchildren—especially those who had never known their grandfather—of Queen Victoria. It was the first sorrowful event in a dreadful year, both personally and in terms of world events. Barely recovered from her brother's death, Frances found herself once again on the witness stand in March, where she amused the press when she insisted that there had been no discussion of the infamous letter at home because "we never discuss painful things. That is our religion, our philosophy."[59] Then, in the spring, she received a card from Teddy's son Herbert informing her of his sister Bertha's sudden death; Teddy was too devastated to write at all. Frances was puzzled by the unexpectedness of this—Bertha had been healthy, and no cause of death was mentioned—and she was "full of anguish for poor Edwina."[60] Only months later she was stunned by even sadder news when they received word that Teddy herself had died. She struggled to write to Teddy's son Herbert, whom she didn't really know, when she had a vision of Teddy awakening on a hillside, embraced by those who had gone before her: her husband

Frank Bridges, Edith's Frank and their little girl Edith, their mother Eliza, Herbert, and Lionel. "Think what it would be," she encouraged Edith.

> Think how they would all love her & laugh for very joy. Oh! what a gladness! Oh what a gladness—after all her sorrow & pain. I feel as if I could see all their faces—their real—real faces—and Edwina not able to believe that such rapturous joy could be. You must think about that all the time. I have thought of nothing else since it came to me [and] I found myself saying in a sort of weird bewildered way "What *are* we staying here for when there is that waiting for us? What are we staying for?" But we stay because there is something for us to do. You have to take care of Ernest and I have to write things that are told to me. You must not think for one moment of anything sad in connection with darling *happy* Teddy![61]

As with the rest of the world, she seesawed with emotion over the war's developments that year. She sent Ella a copy of the *New York Herald* containing President Roosevelt's speech about joining the war and describing "the wild scene at the Metropolitan Opera House when the news arrived. I so loved the man in the gallery who had the sense to call out, 'Three cheers for our Allies!' which seems to have thrown the people into a frenzy of feeling." At the same, "I am absolutely shaken to the soul by a realization of what the Russian Revolution means to the whole world. It gives an enormous hint to slave driven Germany, which is only just beginning to suspect how it has been driven and slaughtered to feed the mere vanity of a mad monster." She was relieved that America was finally entering the war, "ready to pour forth her millions and her aid" even though it "held out so long."[62] She couldn't understand why it would take so long to raise an army, but "the Kaiser knows Roosevelt and he is the one man Germany would be afraid of."[63]

She felt strongly that she had little right to complain about the war when the women in England and France had so much greater sorrows to bear, and when there was so much horrific bloodshed on the battlefields of Europe. The war struck home when she realized that her American publisher Frederick Stokes had two sons in the armed forces, and despite America's sudden patriotic fervour—everyone's car or lapel seemed to sport a flag—her heart was broken, and it seemed "as if this foul, black cloud of War had rolled over the sweet thing of the past and almost blotted them out and made them far off dreams."[64] She continued to help her adopted soldiers and their wives, continuing through the year with gritted teeth as everything seemed to fall apart around her. Vivian, past the age of conscription, collected records to send to soldiers so that they might have music, and Frances sent off letter after letter to English friends.

Through all these sorrows, the machinery of the court case lumbered on. Frances's lawyers appealed to prevent further disclosures in a "bill of particulars," but their request was denied in June. In October 1917, after Annie spent a day on the witness stand, an exasperated state supreme court judge threw out the case, dismissing the action on the grounds that nothing in Frances's letter constituted libel. Annie immediately appealed, and the following May 1918, as the war was winding to its end, the appellate division of the supreme court decided that Frances must stand trial a second time, with the new judge, Justice Dowling, asserting that Frances had "voluntarily interjected herself into a correspondence with which she had no concern, for the purpose of gratifying her malice." He called the letter "virulent in character," blasting her in his decision.[65] It seems laughable now that a private letter, written to a relation by marriage, can constitute grounds for libel action, especially when the contents were divulged to the public not by the so-called slanderer but by the offended person, and Frances's lawyers, the firm of White and Case, were mystified by this turn of events. The case geared up once more, with her attorney, Max D. Steuer, who had won the first round, taking over again when it returned to the trial court on 24 June, "but the black fiendishness of the whole thing is beyond words or endurance."[66] As always, the war put it into perspective, as she well knew. "What is it to the agony of sitting in your sunny, Kentish gardens, and hearing that low, pulsing of the air of which you speak, and which means the far off roaring of the guns of death!" she wrote to Rosamond.[67]

The actual horrors occurring in the wider world and the sorrows surrounding her in her immediate family made the matter shrink to its proper proportions. She went off to the countryside of Quebec with friends that summer, writing little notes to her granddaughter Verity and trying to unwind. She took with her Julia, her African American maid, and found that the "lovely informal & cosy life" agreed with her. "I sleep like a babe until Julia brings me my breakfast. After cigarettes I get up & dress & we have so far gone out to walk each morning & in the afternoon to drive. Today is Sunday & we walked to church & back—as it is proper to go."[68] They had tea with neighbours, and she settled down to work on her new novel, *The Head of the House of Coombe*, by far her longest book, so long in fact that it would have to be broken into two books after its serial publication. Into it she began to pour out her feelings about the war, about the now-lost England she had known and the new Europe that must rise from its ashes. It would take nearly four years to complete this, her last book, and the way it broke into two for publication said it all: *The Head of the House of Coombe*, published in February 1922, tells of an innocent girl named Robin, raised by a flighty mother who ignores her and is mistakenly viewed by the world as the kept lover of an aristocrat. *Coombe* culminates with Robin's first party, when the news arrives of the assassinations at Sarajevo. *Robin*, the second volume, begins during the war itself, when the young men at the party are sent to their doom.

Frances came back from Canada rested, ready even to face further testimony in October, and by the end of the year she was certain all would be well. The case was finally about to be decided in her favour. Then in November she wrote to Rosamond to describe an eventful day, after her return from Canada, when she sat with no one around "but for one elderly colored maid."

It was a morning of heavenly gold and peace and I was writing in my den with the windows open—when suddenly I heard far off steam whistles begin to blow. As we are on the Sound we often hear steamers answering each other on the water, but this was not the signalling of two or even three or four, and it went on and on and increased in wild shrillness, and others joined it and others and others, and then bellowing factory whistles and horns, and more and more—on every side—from every point the shrieking, rioting, frenzied uproar was swelling and spreading. I threw down my pen and stood gasping and staring into the gold leaves. It was so mad it seemed as if it must mean the one—one gorgeous God-blessed thing on earth that would be too *good* to be true. In two seconds I ran to the end of the corridor and called Edith, who was shut up with trunks she was emptying in the attic. I don't know what my voice was like.

"Come and listen," I panted out in a sort of shriek. "Come and listen to the *whistles*! Something—has happened."

Edith flew down the attic stairs—she heard the tumult as she came and it was louder and louder and she dashed to the telephone.

"Central, Central," she shouted. "What are the whistles blowing for? Tell us."

"The war is over! The war is over! Don't ask me another thing," Central shrieked and rang off.

I couldn't possibly remember the things that we did and said—except one. The uproar grew louder and louder—it swelled and shrieked and trumpeted and boomed until every whistle and fog horn and gun on earth seemed to be bursting the heavens. We caught each other in arms. We couldn't hear each other speak; the chauffeur and the cook and the gardener were running up and down. Edith and I clung to each other. "The war's over! The war's over!" we kept sobbing, because there was nothing else immense and wonderful enough to say—but just "The war's over! The war's over!"[69]

At last everything seemed right again with the world. Ernest had a touch of influenza in that year's infamous epidemic, but he seemed to be on the mend even though Edith was running herself ragged with anxiety while nursing him. Frances put her sister firmly to bed, arising herself each morning at 6.30 to prepare Archie's breakfast—not surprisingly, his marriage hadn't weathered the storm—and send him off to work. "The war is over," she wrote to her friend Elizabeth Jordan, "God be thanked."[70]

There was one more battle to be faced, however. Ernest took a turn for the worse and, instead of recovering, died on 31 December 1918.

CHAPTER 21

~

ELIZABETH

1919–1924

B Y THE TIME ERNEST FIRST became ill at the end of 1918, Frances had become completely confident in the belief system she'd so carefully worked out over the years. This belief system—part New Thought, part Christian Science, part positive thinking, and part fairy story—she expressed succinctly in her 1909 children's book *The Land of the Blue Flower*: "The first law of the earth's magic is this one. If you fill your mind with a beautiful thought there will be no room in it for an ugly one."[1] It was this philosophy that amused those who attended her trial and that made even her closest friends sometimes see her as a childlike woman who could not bear ugliness of any kind. When Kitty took her for her first visit to Weber and Field's Musical Hall in New York, Frances felt terribly for the comedian with an enormous hairy mole; it wasn't until the audience laughed that she asked in astonishment, "Is it possible that that horror has been stuck on as being *funny*?"[2] Her aversion to ugliness and misery sometimes made her shrink from them, and one of the first things Kitty had learned about her was that when she saw or heard of something painful during the day, "she must say at once and firmly, 'I will not dream of it!' or else be tormented by it in her sleep."[3] Nevertheless, when Ernest fell ill and seemed to make no recovery, she strode into his bedroom absolutely convinced that she and her beliefs would save him. She sat next to him throughout his final day, willing her soul into him, while "death and Ernest Fahnestock waged a mighty battle" that her nephew lost.[4]

The deepest misery was of course Edith's; she had now lost two husbands, a daughter, and a son and was inconsolable. Frances, believing she had let Edith down, was completely shattered in both her health and her faith, just as she had been after Lionel's death. For the second time since Frank's horrific death in 1911, Plandome was plunged into a stunned mourning, and Frances took Edith to live with her in Manhattan for the winter.

Frances was never quite the same again in spirit or body after this loss, but relief for Edith came from an unexpected source. Archie, who had no particular interest in machinery or inventions, took over Ernest's Fahnestock Electric Company in Long Island City in Queens and drew his mother's interest into making Ernest's business thrive, rescuing her from "the helpless, hopeless depths of despair."[5] Ernest had been just on the verge of success, as he had been so many times, but now it was Archie, the initially rough-edged young man raised in Tennessee and California who had survived a difficult marriage and came down on the side of his mother and aunt, who pulled off the miracle. Throwing himself completely into the business, he turned it around in less than two years, paying his aunt a dividend on her investment in the firm by 1922. Frances was full of admiration, "for the weight fell on your shoulders with a crash, without a moment's warning, it was a thing you knew nothing about; it flung you into work you didn't like, and never had done, and were made as responsible for as if you had been building it up all your life," she told him. "That was a thumping big order, my dear, and if you ever imagined that your little Aunt did not look on, gasping, and pray hard while she watched, you are a misled youth." It was through Archie that Edith decided to live, and Frances recognized that "you have kept Ernest alive for her—you have carried on his work and you have realized a dream he was almost afraid to believe he could realize himself. I am perfectly certain he walks about that factory by your side."[6] She saw in him the spirit of their reputed ancestor, "Cadrad Haard, a Chieftain who sat in the Isle of Anglesea in the 10th Century," whose name they jokingly evoked over the years whenever an obstacle needed to be bravely confronted.

She made a grand effort but something vital had gone out of her after these difficult years. Her health problems increased, whether she was at Plandome or in balmier Bermuda, and now it was Vivian who was always there to help her. If Edith found her support in her only remaining son, so did Frances. He and Constance, along with Edith, were her rock, and their little daughters, Verity and Dorinda, her joys. Verity was everything an older sister could be—helpful, somewhat serious, but elfin and imaginative—and Dorin loved to sing. They both adored their "Nanda," who always sent them special letters from Bermuda and romped with them when she was home. A friend described Frances's bed as "a Matterhorn they climbed every morning, rolling over and around her like ecstatic puppies and taking very small and supposedly prohibited bites of her toast and bacon."[7] Frances spent happy hours making doll's clothes with them, having tea parties, and pretending to be other people, to the girls' delight.

She also doted on their mother, inviting her down to Bermuda when she became stressed and strained; Constance had a tendency to become worn out and depressed, and Vivian, who worked hard himself, worried about her. He worried too about his mother's health, and when he took over much of her business matters in the 1920s, he did so at her request so that she could enjoy her months in Bermuda without worrying about book contracts, taxes, real estate, and house repairs. He found himself constantly reassuring her that she had a great deal of money and that she ought to use it on herself, for her own pleasures, and to feel no obligation to provide for him and his family. Grateful for what she gave—filling the coal bin at Christmas, sending him and his wife out to shop for new clothes—he nevertheless urged her to spend his inheritance.

Somehow, almost inexplicably, a new joy was on the horizon. After two failed marriages and so many family losses, Frances met someone whose affection and vivacity matched her own. In what one might call today a romantic friendship, Elizabeth Jordan offered a deeply important intimacy for the last ten years of Frances's life. Although younger than Frances by fifteen years, she was much more her equal than the Hall sisters, who were more like daughters to her. Elizabeth was strong, talented, and independent. She was brought up by wonderfully supportive and loving parents and had attended a convent school in Milwaukee. Everyone expected her to become a nun or a concert pianist, but she wanted to be a writer. Like Frances, she sold her first story as a teenager, and her parents agreed to let her try her journalistic wings in New York, assuming she would fail. She did not.

Fearless and determined, she worked up to eighteen hours a day in newsrooms, under a series of hard-boiled bosses, and was, in succession, assistant Sunday editor of the *New York World*, editor of the magazine *Harper's Bazar*, and editor at the book publisher Harper and Brothers. She wrote short stories that appeared in the magazine and published a total of twenty-eight books, mainly novels and short stories. She was an ardent feminist, ghosting the autobiography of Dr. Anna Howard Shaw, president of the National American Woman Suffrage Association. As a journalist she travelled alone to the dangerous Big Stone Gap in Virginia, chasing a story, and she covered the famous Lizzie Borden trial and was convinced of the accused axe-murderer's innocence. She shared an apartment in Gramercy Park with two other women, and when her beloved father died, they reshuffled and made room for her mother to move in. In the days before passports were necessary to travel between America and Europe, she frequently travelled abroad on nearly a moment's whim.

It was on the ship taking Frances and the Halls to Europe in 1913 that Elizabeth and Frances cemented their friendship, when "Miss Jordan comes to my cabin to smoke cigarettes after dinner."[8] They had met many times before, usually at social functions, the first time at the home of the novelist Kate Douglas Wiggin, the author of *Rebecca of Sunnybrook Farm*, where they talked animatedly in a corner for more than two hours. Elizabeth had read everything Frances had published, "and there was nothing Mrs. Burnett liked better than to talk about her work."[9] She found Frances the second best woman talker she'd ever met (the first was her friend Josephine Daskam Bacon), and they spent a great deal of time together during the crossing; by the time Frances was in Vienna and Salzburg, they were corresponding regularly, and by the time she returned to America in 1914 and found herself stranded there by the war, Elizabeth was a regular weekend visitor at Plandome.

Elizabeth was much in demand for Friday-to-Monday weekends at friends' houses—on one memorable occasion having no fewer than eighteen invitations—but her weekends with Frances and Edith became a special joy. Friday evenings were spent with Frances and any other family members or friends who happened to be there. They all turned in at about midnight. Saturday mornings, however, belonged to Frances, Elizabeth, and literature. They began with breakfast in Frances's bedroom, with Frances in bed and Elizabeth on a chaise, with a big fire if it was winter. Frances smoked cigarettes held in a silver case Elizabeth had given her, lighting them from the matching lighter. After breakfast, "I would settle myself among my cushions with a deep breath of content. Fluffy, as eager as I, would take up her manuscript with a flamboyant gesture and read aloud what she had written of her novel since my last visit a week or a fortnight earlier," Elizabeth recalled. "Sometimes, if she had been industrious, the reading lasted until luncheon." They both felt like happy children, the one in being read to by someone she admired, the other "weaving tales for an engrossed and appreciative playmate."[10] Sometimes the readings picked up again on Saturday night and again on Sunday morning. On another occasion, while travelling, Elizabeth saw Frances talk nearly non-stop for thirty-six hours, first at a party, then afterwards with Elizabeth; when they'd said their goodnights and Elizabeth was drifting off to sleep, Frances wandered back into her room and talked until nearly four in the morning.

Elizabeth was a sounding board, one whose job was to admire but not to criticize. Frances once recounted in amazement the time she'd read a story to a young man who dared to offer criticism, something Elizabeth would never dream of doing. In fact, the only other time someone had dared such a thing, it ended with his losing his job. Apparently Frances sent the manuscript of one of her novels to the publisher at a time when her editor was unfortunately in Europe. His new young assistant wrote out a list of improvements and passed them on to the equally new assistant editor, who made the mistake of sending it to Frances. "The result," Elizabeth wrote, "was an explosion that shook the building which held the magazine and its employees. Mrs. Burnett gave a magnificent illustration of the tempest that can be aroused in gentle souls." She withdrew the manuscript, to the astonishment of the editor who'd known nothing of what happened, and refused all their calls and letters and cables. By the time it was resolved, months later, Frances had their written agreement that they would continue to publish her work without any alterations whatsoever, as they had all along. When Elizabeth later asked why Frances was so averse to criticism when she averred that stories came from outside herself, the answer was that "I am the custodian of a gift. It is for me to protect its dignity from the driveling of imbeciles!"[11]

Elizabeth never felt comfortable with the name Fluffy that everyone close to Frances used for her. They searched for an alternative term of endearment, ending with Elizabeth's suggesting Querida, the Spanish word for "beloved" or "dearest." "Can one sign oneself 'Querida' as I used to sign myself 'Dearest' to my boys?" Frances wondered. "Or would it be more delicate to sign oneself 'Q?'"[12] Querida it was, and from 1915 on, the two of them used this name exclusively in their letters. They adopted the greeting "Three Rousing Cheers!" (Frances's greeting with Vivian was "Good Hunting!" from Rudyard Kipling's *The Jungle Book*.) When separated by Frances's illnesses, or Elizabeth's summers in Florence, Massachusetts, near Northampton, where her roommate Martha Cutler had a house, or when the demands of her job made it impossible to visit Frances in Bermuda, they wrote constantly. "Dearest Elizabeth," Frances wrote to her in the summer of 1919, "I also have a passionate desire to see you. . . . Why cannot the people who need each other live in a little heavenly group of perfect houses in a perfect place—which would be like the fairy story I made for my place at Vails Gate."

I have told you about it, have nt I [*sic*]? Mountains & low hills would enclose us, & gardens & woods & green spaces would surround us—And each pretty house & its garden would hide itself in its very own corner— And the beloved & understanding people would stroll in & out just when they chose & read to each other under trees on lawns & tell stories on broad porches while the mountains & the clouds & the birds & the flowers would look & listen & delight & always understand what everybody meant because they would all *belong.* I love that fairy story more than [any] I have ever made. There are certain people who need certain others very much—& I am one.[13]

Through Elizabeth, Frances finally contracted to write Lionel's novel *The Fair, Far Country* or *His Friend* for Harper's for a $20,000 advance, on the condition that they not bother her in any way about it, or try to push her towards completion. This book was never to be finished quite in the way she originally imagined so many years before, but in a more interesting and dispassionate way as the ghostly novel *The White People*, which gave her message about love, especially a mother's love for her son, transcending death. She also published with them her last children's book, *The Way to the House of Santa Claus*, a non-religious Christmas story whose charm lay in its modern illustrations and insert-a-name technique to make the children it was read to feel it was written especially for them. It was a very different Christmas book than her previous one, *The Little Hunchback Zia*, about a deformed and leprous boy who is cured by the infant Jesus. No matter how she approached them, she rejoiced that books for children had become so much more appealing and numerous than in her own childhood, and that "now nothing is too good for a child—even a baby."[14]

During the war years, in 1917, Frances had begun *The Head of the House of Coombe*, her last—and longest—adult novel, contracted for as a serial for *Good Housekeeping* magazine, and she carried the manuscript with her everywhere. That winter she spent her weekdays in Manhattan at the Park Avenue apartment and her weekends at Plandome, during the trial, and she tried to work on the novel. She took it to Bermuda in the winters of 1919, 1920, and 1921. It was her constant companion, but it only seemed to get longer and not to get finished. As with *The Shuttle* before, it began its serial run before its completion, but this time she wasn't bothered by not knowing when or how it would end. In fact, she took some satisfaction in its ever-expanding size, believing that only through careful dramatic detail would the story make sense.

One of the reasons it took so long to write was that the war had changed the world. Frances wanted to develop carefully its two halves, to show the world as it used to be and the world as it was becoming. Robin, the sheltered only child of a selfish, beautiful mother, could only be believable in the world as it had existed before 1914, and the social mores that led to her loneliness—the way mothers refused to let their children play with her because they thought her mother was the mistress of Lord Coombe—were thrown out of the window during and after the war. This much Frances could write during the war, but the second half of the novel, chronicling the war years, she could not manage while the war was still going on.

The biggest reason she made little progress with book, however, was her health. Riddled with aches and pains ranging from her legs to her back to her digestive system, and even to the need for stronger glasses, she didn't want people to know just how much and how often she suffered. "Beloved One . . . sometime I am going to reveal to you the details of my double life," she wrote to Elizabeth. "My guilty secret is that I am generally having much more of a devil of a time than it would be worth while owning to people & the greater part of me going into keeping a gaily stiff upper lip & pretending that there is really very little the matter with me." Her letters remained full of jokes and cheerful observations to her family, but to Elizabeth she confessed her frustration at being "sick of this thing which seems to be a law made especially for me. Fifty or sixty years ago I should have lived in a Bath chair & have been spoken of as 'a great sufferer'. We dont do it these days. All this to explain that I have spent a good deal of time in bed or *on* the bed & have been deadly tired & have lied valiantly to keep things cheerful."[15] In November 1919 she spent her seventieth birthday in a Manhattan sanatorium, surrounded by friends, grandchildren, flowers, and gifts. Kitty and Gigi flew in at the end of the day, and when Vivian came in after work he was so delighted to see them that he took them to dinner. Sometimes she made shopping excursions in the company of a nurse, but the rest of the time she received her guests—including "Queen Elizabeth"—from her bed, which "seems at present the only place where one ought to live."[16] The rest did her good, and when she returned home in December the doctor ordered her not to fight against her languor but to enjoy the recuperation. Sure enough, she found herself enough improved at the beginning of 1920 to make the overnight steamer trip to Bermuda with Edith.

Bermuda was a wonderful place for convalescents. Constance and Verity spent several weeks with her in the spring, with Constance returning to health while Frances worked on *Coombe* in her garden. While Constance slept, Frances and her granddaughter developed a happy routine that Frances called their "bed time morning séances." Verity appeared in Frances's bedroom every morning by six o'clock "& we then entertain ourselves until the rest of the household comes down for breakfast. First an apple & a banana— or both—then hair brushed & ribbon tied. Then into bed with Nanda & reading or making wonderful crayon drawings which Nanda is amazed to find at this late hour that she has a talent for. The red birds are fed & Daddy is loved with all our hearts."[17] She worked hard at helping Constance to view life less seriously and to see joy where she tended to see duty, for which Vivian, who remained at home with the younger Dorin, was grateful.

Meanwhile, Vivian was kept busy by his job and her business affairs, and in good weather he took out his boat *Delight* for sails on Long Island Sound. Because she needed to sell the Washington plots she had owned for more than thirty years in anticipation of the city's expansion, and her lawyer Will Dennis had died, Vivian travelled down there to try to dispose of them to her benefit. She was frustrated at the profit the developer had made on her house at 1770 Massachusetts Avenue—after renovating the property he sold it for $90,000, making $50,000 for himself—and she wanted at least to recoup what she'd spent on taxes on the land over the years. Vivian managed this for her. Several offers for her work were coming in, and although she now had a literary agent, Julia Tutwiler, she trusted Vivian's judgment. Through the two of them she contracted out the film rights to *That Lass O'Lourie's* (renamed *The Flame of Life* and starring Priscilla Dean, this was the second Universal Studios film of the novel in seven years) and *The Dawn of a To-morrow*, agreed to a New York production of *T. Tembarom* that seems never to have been produced although it reached the final stages, negotiated the payments for *Coombe,* and arranged other matters.

The famous Mary Pickford film of *Little Lord Fauntleroy*, in which the Hollywood star played both Cedric and Dearest, was in the works; when it opened, Frances at first thought she was not up to attending the premiere, to Pickford's great disappointment. Slipping in after all to her reserved box, she heard the Hollywood star express from the stage her sadness that the author was unable to attend, a misunderstanding they later sorted out. Frances turned down requests for her memoirs and an article on the "changes in women & their lives which the last half century has made. One could write a volume about the thing—if one wanted to."[18] Indeed, although she still worried about money occasionally, the fact was that she was now extremely comfortable financially and her worries were physical rather than monetary. By the end of 1920 she had managed to get to Bermuda for the winter but told Elizabeth that "I am not well—I am not—I am not." Three weeks later she confessed to Vivian that "I have been having increasingly wretched times."[19] She could not eat without tremendous pain afterwards and finally became bedridden for several months. She employed two full-time nurses, could write no letters, and no one except Edith realized that she nearly died.

It was a ghastly winter, but there were joys as well. On 19 January 1921, Kitty Hall, still strikingly beautiful at fifty-seven, surprised them all by marrying the widowed author and critic William Crary Brownell. It was a tiny and "austerely simply, but very cosy" wedding at the Church of the Ascension in Manhattan, and Vivian stood in for Frances. "There were just the few life intimates in the big church and a short service. Kitty very radiant in grey. Much kissing—some tears and then a departure," Vivian reported to his mother in Bermuda. "Gigi is to live permanently with them. It is all surprising and delightful."[20] Then, as Frances lay in bed virtually at death's door, ideas for two novels came to her, and she realized that she might recover. She wrote little notes in extremely feeble handwriting and wondered if the novelistic muse had brought her back to life.

One thing that helped her improve came at Vivian's suggestion: a Christian Science healer named Davis began to treat her. Both Vivian and Constance were active members of the faith and wanted her to give it a try since medical science brought her little relief. At first she wasn't sure he was helping her, but she became very fond of him. He bicycled out to Clifton Heights every morning at nine, puzzling her by speaking in an educated accent with, nonetheless, dropped h's, but bringing her peace and calm. By March she was sleeping well and able to sit out in her garden in a steamer chair, giving instructions to Billy, the new gardener. She didn't fully understand how Davis helped her but there was no doubt of her improvement, and she began to regain some of the beliefs that had deserted her when Ernest died. "I believe that he is going to help me to know what I have strived to learn all my life," she told Vivian and Constance. "But I am not to say 'I believe' I must say simply 'I know.'"[21] Two others who joined Frances in her daily life were a woman named Minna Smith, a former Boston journalist who acted as her companion and amanuensis, and "a young girl—pretty gentle & light colored—name Cordelia—whom she is training to be a maid for me."[22] Under their care she slowly revived and hoped to return to Plandome in July.

Still, her health wavered throughout the spring, and giving Vivian power of attorney, she authorized him to negotiate the book publication of *Coombe*, making sure that he made provision for any moving picture versions that might come along later. The novel was so lengthy that *Good Housekeeping* had made drastic cuts in order to fit the sections into the magazine, so it was with pleasure that a representative of Heinemann, her most recent English publisher, came to America hoping to publish the new novel in its entirety. They were "extremely anxious to do everything possible for the book and they are certainly proud to have it on their list and they have big plans for it," Vivian reported.[23] Meeting with Stokes, who would publish it in America, and Pawling of Heinemann, Vivian and Julia Tutwiler managed to arrange a very good deal for the book, getting her a 25 per cent royalty on the English edition, in addition to the $20,000 she'd received for the serial. The only problem was how to resolve the problem of its formidable length. Frances refused to let the book be cut; Stokes refused to let it be published as a two-volume novel, which might impede sales; so it was Pawling who came up with the brilliant solution of actually publishing it as two separate novels, *The Head of the House of Coombe* and its sequel, *Robin*. It was an inspired move, and booksellers who initially baulked at the notion found themselves scurrying to double and triple their original orders when the sequential books proved so successful.

So near to the end of her life, Frances was in as much demand as she had been more than fifty years before, and *Robin* was her most modern novel. Robin was a twentieth-century girl with a Victorian upbringing. Removed from society though she was throughout her childhood, she still knew how to dance the tango, and wore short tweed skirts. Her disreputable mother was nothing short of a flapper, with bright make-up, above-the-knee dresses in loud colours, and a penchant for excitement, who met her end in a particularly gruesome way when she raced to a rooftop for the thrill of watching a zeppelin dropping bombs on London.

Frances's real message in the book was not modernity, however, but the way the world now embraced notions of psychic phenomena. The restrained Lord Coombe was "amazed to discover that for many years profoundly scientific men had been seriously investigating and experimenting with mysteries unexplainable by the accepted laws of material science . . . . They had written books, scattered through the years, on mesmerism, hypnosis, abnormal mental conditions, the powers of suggestion, even unexplored dimensions and in modern days psychotherapeutics."[24] At a time when high modernists were tackling the war in startlingly new ways in works such as *The Waste Land* and *Jacob's Room*, Frances turned to the occult to define the modern sensibility. Robin's husband, whom everyone but her believed was killed at the front, returns to tell her about an American soldier he'd met. "He believed in a lot of things I'd not heard of except as jokes," Donal tells her. "He called them New Thought and Theosophy and Christian Science. He wasn't clever, but he *believed*."[25] Belief and faith, it seemed, were difficult concepts in these disillusioned postwar years, but her audience was a wide and general one. There is no doubt that her kind of book was not in favour with the postwar intelligentsia, who rejected what they saw as the wordy sentimentalism of the Victorians and Edwardians, as evidenced by the great success of Lytton Strachey's biting social commentary in *Eminent Victorians*. This bothered her not at all. If any good had come from the tragedy of the war, it was vindication of her beliefs.

After postponing her trip home many times because of poor health, something that bothered her more for Edith's sake than for her own because Edith wanted a respite with Archie in New York, she finally returned to Plandome in the middle of the summer. She was never to return to Bermuda. September found her back in the Park Avenue sanatorium, not because of a relapse but in the hope that she could regain her lost energy. Elizabeth herself had been extremely ill and was just now on the mend, and Frances wrote to her that "we must tell each other that we *are* surely better than we were—even if it is only an inch or so. On that inch or half inch we must keep our souls fixed. If we *can* get to each other when we are in New York it will be good for us both. There ought to be *two* sofas in my room & I am wondering if there will be space enough."[26]

Elizabeth visited her at the sanatorium on Christmas Eve, shortly after Vivian and his children left. She found Frances "lying on her back, staring moodily at the ceiling. When she turned her head and recognized me she uttered the crow of a happy child and bounced ecstatically up and down in bed, exactly as the child might have done. For the moment she was five years old."[27] Indeed, she retained until the end her "belief that old age was a 'state of mind,' and that people became old because they accepted old age as an inevitability," and remained as keenly interested in her appearance as she had been in her younger years.[28] Everyone who knew her was so familiar with this aspect of her that Kitty was shocked when she overheard a young man refer to Frances as "old." "She was never old, never could have been," Kitty said. "She was Mrs Burnett—to herself and to us ageless."[29]

When she returned to Plandome, rested, she hired a delightfully vivacious English companion named Agatha Tarenton, who "is—if you please—my chauffeur as well as my companion. She was connected with the Flying Corps in England during the war and did the most amazing work—driving cars and lorries and (incidentally) taking care of a houseful of convalescing officers—catering, cooking, housekeeping for them. What wonders women did in those days. She is a tall, slim Diana of a girl and is too delightful dressed in her khaki overalls, cleaning her engine in the garage and lying on her back under the car."[30] She was heartbroken when the capable Agatha was called back to England to nurse her sick mother, the latest of a string of domestic helpers who seemed to stay at Plandome for shorter and shorter periods, leaving her and Edith to "set our own tables & wash our own dishes. I have no maid & am so ill that I ought to have a trained nurse. Edith is spending the day in town searching the agencies—& God have mercy on her soul."[31]

Throughout these times she rarely put down her pen. Not ready to take up a long book like *Coombe* again, she steadily supplied her "Romantick Lady" columns to *Good Housekeeping*, writing about herself in the third person as she described people she had met throughout her travels. One of her previous articles, in 1920, had been on children's books. And, as always, the outdoors beckoned. She wrote to Elizabeth in the spring of 1922 that she had found a wonderful gardener in Samuel Thompson, who shared her passion for flowers, "& of course you know I am flower drunk. I want millions & I want them always—Spring, Summer, Autumn & Winter—particularly Winter. Thompson & the garden have kept me from dying so far. Most of the time I have been ghastly ill but I have stayed out of doors & by creeping, creeping inches I have covered about four yards on the way to getting well. I massage [and] muscle exercise my face & I obstinately pretend that I am sound & in my right mind & look perfectly well. But only a quarter of me is really alive."[32] She found some relief through her osteopath, Cornelia Walker, but settled into a quiet life at Plandome, never fully free of pain or energetic, and remained involved with the world, making trips into Manhattan, supporting causes (she sent $100 to the new Woodrow Wilson Foundation), and even remaining a member of the Pen and Brush, a New York club made up of women artists and writers. The luncheons she had often attended with reluctance in early years now became nearly unbearable because of her tiredness and pain. At one small one at which she was the guest of honour, she sat silent as the conversation swirled around her, worrying her hostess. Halfway through, Frances "reached with a delicate instinctive hand for the reins of conversation, easily grasped and held them to the end, gaining with every moment in animation, becoming again 'like herself.'"[33] Such efforts, however, sent her to bed for days afterwards.

Life was not without its pleasures. With Vivian and his family next door, her garden to tend, and articles to write, there was plenty to interest her. In 1924 Archie married a Plandome neighbour, Cecelia Schotte, whose relatives stayed with Frances and Edith when they came from Washington state for the wedding. She made regular trips into Manhattan, often lunching with Elizabeth, who still spent many weekends at Plandome. The pain and illness never fully dissipated, however, and by the end of the summer of 1924 she found herself almost completely bedridden, unable to attend the opening of the film version of *The Shuttle* but determined to get well. Elizabeth wrote sympathetically from Massachusetts "to my precious Querida" that "this attack will soon pass, as the others have done, and that very soon you will be feeling like yourself again. No one knows better than I do how many different kinds of discomfort one can have from these digestive disturbances and intestinal troubles; and I know, too, how wretchedly ill one can be, how discouraged one can get—and how well and happy one can also be when it is all over. So cheer up, my beloved, and make the brave fight you always do make."[34]

Worried that Frances wasn't getting better, Elizabeth made a special trip to visit her at Plandome, writing when she returned home that "I want you to know that you are in my thoughts every moment, and deep, deep in my heart. And I am sending you all the health and strength that is in me, to help you in the big fight you are making to throw off this pain and weakness and be well again."[35] She wrote to Frances daily to encourage her, but behind the scenes she and Edith were also corresponding, and their letters took a different tone. Edith's letters broke her heart, Elizabeth told her, for "the situation is indeed terrible for our Fluffy, terrible for you, terrible for all of us here day and night, and I am mentally and emotionally on my knees. If ONLY there was something one could do!"[36] What none of them seems to have known at the time was that Frances's long difficulties with her digestion had a real source: she had colon cancer, and there was nothing anyone could do to cure her.

Years before, when Frances had returned to Washington to nurse Vivian during his bout with typhoid, she went up to her den. Taking out her notebook of writings to Lionel, she thought again about his death and imagined her own.

I have been trying to imagine it—I think it will be like this—I shall be so still and the room will be so silent—and they will stand so quiet—watching me—and *waiting*. The *waiting* is so strange! It seems as if all the world must be waiting when one stands like that by a bedside. It made me sorry to think how sad they will all feel—and that perhaps they cannot help feeling a little afraid of me. But I was not afraid of you, my Lovely One. I only stood there, pouring forth all my whole soul and life in love that folded—and held you and implored Nature to be allowed to help you. But I think people are often a little afraid of the one who is dying.

I wonder who "they" would be. If poor, dear and darling Effie is there I know she will suffer so! I wish I might be allowed to help her past her hour first. She is afraid of dying—and I am not. I wish I might be allowed to die very softly, so that nobody who loves me will be hurt by it. I wish I might be able to say to them quite simply, "Don't think I am minding it—I can tell you truly dears—it is nothing. You need never be the least afraid of it."

I was imagining how I should feel. As if I were *stopping*—I think it will be a quiet feeling—as if one were very *still*—as if everything was so still that nothing could ever begin to move again. And gradually all will darken. But when one tries to picture that it is so difficult not to think of one's mind as going on and analyzing one's sensations as they fade. But that will not be.—The thinking will be ceasing, too—one will not be able to say, "What do I feel? What does it mean?" —All will slip away together.[37]

"I wish I could die in such a way as would made the going seem quite simple and gentle to those who watched," she had written, but that was not to be. In her last difficult months she wrote her final article, "In the Garden," republished posthumously as her last book, in which she penned words that those who loved her remembered for years: "As long as one has a garden one has a future, and if one has a future one is alive," a thought she clung to as the pain wracked her body and filled her with fear.[38]

When Kitty saw her two weeks before she died, the two of them sat in the beautiful Plandome garden. "She had not been well for such a long time that we were strangely—as it seemed later—without alarm or premonition," she remembered. "We had seen her more than once, after reaching for breath like a person suffocating, steady herself and enter a drawing-room in apparently her usual form, receive and give entertainment in her accustomed way. She told me in detail on that autumn day what she had been writing; with her inveterate, never-diminished *Lust zu fabulieren*, she told me a long story, the plot of a book, I think. Before I left she made the round of the garden on the arm of an attendant, pointing out what flowers she wished to have cut, and with these she filled a large box for me. That was one of the pleasures of her garden and one of her last pleasures, symbolic: filling boxes with flowers for her friends."[39] In late October she slipped into long, dark hours of incoherence and what Vivian described as "paroxysms of pain" that brought anguish to the friends who had gathered at Plandome.

She was rarely conscious during her final week. "Believe me, Vivvie, I never could write *anything* that would bring unhappiness into the world," she told Vivian during one of her last alert moments. "There is enough of that in all our lives that we cannot get away from. What we all want is more of the other things—life, love, hope—and an assurance that they are true. With the best that was in me I have tried to write more happiness into the world."[40] A nurse kept watch at night, with instructions to telephone Vivian next door, then to awaken Edith and any friends in the house, when the end approached. At four in the morning of 29 October, they heard the knock they feared. Everyone raced into the hall, where Edith immediately fainted and had to be lifted onto a bed. Somehow Frances waited for them. When she died, several hours later, her sister and her son were by her side.

EPILOGUE

A**T TWO O'CLOCK ON 1 NOVEMBER 1924**, one hundred people gathered at the Plandome house to say goodbye to Frances. The house was filled with flowers, many of them gathered from her own autumn garden. The Rev. C. H. Ricker of Christ Church in Manhasset conducted the service, and Louis Dutton sang a song Frances would have chosen herself, "There Is No Death." She was buried in Roslyn Cemetery with the statue of Lionel she had commissioned so many years before positioned by her grave to watch over her.

Her death inspired those close to her to write. Edith's only publication was an article called "My Sister," commissioned for *Good Housekeeping* by Frances's friend Marguerite Merington, who also had been present at Frances's death. Merington herself wrote Frances's obituary, and two reminiscences of her, before getting embroiled in the long-struggling campaign for the Central Park memorial with Elizabeth Jordan and Kitty Hall Brownell. Anyone who had ever known Frances or had read her books seemed to put their memories of her on paper: Ella Hepworth Dixon, William MacHarg, and Hamilton Williamson all published articles within the first months after her death, and it seemed inevitable that without swift action some less compassionate writer might step forward to write the life of the woman who had spent nearly sixty years in the public eye and had been the subject of so much gossip.

To thwart this, Vivian turned his own life towards memorializing his mother. By December he had taken an office in Manhattan to work on the biography. As her heir he had the means, and now the time, to do this, and he wrote to her closest friends, gathered letters, and set to work. There is no doubt that he wanted to pre-empt the publication of anything that might cast a shadow on her reputation, and indeed today it is impossible to find any negative evidence. Still, something of a sense of her impropriety was passed down in the family. By the time Frances's granddaughters were older women with grandchildren of their own, there were family whispers of Frances as "that woman"; her papers were packed away in boxes in the attic and her name never spoken except as a rather embarrassing secret.

Vivian's biography of his mother received strong reviews, and with that encouragement he tried to publish even more about her, putting together volumes of her letters and unpublished writings, none of which made it past the editors' desks. Constance too took a turn, publishing a young adult biography of her mother-in-law. None of this dissipated Vivian's cast-in-stone reputation as Little Lord Fauntleroy, and his name throughout his life never appeared in a newspaper without the childish sobriquet attached to it.

On 25 July 1937, he was sailing his yawl on Long Island Sound when a sailing boat carrying four passengers capsized. Vivian immediately set about their rescue. When they were all safely on board his boat, he collapsed and had a massive heart attack. He died in front of them, and when the boat was brought back to the dock, all four slipped away after telling of the accident, never to identify themselves or to thank Vivian's family. Every obituary told of how the "Real Little Lord Fauntleroy" died saving others and stilled the taunts that dogged his life. Every one of them told of his fruitless efforts to erase the reputation his mother had unwittingly bestowed upon him. Then, as today, it was the notion and not the reality of Fauntleroy that everyone invoked: the effeminate and syrupy boy who bore no resemblance to the child of Frances's imagination or her heart.

Two months before Vivian's death, Kitty Hall Brownell dedicated the Secret Garden fountain in Central Park, reminding everyone how "fashions change, fashions in writing like other fashions."

> Literary immortality is short at its longest. But because character is formed in the young by what they read, and ideals of conduct are established in the young by the fiction of their day, Mrs. Burnett, enormously read by her generation, and to be read for a long time by some proportion of the generations succeeding, will have a delicate invisible hand in the future. For a long time the ripple will go on widening around the white pebbles she cast, seed of her sowing will go on bringing forth after the sower is forgotten. This earth is better for her having lived; it will never be as if she had not been.[1]

Even Kitty did not foresee that Fauntleroy might be put aside as Frances's most popular work, and that her name and her vision would bloom again and again in the hearts of unimagined generations for a different book. Today, it is the rare person who has read *Little Lord Fauntleroy*, or who knows that it was written by the author of *A Little Princess* and *The Secret Garden*. Certainly few realize that she wrote so much and that so much of what she wrote was for adults. Kitty's perspective on the changing twentieth century allowed her to see that Frances's adult novels now belonged to a world perhaps too different from times in which they were written for them to last long into the future, and that her most enduring books would be thosewritten for children.

Frances's life was quintessentially a writer's life. From her earliest years, she was driven to compose stories and to write them down. Even in the most difficult hours of her many illnesses, she would lie on her back in bed, writing in pencil on a board propped up on her legs. Most of her children's stories she viewed as the sprints between the marathons of her long novels; as she grew older, her long novels became even lengthier. Reading and writing were to her like breathing.

They were, however, also the source of her income and therefore the cause of great anxiety. She worked steadily; the work couldn't be rushed; and yet when it did not come easily, the material things in her life were jeopardized because she had no other source of money. Even so, her earnings grew increasingly throughout her life and surpassed those of writers, especially women writers, whose works may be better known today. Her generosity to her family and friends was as legendary as her love of clothes, houses, and furnishings, and meant that a great deal of what she earned went to supporting others.

Because she was a woman, and one who often wrote for children, we perhaps have complicated expectations for her private life that we might not have for male writers. Her independent spirit was sometimes at odds with her maternity, her fierce love for her sons often at odds with her need to live equally in two countries. She seems to have believed that letters were valid substitutes for her physical presence. Her life was a long juggling of the demands of work and love, and she paid for any mistakes she made with years of guilt, remorse, and generosity. Yet any seeming discrepancy between her own life and the fact that some of her most enduring works are for children can be explained by recalling that although her own childhood was the classic unhappy one, it was cut short by poverty, hard work, and the necessity to grow up quickly. Fairy stories, especially those with happy endings, became her way of making things better.

Frances at the sundial in the grounds of Maytham Hall.
Critic, March 1902.

Frances reading. The photograph was probably taken when she was in her forties.
Library of Congress.

Vivian Burnett as a Harvard student.

Courtesy of Penny Deupree.

Eleanor Robson as Glad in the play *The Dawn of a To-morrow*.

Courtesy of the Billy Rose Theater Collection, New York Public Library, Astor, Lenox and Tilden Foundations.

Caricature of Frances.
Sunday World, 8 August 1909.

Frances's house at Plandome, in Manhasset, Long Island, New York.
Courtesy of Penny Deupree.

Frances's study at Plandome, where she wrote *The Secret Garden*.
Courtesy of Penny Deupree.

ILLUSTRATED BY J. SCOTT WILLIAMS

The world's first view of
The Secret Garden.
American Magazine,
October 1910.

Archie Fahnestock at his home
at Plandome.

Courtesy of Penny Deupree.

Ernest Fahnestock with his son
Ken.

Courtesy of Penny Deupree.

Edith Jordan at Plandome in her
later years.

Courtesy of Penny Deupree.

GROPPER.

Sketched by William Gropper

Frances Hodgson Burnett

Caricature of Frances.

Bookman, October 1922.

Dedication of the Frances Hodgson Burnett Memorial.
Left to right: Park Commissioner Walter Herrick, sculptor Bessie Potter Vonnoh,
Frances's granddaughter Verity Burnett, and New York mayor Fiorello LaGuardia.

Courtesy of the *New York Times.*

Nearly one hundred years have passed since Frances wrote *The Secret Garden*, and the effect of that book on its readers only grows with time. As a novel, a film, and a play—surprisingly, one of her books that she never thought of dramatizing—it continues to move readers and viewers all over the world, and her work has been translated into almost every language. In English, it is consistently cited as one of the most influential books upon generations of readers. In this era of increased opportunities for women, we would do well to remember what tremendous will, devotion, and imagination it took for a woman of her era and talent to achieve this legacy.

NOTES

PROLOGUE

1. "Park Commissioner Defends 'Fauntleroy', Tells Objector to the Burnett Memorials That It Was Wholesome Fiction," *New York Times*, 23 December 1927.

2. Elizabeth Jordan, *Three Rousing Cheers: An Autobiography* (New York: D. Appleton Century, 1938), 327.

3. "Claim Vivian Burnett was the 'Lord Fauntleroy'; Son Does Not Admit It," unidentified newspaper clipping in the McClung Historical Collection, Knoxville, Tenn.

4. Vivian Burnett, "A Story Maker's Notes along the Way, Being a biographical arrangement of selections from the correspondence and unpublished writings of Frances Hodgson Burnett," typescript, Penny Deupree private collection, chap. 2, p. 16.

5. Woolf, "Not One of Us", October 1927, *The Essays of Virginia Woolf*, Vol. 4, 465, ed. Andrew McNeillie (London, The Hogarth Press). It is thirty years since the publication of Ann Thwaite's *Waiting for the Party, the Life of Frances Hodgson Burnett* (New York: Scribner 1974; London: Secker & Warburg 1974), the first biography of Frances to appear in the UK.

6. Gertrude Hall Brownell, "Frances Hodgson Burnett—I", typescript biography, Hargrett Rare Book and Manuscript Collection, University of Georgia Libraries, MA 210, box 4, folder 10, p. 18.

7. FHB, *In the Garden* (Boston and New York: Medici Society of America, 1925), 20.

8. Burnett, *In the Garden*, 30.

CHAPTER I. THE NEW WORLD

1. Frances Hodgson Burnett, *The One I Knew the Best of All* (London: Frederick Warne, 1893), 209. Hereafter, for bibliographic purposes, Burnett is referred to as FHB.

2. Ibid., 221.

3. I am grateful to Katherine P. Hodgson for the information on Herbert Hodgson and his family, and to Knoxville journalist and local historian Jack Neely for the information on Joseph Wood.

4. FHB, *The One I Knew the Best of All*, 221.

5. Ibid., 207; "Dogs of Noted Americans," *Saint Nicholas*, June 1888, 598–599.

6. Edward Everett, "Account of the Fund for the Relief of East Tennessee," 6–7, in Digby Gordon Seymour, *Divided Loyalties: Fort Sanders and the Civil War in East Tennessee* (Knoxville: University of Tennessee Press, 1963), 4.

7. *Brownlow's Knoxville Whig, and Rebel Ventilator*, vol. 2 (28 June 1865), 3.

8. William MacHarg, "The Young Heart, Which Translated, Means Frances Hodgson Burnett," no attribution, but reprinted by permission of *Good Housekeeping* (International Magazine Company, New York) in 1922.

9. FHB, *The One I Knew the Best of All*, 49–51.

10. Elizabeth Gaskell, *Mary Barton* (New York: W. W. Norton, 1958), 91.

11. FHB, *The One I Knew the Best of All*, 235.

12. Frances Trollope, *Domestic Manners of the Americans* (London and New York: Whittaker, Treacher, 1832), 93–94.

13. FHB, "How I Served My Apprenticeship," *Lady's Realm*, November 1896, 75.

14. FHB, *The One I Knew the Best of All*, 234.

15. FHB to Vivian Burnett, June 1897, Penny Deupree private collection.

16. "Mrs. Burnett at Work Again," 24 November 1891, published in an unnamed newspaper on her forty-second birthday.

17. Speech to the Vagabonds, 9 December 1895, quoted in full in Vivian Burnett, *The Romantick Lady (Frances Hodgson Burnett): The Life Story of an Imagination* (New York: Charles Scribner's, 1927), 266–268.

18. "Sketch" of Frances Hodgson Burnett, *Harper's Bazar*, 24 February 1900, 159–160.

19. FHB, *The One I Knew the Best of All*, 237.

CHAPTER 2. A MANCHESTER CHILDHOOD

1. Edith Mary Jordan, "My Sister—An Intimate, loving story of one of the world's most beloved writers," *Good Housekeeping*, July 1925, 142–147.

2. FHB, *The One I Knew the Best of All* (London: Frederick Warne, 1893), 3.

3. Ibid., 209.

4. Ibid., 9.

5. Ibid., 14.

6. Typed draft of FHB's introduction to *Granny's Wonderful Chair*, Penny Deupree private collection.

7. FHB, *The One I Knew the Best of All*, 24–25.

8. Ibid., 19.

9. Ibid., 158.

10. Ibid., 209.

11. FHB, "The Magic in Children's Books," *New York Times*, 14 November 1920, BR3.

12. Vivian Burnett, "A Story Maker's Notes along the Way," typescript, Penny Deupree private collection, chap. 2, p. 2. This typescript includes FHB letters, journals, and miscellaneous writings.

13. FHB, "How I Served My Apprenticeship," *Lady's Realm*, November 1896, 75.

14. Ibid., 75–76.

15. Constance Buel Burnett, *Happily Ever After: A Portrait of Frances Hodgson Burnett* (New York: Vanguard Press, 1965), 19.

16. Henry Hadfield, paper presented to the Manchester Literary Club, 1883, Manchester Central Library, reference ms813.48 Bal, p. 5.

17. FHB, *The One I Knew the Best of All*, 190–191.

18. Vivian Burnett, *The Romantick Lady (Frances Hodgson Burnett): The Life Story of an Imagination* (New York: Charles Scribner's, 1927), 20.

19. *Ibid.*, 21–22.

20. Ibid., 14.

21. FHB to Emily White, 10 March 1863, Penny Deupree private collection.

22. Hadfield, paper presented to Manchester Literary Club, 1883, 5–6.

23. FHB, "The Little Faun," in *Giovanni and the Other* (New York: Charles Scribner's, 1892), 118.

24. FHB, *The One I Knew the Best of All*, 195.

25. Ibid., 201.

26. FHB, draft of introduction to *Granny's Wonderful Chair*.

27. FHB, "My Enemy," *Ladies' Home Journal*, December 1894, 4. This article was first in a series titled "The Man Who Most Influenced Me." All subsequent quotations and facts about Frances's Manchester mentor in this chapter are taken from this article.

28. FHB, *The One I Knew the Best of All*, 188.

29. Ibid.

30. "Mrs. Burnett: A Visit to Her Home in London," *New York* Times, 15 June 1901, 424.

CHAPTER 3. A SHABBY GENTEEL STORY

1. Ada Campbell Larew, "Childhood Recollections of Frances Hodgson Burnett," typescript, McClung Historical Collection, Knoxville Public Library, Knoxville, Tenn.

2. "Dogs of Noted Americans," *Saint Nicholas*, June 1888, 599.

3. Wilma Dykeman, "A Trail of Cherokee Tears—and Death," *Knoxville News-Sentinel*, 27 June 1982.

4. Larew, "Childhood Recollections of Frances Hodgson Burnett."

5. "Famous Story Teller. Side Lights on Marriage of Frances Hodgson Burnett," *Washington Post*, 8 April 1900.

6. Constance Buel Burnett, *Happily Ever After: A Portrait of Frances Hodgson Burnett* (New York: Vanguard Press, 1965), 62.

7. FHB, *The One I Knew the Best of All* (London: Frederick Warne, 1893), 97, 111.

8. Edith Mary Jordan, "My Sister—An Intimate, loving story of one of the world's most beloved writers," *Good Housekeeping*, July 1925, 142–147.

9. Hamilton Williamson, "Frances Hodgson Burnett—'Romantic Lady,'" *Bookman: A Review of Books and Life*, September 1924–February 1925, 712.

10. Larew, "Childhood Recollections of Frances Hodgson Burnett."

11. "Frances Hodgson Burnett, Author, Dies at 74. Romance in Early Life. As a Child She Sold Berries to Buy Paper and Pencil—Won First Fame With 'That Lass of Lowrie's,'" 30 October 1924, De Grummond Collection, University of Mississippi. The publication information is missing.

12. FHB to James Whitcomb Riley, 23 December 1895, Riley MSS, Lilly Library, Indiana University.

13. FHB, handwritten foreword to the 1915 edition of *The One I Knew the Best of All*, sent to Edward L. Burlingame at Scribner's, April 1915, Scribner C0101, box 23, folder 6, Department of Rare Books and Special Collections, Princeton University Libraries.

14. See, e.g., FHB, *In Connection with the DeWilloughby Claim* (New York: Charles Scribner's Sons, 1899), chap. 20, about Tennessee: "There was the spring, when she trotted by Tom's side into the garden and he showed her the little, pale-green points of the crocuses, hyacinths, and tulips pushing their ways up through the moist brown earth, and when he carried her in his big arms into the woods on the hillsides, and they saw the dogwood covered with big white flowers and the wild plum-trees snowed over with delicate blooms, and found the blue violets thick among the wet grass and leaves, and the frail white wind-flowers quivering on their stems. As they went about in this new fairyland, which came every year, and which still seemed always a surprise, it was their habit to talk to each other a great deal. . . . Her child thoughts and fancies might have been those of some little faun or dryad."

15. FHB to Swan Burnett, n.d., quoted in Vivian Burnett, *The Romantick Lady (Frances Hodgson Burnett): The Life Story of an Imagination* (New York: Charles Scribner's, 1927), 47.

16. FHB, ledger book, Special Collections, University of Virginia Library.

17. FHB, "A Real Record," Wilkinson Collection, Department of Rare Books and Special Collections, Princeton University Libraries. Also discussed in Burnett, *Romantick Lady*, 75–76. See also Gertrude Hall Brownell, "Frances Hodgson Burnett—I," typescript biography, Hargrett Rare Book and Manuscript Collection, University of Georgia Libraries, MA 210, box 4, folder 10, which states that after these difficult early years, FHB's health was permanently impaired.

18. Marie A. Belloc, "Mrs. Hodgson Burnett: A Famous Authoress at Home," *Idler* 9 (1896): 645?–648. The article includes a photo by the London photography firm Barraud.

19. Jordan, "My Sister," 55.

20. "Mrs. Francis [*sic*] Hodgson Burnett, *Knoxville Daily Sentinel*, 21 March 1887.

21. Jordan, "My Sister," 55.

22. Margaret Ragsdale, "Author of 'Little Lord Fauntleroy' Found Romance and Happy Home in Knoxville: Burnett Centennial Recalls Early Days," *Knoxville News-Sentinel*, [November 1949], A8.

23. Jordan, "My Sister," 55.

24. Ibid., 142.

25. FHB (The Second, pseud.), "Miss Carruthers' Engagement," *Godey's Lady's Book and Magazine*, October 1868, 311–321.

26. Ibid., 311.

27. "Mrs. Francis [*sic*] Hodgson Burnett," *Knoxville Daily Sentinel,* 21 March 1887.

28. FHB (The Second, pseud.), "Hearts and Diamonds," *Godey's Lady's Book and Magazine,* June 1868, 524–528.

29. Jordan, "My Sister," 55, 142.

30. William MacHarg, "The Young Heart. Which, Translated, Means Frances Hodgson Burnett," n.p., 1922. Although no magazine name is given, the article comes from International Magazine Co. and was reprinted "by permission of *Good Housekeeping.*"

31. Burnett, *Happily Ever After,* 88; FHB, *The One I Knew the Best of All,* 292.

CHAPTER 4. VAGABONDIA

1. Edith Mary Jordan, "My Sister—An Intimate, loving story of one of the world's most beloved writers," *Good Housekeeping,* July 1925, 142.

2. *Helms' Knoxville City Directory* (Knoxville, 1869), 28.

3. Ada Campbell Larew, "Childhood Recollections of Frances Hodgson Burnett," typescript, McClung Historical Collection, Knoxville Public Library, Knoxville, Tenn.

4. This story had multiple incarnations. Although it was published serially in 1873, it first saw life as a novel in a single volume in 1877, when, capitalizing on the success of her novel *That Lass o' Lowrie's,* Porter and Coates of Philadelphia brought it out without her permission as the novel *Dolly.* Angered at their presumption, she made minor changes and reissued it with Scribner's in 1883, renaming it *Vagabondia.* However, one of her English publishers, Frederick Warne, brought it out again in 1893 under its original name of *Dolly.* It was very successful, and this time she had no objections to either its publication or its name.

5. FHB, *Dolly* (London: Frederick Warne, 1893), 2.

6. FHB, ledger book, Special Collections, University of Virginia, 115. She also wrote an early version of "Vagabondia" immediately following this fragment. The ledger book shows her working out her stories, in some cases from youthful attempts to more mature versions in more adult handwriting, or in scraps such as these. In most cases this (and the American spelling) is the only way to date the writings, because the book was used for a variety of purposes in two countries. The page following "Bohemia," for example, shows at the top the 1875 grocery accounts in Swan's handwriting, below which some younger person has practised cursive handwriting.

7. Jack Neely, "Vagabondia Castle," in his weekly "Secret History" column, *Metropulse* (Knoxville), 27 August 1993.

8. FHB, *Dolly,* 43.

9. "The Growth of Knoxville," *Knoxville Daily Tribune,* 13 February 1877; "What a Stranger Thinks of Us," *Knoxville Daily Tribune,* 23 January 1877.

10. Jack Neely, "Finding Vagabondia", in "Secret History" column, *Metropulse* (Knoxville), 18–25 January 1996.

11. "Author of 'Little Lord Fauntleroy' Found Romance and Happy Home in Knoxville," *Knoxville News-Sentinel,* n.d.

12. FHB, *The One I Knew the Best of All* (London: Frederick Warne, 1893), 19.

13. Constance Buel Burnett, *Happily Ever After: A Portrait of Frances Hodgson Burnett* (New York: Vanguard Press, 1965), 91.

14. FHB, *Dolly,* 53.

15. Larew, "Childhood Recollections of Frances Hodgson Burnett."

16. FHB, *Dolly*, 43, 51.

17. Swan Burnett to Edith Hodgson Jordan, 24 August 1881, Penny Deupree private collection.

18. FHB, "How I Served My Apprenticeship," *Lady's Realm*, November 1896, 78.

19. Marie A. Belloc, "Mrs. Hodgson Burnett: A Famous Authoress at Home," *Idler* 9 (1896): 645–648.

20. Fannie E. Hodgson, "The Woman Who Saved Me," *Scribner's Monthly*, March 1873, 560–571.

21. *Letters of Richard Watson Gilder*, ed. Rosamond Gilder (Boston: Houghton Mifflin, 1916), 392.

22. Arthur John, *The Best Years of the "Century": Richard Watson Gilder, "Scribner's Monthly," and "Century Magazine," 1870–1909* (Urbana: University of Illinois Press, 1981).

23. There is no firm agreement on where Vagabondia was located. I am grateful to Jack Neely, a journalist who in his column in Knoxville's *Metropulse* newspaper researches the local history of his subjects, for all this information on Knoxville during FHB's residence there.

24. FHB, *In Connection with the DeWilloughby Claim* (New York: Charles Scribner's, 1899), 216.

25. Ibid., 258, 402.

26. Jack Neely to the author, 24 July 2002.

27. John, *Best Years of the "Century,"* 1–2.

28. Ibid., ix.

29. Bill Nye, quoted ibid., 387.

30. Vivian Burnett, *The Romantick Lady (Frances Hodgson Burnett): The Life Story of an Imagination* (New York: Charles Scribner's, 1927), 53.

31. All the information in this paragraph comes from Arthur John's very informative *Best Years of the "Century,"* 49–61.

32. Jack Neely to the author, 30 July 2002.

33. FHB, *The One I Knew the Best of All*, 68.

34. FHB, "How I Served My Apprenticeship," 78.

35. Richard Watson Gilder to FHB, 23 February 1872, quoted in Burnett, *Romantick Lady*, 54.

CHAPTER 5. THE RELUCTANT BRIDE ABROAD

1. FHB to Vivian Burnett, 25 October 1901, Penny Deupree private collection.

2. Constance Buel Burnett, *Happily Ever After: A Portrait of Frances Hodgson Burnett* (New York: Vanguard Press, 1965), 100.

3. From an article in *Century Magazine* (1909?), after Gilder's death, excerpted in Vivian Burnett, *The Romantick Lady (Frances Hodgson Burnett): The Life Story of an Imagination* (New York: Charles Scribner's, 1927), 65–66.

4. FHB to Richard Watson Gilder, September 1877, Gilder Collection, New York Public Library.

5. FHB to Richard Watson Gilder, 13 November 1872, Gilder Collection.

6. Henry Hadfield, paper presented to Manchester Literary Club, 1883, Manchester Central Library, reference ms813.48 Bal, pp. 7–8.

7. FHB, *Knoxville Journal*, 1 August 1872; reprinted 10 June 1955.

8. Ada Campbell Larew, "Memoirs of Frances Hodgson Burnett," typescript,

McClung Historical Collection, Knoxville Public Library, Knoxville, Tenn.

9. FHB to Rosa Campbell, 16 September 1872, Lennon Papers, Department of Special Collections, University of Tennessee, Knoxville, MS–264. See also Ada Campbell Larew, "The Childhood Recollections of Frances Hodgson Burnett," n.p., n.d., McClung Historical Collection.

10. FHB to Rosa Campbell, 1 January 1873, Lennon Papers.

11. FHB to Richard Watson Gilder, 27 November 1872, Gilder Collection.

12. FHB, 12 July 1874, quoted in Hadfield, paper presented to the Manchester Literary Club, 8–12. One of the most puzzling aspects of this wedding is its date. The marriage certificate declares it to be 7 September 1874, fully a year after the date commonly given for it, and only two weeks before the birth of their first child. It is recorded in the bound official records for that year. However, at that time there was no requirement that a marriage be recorded when it took place, and all the detailed newspaper accounts of the wedding appear in the September 1873 editions, so we can assume that the marriage indeed took place then and that Frances was not a pregnant bride.

13. Mamie B. Foust to Vivian Burnett, quoted in Burnett, *Romantick Lady*, 67.

14. Hadfield, paper presented to Manchester Literary Club, 8–12.

15. Edith Mary Jordan, "My Sister—An Intimate, loving story of one of the world's most beloved writers," *Good Housekeeping*, July 1925, 143.

16. Burnett, *Happily Ever After*, 106; Hadfield, paper presented to Manchester Literary Club.

17. Mr. Fraice to Henry Hadfield, 22 September 1882, quoted in Hadfield, paper presented to Manchester Literary Club, 16.

18. Jordan, "My Sister," 143–145.

19. Ibid.

20. Hadfield, paper presented to Manchester Literary Club, 17–18.

21. FHB, "Will You Know," 7 March 1876, Penny Deupree private collection.

22. FHB to Edith Fahnestock, April 1876, quoted in Jordan, "My Sister," 143–145.

23. Ibid.

24. Ibid., 143.

25. *Literary World*, May 1876, 198.

26. FHB, *The One I Knew the Best of All* (London: Frederick Warne, 1893), 70–71.

CHAPTER 6. PIRACY AND A PLAY

1. Fraice to Henry Hadfield, 22 September 1882, as quoted in Henry Hadfield, paper presented to Manchester Literary Club, 1883, Manchester Central Library, reference ms813.48 Bal, pp. 14–17.

2. FHB, *In Connection with the DeWilloughby Claim* (New York: Charles Scribner's, 1899), 281.

3. Swan Burnett to Edith Fahnestock (Jordan?), 24 August 1881, Penny Deupree private collection.

4. FHB to Richard Watson Gilder, 12 December 1876, Gilder Collection, New York Public Library.

5. Ibid.

6. Ibid.

7. FHB to Swan Burnett, 12 November [1876], Penny Deupree private collection.

8. FHB to Richard Watson Gilder, [1877], Gilder Collection.

9. Scribner's to Mr. Welford, 2 March 1877, Scribner Letter Books for JBS (J. Blair Scribner), October 1876–September 1877, letter book no. 5, Department of Rare Books and Special Collections, Princeton University Libraries.

10. FHB to Richard Watson Gilder, 8 March 1877, Gilder Collection.

11. Scribner's to Dr. R. Sheldon Mackenzie, 25 April 1877, Scribner letter book no. 5, Department of Rare Books and Special Collections, Princeton University Libraries.

12. Press notices at the back of FHB, *Haworth's* (New York: Charles Scribner's, 1879).

13. Scribner's to FHB, 28 April 1877, Scribner letter book no. 5, Department of Rare Books and Special Collections, Princeton University Libraries.

14. FHB to Richard Watson Gilder, 30 April 1877, Gilder Collection.

15. "That Lass 'o Towery 's!" *Punch,* 20 October–17 November 1877.

16. Vivian Burnett, *The Romantick Lady (Frances Hodgson Burnett): The Life Story of an Imagination* (New York: Charles Scribner's, 1927), 77.

17. FHB to Julia Schayer, in Vivian Burnett, "A Story Maker's Notes along the Way," typescript, Penny Deupree private collection, chap. 5, pp. 2–4 and 12.

18. Unidentified newspaper account, quoted in Hadfield, paper presented to Manchester Literary Club, 19.

19. FHB, "A Real Record," Wilkinson Collection, Department of Rare Books and Special Collections, Princeton University Libraries. Also quoted in Burnett, *Romantick Lady,* 75–76.

20. Swan Burnett to Scribner's, 29 September 1878, Scribner Colol, box 23, folder 2 (AM19189), Department of Rare Books and Special Collections, Princeton University Libraries.

21. "Gradations in Inanity," no publication or author information, Gilder Collection.

22. FHB to Mary Bucklin Claflin, 14 July 1882, Overbury Collection, Barnard College.

23. FHB to Richard Watson Gilder, September 1877, Gilder Collection.

24. Swan Burnett to Scribner's, 29 September 1878.

25. "Novels," *Literary World* 8 (1877): 193.

26. Unidentified critic, as quoted in Burnett, *Romantick Lady,* 87.

27. "Mrs. Frances H. Burnett: The Youth and First Efforts of the Author of 'That Lass o' Lowrie's,'" *Cincinnati Enquirer,* 23 December [1877].

28. Swan Burnett to Charles Warren Stoddard of Scribner's, 12 October 1877, Anthony Collection, New York Public Library.

29. FHB to Richard Watson Gilder, 23 October 1877, Gilder Collection.

30. *New York Times,* 31 October 1878, p. 4, col. 3.

31. Ibid.

32. "Another Burst of Anger. Charles Reade and His Critics. How the Novelist and Playwright Claims to Have Dealt With Brother Writers," *New York Times,* 2 October 1879, 2; article reprinted from the Manchester *Examiner,* 15 September 1879.

33. FHB to Richard Watson Gilder, [1877], Gilder Collection.

34. Joseph Hatton and Arthur Matthison, *Liz: A Drama, in four Acts, Founded Upon The Novel Of "That Lass o' Lowrie's" (By Permission of the Author), and Adapted to the Stage by Joseph Hatton and Arthur Matthison. First produced in London at the Opera Comique, Sept. 1, 1877, under the management of Mr. John Radcliff* (London and New York: Samuel French, n.d.).

35. See reviews in the *Daily Sun* (Philadelphia), 29 October 1878, and the *New York*

Dramatic News, October 1878.

36. FHB to Julia Schayer, [autumn 1878], quoted in Burnett, *Romantick Lady,* 102–103.

37. FHB to Richard Watson Gilder, in Burnett, "A Story Maker's Notes along the Way," chap. 4, p. 3.

CHAPTER 7. A CITY OF GROVES AND BOWERS

1. FHB, "A City of Groves and Bowers," *Saint Nicholas,* June 1893, 563–571.

2. Constance McLaughlin Green, *Washington: A History of the Capital, 1800–1950* (Princeton: Princeton University Press, 1962), 77.

3. FHB, "City of Groves and Bowers," 565.

4. Green, *Washington,* 84.

5. Vivian Burnett, *The Romantick Lady (Frances Hodgson Burnett): The Life Story of an Imagination* (New York: Charles Scribner's, 1927), 72.

6. FHB, "The Little Faun," in *Giovanni and the Other* (New York: Charles Scribner's, 1892), 120, 126.

7. FHB, "City of Groves and Bowers," 565.

8. Ibid.

9. FHB to Vivian Burnett, 6 April 1906, Penny Deupree private collection.

10. FHB to Richard Watson Gilder, May or June 1877, Gilder Collection, New York Public Library.

11. FHB to Richard Watson Gilder, 23 October 1877, Gilder Collection.

12. FHB to Richard Watson Gilder, September 1877, Gilder Collection.

13. FHB to Richard Watson Gilder, 5 February 1878, Gilder Collection.

14. FHB to Richard Watson Gilder, [1878], Gilder Collection.

15. Burnett, *Romantick Lady,* 78.

16. Ibid., 82.

17. Samuel Joseph Platt and Mary Louise Ogden, *Medical Men and Institutions of Knox County, Tennessee, 1789–1957* (Knoxville: Prepared for the Centennial Celebration of the Knoxville Academy of Medicine, 1969), 235–236.

18. Elizabeth Elliot, "Smiling Memories of Mrs. Burnett," *Literary Digest International Book Review,* n.d., 160–161.

19. FHB to Mary Hooker Burton, n.d., Stowe–Day Foundation. "Mrs. Cimabue Brown" was a character created by *Punch* illustrator and satirist George DuMaurier as a parody of the Aesthetic movement.

20. FHB to Richard Watson Gilder, 5 May 1878, Gilder Collection.

21. Burnett, *Romantick Lady,* 78.

22. FHB to Richard Watson Gilder, 5 May 1878.

23. Ibid.

24. FHB to Richard Watson Gilder, 20 September 1878, Gilder Collection.

25. FHB to Richard Watson Gilder, [1878, probably a later letter than that cited in n. 14], Gilder Collection.

26. FHB to Richard Watson Gilder, 20 September 1878.

27. FHB to Mary Mapes Dodge, n.d., Laurence Hutton Correspondence, box 2, folder 46, Department of Rare Books and Special Collections, Princeton University Libraries.

28. See http://www.lake-lure.com/big%20house.html, and http://www.ls.net/~newriver/nc/wnc23.htm for more on Logan House and Lake Lure.

29. FHB to Richard Watson Gilder, n.d., Gilder Collection.

CHAPTER 8. IN THE COMPANY OF WOMEN

1. FHB to Richard Watson Gilder, 4 February 1879, Gilder Collection, New York Public Library.

2. Ibid.

3. FHB, "Birdie," in *Giovanni and the Other* (New York: Charles Scribner's, 1892), 158.

4. FHB to Lady Dorothy Nevill, [1890], Lilly Library, Indiana University, Lilly PZ 7.B964 L7 1890.

5. FHB, "The Proud Little Grain of Wheat," *Saint Nicholas,* January 1880, 193–197.

6. Mary Mapes Dodge to FHB, 10 February 1879, quoted in Vivian Burnett, *The Romantick Lady (Frances Hodgson Burnett): The Life Story of an Imagination* (New York: Charles Scribner's, 1927), 93.

7. FHB, n.d., in Vivian Burnett, "A Story Maker's Notes along the Way," typescript, Penny Deupree private collection, chap. 5, p. 5.

8. John Boyle O'Reilly to FHB, 14 March 1879, quoted in Burnett, *Romantick Lady,* 94–95.

9. Swan Burnett to Scribner's, 15 January 1879, C0101, box 23, folder 2 (AM19189), Department of Rare Books and Special Collections, Princeton University Libraries.

10. Letter to Scribner's, 25 September 1879, C0101, box 23, folder 2 (AM19189), Department of Rare Books and Special Collections, Princeton University Libraries.

11. FHB to Mr. Warner, 11 April 1878, Mark Twain House, Hartford, Conn.

12. Isabella Beecher Hooker, "The Constitutional Rights of the Women of the United States: An Address before the International Council of Women," Washington, D.C., 30 March 1883 (http://users.ntropolis.net/slummit/machine/Suffrage/speech1.htm/).

13. Joseph S. Van Why, *Nook Farm,* ed. Earl A. French (1962; reprint, Hartford, Conn.: Stowe–Day Foundation, 1975), 36–37.

14. Joan D. Hedrick, *Harriet Beecher Stowe: A Life* (New York: Oxford University Press, 1994), 368.

15. Harriet Beecher Stowe to Mary Claflin, 24 December 1872, quoted ibid., 377.

16. Ibid., 354, 370.

17. FHB to Isabella Beecher Hooker, 25 May 1880, Stowe–Day Foundation, Hartford, Conn. Whether or not the children actually went to Tennessee is confusing. She refers in the same letter to needing to arrange for a local laundress in Hartford, for "with my two small boys . . . washing is an item of importance." Hooker, in a letter to Alice Day, mentions that only a small group is at Nook Farm, including Frances and Vivian, and when FHB gets to Nook Farm she writes to tell Mary Claflin that "we" arrived safely.

18. The *Critic* noted this collaboration in its 18 June 1881 issue: "For several months past Mrs. Burnett has been engaged with Mr. W. H. Gillette in constructing a play from two of her short stories, 'Lodusky' and 'Esmeralda.' She will spend the Summer near New York in rehearsing the piece, which is to be brought out at the Madison Square Theatre in the Fall. Mrs. Burnett is also at work on two new novels, one dealing with scenes and characters at Washington." Apparently the play of "Lodusky" never materialized.

19. FHB to Richard Watson Gilder, June 1880, Gilder Collection.

20. FHB to Isabella Beecher Hooker, 29 June 1880, Stowe–Day Foundation.

21. FHB to Richard Watson Gilder, [October 1881], Gilder Collection.

22. FHB to Mary Bucklin Claflin, [August 1880], Overbury Collection, Barnard College.

23. FHB to Richard Watson Gilder, [summer 1880], Gilder Collection.

24. Mary Hooker Burton to FHB, 21 September 1880, Stowe–Day Foundation.

25. FHB to Mary Hooker Burton, [1880], Stowe–Day Foundation.

26. Burnett, *Romantick Lady*, 120, 121.

27. FHB, *Through One Administration* (reprint, Ridgewood, N.J.: Gregg Press, 1967; New York: Charles Scribner's, 1881), 82, 86.

28. FHB to Julia Schayer, [July 1881], quoted in Burnett, *Romantick Lady*, 122–124.

29. FHB to [George?] Warner, [winter 1880], Mark Twain House, Hartford, Conn.

30. "Mrs. Frances H. Burnett. The Youth and First Efforts of the Author of That Lass o' Lowrie's, from the *Cincinnati Enquirer*," Washington D.C., 23 December 1881. This article was clearly reprinted, but the name of the newspaper is unavailable.

31. FHB to Mary Hooker Burton, [autumn 1880], Stowe–Day Foundation.

32. FHB to Richard Watson Gilder, n.d., Gilder Collection.

33. Lucretia Garfield to FHB, 13 November 1880, quoted in Burnett, *Romantick Lady*, 113.

34. FHB to Mary Hooker Burton, 25 November 1880, Stowe–Day Foundation.

35. FHB to Richard Watson Gilder, [March 1881], Gilder Collection.

36. FHB to Julia Schayer, [July 1881], quoted in Burnett, *Romantick Lady*, 123. This same story of staying in a beach hotel without luggage, sharing a comb chastely between rooms, was repeated years later by Frances in a letter to Vivian, when Frances spent the night in Bournemouth with Stephen Townesend.

37. FHB to Richard Watson Gilder, Monday [summer 1881], Gilder Collection.

38. FHB to Julia Schayer, [July 1881], quoted in Burnett, *Romantick Lady*, 122–124.

39. Swan Burnett to Edith Jordan, 24 August 1881, Penny Deupree private collection.

40. FHB to Richard Watson Gilder, [summer 1881], Gilder Collection.

41. FHB to Louise Krutch, [spring 1881], in Burnett, "Story Maker's Notes along the Way," chap. 5, p. 13.

42. "A Fair Barbarian," *Critic*, 26 March 1881.

43. FHB to Mary Bucklin Claflin, [spring 1882], Overbury Collection.

44. FHB to Isabella Beecher Hooker, 9 December 1882, Stowe–Day Foundation.

45. Ibid.

46. Review of *Through One Administration*, *Saturday Review*, 30 June 1883, 838.

47. "Frances Hodgson Burnett," *Critic*, 17 December 1881, 346–347.

CHAPTER 9. FAUNTLEROY

1. Vivian Burnett, *The Romantick Lady (Frances Hodgson Burnett): The Life Story of an Imagination* (New York: Charles Scribner's, 1927), 134–135. Gertrude Hall Brownell, in her handwritten introduction for a new edition of *Little Lord Fauntleroy*, says that it was a bearskin rug, not a pillow.

2. Vivian Burnett to FHB, 20 May 1897, Penny Deupree private collection.

3. See "The Boston Mind Cure: Differing Impressions of Two Popular Women Writers," *New York Times*, 8 July 1885.

4. FHB to Maria S. Porter, Wednesday, n.d., Special Collections, University of Virginia Library, MSS 6817–d, ALS.

5. Gertrude Hall Brownell, "Frances Hodgson Burnett—II," typescript biography, Hargrett Rare Book and Manuscript Collection, University of Georgia Libraries, MA 210, box 4, folder 10, p. 15.

6. Gertrude Hall Brownell, "Frances Hodgson Burnett—I," typescript biography, Hargrett Rare Book and Manuscript Collection, MA 210, box 4, folder 10, p. 1.

7. FHB to Edna Hall, 30 May 1886, in Vivian Burnett, "A Story Maker's Notes along the Way," typescript, Penny Deupree private collection, chap. 5, pp. 20–21.

8. Brownell, "Frances Hodgson Burnett—I," 2.

9. Burnett, *Romantick Lady*, 151.

10. FHB to Kitty Hall (Gertrude Hall Brownell), March 1887, in Burnett, "Story Maker's Notes along the Way," chap. 5, pp. 22–23.

11. Brownell, "Frances Hodgson Burnett—I," 6.

12. Constance Buel Burnett, *Happily Ever After: A Portrait of Frances Hodgson Burnett* (New York: Vanguard Press, 1965), 125–126.

13. "Authors At Work—III," in *The Book Buyer: A Review and Record of Current Literature* (New York: Charles Scribner's, 1886), 21.

14. Brownell, "Frances Hodgson Burnett—I," 1–2.

15. FHB to Vivian Burnett, 25 November 1900, Penny Deupree private collection.

16. Brownell, "Frances Hodgson Burnett—I," 6.

17. Burnett, *Happily Ever After*, 129–130.

18. FHB, "How Fauntleroy Really Occurred, and a Very Real Little Boy Became an Ideal One," *Ladies' Home Journal*, serialized beginning December 1893; reprinted in FHB, *Piccino and Other Child Stories* (New York: Charles Scribner's, 1894).

19. Ibid.

20. FHB, "A Domestic Drama Entitled *The Hatchet*," in Burnett, "Story Maker's Notes along the Way," chap. 3, pp. 1–4.

21. FHB to Mary Mapes Dodge, Saturday [April 1885], Mary Mapes Dodge Collection, Wilkinson Dodge, CO114, box 2, folder 6, Department of Rare Books and Special Collections, Princeton University Libraries.

22. Mary Mapes Dodge to FHB, 12 June 1885, Mary Mapes Dodge Collection.

23. FHB, "The Boy Who Became a Socialist," in *Giovanni and the Other* (New York: Charles Scribner's, 1892), 140.

24. Samuel Clemens to Rev. F. V. Christ, August 1908, in *Mark Twain's Letters*, 2 vols., ed. Albert Bigelow Paine (New York: Harper and Brothers, 1917), 2:813–814.

25. "King Plagiarism and His Court," *Fortnightly Review* 47 (1 January–1 June 1890): 435–436. I have found no evidence yet of the earlier supposed plagiarism, although her experience in offering in 1904 to rewrite the stories in *Granny's Wonderful Chair*, a book from her childhood, makes this seem possible but unintentional.

26. "Correspondence. A Commentary in an Easy-Chair. Plagiarism—The Criticism of the Unsuccessful—the Scorn of the Successful—A Case in Point," *Spectator*, 1 February 1890, 164–165. I have been unable to locate Frances's letter or Edmund Gosse's response to it.

27. "The Pleasure of Paragraphs," *Saturday Review*, 23 March 1889, 334.

28. FHB to Kitty Hall (Gertrude Hall Brownell), April 1886, Penny Deupree private collection.

29. Vivian Burnett to FHB, Wednesday, n.d., Penny Deupree private collection.

30. Lionel Burnett to FHB, 26 October 1886, Penny Deupree private collection.

31. FHB to Dorothea Gilman, 23 February 1887, Special Collections, University of Virginia Library, MSS 6817–d, ALS.

32. FHB to Arthur Gilman, 23 February 1887, Special Collections, University of Virginia Library, MSS 6817–d, ALS.

33. Burnett, *Romantick Lady*, v.

34. Brownell, "Frances Hodgson Burnett—I," 8.

35. FHB to Kitty Hall (Gertrude Hall Brownell), [March 1887], quoted in Burnett, *Romantick Lady*, 148–150.

36. "Mrs. Francis [*sic*] Hodgson Burnett, An Interesting Sketch," *Knoxville Daily Sentinel*, 21 March 1887.

CHAPTER 10. RETURN TO EUROPE

1. "The Tinker's Tom," in *Giovanni and the Other* (New York: Charles Scribner's, 1892), 173.

2. Ibid., 162–163.

3. FHB to Owen Lankester, quoted in Vivian Burnett, *The Romantick Lady (Frances Hodgson Burnett): The Life Story of an Imagination* (New York: Charles Scribner's, 1927), 154–156.

4. FHB, "Eight Little Princes," in *Giovanni and the Other*, 96.

5. FHB to Elizabeth Jordan, 9 October 1913, Elizabeth Jordan Collection, New York Public Library.

6. FHB to Vivian Burnett, 3 June 1917, Penny Deupree private collection.

7. FHB cable to Scribner's, 9 January 1888, Scribner C0101, box 24, folder 8, Department of Rare Books and Special Collections, Princeton University Libraries.

8. Frederick Warne to Scribner's, 14 March 1888, Scribner C0101, box 24, folder 8, Department of Rare Books and Special Collections, Princeton University Libraries.

9. "Dogs of Noted Americans," *Saint Nicholas*, June 1888, 598–600.

10. Carl Van Vechten, *The Tiger in the House* (New York: Alfred A. Knopf, 1920), 298.

11. Vivian Burnett, "A Story Maker's Notes along the Way," typescript, Penny Deupree private collection, chap. 7, p. 10.

12. FHB to Owen Lankester, [1887], quoted in Burnett, *Romantick Lady*, 162–163.

13. *Critic*, 20 April 1889, 197. This article also reports that "Mrs. Burnett had no intention of dramatizing 'Little Lord Fauntleroy' even after Mr. Seebohm's version of it was brought out in London, until some of her theatrical acquaintances got at her and told her that she was losing a great opportunity."

14. FHB to Lionel and Vivian Burnett, [April 1888], in Burnett, "Story Maker's Notes along the Way," chap. 3, p. 8.

15. "Playwriting, a Handbook for Would-be Dramatic Writers. By a Dramatist" (http://gaslight.mtroyal.ab.ca/plywrt11.htm).

16. FHB to Gertrude Hall ("my darling Kitten"), n.d., in Burnett, "Story Maker's Notes along the Way," chap. 7, p. 2.

17. William Archer, *World*, 23 May 1888. See also Burnett, *Romantick Lady*, 168. For further information, see "High Court of Justice. Chancery Division, Warne and Co. v. Seebohm," *Times* (London), 25 April, 1888, 11; and "High Court of Justice. Chancery

Division. (Before Mr. Justice Stirling.) Warne v. Seebohm," *Times* (London), 11 May 188, 3.

18. FHB to Louise Krutch, n.d., in Burnett, "Story Maker's Notes along the Way," chap. 5, p. 15.

19. FHB to Nora Phillips, [July 1888], Department of Manuscripts and Letters, National Library of Wales.

20. Burnett, *Romantick Lady*, 172.

21. FHB to Lionel and Vivian Burnett, [1888], in Burnett, "Story Maker's Notes along the Way," chap. 3, p. 8.

22. Burnett, *Romantick Lady*, 175.

23. Oliver Wendell Holmes to FHB, 28 October 1888, Special Collections, Boston University Library, no. 1444, box 1, folder 1.

24. John Nicholas Beffel, "The Fauntleroy Plague," *Bookman: A Review of Books and Life*, March 1927–August 1927. This is the article that appeared during the planning of the Burnett Central Park memorial, causing the park commissioner's response.

25. "Effort to Stabilize the Wool Industry before Seeking Expansion," *Advertisers' Weekly*, 31 March 1928, 3. The illustration of Cedric and his grandfather bears the caption "Celebrated picture that hurt wool in favor of velvet."

26. "The Pleasure of Paragraphs," *Saturday Review*, 23 March 1889, 334–345.

27. "Mrs. Burnett Protests," *Critic*, 2 March 1889, 106–107.

28. "The Right to Privacy," *New York Times*, 15 March 1889, p. 4, col. 5.

29. *Washington Post*, 30 December 1888, 9.

30. "Mrs. Burnett Protests," 106–107.

31. FHB to Owen Lankester, [November 1888], quoted in Burnett, *Romantick Lady*, 176–177.

32. FHB to Kitty Hall (Gertrude Hall Brownell), November 1888, quoted ibid., 175–176.

33. Burnett, *Romantick Lady*, 177–178.

34. Mary Mapes Dodge to FHB, 5 January 1889, Mary Mapes Dodge Collection, Wilkinson Dodge, C0114, box 2, folder 6, Department of Rare Books and Special Collections, Princeton University Libraries.

35. See Elisabeth Marbury, *My Crystal Ball: Reminiscences* (New York: Boni and Liveright, 1932), chap. 10.

36. FHB to Emma Daniels, 16 December 1888, quoted in Burnett, *Romantick Lady*, 182–183.

37. The *Washington Post* for 28 November 1888 reported that the house she bought was at 1756 Massachusetts Avenue and was the former residence of William B. Allis.

CHAPTER 11. LIONEL

1. *Critic*, [December 1889], 282.

2. "The Lounger," *Critic*, 26 January 1889, 44–45.

3. *Washington Post*, 19 May 1889, 5. "Mrs. Frances Hodgson Burnett, just previous to her departure for England, selected a most picturesque and charming location at Sorrento as the site for a summer house for her family. The situation is one of great natural beauty, being partly covered with beautiful forest trees extending from the top of a high cliff overlooking the bay to the bench at the foot. A sweep of fine grass land extends down to the front of the lot, which is on Bay View avenue. If Mrs. Burnett's business engagements will permit her to return early in the fall, it is her intention to visit Sorrento

and arrange for the building of her cottage." It is not clear that she actually planned to build a cottage there.

4. FHB, "The Boy Who Became a Socialist," in *Giovanni and the Other* (New York: Charles Scribner's, 1892), 144–145.

5. FHB to Lionel and Vivian Burnett, [1889], in Vivian Burnett, "A Story Maker's Notes along the Way," typescript, Penny Deupree private collection, chap. 3, p. 9.

6. FHB to Owen Lankester, [summer 1889], three letters, ibid., chap. 7, p. 4.

7. "Mrs. Burnett's Power," *Boston Traveller*, 11 July 1889.

8. *Washington Post*, 1 July 1889, 4; reprinted from the *New York World*.

9. FHB, "Illustrissimo Signor Bébé," in *Giovanni and the Other*, 55.

10. Lionel Burnett to FHB, 27 June 1889, Penny Deupree private collection.

11. "Mrs. Burnett's Power," *Boston Traveller*, 11 July 1889.

12. *Critic*, 10 August 1889, 64.

13. FHB to Lionel Burnett, [summer 1889], in Burnett, "Story Maker's Notes along the Way," chap. 3, p. 10.

14. FHB to Edmund Gosse, [summer 1889], Brotherton Library, University of Leeds.

15. FHB to Owen Lankester, [summer 1889], quoted in Vivian Burnett, *The Romantick Lady (Frances Hodgson Burnett): The Life Story of an Imagination* (New York: Charles Scribner's, 1927), 188–189.

16. Lionel Burnett to FHB, 17 July 1889, Penny Deupree private collection.

17. Lionel Burnett to FHB, 19 July 1889, Penny Deupree private collection.

18. Burnett, *Romantick Lady*, 189.

19. FHB, "When He Decides," in *Before He Is Twenty: Five Perplexing Phases of the Boy Question Considered* (New York: F. H. Revell, ca. 1894). The other contributors are Robert J. Burdette, Edward Bok, Mrs. Burton Harrison, and Abby F. Hamlin Abbott.

20. FHB to Owen Lankester, [summer 1889], quoted in Burnett, *Romantick Lady*, 188.

21. FHB to Kitty Hall (Gertrude Hall Brownell), [November or December 1889], quoted ibid., 192–193.

22. Lionel Burnett to FHB, 6 September 1889, Penny Deupree private collection.

23. Lionel Burnett to Swan Burnett (he calls him P.O.D.), 6 September 1889, Penny Deupree private collection.

24. Lionel Burnett to FHB, 20 September 1889, Penny Deupree private collection.

25. *Ladies' Home Journal*, September 1889, 24.

26. Gertrude Hall Brownell, "Frances Hodgson Burnett—I," typescript biography, Hargrett Rare Book and Manuscript Collection, University of Georgia Libraries, MA 210, box 4, folder 10, p. 3.

27. FHB, "The Daughter of the Custodian," in *Giovanni and the Other*, 76–77.

28. Lionel Burnett to FHB, 29 September 1889, Penny Deupree private collection.

29. *Washington Post*, 18 April 1890, 2.

30. Lionel Burnett to FHB, 9 October 1889, Penny Deupree private collection.

31. Luisa Chiellini to Lionel Burnett, 11 October 1889, Penny Deupree private collection.

32. Ibid.

33. FHB to Kitty Hall, [November or December 1889].

34. Lionel Burnett to FHB, 9 December 1889, Penny Deupree private collection.

35. Lionel Burnett to FHB, 12 January 1890, Penny Deupree private collection.

36. Vivian Burnett to FHB, 24 February 1890, Penny Deupree private collection.

37. Lionel Burnett to FHB, 26 February 1890, Penny Deupree private collection.

38. FHB to Lionel Burnett, 28 March 1890, Penny Deupree private collection.

39. FHB to Lionel Burnett, 29 March 1890, Penny Deupree private collection.

40. Lionel Burnett to FHB, 12 April 1890, Penny Deupree private collection.

41. FHB, "A Pretty Roman Beggar," in *Giovanni and the Other*, 88.

42. *Washington Post*, 18 April 1890, 2.

43. Ibid. A script of the play, perhaps for the copyright performance, exists in the British Library. It takes place in Paris and bears little resemblance to the original story.

44. FHB to Mr. Scribner, [late July 1890; received 4 August 1890], Scribner C0101, box 24, folder 8, Department of Rare Books and Special Collections, Princeton University Libraries.

45. FHB to Euphemia Macfarlane, [spring or summer 1890], in Burnett, "A Story Maker's Notes along the Way," chap. 3, p. 15.

46. Vivian Burnett to Swan Burnett, [August 1890], Penny Deupree private collection.

47. FHB, "What Use Is a Poet?" in *Giovanni and the Other*, 135.

48. Ibid., 138.

49. FHB to Vivian Burnett, [late October 1890], Penny Deupree private collection.

50. FHB to Lionel Burnett, 3 October 1890, Penny Deupree private collection.

51. FHB to Lionel Burnett, 7 October 1890, Penny Deupree private collection.

52. FHB to DeVin Finckel, [1890], in Burnett, "Story Maker's Notes along the Way," chap. 3, p. 18.

53. FHB to Lionel Burnett, 11 October 1890, Penny Deupree private collection.

54. FHB to Lionel Burnett, 13 October 1890, Penny Deupree private collection.

55. FHB to Vivian Burnett, [late October 1890], Penny Deupree private collection.

56. FHB, [1890], Overbury Collection, Barnard College.

57. FHB, "His Friend," quoted in Burnett, *Romantick Lady*, 205.

58. FHB to her cousin Emma Daniels, n.d., quoted ibid., 211–212.

59. There is some confusion about where Lionel is buried. Since there is no St. Germain cemetery in Paris, it is likely that his grave is in St. Germain-des-Près.

60. Brownell, "Frances Hodgson Burnett—I," 10.

CHAPTER 12. DRURY LANE

1. FHB, "To Her Boy in the Fair, Far Country," in Vivian Burnett, "A Story Maker's Notes along the Way," typescript, Penny Deupree private collection, chap. 8, p. 14.

2. FHB, 6 March 1891, ibid., p. 2.

3. Ibid.

4. FHB, 7 March 1891, ibid., p. 3.

5. FHB, 11 March 1891, ibid., p. 5.

6. FHB, 12 March 1891, ibid., p. 6.

7. FHB, 6 March 1891, ibid., p. 2.

8. FHB, 11 March 1891, ibid., p. 5.

9. FHB to DeVin Finckel, [1891], ibid., chap. 3, pp. 17–19.

10. *Washington Post*, 8 December 1890; reprint, *New York Times*, 10 December 1890.

11. FHB to Swan Burnett, 29 March 1891, Penny Deupree private collection.

12. FHB to Vivian Burnett, 10 March 1891, Penny Deupree private collection.

13. FHB to Vivian Burnett, 6 September 1891, Penny Deupree private collection.

14. FHB, 12 March 1891.

15. FHB, 20 September 1891, in Burnett, "Story Maker's Notes along the Way," chap. 8, p. 11.

16. FHB, 8 and 10 March [1891], ibid., pp. 3–4.

17. FHB, Tuesday, [September 1891?], ibid., p. 12.

18. Ibid., p. 13.

19. FHB, [April 1891], ibid., p. 7.

20. Ibid., p. 8.

21. Gertrude Hall Brownell, "Frances Hodgson Burnett—I," typescript biography, Hargrett Rare Book and Manuscript Collection, University of Georgia Libraries, MA 210, box 4, folder 10, p. 10.

22. FHB, Tuesday, [1891], in Burnett, "Story Maker's Notes along the Way," chap. 8, p. 9.

23. FHB, 20 September 1891.

24. "The Drury Lane Boys' Club," written by FHB, contains all this information. It was published by Vivian Burnett on his home printing press in 1892 and also appeared in *Scribner's Monthly* in 1892.

25. Victoria Mary, duchess of Teck, to FHB, 19 May 1891, Special Collections, Boston University Library, no. 1444, box 1, folder 1.

26. FHB, [1892], in Burnett, "Story Maker's Notes along the Way," chap. 8, p. 11.

27. Playbill for *Nixie*, 11 April 1890.

28. FHB to Kitty Hall (Gertrude Hall Brownell), 20 November 1891, in Vivian Burnett, *The Romantick Lady (Frances Hodgson Burnett): The Life Story of an Imagination* (New York: Charles Scribner's, 1927), 222.

29. FHB to Vivian Burnett, 29 November 1891, Penny Deupree private collection.

30. "Mrs. Burnett at Work Again," *New York Times*, 24 November 1891.

31. FHB to Vivian Burnett, 31 October 1891 [she mistakenly writes 1890 on the letter], Penny Deupree private collection.

32. FHB to Vivian Burnett, 23 November 1891, Penny Deupree private collection.

33. FHB to Kitty Hall (Gertrude Hall Brownell), 20 November 1891, quoted in Burnett, *Romantick Lady*, 221–222.

34. FHB to Vivian Burnett, 5 [?] December 1891, Penny Deupree private collection.

35. FHB to Vivian Burnett, Monday, [December 1891], Penny Deupree private collection.

36. FHB to Vivian Burnett, [February 1892], Penny Deupree private collection.

CHAPTER 13. "GREAT LONDON ROARS BELOW"

1. "Talk with Mrs. Burnett: Her Literary Work and Social Life in London," *New York Times*, 13 March 1892, 3.

2. FHB, "To Her Boy in the Fair, Far Country," in Vivian Burnett, "A Story Maker's Notes along the Way," typescript, Penny Deupree private collection, chap. 8, pp. 13–14.

3. FHB, "As Fairy God-Mother," ibid., chap. 16, p. 2.

4. FHB to Ernest Fahnestock, 26 March [1892], Penny Deupree private collection.

5. FHB, 2 March [1892], in Burnett, "Story Maker's Notes along the Way," chap. 8, p. 18.

6. FHB, Sunday [1892], ibid., p. 17.

7. FHB, Tuesday [1892], ibid., p. 19.

8. "A Column for Women," *Brooklyn Eagle*, 12 February 1898, 11.

9. *Athenaeum*, 16 April 1892, 499.

10. FHB to Edward Burlingame, [March or April 1892], Scribner C0101, box 23, folder 4, Department of Rare Books and Special Collections, Princeton University Libraries.

11. FHB to Edward Burlingame, [April 1892], Scribner C0101, box 23, folder 4, Department of Rare Books and Special Collections, Princeton University Libraries.

12. FHB to Edward Burlingame, 18 May 1892, Scribner C0101, box 23, folder 3, Department of Rare Books and Special Collections, Princeton University Libraries.

13. FHB, "The Child of This Century," in Burnett, "A Story Maker's Notes along the Way," chap. 3, pp. 6–7.

14. FHB, "To Her Boy in the Fair, Far Country," 13.

15. Edward Burlingame to Scribner's, 1 June 1892, Scribner C0101, box 23, folder 3, Department of Rare Books and Special Collections, Princeton University Libraries.

16. FHB to Edward Burlingame, 4 June 1892, Scribner C0101, box 23, folder 3, Department of Rare Books and Special Collections, Princeton University Libraries.

17. FHB, "To Her Boy in the Fair, Far Country," 13–14.

18. FHB to Edward Burlingame, 26 July 1892, Scribner C0101, box 23, folder 3, Department of Rare Books and Special Collections, Princeton University Libraries.

19. Vivian Burnett to Swan Burnett, 8 July 1892, Penny Deupree private collection.

20. FHB to Vivian Burnett, [1892], Penny Deupree private collection.

21. See Sir Francis Dowley Burnand to FHB, 11 December 1892, no. 1444, box 1, folder 1, Boston University Library Special Collections; and FHB to Edward Burlingame, 19 January 1893, Scribner C0101, box 23, folder 3, Department of Rare Books and Special Collections, Princeton University Libraries.

22. Delia T. Davis, "The Romance of a Young Artist," *Illustrated American*, 28 August 1897, 279–280. See also "Mrs. Burnett as a Patron of Art," in "General Gossip of Authors and Writers," *Current Literature*, November 1897, 404–405.

23. Davis, "Romance of a Young Artist," 279–280. See also "Mrs. Burnett as a Patron of Art," 404–405.

24. FHB, Sunday [December 1892], in Burnett, "Story Maker's Notes along the Way," chap. 8, p. 15.

25. FHB, Tuesday [December 1892], ibid., p. 14.

26. FHB to Miss Flaske [?], 25 February 1893, uncatalogued letter, Department of Special Collections, University of Tennessee at Knoxville Library.

27. "The Women's Building at the 1893 Exposition: Architecture, Statuary, Murals" (http://faculty.pittstate.edu/~knichols/cassatt5.html).

28. "The Book of the Fair/Woman's Department," in "World's Columbian Exposition" (http://columbus.gl.iit.edu/bookfair/ch11.html).

29. FHB to Scribner's, 4 May 1893, Scribner C0101, box 23, folder 3, Department of Rare Books and Special Collections, Princeton University Libraries.

30. List of the books in the library of the Woman's Building, World's Columbian Exposition, 1893, in "A Celebration of Women Writers" (http://digital.library.upenn.edu/women/clarke/library/library.html).

31. Eleanor Robson Belmont, *The Fabric of Memory* (New York: Arno Press, 1980), 67.

32. FHB, "Snatches and Remainders," in Burnett, "A Story Maker's Notes along the Way," chap. 19, p. 8.

33. Vivian Burnett to FHB, 11 September 1893, Penny Deupree private collection.

34. FHB to Kitty Hall (Gertrude Hall Brownell), 6 September 1893," in Burnett, "Story Maker's Notes along the Way," chap. 9, p. 3.

35. FHB to Ernest Fahnestock, 26 January 1894, Penny Deupree private collection.

36. FHB to Edward Burlingame, 1 May 1894, Scribner Co101, box 23, folder 3, Department of Rare Books and Special Collections, Princeton University Libraries.

37. FHB, preliminary study for *My Robin,* in Burnett, "A Story Maker's Notes along the Way," chap. 7, pp. 7–8, 9–10.

CHAPTER 14. THE NEW WOMAN

1. Vivian Burnett to FHB, 29 May 1894, Penny Deupree private collection.

2. FHB to Frank and Edith Jordan, Tuesday, [May 1894], Penny Deupree private collection.

3. Vivian Burnett to FHB, 1 July 1894, Penny Deupree private collection.

4. Ibid.

5. Israel Zangwill to FHB, 24 August 1894, Special Collections, Boston University Library, no. 1444, box 1, folder 1.

6. FHB, 13 August 1894, in Vivian Burnett, "Story Maker's Notes along the Way," typescript, Penny Deupree private collection, chap. 8, p. 21.

7. FHB, 28 August 1894, ibid.

8. "At the Bedside of Her Son," *Washington Post,* 25 August 1894, 5.

9. FHB, 25 September 1894, in Burnett, "Story Maker's Notes along the Way," chap. 8, p. 23.

10. FHB, 28 August 1894, ibid., p. 22.

11. FHB to Vivian Burnett, October 1894, Penny Deupree private collection.

12. FHB to Vivian Burnett, 8 January 1895, Penny Deupree private collection.

13. Ibid.

14. FHB to Vivian Burnett, 19 February 1897, Penny Deupree private collection.

15. FHB to Vivian Burnett, [January or February 1895], Penny Deupree private collection.

16. Elizabeth Elliot, "Smiling Memories of Mrs. Burnett," *Literary Digest International Book Review,* [1925?], 160–161.

17. FHB to Vivian Burnett, 8 January 1895.

18. Edward L. Burlingame to Charles Scribner, 23 April 1895, Scribner Co101, author files, box 133, folder 8, Department of Rare Books and Special Collections, Princeton University Libraries.

19. FHB to Mrs. Edmund Gosse, [26 April] 1895, Cambridge University Library, Add 7022, Letters of Edmund Gosse, vol. 4, 1891–95, 120.

20. FHB to Vivian Burnett, 14 March 1895, Penny Deupree private collection.

21. FHB to Vivian Burnett, 8 January 1895.

22. FHB to Israel Zangwill, n.d., quoted in Vivian Burnett, *The Romantick Lady (Frances Hodgson Burnett): The Life Story of an Imagination* (New York: Charles Scribner's, 1927), 249–250.

23. FHB to Vivian Burnett, 29 March 1895, Penny Deupree private collection.

24. Vivian Burnett to FHB, 25 April 1895, Penny Deupree private collection.

25. FHB to Vivian Burnett, 5 May 1895, Penny Deupree private collection.

26. "A Chat with Frances Hodgson Burnett," *Illustrated American,* 28 March 1896, 404–405.

27. FHB to Vivian Burnett, 4 April 1895, Penny Deupree private collection.

28. FHB to Vivian Burnett, 5 May 1895.

29. Mary Simmons [Mrs. G. W. Simmons] to Edith Jordan, 31 December 1924, Penny Deupree private collection.

30. Stephen Townesend to Scribner's, 22 October [1895], Scribner C0101, box 23, folder 5, Department of Rare Books and Special Collections, Princeton University Libraries.

31. FHB to Ernest Fahnestock, 10 November 1895, Penny Deupree private collection.

32. FHB to Vivian Burnett, 2 November 1895, Penny Deupree private collection.

33. FHB to Vivian Burnett, 18 January 1896, Penny Deupree private collection.

34. Vivian Burnett to FHB, 3 November 1895, Penny Deupree private collection.

35. Vivian Burnett to FHB, 25 April 1895.

36. FHB to Vivian Burnett, 18 January 1896.

37. "Dr. Burnett's Positive Denial," *Washington Post*, 12 September 1895, 3.

38. "Dr. Burnett's Strong Denial," *New York Times*, 13 September 1895.

39. FHB to Vivian Burnett, 24 November 1895, Penny Deupree private collection.

40. Israel Zangwill to FHB, 30 November 1895, Special Collections, Boston University Library, no. 1444, box 1, folder 1.

41. FHB to Vivian Burnett, 13 December 1895, Penny Deupree private collection.

42. *The Queen*, as quoted in Burnett, *Romantick Lady*, 266–268.

43. Stephen Townesend to Scribner's, 5 February 1896, Scribner C0101, box 24, folder 8, Department of Rare Books and Special Collections, Princeton University Libraries.

44. Vivian Burnett to FHB, [January 1896], Penny Deupree private collection.

45. "A Speech by Mrs. Burnett," *New York Times*, 16 August 1896, p. 23, col. 6; also "Guests of the English Authors, A Dinner to Mrs. Burnett," *Critic*, [August?] 1896; both reprinted from the London *Daily Chronicle*, 17 July 1896.

46. FHB to Vivian Burnett, [March 1896], Penny Deupree private collection.

47. All these quotations are from the script of *A Lady of Quality* in the Lord Chamberlain's Play Collection, British Library.

48. Marie A. Belloc, "Mrs. Hodgson Burnett. A Famous Authoress at Home," *Idler* 9 (1896): 645–648.

CHAPTER 15. LADIES OF QUALITY

1. FHB to Vivian Burnett, 17 November 1895, Penny Deupree private collection.

2. FHB to Vivian Burnett, 1 December 1895, Penny Deupree private collection.

3. FHB to Vivian Burnett, 27 September 1895, Penny Deupree private collection.

4. Israel Zangwill to FHB, 8 September 1895, Special Collections, Boston University Library, no. 1444, box 1, folder 1.

5. Henry James to FHB, n.d., quoted in Vivian Burnett, *The Romantick Lady (Frances Hodgson Burnett): The Life Story of an Imagination* (New York: Charles Scribner's, 1927), 251.

6. "Noticeable Books: A Lady of Quality," *Nineteenth Century*, November 1896, 771–772.

7. "A Servants' Hall Vision," *Saturday Review*, 10 June 1896, 627.

8. FHB to Vivian Burnett, 15 March 1896, Penny Deupree private collection.

9. FHB to Vivian Burnett, 30 March 1896, Penny Deupree private collection.

10. FHB to Vivian Burnett, 1 December 1895.

11. FHB to Kitty Hall (Gertrude Hall Brownell), 2 January 1896, quoted in Burnett, *Romantick Lady*, 271.

12. Earl of Crewe to FHB, 8 February 1896, Special Collections, Boston University Library, no. 1444, box 1, folder 1.

13. Henry James to FHB, quoted in Burnett, *Romantick Lady*, 250.

14. Henry James to FHB, ibid., 240. The letters from James to her are housed in the Houghton Library at Harvard University.

15. FHB to Vivian Burnett, 26 April 1896, Penny Deupree private collection.

16. Vivian Burnett to FHB, 23 May 1896, Penny Deupree private collection.

17. FHB to Vivian Burnett, [May 1896], Penny Deupree private collection.

18. FHB to Vivian Burnett, 29 May 1896, Penny Deupree private collection.

19. Vivian Burnett to FHB, [21] August 1896, Penny Deupree private collection.

20. FHB to Vivian Burnett, [early September 1896], Penny Deupree private collection.

21. FHB to Douglas Sladen, 19 November 1896, Douglas Sladen Papers, London Borough of Richmond upon Thames Library, 82.

22. "Mrs. Burnett Returns Home," *New York Times*, 29 November 1896, p. 11, col. 5.

23. FHB to Vivian Burnett, 10 December 1896, Penny Deupree private collection.

24. FHB to Vivian Burnett, 27 February 1897, Penny Deupree private collection.

25. FHB to Vivian Burnett, 1 January 1897, Penny Deupree private collection.

26. FHB to Vivian Burnett, [January 1897], Penny Deupree private collection.

27. "Theatrical Chat," *Washington Post*, 22 April 1897, 7.

28. "Scenes from Frances Hodgson Burnett and George Fleming's New Play 'The First Gentleman of Europe," *Harper's Weekly*, 13 February 1897; "Player Folk," *Leslie's Weekly*, 4 March 1897; "The Drama: 'The First Gentleman of Europe,'" *Critic*, 30 January 1897.

29. FHB poem to Vivian Burnett, 4–5 April 1897, Penny Deupree private collection.

30. FHB to Vivian Burnett, 4 April 1897, Penny Deupree private collection.

31. FHB to Vivian Burnett, 25 June 1897, Penny Deupree private collection.

32. FHB to Vivian Burnett, 4 April 1897.

33. FHB to Vivian Burnett, 10 August 1897, Penny Deupree private collection.

34. FHB to Vivian Burnett, 3 May 1898, Penny Deupree private collection.

35. FHB to Vivian Burnett, [May 1897], Penny Deupree private collection.

36. Stephen Townesend to Edward Burlingame, 1 October [1897], Scribner C0101, box 23, folder 5, Department of Rare Books and Special Collections, Princeton University Libraries.

37. "Thanks to Julia Arthur," *New York Times*, 19 October 1897, 7.

38. FHB to Vivian Burnett, postmarked 27 October 1897, Penny Deupree private collection.

39. "Mrs. Burnett to Marry Her Stage Manager," *New York Telegraph*, 25 May 1898. One must take this story, as with many others about her in the press, with a pinch of salt. Among other things, it claims she is marrying Stephen only weeks after her divorce from Swan. However, Stephen's temper is well-enough documented for the story to ring true.

40. FHB to Vivian Burnett, postmarked 7 November 1897, Penny Deupree private collection.

41. "A New Stage Heroine," *New York Times*, 2 November 1897; "The Drama. 'A Lady of Quality,'" *Critic*, November 1897; "The Drama," *New York Times*, 7 November

1897, SM8.

42. "Mrs. Burnett on 'A Lady of Quality,'" *Critic*, December 1897, 346–347.

43. "At the New York Theatres. Saturday Even, November 19—Wallack's Theatre: Mrs. Frances Hodgson Burnett's 'A Lady of Quality,'" *Forum* 26: 752–753.

44. FHB to Vivian Burnett, 6 December 1897, Penny Deupree private collection.

45. See "'The Lady of Quality' Retold," *Public Opinion*, 2 December 1897, which says that "not one aspect of the first telling of the story has been changed."

46. "The Literary Women of Washington," *Chautauquan* 27 (September 1898): 582.

CHAPTER 16. MAYTHAM HALL

1. "Personal Mention," *Brooklyn Eagle*, 11 September 1895, 11.

2. "Mrs. Burnett Seeks Divorce," *New York Herald*, 20 March 1898.

3. "London Literary Letters," *New York Times*, 1 October 1898, 17.

4. "A Chapter in Her Life: Frances Hodgson Burnett Sues for Absolute Divorce," *Washington Post*, 20 March 1898.

5. Ibid.

6. FHB to Vivian Burnett, 28 February 1898, Penny Deupree private collection.

7. "Divorce for Mrs. Burnett," *Washington Post*, 11 May 1898, 12.

8. FHB to Vivian Burnett, 28 February 1898.

9. FHB to Vivian Burnett, 22 July 1898, Penny Deupree private collection.

10. FHB to Vivian Burnett, 10 June 1898, Penny Deupree private collection.

11. FHB to Vivian Burnett, 22 July 1898.

12. FHB to Vivian Burnett, 28 July 1898, Penny Deupree private collection.

13. FHB to Edith Jordan, [1 November 1898], Penny Deupree private collection.

14. Vivian Burnett, "A Story Maker's Notes along the Way," typescript, Penny Deupree private collection, chap. 4, p. 11.

15. FHB to Edith Jordan, 6 November [1898], Penny Deupree private collection.

16. FHB to Edith Jordan, [3 November 1898], Penny Deupree private collection.

17. FHB to Edith Jordan, 6 November [1898].

18. Ibid. FHB wrote the same letter, no doubt copied, to Annie Russell also (New York Public Library).

19. FHB to Edith Jordan, 1 February [1899], Penny Deupree private collection.

20. FHB to Edith Jordan, 6 November [1898]. The letters from Frances to Edith about the friendship with James, as well as James's letters to Frances, dispel the notion that James somehow disliked and avoided her. However, Frances's reflect her own take on things, in which she was anxious to be associated with the great man, and James's are written in an exaggeratedly friendly style. It may be that he preferred her company on paper.

21. FHB to Edith Jordan, 23 November [1898], Penny Deupree private collection.

22. Ella Hepworth Dixon, quoted in Ann Thwaite, *Waiting for the Party, the Life of Frances Hodgson Burnett* (reprint, Boston: David R. Godine, 1991; London: Faber & Faber, 1991), 187.

23. See Thwaite, *Waiting for the Party*, 78–79 and 184–187; and Ella Hepworth Dixon, *"As I Knew Them": Sketches of People I Have Met on the Way* (London: Hutchinson, 1930).

24. FHB to Vivian Burnett, 5 June 1898, Penny Deupree private collection.

25. FHB to Edith Jordan, 12 December [1898], Penny Deupree private collection.

26. FHB to Edith Jordan, [January 1899], Penny Deupree private collection.

27. "'A Lady of Quality' in London," *Washington Post*, 9 March 1899, 7.

28. "Drama. The Week. Comedy [Theatre]—'A Lady of Quality,' a Play in Five Acts. By Frances Hodgson Burnett and Stephen Townsend [*sic*]," *Athenaeum*, 18 March 1899, 347.

29. FHB to Edith Jordan, [March 1899], Penny Deupree private collection.

30. FHB to Frank Jordan, 22 March 1899, Penny Deupree private collection.

31. "Drama. The Week. Comedy [Theatre]—'A Lady of Quality,'" 347.

32. FHB to Edith Jordan, [March 1899].

33. Vivian Burnett to FHB, 26 March 1899, Penny Deupree private collection.

34. "Mrs. Burnett's New Story: A Beautiful One with a Long Title," *New York Times*, 2 December 1899; "Topics of the Week," *New York Times*, 14 October 1899; "The DeWilloughby Claim," *New York Times*, 16 December 1899.

35. "Sketch: Frances Hodgson Burnett," *Harper's Bazar*, 24 February 1900, 159–160.

36. FHB to Annie Russell, 10 September 1899, Annie Russell Papers, New York Public Library.

37. FHB to Kitty Hall (Gertrude Hall Brownell), 13 November 1899, quoted in Vivian Burnett, *The Romantick Lady (Frances Hodgson Burnett): The Life Story of an Imagination* (New York: Charles Scribner's, 1927), 296.

38. FHB to Kitty Hall, 22 December 1899, ibid., 297.

39. "Social Whirl Is Slackened," *Brooklyn Eagle*, 4 March 1900, 37.

CHAPTER 17. STEPHEN

1. FHB to Edith Jordan, 22 March 1900, Penny Deupree private collection.

2. "Love's Afternoon in the Life of Little Lord Fauntleroy's Mamma," *New York Journal and Advertiser*, 25 March 1900. See also *New York Times*, 15 March 1900, 1; *Daily News*, 16 March 1900.

3. "Famous Storyteller. Side Lights on Marriage of Frances Hodgson Burnett. Did Not Wed Private Secretary," *Washington Post*, 8 April 1900, 22.

4. "A Doctor in the Family," *Brooklyn Eagle*, 17 April 1900; reprinted from *Cleveland Plain Dealer*.

5. "Famous Storyteller," 22.

6. FHB to Edith Jordan, 22 March 1900.

7. FHB to Edith Jordan, 20 May 1900, Penny Deupree private collection. See also "London Mad With Joy. Hears of Mafeking's Relief," *Chicago Record*, 19 May 1900, for an account of the British frenzy over this victory. Also on the Web at http://www.scoutingarchives.com/np/bp000519.jpg.

8. FHB to Katherine Thomas, 24 May 1900, Special Collections, University of Virginia Library, MSS 6817–d. These remarks cancel out those of Angus Wilson in 1974: "her second husband, an actor 10 years younger, married her for her money (surely, though Mrs. Thwaite doesn't say so, he must have been homosexual—Frances Burnett seemed fated to become what later generations would have called a queen's moll). I suspect that like many Edwardian women she wanted romance, even affairs, but not really sex" ("Fauntleroy's Creator," *Observer*, 2 June 1974). Although there is no way to know more about Stephen's sexual orientation, his repeated pleas for her to love him and her refusal to do so certainly indicate that she wasn't in the mood for romance with him.

9. FHB to Katherine Thomas, 24 May 1900.

10. FHB to Edith Jordan, 30 May 1900, Penny Deupree private collection.

11. Ibid.

12. E. Kenneth Campbell to Herbert Hodgson, 1 August 1900, Katherine P. Hodgson private collection.

13. FHB to Katherine Thomas, 24 May 1900.

14. FHB to Edith Jordan, 30 May 1900.

15. Ella Hepworth Dixon, "Frances Hodgson Burnett," in *"As I Knew Them": Sketches of People I Have Met on the Way* (London: Hutchinson, 1930), 98.

16. FHB to Richard Watson Gilder, 10 August 1900 [mailed 17 August], Century Collection, New York Public Library.

17. "'Little Lord Fauntleroy' a Reporter," *New York Times*, 20 January 1901, 7.

18. FHB to Vivian Burnett, 28 September 1900, Penny Deupree private collection.

19. Vivian Burnett to FHB, 9 October 1900, Penny Deupree private collection.

20. "Famous Storyteller," 22.

21. FHB to Vivian Burnett, 25 October 1900, Penny Deupree private collection.

22. FHB to Vivian Burnett, 25 November 1900, Penny Deupree private collection.

23. FHB to Vivian Burnett, 16 December 1900, Penny Deupree private collection.

24. FHB to Richard Watson Gilder, 4 December 1900, Gilder Collection, New York Public Library.

25. "Mrs. Burnett: A Visit to Her Home in London," *New York Times*, 15 June 1901.

26. "A Dog's Tale," *New York Times*, 21 September 1901.

27. "Dogs of Noted Americans," *Saint Nicholas*, June 1888, 600.

28. David Murray to FHB, 13 June 1899, Special Collections, Boston University Library, no. 1444, box 1, folder 1.

29. "Mrs. Burnett: A Visit to Her Home in London."

30. FHB, "One Woman of the Nineteenth Century," typescript, New York Public Library, 62M56, p. 6.

31. FHB to Richard Watson Gilder, 8 May 1901, Century Collection.

32. Review of *The Making of a Marchioness*, *New York Times Book Review*, 12 October 1901, BR4.

33. FHB to Richard Watson Gilder, 8 May 1901.

34. FHB, "One Woman of the Nineteenth Century," typescript, New York Public Library, 62 M 56, pp. 3 and 7.

35. FHB to Richard Watson Gilder, 31 March 1901, Century Collection.

36. "Mrs. Frances Hodgson Burnett (Mrs. Stephen Townsend [*sic*]) has transferred her publishing business, for the time being, from Messrs Scribner to the F. A. Stokes Co," in "The Lounger," *Critic*, June 1901, 499.

37. "Mrs. Frances Hodgson Burnett at Home. A Visit to Maytham Hall, Rolvenden, Kent," *Critic*, March 1902, 230–234.

38. Ann Thwaite, *Waiting for the Party: The Life of Frances Hodgson Burnett* (reprint, Boston: David R. Godine, 1991; London: Secker and Warburg, 1974), 193.

39. FHB to Vivian Burnett, 27 [July] 1901, Penny Deupree private collection.

CHAPTER 18. RECOVERY AND NEW THOUGHTS

1. FHB to Vivian Burnett, 25 June 1904, Penny Deupree private collection.

2. "Second Marriage Is Also a Failure," *New York Times*? [11 January 1902].

3. "Not to Get a Divorce," *Washington Post*, 12 January 1902, 6.

4. FHB to Vivian Burnett, [January 1902], Penny Deupree private collection.

5. Ibid.

6. Vivian Burnett to FHB, 11 May 1902, Penny Deupree private collection.

7. Vivian Burnett to FHB, 24 June 1902, Penny Deupree private collection.

8. Vivian Burnett to FHB, 29 June 1902, Penny Deupree private collection.

9. FHB to Mr. Dickey, 26 November 1902, Dickey MSS, Manuscripts Department, Lilly Library, Indiana University.

10. FHB to Vivian Burnett, n.d., in Vivian Burnett, "A Story Maker's Notes along the Way," typescript, Penny Deupree private collection, chap. 17, p. 4.

11. FHB to Edward Burlingame, 17 July 1903, Scribner C0101, box 23, folder 6, Department of Rare Books and Special Collections, Princeton University Libraries.

12. "Mrs. Burnett's New Play," *New York Times*, 26 January 1904, 5.

13. "Mrs. Frances Hodgson Burnett, Novelist & Dramatist Says That It Is Fascinating to Write Plays, But That It Is Bitterly Disappointing to See Them Acted," *New York Herald*, 24 January 1904.

14. FHB to Vivian Burnett, 16 March 1904, Penny Deupree private collection.

15. FHB, "The Story of the Lost Fairy Book," in Frances Browne, *Granny's Wonderful Chair* (New York: McClure, Phillips, 1904), xxxii.

16. FHB to Vivian Burnett, 22 August 1904, Penny Deupree private collection.

17. FHB to Vivian Burnett, 22 September 1904, Penny Deupree private collection.

18. FHB to Vivian Burnett, 19 August 1904, Penny Deupree private collection.

19. Gertrude Hall Brownell, "Frances Hodgson Burnett—I," typescript biography, Hargrett Rare Book and Manuscript Collection, University of Georgia Libraries, MA 210, box 4, folder 10, p. 6.

20. Marion Percival Smith to FHB, 4 September 1904, Special Collections, Boston University Library, no. 1444, box 1, folder 1.

21. FHB to Vivian Burnett, 17 October 1904, Penny Deupree private collection.

22. I am grateful to Jack Neely for this information on John George Hodgson.

23. FHB to Vivian Burnett, 14 November 1904, Penny Deupree private collection.

24. Ibid.

25. FHB, "Christmas in the Fog," a "Romantick Lady" column, in *Good Housekeeping*, December 1914, 661–671.

26. FHB to Edward Burlingame, 10 July 1905, Scribner C0101, box 23, folder 6, Department of Rare Books and Special Collections, Princeton University Libraries.

27. FHB to Vivian Burnett, n.d., in Burnett, "A Story Maker's Notes along the Way," chap. 17, p. 6.

28. Ibid., 6–7.

29. For more on New Thought, see http://religiousmovements.lib.virginia.edu/nrms/Newthoug.html.

30. FHB, *The Dawn of a To-Morrow* (New York: Charles Scribner's, 1906), 91.

31. See, e.g., "'There is No Devil,'" Asserts Mrs. Frances Hodgson Burnett," *Kansas City Post*, [31 October?] 1910; "'Hell is Worse Than Archaic, It's Rococo' Declares Mrs. Frances Hodgson Burnett," *New Jersey Evening World*, 26 November 1910. The story was picked up by the wire services after appearing in a Chicago newspaper article.

32. FHB to Archer Fahnestock, n.d., in Burnett, "Story Maker's Notes along the Way," chap. 17, p. 8.

33. "Mrs. Frances Hodgson Burnett Finds a New Field for Her Pen," *New York Times*, 20 May 1906.

34. FHB, *The Troubles of Queen Silver-Bell* (New York: Derrydale Books, 1992), 22–26.

35. Laurence Alma Tadema, "To My Mother," n.d., Bodleian Library, Oxford University, MS Eng.misc.c.790, 88.

36. FHB to Laurence Alma Tadema, 30 May 1905, Bodleian Library, MS Eng.misc. c.790 (fols. 5–31).

37. Laurence Alma Tadema, "Mrs. Hodgson Burnett and Great Maytham," letter to the editor, *Times* (London), 15 August 1936, 6.

38. FHB to Laurence Alma Tadema, [January 1906], Bodleian Library, MS Eng. misc.c.790 (fols 5–31).

39. "Mrs. Frances Hodgson Burnett. The Authoress of 'Little Lord Fauntleroy' Has Something to Say About Children and Children's Books," *Brooklyn Eagle*, 3 December 1906.

40. FHB to Vivian Burnett, 18 January 1906, Penny Deupree private collection.

41. FHB to Vivian Burnett, [April 1906], Penny Deupree private collection.

42. Ibid.

43. FHB to Vivian Burnett, 28 July 1906, Penny Deupree private collection.

44. FHB to Vivian Burnett, 25 August 1906, Penny Deupree private collection.

45. FHB to Vivian Burnett, 26 April 1906, Penny Deupree private collection.

46. FHB to Richard Watson Gilder, 10 August 1900, Century Collection, New York Public Library.

47. FHB, *The Shuttle* (New York: Frederick A. Stokes, 1907), 39.

48. FHB to Richard Watson Gilder, 11 September 1900, Century Collection.

49. FHB to Vivian Burnett, 17 February 1901, Penny Deupree private collection.

50. Vivian Burnett to FHB, 10 August 1904, Penny Deupree private collection.

51. FHB to Vivian Burnett, 4 November 1906, Penny Deupree private collection.

52. FHB to Vivian Burnett, [January 1907], Penny Deupree private collection.

53. FHB to Vivian Burnett, 11 July 1906, Penny Deupree private collection.

54. FHB, *Shuttle*, 436.

55. "Mrs. Burnett Robbed. Authoress Loses Silverware Valued at $14,000. Famous English Plate Gone. Writer of 'Little Lord Fauntleroy' on Return Home Finds House Looted. Convinced that It Was an 'Inside Job,' but Unable to Recover her Property She Appeals to New York Police," *Washington Post*, 18 October 1907, 12. See also "Get Mrs Burnett's Silver. Noted Author Victim of Thieves, Who Take Nearly All of Collection Valued at Over $14,000," *Boston Globe*, 17 October 1907.

CHAPTER 19. THE END OF AN ERA

1. Edith Jordan to Laurence Alma Tadema, [30 December 1906], Bodleian Library, Oxford University, MS Eng.misc.c.790.

2. FHB to Vivian Burnett, 4 November 1906, Penny Deupree private collection.

3. FHB to Vivian Burnett, 14 October 1906, Penny Deupree private collection.

4. FHB to Mrs. David Thompson, 8 June 1908, Carson Newman College.

5. FHB to Vivian Burnett, 16 February 1907, Penny Deupree private collection.

6. FHB to Laurence Alma Tadema, 20 September 1907, Bodleian Library.

7. FHB to Laurence Alma Tadema, 18 October 1907, Bodleian Library.

8. FHB to Laurence Alma Tadema, 4 July 1907, Bodleian Library.

9. To FHB from the Maytham servants, 21 March 1907, Special Collections, Boston University Library, no. 1444, box 1, folder 1.

10. FHB to Eleanor Robson, n.d., Spec. MS Coll. Belmont, Special Collections, Columbia University Libraries.

11. Eleanor Robson Belmont, *The Fabric of Memory* (New York: Arno Press, 1980), 67.

12. FHB to Eleanor Robson [Belmont], 19 May 1908, Spec. MS Coll. Belmont.

13. There is some confusion about when she became an American citizen. Letters seem to indicate that she took out papers in 1908 when she acquired the Plandome property. Ann Thwaite and others state that she became a citizen in 1905, but the only evidence I find for that date is the ship's manifest for her trip to America that year, which lists her as an American citizen. She may have become naturalized that year, but it is also possible that she took out the papers in 1905 and declared herself American, but did not become official until several years later. Will Dennis's concern about her status suggests either that she acquired citizenship in 1908 or that, as an American citizen still married to a British citizen, her ability to own property in New York was compromised.

14. Gertrude Hall Brownell, "Frances Hodgson Burnett—I," typescript biography, Hargrett Rare Book and Manuscript Collection, University of Georgia Libraries, MA 210, box 4, folder 10, p. 7.

15. FHB to Edith Jordan, 5 July 1908, Penny Deupree private collection.

16. FHB to "family," 24 June [1908], Penny Deupree private collection.

17. *Book Buyer*, [May 1900?], 12–13.

18. FHB to Vivian Burnett, [July 1908], Penny Deupree private collection.

19. FHB to Vivian Burnett, 20 July 1908, Penny Deupree private collection.

20. FHB to Vivian Burnett, 9 September 1908, Penny Deupree private collection.

21. FHB to Edith Jordan, 25 September 1908, Penny Deupree private collection.

22. FHB to Edith Jordan, 3 October 1908, Penny Deupree private collection.

23. FHB to Vivian Burnett, 29 October 1908, Penny Deupree private collection.

24. FHB to Edith Jordan, 2 November 1908, Penny Deupree private collection.

25. FHB to Eleanor Robson [Belmont], n.d., Columbia University Libraries.

26. Louis V. De Foe, "The New Thought Mixed with Fantasy Is Served in Guise of Melodrama," *New York World*, 31 January 1909.

27. "Another Play of Slum Life," *New York Times*, 19 December 1908.

28. De Foe, "New Thought Mixed with Fantasy Is Served in Guise of Melodrama."

29. "Clean Plays are Most Successful. Mrs. Frances Hodgson Burnett Discusses the Good and Evil Drama. Author Believes in Stage Censor," *Philadelphia Times*, 14 February 1909.

30. "Mrs. Frances Hodgson Burnett on the New Drama. The Author of 'The Dawn of a To-morrow' Traces Through Various Fields of Art an Awakened Ideal Which is Reflected on the Stage To-day," *New York Times*, 31 January 1909, SM9.

31. "Mrs. Burnett Not a Christian Scientist," *Chicago Post*, 10 April 1909.

32. FHB to Edward Burlingame, 10 July 1905, Scribner Co101, box 23, folder 6, Department of Rare Books and Special Collections, Princeton University Libraries.

33. "Mrs. Burnett Not a Christian Scientist."

34. Vivian Burnett, "A Story Maker's Notes along the Way," typescript, Penny Deupree private collection, chap. 17, pp. 3–4.

35. FHB to Archer Fahnestock, [1908], ibid., 8.

36. FHB to Ella and Madge Hepworth Dixon, 29 June 1909, quoted in Vivian Bur-

nett, *The Romantick Lady (Frances Hodgson Burnett): The Life Story of an Imagination* (New York: Charles Scribner's, 1927), 325–326.

37. FHB to Emma Daniels, 15 January 1911, in Burnett, "Story Maker's Notes along the Way," chap. 9, p. 13. The article by Jeannette Cascaden Klauder, "Country House of Frances Hodgson Burnett. A handsome home on the Shores of Manhasset Bay, Long Island, that reflects the Individuality of its owner," was in *American Suburbs*, January 1911, 139–141.

38. FHB to Ella and Madge Hepworth Dixon, [early 1910], quoted in Burnett, *Romantick Lady*, 339.

39. FHB to Vivian Burnett, 19 May 1910, Penny Deupree private collection.

40. FHB to Vivian Burnett, 20 April 1910, Penny Deupree private collection.

41. FHB to William Heinemann, 9 October 1910, in Burnett, "Story Maker's Notes along the Way," chap. 18, p. 11.

42. FHB to Ella Hepworth Dixon, n.d., ibid., p. 12.

43. All these reviews can be found s.v. "Frances Hodgson Burnett," *Dictionary of Literary Biography* (Detroit: Gale Publishing, 1996), 41–44. The individual reviews quoted are from ALA *Booklist*, 8 October 1911, 76; *Nation*, 28 September 1911, 290; and R. A. Whay, in *Bookman*, October 1911, 183–184.

44. Advertisement for a letter by FHB, 19 October 1910. Offered for sale by Argosy Book Store (UR no. R21430).

45. "Interesting People," *American Magazine*, October 1910, 748–750.

46. Magda Frances West, "'There is No Devil,' Asserts Mrs. Frances Hodgson Burnett," *Kansas City Post*, [31 October?] 1910; article originally published in Chicago, 31 October 1910.

47. "Mrs. Frances Hodgson Burnett," *Pittsburgh Post*, 28 July 1910.

48. "Name for Suffrage Cause," *New York Times*, 5 November 1910.

49. FHB to Ella Hepworth Dixon, n.d., from Bermuda, in Burnett, "Story Maker's Notes along the Way," chap. 18, p. 11.

50. Burnett, *Romantick Lady*, 326.

51. "Burnett Memorabilia Presented to School. Son Gives 'Secret Garden' Notes, Photographs, Painting and Book to Institution for Deaf," *New York Times*, 31 January 1929. The librarians and archivist of the school have made several thorough searches for these items, but the materials have utterly vanished.

52. For a complete account of the accident, see "2 Die, 3 Hurt in Auto. Trolley Hits Mrs. Frances Hodgson Burnett's Car. Her Brother-in-Law Killed," *Washington Post*, 14 July 1911, 1. See also "Serious Motor-Car Accident," *Times* (London), 14 July 1911, 5.

CHAPTER 20. AT HOME AND ABROAD

1. "Among the Authors," *New York Times*, 9 February 1913, BR64.

2. FHB to Vivian Burnett, 23 January 1912, Penny Deupree private collection.

3. FHB to Vivian Burnett, 31 March 1912, Penny Deupree private collection.

4. FHB to Vivian Burnett, [7?] February 1913, Penny Deupree private collection.

5. FHB to Robert Underwood Johnson, 13 November 1912, Manuscript Collection, House of Books, Columbia University Libraries.

6. "Fact and Fairy Tale. Mrs. Burnett's 'T. Tembarom' a Delightful Blending of familiar Modern Conditions and Romance," *New York Times*, 26 October 1913.

7. FHB to Robert Underwood Johnson, 18 April 1912, Riley MSS, Lilly Library,

Indiana University.

8. FHB, "My Toy Cupboard," *Ladies' Home Journal*, April 1915, 10–11.

9. "Racketty-Packetty House," in "At the Children's Matinée," *Saint Nicholas*, February 1912, 352.

10. FHB to Vivian Burnett, 18 April 1912, Penny Deupree private collection.

11. FHB to Vivian Burnett, 7 August 1913, Penny Deupree private collection.

12. Ibid.

13. FHB to Herbert Hodgson, 6 November 1913, Katherine P. Hodgson private collection.

14. "Mrs. Burnett and the Occult. The Noted Novelist Explains Some of Her Beliefs and Opinions on Other World Matters," *New York Times*, 12 October 1913, BR542.

15. Gertrude Hall Brownell, "Frances Hodgson Burnett—I," typescript biography, Hargrett Rare Book and Manuscript Collection, University of Georgia Libraries, MA 210, box 4, folder 10, p. 8.

16. FHB to Vivian Burnett, Edith Jordan, and Effie Macfarlane, 19 October 1913, Penny Deupree private collection.

17. FHB to Vivian Burnett, 14 December 1913, Penny Deupree private collection.

18. Mystery surrounds Stephen's life. Like the vanished notes to *The Secret Garden*, nearly everything about Stephen has disappeared: copies of his obituary in an antivivisectionist magazine; his clipping file at the Performing Arts Collection of the New York Public Library; the books containing biographical information; his correspondence with Frances.

19. Ann Thwaite, panel discussion, "Beyond *The Secret Garden*" conference, Fresno State University, Fresno, Calif., April 2003; and see *Waiting for the Party* (op. cit.), 191.

20. Stephen Townesend, *Dr. Tuppy* (London: Hodder and Stoughton, 1912), 33.

21. "The Brown Dog," in "Letters to the Editor," *Times* (London), 16 December 1907, 11.

22. Townesend, *Dr. Tuppy*, 312–313.

23. FHB to Rosamond Campbell, [1921 or 1922], in Vivian Burnett, "A Story Maker's Notes along the Way," typescript, Penny Deupree private collection, chap. 9, p. 19.

24. Edith Jordan to FHB, 1 January 1914, Penny Deupree private collection.

25. FHB to Edith Jordan, 1 January 1914, Penny Deupree private collection.

26. Edith Jordan to FHB, 22 January 1914, Penny Deupree private collection.

27. All quotations from the letter in this and the following paragraphs are taken from a newspaper account, "Mrs. Burnett's Pen Turned Upon Niece," *New York Times*, 16 February 1916.

28. Edith Jordan to FHB, 23 February 1914, Penny Deupree private collection.

29. FHB to Edith Jordan, 6 March 1914, Penny Deupree private collection.

30. FHB to Kitty and Gigi Hall, 27 July 1914, quoted in Vivian Burnett, *The Romantick Lady (Frances Hodgson Burnett): The Life Story of an Imagination* (New York: Charles Scribner's, 1927), 358.

31. FHB to Elizabeth Jordan, 14 July 1914, Elizabeth Jordan Papers, New York Public Library.

32. Elizabeth Jordan, *Three Rousing Cheers: An Autobiography* (New York: D. Appleton Century, 1938), 325–326.

33. FHB, "The House in the Dismal Swamp," *Good Housekeeping*, April 1920, 17.

34. FHB to Elizabeth Jordan, [August 1914], Elizabeth Jordan Papers.

35. Vivian Burnett to FHB, 16 February 1915, Penny Deupree private collection.

36. Ibid.

37. Burnett, "Story Maker's Notes along the Way," chap. 15, p. 1.

38. FHB to Josephine Brown, 4 October 1915, ibid.

39. FHB to Ella Hepworth Dixon, 9 November 1915, ibid., chap. 15, p. 2.

40. "A World of Dreams in Leading Novels," *New York Times*, 17 October 1915, BR1.

41. FHB to Ella Hepworth Dixon, 9 November 1915.

42. FHB, "House in the Dismal Swamp," 17.

43. Conversation with Herbert's granddaughter, Katherine P. Hodgson.

44. FHB to Vivian Burnett, 30 April 1915, Penny Deupree private collection.

45. Ibid.

46. FHB to Vivian Burnett, 18 September 1915, Penny Deupree private collection.

47. FHB to Anna Branch, 28 October 1915, Anna Hempstead Branch Papers, Smith College.

48. FHB to Ella Hepworth Dixon, 9 November 1915.

49. FHB to Josephine Brown, 4 October 1915.

50. FHB to Ella Hepworth Dixon, 9 November 1915.

51. FHB to Elizabeth Jordan, [20 October 1915], Elizabeth Jordan Papers.

52. FHB to Vivian Burnett, 9 May 1915, Penny Deupree private collection.

53. FHB to Vivian Burnett, 18 September 1915.

54. "Niece Sues Mrs. Burnett," [*New York Times?*], Billy Rose Theater Collection, New York Public Library, FHB clippings file.

55. FHB to Edith Jordan, 20 February 1916, Penny Deupree private collection.

56. FHB, *The White People* (New York and London: Harper and Brothers, 1917), 105–106.

57. FHB to Elizabeth Jordan, 15 August 1916, Elizabeth Jordan Papers.

58. Herbert Hodgson obituary, *Virginian Pilot and Norfolk Landmark*, [11 January 1917].

59. "Banned _____ [word cut off] Talk, Says Author," *New York Telegraph*, 11 March 1917. Some of these newspaper accounts need to be taken with a large pinch of salt. The same article claims she testified that she was born in Ireland.

60. FHB to Edith Jordan, [1917], Penny Deupree private collection.

61. FHB to Edith Jordan, 13 June 1917, Penny Deupree private collection.

62. FHB to Ella Hepworth Dixon, 6 April 1917, in Burnett, "Story Maker's Notes along the Way," insert to chap. 15.

63. FHB to Josephine Brown, 22 May 1917, ibid., chap. 15, p. 3.

64. FHB to Ella Hepworth Dixon, 6 February 1917, ibid.

65. "Court Lashes Mrs. Burnett," *New York American*, 18 May 1918.

66. FHB to Rosamond Campbell, 23 June 1918, in Burnett, "Story Maker's Notes along the Way," chap. 15, p. 9.

67. Ibid.

68. FHB to Edith Jordan, 24 August 1918, Penny Deupree private collection.

69. FHB to Rosamond Campbell, 16 November 1918, in Burnett, "Story Maker's Notes along the Way," chap. 15, p. 9.

70. FHB to Elizabeth Jordan, 19 and 23 December 1918, Elizabeth Jordan Papers.

CHAPTER 21. ELIZABETH

1. FHB, *The Land of the Blue Flower* (New York: Moffat, Yard, 1909), 66.

2. Gertrude Hall Brownell, "Frances Hodgson Burnett—I," typescript biography, Hargrett Rare Book and Manuscript Collection, University of Georgia Libraries, MA 210, box 4, folder 10, p. 4.

3. Gertrude Hall Brownell, "Frances Hodgson Burnett—II," typescript biography, Hargrett Rare Book and Manuscript Collection, p. 16.

4. Elizabeth Jordan, *Three Rousing Cheers: An Autobiography* (New York: D. Appleton Century, 1938), 328.

5. FHB to Archer Fahnestock, 1 January 1922, in Vivian Burnett, "A Story Maker's Notes along the Way," typescript, Penny Deupree private collection, chap 9, pp. 8–9.

6. Ibid.

7. Jordan, *Three Rousing Cheers*, 308.

8. FHB to Vivian Burnett, n.d., Penny Deupree private collection.

9. Jordan, *Three Rousing Cheers*, 186.

10. Ibid., 316.

11. Ibid., 324–325.

12. FHB to Elizabeth Jordan, [7 or 8] April 1915, Elizabeth Jordan Papers, New York Public Library.

13. FHB to Elizabeth Jordan, 22 August 1919, Elizabeth Jordan Papers.

14. FHB, "The Magic in Children's Books," *New York Times*, 14 November 1920, BR3.

15. FHB to Elizabeth Jordan, 24 April 1920, Elizabeth Jordan Papers.

16. FHB to Elizabeth Jordan, n.d, Elizabeth Jordan Papers.

17. FHB to Vivian Burnett, [April 1920], Penny Deupree private collection.

18. FHB to Elizabeth Jordan, 24 April 1920.

19. FHB to Elizabeth Jordan, 8 December 1920, Elizabeth Jordan Papers; and FHB to Vivian Burnett, 28 December 1920, Penny Deupree private collection.

20. Vivian Burnett to FHB, 27 January 1921, Penny Deupree private collection. See also wedding announcement in the *New York Times*, 20 January 1921, 9.

21. FHB to Vivian and Constance Burnett, 21 March 1921, Penny Deupree private collection.

22. FHB to Vivian Burnett, 29 April [1921], Penny Deupree private collection.

23. Vivian Burnett to FHB, 19 May 1921, Penny Deupree private collection.

24. FHB, *Robin* (New York: A. L. Burt, 1922), 252–253.

25. Ibid., 340.

26. FHB to Elizabeth Jordan, 2 September 1921, Elizabeth Jordan Papers.

27. Jordan, *Three Rousing Cheers*, 328.

28. Vivian Burnett, *The Romantick Lady (Frances Hodgson Burnett): The Life Story of an Imagination* (New York: Charles Scribner's, 1927), 387.

29. Brownell, "Frances Hodgson Burnett—I," 9.

30. FHB to Elizabeth Jordan, 4 October 1921, Elizabeth Jordan Papers.

31. FHB to Elizabeth Jordan, 11 May 1922, Elizabeth Jordan Papers.

32. FHB to Elizabeth Jordan, 26 June 1922, Elizabeth Jordan Papers.

33. Brownell, "Frances Hodgson Burnett—II," 8.

34. Elizabeth Jordan to FHB, 14 October 1924, Elizabeth Jordan Papers.

35. Elizabeth Jordan to FHB, 19 October 1924, Elizabeth Jordan Papers.

36. Elizabeth Jordan to Edith Jordan, 27 October 1924, Elizabeth Jordan Papers.

37. FHB, December 1892, in Burnett, "Story Maker's Notes along the Way," chap. 8, pp. 15–16.

38. Frances Hodgson Burnett, *In the Garden* (Boston and New York: Medici Society of America, 1925), 30.

39. Brownell, "Frances Hodgson Burnett—I," 9.

40. Burnett, *Romantick Lady*, 409–410.

EPILOGUE

1. Gertrude Hall Brownell, "Frances Hodgson Burnett—II," typescript biography, Hargrett Rare Book and Manuscript Collection, University of Georgia Libraries, MA 210, box 4, folder 10, p. 18.

ACKNOWLEDGMENTS

My particular appreciation goes to Penny Deupree, great-granddaughter of Frances and granddaughter of Vivian, for her friendship, unstinting cooperation, and interest in this book, and for her permission to publish from the materials in her private collection, and to Tom Deupree, for his warm encouragement. I wish also to thank Katherine P. Hodgson, granddaughter of Frances's brother Herbert, for the use of materials from her private collection, and for the family information and stories she shared. Great appreciation goes to Ann Thwaite, whose groundbreaking research and resulting biography, *Waiting for the Party,* paved the way for those of us who followed.

I am grateful to the National Endowment for the Humanities for a summer stipend that allowed me to do the initial travel and research for this book; to Vassar College, for a series of research grants; and to Barnard College, Columbia University, for research funds.

I would like to thank the following librarians, archivists, students, and friends for their invaluable help: Victoria Bond, Victoria Brown, Lucinda Dubinski, Jane Livingston, and Tiffany Tsang at Vassar College; Sally Brown, Manuscripts Division, British Library; Angelica Carpenter at the Fresno State Library; Tamar Dougherty, formerly of the Princeton University Library; Paddy and George Ferrier at Great Maytham Hall; Regenia Gagnier and Helen Taylor at the University of Exeter; Peggy Haile-McPhillips at the Norfolk, Virginia, Public Library; Alexa Jaffurs and Janet M. Jourdain at the Amherst College Library; Karen Kukil at the Neilson Library, Smith College; Elinor Lipman, for her reading of the manuscript and unflagging enthusiasm; Tom Mallon, for his insights and information on Washington, D.C.; Carrie McBride for her eagle eye and impeccable index; Ann Mulloy

Ashmore at the de Grummond Collection, McCain Library and Archives, University of Southern Mississippi; Jack Neely at *Metropulse* in Knoxville, Tennessee; Sally R. Polhemus, special materials librarian, Steve Cotham, manager, and Danette Welch, reference assistant, all at the C. M. McClung Historical Collection; and Florine Polner at the Manhasset Public Library.

The following libraries opened their collections to me and/or gave me permission to publish from their materials: Archives and Special Collections, Amherst College Library; Special Collections of the Barnard College Library; the Mark Twain Project, Bancroft Library, University of California at Berkeley; the Bodleian Library, Oxford University; Special Collections, Boston University; the British Library; Carson-Newman College; Cambridge University Library; August Belmont Papers, Rare Book and Manuscript Library, Columbia University; the Lilly Library of Indiana University; Special Collections at the University of Iowa Library; the Brotherton Collection, Leeds University Library; Manhasset Public Library; Manchester Central Library; the Mark Twain House; the University of Massachusetts at Amherst; C. M. McClung Historical Collection; Billy Rose Theater Collections and Department of Special Collections, New York Public Library; Manuscripts and Archives Division, New York Public Library; Manuscripts Division, Department of Rare Books and Special Collections, Princeton University Library; Library of the London Borough of Richmond Upon Thames; Mortimer Rare Book Room and the Sophia Smith Collection of the Neilson Library, Smith College; McCain Library and Archives, University of Southern Mississippi; Special Collections, Stanford University Libraries; the Harriet Beecher Stowe House and the Stowe-Day Library of the Harriet Beecher Stowe Center; Special Collections, the University of Tennessee at Knoxville; the Mark Twain Department of Rare Books and Manuscripts, University of Virginia Library; National Library of Wales; and the Watkins-Loomis Agency.

Finally, I wish to thank the agents and editors who believed in this project and made it possible: Caroline Dawnay, Neeti Madan, Leslie Mitchner, Ann Rittenberg, and Alison Samuel.

GENERAL INDEX

Adams, Maude, 235
Addams, Jane, 166
African Americans, 32, 172, 269; in
  American South, 5, 7, 25, 43, 233;
  employed by FHB, 56, 79, 108, 268,
  287–288, 298; in FHB's works, 44, 88,
  118; in Washington, 78–79. *See also*
  FHB: and race
Aïdé, Hamilton, 192
Ainsworth, Harrison, 17
Alabama, 233
Alcott, Louisa May, 87–89, 103–104
Alexandra of Denmark (Princess of
  Wales), 20
Algiers, 271
Alma Tadema, Lady, 256
Alma Tadema, Laurence, 243, 251, 253
Alps, the, 272
Amberley, Viscount, 3
American Indians, 6, 26, 118
American Magazine, 255, 262
Anthony, Susan B., 166
antivivisection. *See under* Townesend,
  Stephen
Arizona, 233
Arnold, Matthew, 45
Arthur, Julia, 195, 199, 200, 208–210, 257
Athenaeum, 160, 209
Atlantic Monthly, 43, 45, 92

Australia, 280
Austria, 264, 270, 272–273, 276, 293
Authors' Club (London), 185, 194
aviation, 273, 300

Bacon, Josephine Daskam, 293
Ballou's Magazine, 34
Barrett (solicitor), 273
Beecher, Catharine E., 91
Beecher, Henry Ward, 92
Belgium, 229
Belmont, August, 256
Berenson, Bernard, 193
Beringer, Vera, 121
Bermuda, 10, 267–268, 273, 276–278,
  283, 292, 296–297, 300; FHB's health
  in, 270, 291; FHB starts garden in,
  268; FHB writes in, 270, 279, 284, 295
Besant, Sir Walter, 192
Bigelow, Poulteney, 207
Birch, Reginald, 29, 109–10, 122
blacks. *See* African Americans
Blackwood's Magazine, 27–28
Bloomsbury group, 38
Boer War, 217
Bookman, 263
Boond, Emily, 20
Boond, Fred, 38–39
Boond, Hanna, 12, 14, 16

Boond, William (uncle), 3, 5–6, 24
Boond, William (grandfather), 12
Boston, 89–91, 93, 103–105, 111, 122, 163, 173–174. *See also* Massachusetts
Boston mind cure, 103–104, 111–112, 259. *See also* metaphysical healing
Boston Press Club, 166
Boston Transcript, 67
Boston Traveller, 10, 129
Brady, Kate, 133
Brady, Margaret, 133, 204
brain science, 198–199
Bridges, Bertha, 40, 280, 285
Bridges, Edwina (Teddy). *See* Hodgson, Edwina (Teddy)
Bridges, Frank (brother-in-law), 38–40, 62, 94, 286
Bridges, Frank (nephew), 94, 244
Bridges, Herbert, 62, 280, 285
Brontë, Charlotte, 117
Brooks, Noah, 118
Brown, Josephine, 248, 262, 264, 281, 283
Browne, Frances, 237
Brownell, Gertrude (Kitty) Hall, xiii, 104–105, 107 109, 111, 134, 142, 162–163, 173, 194–195, 219, 232, 237, 255, 270–271, 273, 274, 290, 296, 306; and Central Park memorial, 2, 304–305; in England, 113–114, 120, 193; in Italy, 115, 145–147, 150; letters to, 106, 121, 135, 153, 155, 192, 214, 279; marries, 297–298
Brownell, William Crary, 297–298
Browning, Robert, 68
Buckingham, Andrew, 151–152
Buel, Clarence Clough, 279
Bulwer-Lytton, Edward, 46
Bunyan, John, 166
Burlingame, Edward, 161, 176–178, 190, 199, 235, 241, 260
Burnett, Constance Buel, x, 104, 279–280, 284, 291–292, 296–298, 305
Burnett, Dorinda, 104, 291–292, 297
Burnett, Frances Eliza Hodgson: absence from family, xii, 55, 65, 87, 91, 93–94, 96, 98–100, 103, 107, 111, 113, 116, 120–122, 125, 127, 130, 133, 136, 140–141, 154–156, 202; accent, 8, 11, 49, 211; on

America, xi, 6–7, 51, 246; America/England in writing style and works, x, 34, 42, 46, 66, 93, 102, 109, 122, 225–226, 263, 269; biographies of, x, 29, 96, 304–305; birth, 13; charity to children, 137, 141, 150–152, 156, 159, 163–164, 206, 213, 228, 240, 279; childhood and adolescence, x, 4, 7, 12–28, 31, 39, 60, 160; colonialism in works of, 117–118; countryside and nature, love of, 7, 9–10, 13, 25–26, 28–29, 114–115, 131, 272, 294; death and burial, ix, xiii, 303–304; death of father, 14–15, 29–30, 118; death of mother, 39, 48, 118; decorates homes, 78, 81, 83, 117, 121, 124–125, 129–130, 151, 169, 176–177, 183, 205, 227, 243, 261, 270, 276, 306; dialect in works of, 46–7, 60, 66–67, 90, 118, 236; and dogs, 4, 25–26, 119, 224–225 (*see also* dogs); dress and fashion, xii, 17, 36, 51–52, 54, 57, 78, 83–84, 97, 105, 112–113, 134, 185, 245, 306; early reading, 14, 16–18, 21–22; education, 10, 16–18, 23–24; on England, xi, 51, 157, 169–170, 227; fairy theme in life and works, xii, 112, 228, 242–243, 279, 285, 290, 294–295, 306; financial support of family and relatives, x, xii, 4, 9, 14, 30, 34–35, 39, 46, 56–59, 65, 88, 159, 174, 176, 183, 196, 204, 211, 238–239, 270, 277–278, 280, 282, 306; first mentor, 21–24; first publication, 34–35; flirtations, 99, 105, 155, 220, 303; and gardens and gardeners, xii, xiii, 2, 13, 37, 51, 121, 201, 204–207, 212, 216, 227, 229, 231, 243, 248, 261–263, 267–268, 283, 294, 296, 298, 301, 303–304; gender in works of, 102, 178–180, 187, 246; gossip and rumours about, x, 97, 99, 123–125, 130, 133–134, 183–184, 189–190, 202, 204, 215–216, 232, 305; health, physical and mental, xiii, 30, 48, 50–52, 55, 57–59, 69, 74, 78, 80, 86–87, 93, 97–98, 100, 102–104, 106–107, 109, 111–113, 120, 132–138, 147–148, 150, 152, 154, 157, 171, 193–194,

197, 214, 216, 221, 229, 232–234, 237, 244, 245, 247, 255–256, 258–259, 265, 267, 270–272, 290–291, 296–298, 300–302, 306; keeps journal for Lionel after death, 145, 149, 158–159, 161–162, 164–165, 172, 199, 241, 302–303; libel lawsuit against, 278, 283–285, 287–288, 290; literary reputation of, xi, 10, 11, 60, 63, 67, 70–74, 111, 220, 264; on marriage, 28, 40, 48, 94–96, 100, 187, 196, 202–203, 218, 220, 222, 225–226, 265; and money matters, 9, 30, 35, 41–42, 55, 57, 59, 63, 107, 125, 127, 133–134, 157, 169, 175, 180–183, 189, 191–192, 194, 196, 211, 222, 228, 237, 249, 252, 264, 274, 297 (see also FHB: financial support of family and relatives); as mother, xii, 80, 95, 97–98, 112, 124, 140–142, 146, 154–155, 175, 198, 306; mourns Lionel, 145–150, 155, 173; move to America, 3–6, 11, 24, 31; and music, 37, 39, 82–83, 97, 99, 105, 130, 162, 200, 207, 223, 229, 281; national identity of, x, 8, 10–11, 34, 46, 52, 114, 160, 170, 184, 190, 212, 225, 246–247, 253, 255; nicknames for, xiv, 27, 65, 105, 108, 129, 294; and occult, 83, 199, 234, 260, 264, 272, 299; philanthropy of, xii, 148, 150, 159, 168, 206, 217, 229, 265, 282, 301 (see also FHB: charity to children); physical appearance, 9, 11, 18, 68–69, 105–106, 228, 244–245, 254, 271; plagiarism accusations, 110–111, 236; poverty of Hodgson family, 5–8, 15–6, 24, 26, 30, 32, 39, 306; pressure to write, xv, 9, 30–31, 48, 51, 57, 69–70, 101; pronunciation of name, x; pseudonyms of, 19, 34–35, 41, 64–65; public speaking of, 184–186, 194; and race, 44, 56, 68, 78–79, 90, 117–118, 122, 146, 172; as reader, 10, 16, 18, 21–22, 27–28, 80, 85, 107–108; relationship with Edith, 14, 69, 159, 168, 171, 189, 197, 206, 267, 278, 284; relationship with Herbert, 20, 22, 32, 36; relationship with John, 20, 22, 32, 238; relations with children, 26, 48, 52, 88,

112, 119, 125, 128, 137, 141, 147, 149, 150, 156, 165, 206, 228; relations with publishers, xi, 4, 34, 41–42, 45, 55, 64, 70–72, 119, 161–162, 165, 177–178, 182, 196, 212, 228, 294, 299; religious beliefs of, 31, 39, 89, 104, 117, 119, 149, 199, 206, 240–242, 253, 259–260, 263–264, 286–287, 290, 298–299; remembered as children's author, xi, xii, 86, 109, 119, 157, 187, 190, 306; and reporters, xi, 72, 101, 111, 123–125, 134, 138, 157, 195, 201–204, 214, 216, 228, 231–232, 264; as schoolteacher, 9; sense of humour, 23, 28, 40, 52, 78, 80, 82, 105, 296; and servants, 13, 56–57, 60, 63, 79, 88, 108, 114, 117, 122, 130, 186, 205, 207, 215–216, 224, 228–229, 236–238, 244, 249–250, 253, 255, 258, 271, 277, 287–288, 298; shabby genteel theme in life and works, 3, 26, 30–31, 37–38, 54, 60, 226; shift in fortune theme in work, xi, 61, 118, 269; smoking, 20, 180, 190, 204, 224, 248, 263, 265, 271, 287, 293; as storyteller, 2, 5, 9, 16, 18, 20–21, 26–27, 108–109, 160, 177, 181, 303; and Stephen Townesend, 10, 131–132, 138, 148, 152, 154–155, 163, 176, 180, 186, 189–190, 192, 195, 199, 201, 204, 206, 213, 216, 217–220, 229–231, 237, 245–249, 255, 264, 275; and Swan Burnett, 10–11, 27–30, 40–41, 48, 52–55, 57, 59, 62, 64–65, 68–69, 73, 76, 80–82, 85, 89, 93–94, 96–97, 99–101, 107, 111, 115, 120, 125, 127, 131, 138, 142, 147, 154, 156, 158, 163, 183, 189, 196–198, 201–204, 218, 221–222, 244; travel, xi, 49, 51, 57, 61, 90, 104, 115, 229, 231, 233, 248, 264, 270–273, 283, 301; unable to write, 102–103, 106, 247; unauthorized printing of works, 70–73, 120 (see also copyright); writes for money, 31, 34, 56–57; on writing as "gift," 10–11, 16, 20–21, 294; writing habits, 33, 35, 42, 51, 80–82, 109, 123, 141, 148, 162, 207, 212, 236, 261, 266, 288, 296, 306. See also Index of Works

Burnett, John M., 27, 53, 98, 158

Burnett, Lionel, 55–57, 59–60, 63, 82, 85–86, 93, 97–98, 104, 114–116, 120–121, 151, 159, 163, 192, 216, 244, 272, 286, 304; in Atlantic City, 130–131, 133; death, 142; fairy box for, 140–141; health and illness of, 100, 111, 116, 130–131, 133, 136–142; and reporters, 123–124, 127, 134; represented in FHB's works, 88, 108–109, 150, 263–264, 284; in Washington, 80, 103, 128, 135. *See also* FHB: keeps journal for Lionel after death

Burnett, Lydia Ann Peck, 27, 53, 100, 158

Burnett, Swan Moses, 54–56, 59, 62–65, 68–70, 73–74, 76, 78, 80–81, 83–85, 91, 93, 96–101, 104, 111, 113, 115, 120, 122, 125–127, 130–131, 133, 135–137, 142, 148, 160, 162, 201, 233, 280; courtship with and marriage to FHB, 10, 40–41, 48, 52–54; death, 204, 244; divorce from FHB, 202–204; education and career, 28, 40, 55–57, 63, 82; as father, 60, 107, 147, 156, 173, 193, 198; as FHB's manager, 64, 66, 71–72, 75, 90, 96, 127, 163; FHB's nicknames for, 30, 54; health of, 171, 221; marriage troubles, 107, 158, 163, 183, 189, 197, 201, 221–222; and money matters, 107, 175, 180, 183, 211; in New Market, 11, 27–29; remarries, 239; and reporters, 183–184. *See also* FHB: and Swan Burnett

Burnett, Verity, 104, 284, 287, 291–292, 296

Burnett, Vivian, x, xiii, 56, 78, 104, 123–124, 146–148, 151, 155–156, 158, 171–172, 181–183, 185, 190, 193, 200–201, 204, 210, 219, 223–224, 229, 238, 245, 252, 258, 266, 270, 274, 276, 286–287, 296–298, 301, 303; arranges FHB's housing, 253, 256, 258; biography of FHB, x, 96, 304–305; childhood and adolescence, 59, 63, 68, 80, 82, 86, 93, 97, 100, 103, 108, 114–115, 120–121, 127–128, 130, 133, 135–136, 138–139, 162–163; and Christian Science, 104, 242, 298; death, 305; and *Fauntleroy*, 108–110, 122–123, 134, 169, 193, 221,

305; as FHB's manager, 237, 247, 292, 297–298; at Harvard, 173, 176, 180–181, 191, 193; health, 172–173, 193, 229; honeymoon tour to Asia, 233, 280; involvement in theatre, 193, 196–197; as journalist, 209, 211, 221, 232–233; letters to, 2, 9, 107, 140–141, 153–154, 175, 189, 197–198, 203, 222, 245, 268, 274, 294; marriage, 279; as publisher, 257, 280; relationship with FHB, 111, 154, 156, 168, 173–174, 180, 194, 197–198, 213, 221, 239, 257, 291; represented in FHB's works, 8, 150 (*see also Little Lord Fauntleroy*)

Burroughs, John, 45

Burton, Mary Hooker, 94–95

Byron, Lady, 92, 95

Byron, Lord, 92

Calcagni, Giovanni, 149–150

Calhoun, Eleanor, 194–195, 199, 201, 208–210, 214, 224, 257, 281

California, 62, 99, 158, 233, 280. *See also* San Francisco

Campbell, Ada, 26, 39–40

Campbell, Dr. and Mrs., 39, 52

Campbell, Kenneth, 186, 206, 218, 224, 237

Campbell, Rosa, 39, 52

Campbell, Rosamond, 186, 206–207, 212, 218, 224, 248, 258, 275, 287–288

Canada, 4–5, 90, 185, 287–288

Carlyle, Thomas, 4

Carnegie, Andrew, 45

Carr, Comyns, 131, 155

Central Park memorial, ix, x, xii, 2, 304–305

Century magazine, 43, 45, 101, 227, 247, 269, 279, 284

Chiellini, Luisa ("Liza" or "Lisa"), 116, 120, 127, 129–130, 132, 135–136, 138–141, 150, 155

Children's Magazine, 257

China, 233, 280

Christian Science, 104, 241–242, 272, 290, 298–299

Civil War, U.S., 3–6, 24, 26, 43, 78, 233

Claflin, Mary Bucklin, 92, 94, 101
Clarence, duke of, 156
Clarke, Fayal, 284
Classical Dictionary (Lemprière), 20
Cleveland, Grover, 105
Coleridge, Samuel Taylor, 28
Collins, Wilkie, 121
Colorado, 209, 211, 213
Connecticut, 91–92, 94–95, 101, 259. *See also* Nook Farm
Cooper, James Fenimore, 6
copyright, 73–75, 86, 90, 94, 119–121, 129–130, 181, 185–186, 191. *See also* FHB: unauthorized printing of works
Cornhill, 23, 227
Cranbrook, earl of, 205
Crewe-Milnes, Robert Offley Ashburton (earl of Crewe), 192
Critic, 102, 120, 123, 125, 130, 197, 200, 228
Crossland, Cecil, 156
Cutler, Martha Hill, 294

Daily Telegraph, 191
Daniels, Emma, 204, 261
Daniels, Willie, 204
Davidge, William, 75
Davis, Delia T., 159
Dean, Priscilla, 297
Defoe, Daniel, 110
DeManger, Monsieur (teacher), 115–116
Dennis, Will (pseud. for Stephen Townesend), 153
Dennis, William (Will) Henry (lawyer), 80, 96, 153, 189, 192, 201, 203, 210, 238, 255
Denver Republican, 211
DeQuincy, Thomas, 68
Derby, earl of, 13
de Wolfe, Elsie, 238, 256
Dickens, Charles, 23, 27, 35, 46–47, 54, 71, 102, 263, 269
Dick Sheridan (play), 155
Dixon, Ella Hepworth, 207–208, 218–219, 237, 260, 262, 283, 286, 304
Dixon, Madge (Maddie) Hepworth, 207–208, 218, 237, 261

Dr. Tuppy (Townesend), 274–275
Dodge, Mary Mapes, 86–90, 97, 109–110, 125
dogs, 223–224, 275. *See also* FHB: and dogs
Douglass, Frederick, 78
Drury Lane Boys' Club, 151–152, 156
Dunbar, Paul Lawrence, 47
Dutton, Louis, 304

Eddy, Mary Baker, 104, 241, 259
Edwards, Howard Parnell, 204, 239, 248, 251, 257
Edward VII (king of England) (formerly Albert Edward, Prince of Wales), 20, 261
Eliot, George, 67
Elite List, 78
Elliot, Elizabeth, 82, 176–177, 279
Elliott, Gertrude, 261
Elm Farm, Suffolk, 114–115
Emerson, Ralph Waldo, 68, 89, 241
Emery, Winifred, 228
England, 11, 48–49, 57, 167; Buckinghamshire, 193; Chester, 51; Haslemere, 172; Isle of Wight, 256; Kent, 10, 194; Liverpool, 4, 261; Salford, 12, 16; York, 12, 192. *See also* Elm Farm, Suffolk; Glade, The, Surrey; Joss Farm, Thanet; London; Manchester; Maytham Hall; Portland Place
Examiner (Manchester), 73

Fahnestock, Abby, 270, 276–277
Fahnestock, Annie (née Prall), 252, 270–271, 276–278, 283, 287
Fahnestock, Archer Pleasant (brother-in-law), 38–40, 52, 62, 158
Fahnestock, Archie (nephew), 40, 159, 169, 171, 174–176, 182, 190, 196, 224, 234, 242, 252, 260, 268, 270, 276–278, 289, 291, 301
Fahnestock, Benjamin, 62
Fahnestock, Cecelia (née Schotte), 301
Fahnestock, Ernest, 62, 158–159, 169, 196, 210–211, 234, 270, 276–277, 289–290, 298

Fahnestock, Francis, 276
Fahnestock, Kenneth, 270, 276
Faulkner, William, 44
feminism. *See* women's issues
Field, Eugene, 167
Finckel, DeVin, 133, 135, 146–147
Fischer, Hiram, 80
Fleming, George. *See* Fletcher, Constance
Fletcher, Constance (pseud. George
    Fleming), 190, 196–197, 224
Fortnightly Review, 110
Fraice, Mr., 56, 63
France, 55, 57, 264; FHB stories set in,
    64; Le Havre, 137. *See also* Paris
Frank Leslie's Illustrated Newspaper, 31
French, Henry, 125
Frohman, Charles, 191
Frohman, Daniel, 127, 189, 194–195, 259
Fry, Dr., 244–245
Fuller, Margaret, 89
F. Warne and Company, 67, 74, 110, 113,
    119, 151, 162–163, 182, 199, 210, 228. *See
    also* Warne, Frederick

gardens. *See* FHB: and gardens and
    gardeners
Garfield, James, 79, 82, 97
Garfield, Lucretia Rudolph, 97
Gaskell, Elizabeth, xiii, 7, 66, 71
Gates, Dr., 198
gender. *See* FHB: gender in works of;
    women's issues
Georgetown University medical school, 82
George V (king of England), 152
Germany, 57, 130, 133, 138, 189, 210, 255,
    272, 276
Gibraltar, 215, 231
Gilder, Helena, 44–45, 80, 84, 96, 99
Gilder, Jeanette, 274
Gilder, Richard Watson, 43–45, 47, 52, 55,
    61, 64, 66, 73, 88, 96, 99, 101, 141, 207,
    247, 261; encourages FHB, 45, 47, 95;
    FHB visits in New York, 89, 98; letters
    to, 52, 65, 67–68, 75–76, 80–81, 87,
    93–94, 97, 100, 220, 223, 225–226,
    245–246, 249; relationship with FHB,
    44, 49–50, 52–53, 84–85, 228

Gilder, Rodman, 80
Gillette, Francis, 91
Gillette, William, 89, 91, 93, 96, 98–99
Glade, The, Surrey, 131, 135, 168, 190
Gladstone, Catherine Glynne, 116
Gladstone, William, 116, 139
Godey's Lady's Book and Magazine, 17, 31,
    34–35, 41, 43, 46, 49
Good Housekeeping, 282, 295, 298, 301,
    304
Gordon, Marie, 74
Gosse, Edmund, 121, 131, 181
Gower, Lord Ronald, 192, 237, 248, 262,
    264, 284
Granny's Wonderful Chair (Browne),
    236–237
Grant, Ulysses S., 79
Grundy, Sydney, 132

Haberton, Joseph, 119
Hadfield, Alice, Jane, and Sarah, 17,
    23–24, 51–52, 63, 160
Hadfield, Annie, 17, 51–52, 63
Hadfield, Henry, 17, 51–52, 56–57, 63
Hague, Alice and Mary, 16
Hall, Dame Edna, 105, 181, 195
Hall, Gertrude (Kitty). *See* Brownell,
    Gertrude (Kitty) Hall
Hall, Grace (Gigi), 105, 195, 232, 255,
    270–272, 279, 296–297
Hall, Marguerite (Daisy), 105, 114, 163,
    190, 232, 255–256
Hardy, Thomas, 84
Harper and Brothers (publisher), 292,
    295
Harper's Bazar and *Harper's Weekly,* 11, 50,
    52, 65, 197, 271, 292
Harris, George Washington, 44
Harte, Bret, 121, 192
Hartford Courant, 67
Harwood, Charlotte, 228–229
Hatton, Joseph, 73–74
Hawaii, 280
Hayden, Sophia, 166
Haynes, Charles, 39
Hearth and Home, 88
Heinemann (publisher), 249, 262, 298

Henry Holt (publisher), 271
Herford, Beatrice, 190, 196
Hillier, Sam, 128
Hird, Frank, 237, 248, 262, 264
Hodder and Stoughton (publisher), 274
Hodgson, Albert Edwin, 158
Hodgson, Alfred Eldridge, 210
Hodgson, Ann (née Burnett), 39–40, 158
Hodgson, Bert Cecil, 158
Hodgson, Edith (later Fahnestock and
    Jordan), 5, 8, 12, 20, 28, 31, 40, 49,
    52–54, 59–60, 62, 69, 159, 175, 189, 197,
    200, 219, 221, 234, 236, 239, 244, 247,
    252–253, 257, 266, 273, 280, 288–291,
    300, 302–303); in Bermuda, 267, 270,
    277, 278, 284, 296; in California, 94,
    99, 158; childhood and adolescence, 13,
    25–27, 32, 35–36, 39, 46; in England,
    168–169, 201, 204–206, 222, 227, 229,
    231, 238, 243, 251, 261; and libel lawsuit,
    276–278, 283–284; on Long Island, NY,
    233, 268, 270–271; in Washington, 171,
    176, 183; writes "My Sister," 304. See
    also FHB: relationship with Edith
Hodgson, Edwin (father), 10, 12–15, 23
Hodgson, Edwin (nephew), 40, 158
Hodgson, Edwina (Teddy) (later
    Bridges), 39–40, 49, 53, 238, 239, 277,
    285–286; in California, 62, 94, 158, 233,
    244, 280; childhood and adolescence,
    8, 15, 25–27, 31–32, 35
Hodgson, Eliza Boond, 3, 4, 6, 8–10,
    12–13, 15–17, 19–20, 23–24, 35–36, 38,
    286
Hodgson, Frances Burnett (niece), 158,
    201, 211, 239, 272, 282
Hodgson, Frank Bridges, 158
Hodgson, Harry, 158
Hodgson, Herbert (brother), 3, 4, 6, 8–9,
    13–5, 17, 20, 22–23, 25, 30, 32, 35–40,
    158, 200, 210–211, 219, 223, 238, 259,
    272, 277, 281–283, 285–286. See also
    FHB: relationship with Herbert
Hodgson, Herbert (nephew), 158
Hodgson, John George, 4–6, 8–9, 13–4,
    17, 20, 22, 23, 25, 32, 35–40, 158, 223,
    238. See also FHB: relationship with

John
Hodgson, Lillian, 158
Hodgson, Medora, 158, 211, 272, 282–283,
    285
Hodgson, Vivian Burnett (nephew), 158
Holland, Josiah Gilbert, 42, 46–47, 49,
    53, 101
Holmes, Oliver Wendell, 122
Holmes, Richard, 2
Hooker, Isabella Beecher, 91–92, 94, 101
Hooker, John, 91
Hughes, Annie, 120
Hungary, 270, 272–273
Hutchison, Dave, 80, 84

Idler, 187
Illinois, 165–167, 179, 211
Illustrated News, 151
Incorporated Authors, 121
India, 117–118
Indians. See American Indians
intellectual property. See copyright
Italy, 57, 115–116, 134, 145, 148, 216; Alps,
    264; FHB marries in, 11, 214–215; FHB
    recuperates in after Lionel's death,
    146–150; Florence, 115, 120, 139, 231;
    Genoa, 11; Lake Como, 231; Lake
    Garda, 264; Milan, 231, 264; Rome,
    137; San Remo, 146–147, 149; Sorrento,
    127; Trieste, 271; Venice, 231, 264

James, Henry, 45, 85, 101–102, 129, 150,
    191–193, 208, 219
James, Nellie, 150
James, William, 241
Jane Eyre (Brontë), 117, 262
Japan, 233, 280
Jefferson, Joe, 45
Jekyll, Gertrude, 268
Jenkins, family, 8
Johnson, Mary, 27
Johnson, Robert Underwood, 269
Johnstone, Edith, 266
Johnstone, Mildred, 266
Jordan, Edith, 159, 286
Jordan, Elizabeth Garver, ix, xii, 271, 289,
    292–294, 296–297, 300–302, 304

Jordan, Frank T., 94, 99, 158–159, 171, 174–176, 183, 189, 196, 200, 216–217, 231, 234, 239, 243, 253, 255, 266, 276, 279, 286, 291
Jordan Marsh (publisher), 119
Joss Farm, Thanet, 121

Kaye and Guedella (law firm), 120, 140
Keats, John, 28, 134
Kellogg, Clara Louise, 45
Kendal, Madge, 121
Kipling, Rudyard, 294
Klauder, Jeannette Cascaden, 261
Knorr, Emma, 277, 283
Knoxville College, 25, 43
Knoxville Daily Sentinel, 113
Knoxville Journal, 51
Knoxville Whig, 5–6
Korea, 280
Krutch, Louise, 100
Ku Klux Klan, 43

Ladies' Halfpenny Journal, 17
Ladies' Home Journal, 133, 169
Lampé, Dr., 255–257
Lankester, Owen, 114–115, 119, 129, 132, 150, 168, 274
Lee, Robert E., 233
Leigh, Augusta, 92
Leighton, Robert, 118
Leslie, Elsie, 110, 122, 125
Leslie's Weekly, 197
Lewis, Arthur, 200
Lewis, Ida. *See* Arthur, Julia
Lincoln, Abraham, 4–5, 91
Lippincott's Monthly Magazine, 37, 113, 119
Literary Society (Washington), 166
Literary World, 60, 72
London, 10, 38, 51, 113, 121, 127, 130–131, 135, 141, 150–151, 156, 161, 167, 175, 191, 204, 222–223, 229, 264, 273. *See also* Portland Place
Long Island, 10, 98–99, 233–234, 252–253; Plandome, 255–258, 260–261, 265–266, 268, 270, 276–277, 279, 281–282, 291, 293, 295, 300–304
Lord Chesterfield's Letters, 174

Lupton, F. M. (publisher), 70
Lutyens, Sir Edwin, 204

MacArthur, Hugh, 215, 218
Macfarlane, Emma, 80
Macfarlane, Euphemia (Effie), 80, 107, 122, 135, 138, 189, 200, 219, 234, 252, 271, 302
Macfarlane, Rachel, 80
Macfarlane, Virginia Prall, 80
MacHarg, William, 304
Macmillan (publisher), 90
Magnus, Julian, 74
Maguire, Mr. (theatre manager), 90
Maitland, Lady, 237
Manchester, x, xiii, 3, 4, 7–10, 12, 16, 24, 27, 32, 49–50, 52, 55–6, 63, 115, 160, 204, 261
Marbury, Elisabeth, 125–127, 186, 189, 191, 238, 254, 256–258
Mary Barton (Gaskell), 7, 66
Massachusetts, 89, 103, 162–163, 197, 294; Berkshires, 283. *See also* Boston
Matthison, Arthur, 73
Maude, Cyril, 228, 238
Maude, Pamela, 228
Maytham Hall, 204–209, 212–213, 217–218, 222, 224, 227–229, 231, 237, 240–243, 245, 247–248, 250–253, 256–258, 260, 262, 264, 266, 275
McClure's, 161, 234, 237, 239
Mechanics' Institute, 17
memorial. *See* Central Park memorial
Meredith, George, 46, 121
Merington, Marguerite, 304
metaphysical healing, 103–104, 199
Michigan, 196, 199
Mill, John Stuart, 91
Mitchell, Donald Grant, 88
Modjeska, Helen, 45, 87
Morans, the, 277
Mudieman, Marmaduke, 18
Munsey's, 245
Murray, David, 225

Nation, The, 45, 263
Nelson, Thomas, 118

Netherlands, the, 57
New Jersey, 130, 138
Newman, Mrs. (metaphysical healer), 103–104
newsreels, 273
New Thought, 260, 263, 290, 299. *See also* FHB: religious beliefs
"New Woman," 184, 191, 203
New York: Fishkill Landing, 229, 232–233; New Windsor-on-Hudson, 283, 285. *See also* Long Island; New York City
New York City, 40, 44, 49, 53, 72, 84, 87, 90, 95, 98, 122, 124–125, 127, 157, 189, 195–196, 229, 231–232, 234, 237–240, 243–244, 247, 249, 255, 269, 283, 286, 290–291, 295–296, 300–301
New York Herald, 67, 200, 286
New York Times, 44, 73, 124–125, 134, 153, 183, 200, 203
New York World, 191, 292
Nineteenth Century, 191
Nook Farm, 91–95, 101
North Carolina, 85, 90, 93, 236
Norway, 191–193

Ochs, Adolph, 44
O'Connor, Flannery, 44
Ohio, 28, 40
Olmsted, Frederick Law, 77
Oregon, 158
O'Reilly, John Boyle, 87, 90
Osgood, James R. (publisher), 98, 160

Pall Mall Magazine, 114, 208
Palmer, Bertha Potter, 166
Panama, 280
Papyrus Club, 87–88, 94
Paris, 51, 52, 55, 57, 88, 115, 130, 136, 139, 145, 186, 231; St. Germain Cemetery, 142, 145. *See also* France
Pawling, Sydney, 298–299
Pégoud, Adolphe, 273
Pen and Brush (club), 301
Penman and Butt, 24
Pennsylvania, 75, 87, 138
Pepys, Samuel, 167
Peters, the, 8

Peterson, Charles J., 41–42, 55–56, 58, 64–65, 70–72, 75, 89
Peterson's Monthly Magazine, 31, 37, 41, 43, 45–46, 49, 50, 52, 54–56, 58, 60, 64–65, 70, 113, 165
Pfalz, Prince Ruprecht of (portrait), 272
Philadelphia Press, 67
Phillips, Nora, 121
Pickford, Mary, 279, 297
plagiarism. *See* FHB: plagiarism accusations
Porter, Maria S., 104
Porter and Coates (publisher), 71
Portland Place, 113–114, 168–169, 176–177, 180, 183, 192, 194, 196, 205, 208. *See also* London
Portugal, 231
Post (London), 130
Punch, 68, 163
Putnam's Magazine, 95

Queen, The, 185
Quimby, Phineas Parkhurst, 241

Raymond, John T., 74
Reade, Charles, 73–74
Reid, Capt. Mayne, 16
Rhode Island, 68, 90, 189
Rice, Charles Edward, 80, 83, 96, 99, 135, 198, 271, 284
Ricker, Rev. C. H., 304
Riley, James Whitcomb, 47, 234
Rimmer, Emma, 13, 15
Robinson Crusoe (Defoe), 110
Robson, Eleanor (later Belmont), 253–254, 256–259, 261
Romance Magazine, 165
Roosevelt, Theodore, 286
Rossetti, William, 121
Royces, the, 285
Russell, Annie, 213
Russell, Tommy, 125

Sackville-Cresswells, the, 205
Saint-Gaudens, Augustus, 45
St. James Gazette, 110
Saint Nicholas, 78, 86, 88, 108–110, 112,

116–117, 119, 125, 165, 242

Samuel McClure (publisher), 125

San Francisco, 62, 90, 94, 233, 244

Saturday Review, 102, 111, 130, 189

Schayer, Julia, 68, 75, 80, 99, 107

Scott, Sir Walter, 17, 27–28

Scribner, Arthur, 207

Scribner, Charles, 138, 177

Scribner, Helen, 207

Scribner and Company, 43, 64, 66–67,
　72, 90, 110, 118–119, 160–162, 165–166,
　169, 176, 182, 185, 196, 199, 210, 212,
　220, 228

Scribner's Monthly, 42–47, 49–50, 53, 55,
　60–61, 63–65, 70, 72, 85, 90, 95, 98,
　113, 156, 160, 178, 190, 194, 227

Seebohm, E. V., 120–121

Select Seminary for Young Ladies and
　Gentlemen (Manchester), 17,
　23–24

Shackleton, Francis, 261–262

Shakespeare, William, 28

Shaw, Anna Howard, 292

Shaw, George Bernard, 254

Shelley, Percy Bysshe, 134

Sherson, Erroll, 116, 174

ships: *Britannic,* 173; *Campania,* 194;
　Cedric, 239; *Ems,* 113; *Etruria,* 194;
　Gascogne, 137; *Kaiser Franz Joseph I,*
　271; *The Lahn,* 168; *Lusitania,* 283;
　Minneapolis, 247; *Minnewaska,* 274;
　Paris, 169; *Parthia,* 53; *St. Paul,* 214;
　Teutonic, 157; *Zeeland,* 255

Silesia, Göbersdorf, 138

Simmons, George, 105, 181–183, 191, 199,
　210

Simmons, Mary, 181

Sir Isaac Pitman's Metropolitan School
　(London), 175

Sladen, Douglas, 193–194

smallpox, 62, 158

Smith, Elder and Co. (publisher), 228

Smith, Minna, 298

Society of British Authors, 121

Solberg, Thorvald, 80, 84

South Carolina, 27, 233

Spectator, 111

Spirit of the Times, The (London), 129

Springfield Republican, 42

stageright. *See* copyright

Stanley, Robert A., 231, 235–236

Stanton, Elizabeth Cady, 91, 166

Stephen, Leslie, 38

Steuer, Max D., 287

Stoddard, Charles Warren, 72

Stokes, F. A. (publisher), 228, 248–249,
　260, 286

Stokes, Frederick, 247, 298–299

Stowe, Harriet Beecher, 6, 44, 88, 91–92,
　94–95, 104, 166

Strachey, Lytton, 299

suffrage. *See* women's issues

Swedenborg, Emmanuel, 241

Switzerland, 231, 248, 253, 264

Tarenton, Agatha, 300

Tatler, 167

Tennessee, 3, 5–9, 24, 31, 62, 65; Clinton
　Pike, 25, 28, 30–33, 36, 39; Knoxville,
　3–6, 8, 24–25, 27–28, 30, 32, 35–40,
　43–44, 46, 53–54, 59, 62, 158, 238; New
　Market, 5, 6, 8–10, 25, 27–28, 53, 62–
　64, 67, 88, 98, 100

Tennyson, Alfred, Lord, 164

Terry, Ellen, 195

Thackeray, William Makepeace, 15, 27,
　30, 46, 102, 108, 117

theatres: Adelphi, 155; Avenue, 235;
　Baldwin's, 90; Booth, 74; Broadway,
　125, 133; Comedy, 155, 209; Court, 131,
　155; Criterion, 234; Crystal Palace, 131;
　Garrick, 155; Lyceum, 127, 189, 197,
　259; Lyric, 279; Prince of Wales, 120;
　Royal, 193; Savoy, 235; Shaftesbury,
　234; Strand, 120, 152; Terry's, 120–121,
　153, 235

Thomas, Augustus, 122

Thoreau, Henry David, 89

Thoroughbred Mongrel, A (Townesend),
　223–225

Times (London), 275

Townesend, Stephen, 131–132, 138–141,
　148, 152, 155, 163, 175, 186, 199, 201,
　206, 209–210, 217, 221–222, 225,

227–231, 237, 245–247, 249; as actor, 132, 153, 155, 189, 197, 200, 229; and antivivisection, 218, 223–224, 230, 274–275; as author, 131, 223–225, 230, 274–275; as co-author with FHB, 140, 152–153, 186, 189, 193, 196, 200, 219, 264; death, 274; as FHB's adviser and manager, 138, 153, 176,180, 182, 185–186, 190–193, 196, 199, 212, 228, 248; gossip about, 189, 190, 204, 216; marriage to FHB, 214–215; temper, 153–154, 189–190, 216–223
Trollope, Anthony, 46, 115
Trollope, Frances, 7–8
Tutwiler, Julia, 297–8
Twain, Mark, 44, 47, 91, 95, 110
Twelfth Night Club, 197

Uhl, Simon Jerome, 163–164
Uncle Tom's Cabin (Stowe), 6–7, 44, 88, 110, 166

Vagabonds Club (London), 11, 184
Vanderbilt, Consuelo, 245
Vanity Fair (Thackeray), 15, 117
Ver Beck, Mrs., 273
Victoria (queen of England), 156, 225, 227, 285
Victoria Mary, duchess of Teck, 152
Virginia, 85, 90, 93–94, 158, 259, 281–283

Walker, Cornelia, 272, 301
Waltman, Harry Franklin, 163–164
Ward, Lock, and Company (publisher), 111
Warne, Frederick, 67, 70, 189. *See also* F. Warne and Company
Warne, Harold, 191
Warner, Charles Dudley, 101
Washington, Booker T., 43
Washington, D.C., 10, 55, 62–63, 65, 68–70, 77–79, 81, 85, 87, 90–96, 100, 103, 107, 109, 113, 121, 123, 124–126, 135, 138, 147, 154, 156, 159, 161, 164, 169, 171, 173–174, 201, 213, 244, 255, 297; 1770 Massachusetts Avenue, 126–127, 176, 183, 211, 252, 258, 285, 297

Washington Post, 124, 147, 183, 202, 209
White, Emily, 20
White and Case (law firm), 287
Whitwell, William, 232–233
Who's Who, 194–195
Wiggin, Kate Douglas, 293
Wilde, Oscar, 96, 121
Wilkins, Emily J., 166
Williamson, Hamilton, 304
Wilson, Carlos, 151–152
Winthrop, A. T., 110
women's issues, xiii, 87, 91–92, 95, 166, 179, 185–188, 202–203, 249, 265, 283, 292, 297, 307. *See also* FHB: gender in works of; FHB: on marriage; "New Woman"
Wood, Florence, 75
Wood, Joseph, 3–4, 36
Woodhull, Victoria, 91–92
Woodrow Wilson Foundation, 301
Woolf, Virginia, xiii, 38, 186
Wordsworth, William, 160
World (London), 121, 129, 134
World War I, 276, 279–284, 286–289, 295
Worth (couturier), 134

Zangwill, Israel, 114, 172, 179–180, 184, 190, 254

INDEX OF WORKS

ARTICLES AND ESSAYS

"How Fauntleroy Really Occurred," 169
"My Toy Cupboard," 270
"One Woman of the Nineteenth Century," 227
"Romantick Lady" articles, 281, 300–301
"The Story of a Beautiful Thing," 156
"What Use Is a Poet?" (sketch), 138–9
"When He Decides," 132

BOOKS

Bettina (see *The Shuttle*)
Children I Have Known, 160
The Dawn of a To-morrow, ix, 240–242, 260, 263–264
Dolly, 37, 40–41, 71–72, 75, 130, 163
Earlier Stories, First Series, 71–72, 166
Earlier Stories, Second Series, 71–72, 166
Editha's Burglar: A Story for Children, 119, 153
Emily Fox-Seton, 227
A Fair Barbarian, 93–95, 97–98, 101, 122, 166
The Fair, Far Country or *His Friend,* 295
The Fortunes of Philippa Fairfax, 119, 127, 129
Giovanni and the Other, 160, 162, 165–166
Haworth's, 70, 75–76, 81, 84, 90, 119, 166, 179
The Head of the House of Coombe, 287–288, 295–299 (see also *Robin*)
His Grace of Osmonde, 197, 199, 201, 210
In Connection with the De Willoughby Claim, 43, 63, 79, 93, 95, 100, 117–118, 181–182, 186, 193–194, 197, 199, 212, 220, 228, 235, 265
In the Closed Room, 234–235, 260

In the Garden, xiii, 303
A Lady of Quality, 176–182, 185–186, 189–191, 194, 197, 199, 210, 215, 220, 236, 264
The Land of the Blue Flower, 290
The Little Hunchback Zia, 295
Little Lord Fauntleroy, ix, x, xi, xii, 106, 109–110, 112, 116, 118, 120, 122–123, 124, 127,
   131, 157, 166, 169, 216, 220, 263, 280, 306 (*see also under* Burnett, Vivian in
   General Index)
A Little Princess, ix, 109, 116, 118, 235, 238, 242, 247, 263, 306 (*see also* books: *Sara
   Crewe*; stories: "Sara Crewe")
Little Saint Elizabeth, 165, 166
The Lost Prince, 272, 279, 281
Louisiana, 90, 166
The Making of a Marchioness, 225–228, 238, 242, 247
The One I Knew the Best of All, 29, 117, 160, 162, 165, 199
Piccino and Other Child Stories, 165
Pretty Polly Pemberton, 71, 75
The Pretty Sister of José, 166
Robin, 288, 299 (*see also The Head of the House of Coombe*)
Sara Crewe, 118–119, 166, 179
The Secret Garden, ix, xii, xiii, 46, 117–118, 165, 260–263, 265–266, 271, 306–307
The Shuttle, 220, 225, 238–239, 245–249, 263–264, 268–269
Surly Tim and Other Stories, 70–72, 74, 113, 166
That Lass o' Lowrie's, 64, 66–68, 70–71, 74–75, 90, 166, 179
Through One Administration, 95, 98, 100–103, 116, 118, 127, 166, 177, 179, 221
The Tide on the Moaning Bar, 71
T. Tembarom, 263, 269, 277, 281, 297
Two Little Pilgrims' Progress, 166, 181
Vagabondia, 37, 40, 130, 166
The Way to the House of Santa Claus, 295
The White People, 284, 295
A Woman's Will; or Miss Defarge, 113, 119, 263

EARLY WRITING, 4, 9–11, 16–22, 32–33

FILMS BASED ON WORKS, 273, 297

   The Dawn of a To-morrow, 297
   Little Lord Fauntleroy, 273–274, 279, 297
   The Shuttle, 301
   That Lass o' Lowrie's (renamed *The Flame of Life*), 297

PLAYS ADAPTED BY FHB OR BASED ON WORKS

   Clorinda, 193–195
   The Dawn of a To-morrow, 253–254, 256–259, 261, 264, 284
   Editha's Burglar, 122, 138
   Esmeralda, 85, 93–94, 98, 101–102, 208
   Glenpeffer, 238

A Lady of Quality, 182, 186–187, 187, 196, 197, 199–201, 208–210
Little Lord Fauntleroy, 120–122, 125–126, 128, 130, 138, 155, 181, 189, 229
A Little Princess, 234–235, 237
Liz, 74
Phyllis, 127–130, 208
The Pretty Sister of José, 235, 238, 247
Racketty-Packetty House, 269–270
That Lass o' Lowrie's, 73, 75, 90, 93
That Man and I, 235–236, 247

PLAYS BASED ON WORKS

Editha's Burglar, 122, 138
Little Lord Fauntleroy, 181, 189, 229
Liz, 74
That Lass o' Lowrie's, 73, 75, 90

PLAYS WRITTEN OR CO-WRITTEN

The First Gentleman of Europe, 190–191, 194–197
Nixie, 140, 153, 155
The Showman's Daughter, 152–153, 156–157, 163

POEMS, 16–18, 20, 58–59, 69, 97, 181, 197

STORIES

"After Josh Billings," 46
"After Thirty Years," 56
"As Good as a Mile," 56
"Aunt Portia's Diamond," 34, 55
"The Ban-Dog," 225
"Behind the White Brick," 88, 165
"The Captain's Youngest," 165
"The Curate of St. Mary's," 46
"Dolores," 37, 52, 71 (*see also* books: *Dolly*)
"Dorothea," 37, 71 (*see also* books: *Dolly*)
Emily Fox-Seton stories, 117, 225
"Esmeralda," 64, 85, 93
"Ethel's Sir Lancelot," 40–41
"The Fire at Grantley Mills," 55, 65
"Giovanni and the Other," 150 (*see also* books: *Giovanni*)
"Hearts and Diamonds," 35
"Her Secret," 52
"How Denis Scarbrough Married for Money," 34
"How Lottie Elected the President," 97
"In Spite of Themselves," 46
"Jarl's Daughter," 46
"Kathleen's Love Story," 41

"Lindsay's Luck," 50, 71
"Lisabel Cray's Punishment," 34
"Lisa's Little Story," 58
"Little Betty's Kitten," 165
"Little Polly Lambert," 33, 46, 49
"Little Saint Elizabeth," 125
"The Little Shop at Gowanham," 55
"Louisiana," 134, 153
"The Men Who Love Elizabeth," 56
"Mère Giraud's Little Daughter," 64
"Merely an Episode," 60
"Miss Carruthers' Engagement," 33–35
"Miss Crespigny's Absurd Flirtation," 60, 64
"Miss Jerningham's Version," 56
"Miss Vernon's Choice," 49, 70
"My Cousin Katherine," 58
"My Dear Friend Barbara Sharpless," 60
"My Robin," 266–267
"The New Governess," 46
"Norah Ferguson's Story," 52
"One Day at Arle," 50
"One Quiet Episode," 52
"The Pretty Sister of José," 127, 235
"The Proud Little Grain of Wheat," 88, 108, 165
"A Quiet Life: A Pathetic Love Story," 71
"Racketty-Packetty House," 242–243
"Sara Crewe," 109, 113, 116–118, 234
"Sir Patrick's Romance," 46
"Smethurstses," 72
"The Story of Prince Fairyfoot" (a k a "Little Prince Fairyfoot"), 112, 165, 236
"Surly Tim's Trouble," 47, 49, 60
"That Lass o' Lowrie's," 61, 63–64, 66–68, 72
"Theo," 54, 70–71
"The Tide on the Moaning Bar," 56, 65, 71
"Tom Halifax, M.D.," 46, 49
"The Tragedy of a Quiet Life," 46
"The Troubles of Queen Silver-Bell," 242–243
"Wanted—A Young Person," 58, 70
"What Might Have Been Expected," 60
"The Woman Who Saved Me," 42, 45, 47, 50, 52

UNPUBLISHED, 167, 169–170

"Bohemia," 37
"The Child of This Century" (fragment), 160–161
"The Hatchet" (sketch), 108–109
"His Friend," 142, 148, 173

"How Donna Scarborough Married for Money," 17
"In a Fair, Far Country," 148, 263–264, 284
"Lady Judith" (a k a "Judy O'Hara"), 236
"A Real Record," 69